INFORMATICS AND THE FOUNDATIONS OF LEGAL REASONING

Law and Philosophy Library

VOLUME 21

The titles published in this series are listed at the end of this volume.

INFORMATICS AND THE FOUNDATIONS OF LEGAL REASONING

Edited by

ZENON BANKOWSKI
The University of Edinburgh, Scotland, U.K.

IAN WHITE
University of Cambridge, Cambridge, U.K.

and

ULRIKE HAHN
The University of Edinburgh, Scotland, U.K.

KLUWER ACADEMIC PUBLISHERS
DORDRECHT / BOSTON / LONDON

A C.I.P. Catalogue record for this book is available from the Library of Congress

ISBN 0-7923-3455-8

Published by Kluwer Academic Publishers,
P.O. Box 17, 3300 AA Dordrecht, The Netherlands.

Kluwer Academic Publishers incorporates
the publishing programmes of
D. Reidel, Martinus Nijhoff, Dr W. Junk and MTP Press.

Sold and distributed in the U.S.A. and Canada
by Kluwer Academic Publishers,
101 Philip Drive, Norwell, MA 02061, U.S.A.

In all other countries, sold and distributed
by Kluwer Academic Publishers Group,
P.O. Box 322, 3300 AH Dordrecht, The Netherlands.

Printed on acid-free paper

Printed in the Netherlands

CONTENTS

PREFACE vii

CONTRIBUTORS xi

INTRODUCTION
Zenon Bankowski, Ian White & Ulrike Hahn 1

POLICY ARGUMENTS AND LEGAL REASONING
John Bell 73

DEFEASIBILITY IN LAW AND LOGIC
Neil MacCormick 99

DEFEASIBILITY IN LEGAL REASONING
Giovanni Sartor 119

ON SOME PROBLEMS OF
THE THEORY OF LEGAL ARGUMENTATION
Eric Hilgendorf 159

ANALOGICAL REASONING AND LEGAL INSTITUTIONS
Zenon Bankowski 177

THE REDUNDANCY OF REASONING
S.C. Smith 191

ONTOLOGY AND DIMENSION IN LEGAL REASONING
Geoffrey Samuel 205

COMMON LAW CONCEPTS:
THE PROBLEM OF INDEFINABILITY
Gregory Pipe 225

FORMALIZATION, INVENTION, JUSTIFICATION
Garrett Barden 245

ON THE RÔLE OF DEONTIC LOGIC
IN THE CHARACTERIZATION OF NORMATIVE SYSTEMS
Andrew J.I. Jones & Marek Sergot. 271

AI, LEGAL THEORY AND EC LAW:
A MAPPING OF THE MAIN PROBLEMS
Joxerramon Bengoetxea 291

BUILDING AN INTESTATE SUCCESSION ADVISER:
COMPARTMENTALISATION AND CREATIVITY
IN DECISION SUPPORT SYSTEMS
Lilian Edwards. 311

LEGISLATION AS LOGIC PROGRAMS
Robert A. Kowalski. 325

USING INFORMATION TECHNOLOGY AS A DETERMINER
OF LEGAL FACTS
Sandra Dewitz 357

INDEX 371

PREFACE

In 1988 an international team of legal theorists and computer scientists, from a dozen universities and research institutes in half a dozen European countries, came together to propose a collaborative project of work under the Basic Research section of *ESPRIT II*. This was the second stage of the European Commission's *European Strategic Programme for Research and Development in Information Technology*. The intended task of the proposers was to carry out a fundamental and systematic analysis of legal reasoning, from a point of view which combined computer science with formal logic, legal philosophy and the study of legal practice. The aim was to determine the extent to which the law was amenable to formal modelling, and the extent to which the formal models were amenable to computation; thus to identify the proper rôle of informatics in law, and to picture how this rôle could be filled.

The project was formulated on the principle that research, because it is basic, is not therefore remote from practical application. It appeared to proposers that, on the contrary, research that is fundamental to the domain of application is what has the most practical import for making well conceived and therefore effective uses of information technology.

The proposal was extremely ambitious, and was not fully funded as a project. It was, however, approved by the European Commission, to be set up as the *Basic Research Working Group on the Foundations of Legal Reasoning*. Funding, for two and a half years, covered the costs of members' travel to meetings and the costs of administration, but not the costs of the actual research itself. So the tasks envisaged in the original proposal were cut down to something less grand. However, the members of the group were determined to stick to the plan of doing basic work and having as large a cross-disciplinary mixture as possible. The aim was at least to identify the essential areas. The effect of the collaboration was to focus on a number of central issues to which different members could make complementary contributions, or on which they could engage in constructive debate.

The members of the Group met formally twice a year at different sites, and also made individual visits or organized smaller seminars. The emphasis of the meetings was on freedom and continuity of discussion, and in the course of the project the work of the members became more and more interconnected.

An essential function of the Working Group was to add a collaborative dimension to other research projects in which the members were severally or jointly engaged. Important here in the sphere of legal reasoning was the International Statutory Interpretation Project: some of its members were active in the Group, and its work touched on the Group's area of interest. On the informatics side, mention must also be made of the Automated Analysis of Legislation Project of the Istituto per la Documentazione Giuridica and the JURISTAR project of the University of Tubingen. There has been close contact with other ESPRIT Projects such as DRUMS, MEDLAR, and NOMOS.[1] The co-ordinating partner, with other members of the Group and additional partners, also proposed and then carried out the ESPRIT Exploratory Action ALDUS, to investigate the feasibility of an artificial legal draftsman to assist the formation of international contracts of sale. Members of the Group, collaborating with distinguished American researchers, were the founders of the International Association for Artificial Intelligence and Law; and also initiated ΔEON, a new seriesof International Workshops on Deontic Logic in Computer Science.

Considerable interest was aroused by the work of the Group. Some external observers were invited and several additional members were recruited over the two and a half years, including visitors from outside the European Community. However the group was still kept relatively small in the number of people involved but relatively large in the number of institutions, countries and disciplines represented.[2]

The project, as far as we are able (or entitled) to judge, has been extremely fruitful. A substantial body of papers was written during its course. Throughout the life of the project our work become more and more interconnected. The work of the Group has been presented at seminars to students at several centres, and at national and international meetings, and has formed the basis of a series of educational television programmes. Members of the group have been involved in building, or further developing, a number of prototype computer systems.[3]

Much of the work has been published in journals, books, or the proceedings of other conferences at which the work of the Group has been disseminated. We present here a selection of the papers from the project as representing some of the work that had been done and is largely unpublished. Much more, we hope, will come out of the project, since this was, as is the nature of fundamental research, a 'seed corn' which has stimulated our thinking further and in other directions.

Our acknowledgements are due, first of all, to the European Commission, for their financial support under the ESPRIT Programme, and in particular, for their help and their patience, to Mr Simon Bensasson and Mr David Cornwell of the ESPRIT office in Brussels, who were successively the Project Officers of the Group.

We should also like to thank all the members of the Group itself, especially those who are not represented in this collection of papers, but to whom we and the contributors owe a great deal, in the way both of inspiration and of criticism, for the published and unpublished work which they presented at the Group's meetings, and for the part they played in discussions.

We are grateful to Dr Tony Holden (a member of the Group) and the Decision Support Group in the Department of Engineering at the University of Cambridge, who provided invaluable technical assistance and facilities for the preparation of the book.

[1] ESPRIT Research Projects: DRUMS (Defeasible Reasoning and Uncertainty Management), MEDLAR (Mechanizing Deduction in the Logics of Practical Reasoning), and NOMOS (Knowledge Acquisition for Normative Reasoning Systems).

[2] The institutions from within the European Community represented in the Working Group were the Universities of the Basque Country, Bologna, Cambridge, Cork, Edinburgh, Ferrara, Granada, Kiel, Lancaster, Leeds, Tübingen, the Technical University of Denmark, Imperial College, London, the European University Institute and the Istituto per la Documentazione Giuridica, Florence. Also represented at the meetings were the Universities of Buenos Aires, Nitra in Slovakia, Oslo, Salzburg, South Carolina, and Texas at Austin.

[3] A complete list of the papers presented at the Group's meetings, and publications and other work by members of the Group, is contained in the *Report to the European Commission (BRA 3152)*, I. White (ed.), 1992.

CONTRIBUTORS

Prof. Zenon Bankowski
Faculty of Law
University of Edinburgh
Old College
South Bridge
Edinburgh EH8 9YL
Scotland

Prof. Garrett Barden
Arts Faculty Office
University College Cork
Cork
Ireland

Prof. John Bell
Department of Law
University of Leeds
Liddon Terrace
Leeds LS2 9JT
England

Dr Joxerramon Bengoetxea
Departamento de la Filosofia del Derecho
Facultad de Derecho
University of the Basque Country
20009 San Sebastian-Donostia
Spain

Mrs Sandra Donaldson Dewitz
School of Business: Marketing/Quantitative Studies
One Washington Square
San José
California 95192-0069
United States of America

Ms Lilian Edwards
Faculty of Law
University of Edinburgh
Old College
South Bridge
Edinburgh EH8 9YL
Scotland

Ms Ulrike Hahn
Centre for Cognitive Science
University of Edinburgh
South Bridge
Edinburgh
Scotland

Mr Eric Hilgendorf
Juristische Fakultät
Universität Tübingen
Wilhelmstraße 7 / Neue Aule
7400 Tübingen 1
Germany

Prof. Andrew Jones
Norwegian Research Centre for Computers and Law
St Olavs Plass 5
0130 Oslo
Norway

Prof. Robert Kowalski
Department of Computing
Imperial College
180 Queen's Gate
London SW7 2BZ
England

Prof. Neil MacCormick
Faculty of Law
University of Edinburgh
Old College
South Bridge
Edinburgh EH8 9YL
Scotland

Mr Gregory Pipe
Department of Law
University of Leeds
Liddon Terrace
Leeds LS2 9JT
England

Dr Geoffrey Samuel
Department of Law
University of Lancaster
Lancaster LA1 4YN
England

Dr Giovanni Sartor
CIRFID
Università degli Studi di Bologna
Via Zamboni 27/29
40126 Bologna
Italy

Dr Marek Sergot
Department of Computing
Imperial College
180 Queen's Gate
London SW7 2BZ
England

Mr S.C. Smith
Emmanuel College
Cambridge CB2 3AP
England

Mr Ian White
c/o St John's College
Cambridge CB2 1TP
England

ZENON BANKOWSKI, IAN WHITE & ULRIKE HAHN

INTRODUCTION

Our aim here is to do two things. First of all to give a brief outline of the papers that go into this book to enable readers to see, fairly quickly, which pieces they might be particularly interested in. Secondly, and building on this, we try to present a more critical and explanatory survey of the issues raised. We show how the articles converge on common problems which were the subject of discussion in the Group's meetings. We fill in some of the background of work done in this area, including other work by the contributors and work by other members of the Group not represented in this collection. Finally, we try to suggest points for further discussion.

1. OUTLINE

The common starting-point of the contributors to this volume is the representation of any piece of legal reasoning as the so-called *legal syllogism*, in which a legal norm in the form of a conditional rule figures as the major premise, and the application of the norm is carried out by adding a minor premise that subsumes the given case under the antecedent of the rule. The major premise has a double rôle: it is at the same time universal, securing uniformity over many cases, and also hypothetical with a normative consequent, serving in each case to attach *legal* consequences to *factual* conditions. The deductive nature of the syllogism suggests that it will lend itself to formalization, and that it is accordingly here that computers will find their legal application.

The contributors do not endorse this picture of legal reasoning without qualification, if at all: on the contrary, they are concerned in various ways to elaborate it, to define its limitations, to criticize it, even to replace it. When they do broadly accept it, they do so on the lines of the more sophisticated analyses offered, for example, by Karl Engisch, Jerzy Wróblewski and Ota Weinberger. Even then, the syllogistic representation, when seen as a model of legal reasoning, encounters many difficulties. In particular, it appears that the minor premise, by which a case is subsumed under a general rule, is especially resistant to formalization. But the adequacy of the major premise, the general rule, can also be queried.

John Bell studies an aspect of legal justification, 'policy argument', which introduces wider considerations than those found in the standard sources of

Z. Bankowski et al. (eds.), Informatics and the Foundations of Legal Reasoning, 1–71.

law, such as statutes and cases. Legal certainty is an important value in the rule of law, met by a programmable set of rules and exceptions and moves. But there are other public values which the law must also serve. The rule of law institutionalizes these values, in the strong sense that it handles them though the device of legal institutions. Policy arguments are based on the functions law serves. As 'extra-legal' considerations they make the analysis of a problem in terms of legal rules potentially defeasible. Thus, they move legal reasoning beyond a simple rule-based process. This makes for limitations in the design of decision support systems in law, and Bell offers specific suggestions as to how 'policy' might be incorporated.

Bell shows, in any case, that making the content of legal source materials available in a formalized system entails a substantial task of legal interpretation, and that the language of legal draftsmen should be considered in relation to how and by whom it is to be understood. These topics are taken up by Bengoetxea and Kowalski. This was also an aspect of the work of several other members of the Group that related it to the International Statutory Interpretation Project, of which some of them were members.[1]

Neil MacCormick further investigates the concept of defeasibility in Law. Firstly, he considers explicit and implicit defeasibility in the legal system. He then highlights the differences between legal qualifications and exceptions. These turn out to be primarily pragmatic, concerning, for example, allocation of the burden of proof. Drawing on this, he argues that all cases of defeasibility ought primarily to be understood in terms of pragmatics. This perspective is then submitted to possible realist challenges, and developed by an extensive treatment of the notion of a legal power. Thus it is demonstrated how defeasibility, pragmatically viewed, allows compromise between 'the need for reasonable security in human plans and the need to uphold principles of deep importance in a given view of socio-legal order'.

Giovanni Sartor provides a detailed logical analysis of defeasibility in legal reasoning. Legal norms, in general, subordinate a legal effect —an obligation, right, etc.— to a legal condition. Some conditions may need to be proved; others may need only not to be disproved. This distinction underlies the defeasibility of legal norms, and makes legal reasoning non-monotonic, i.e. consequences derivable from a set of premises can be invalidated by additional information which, for example, establishes an exception to a rule. Sartor provides an introduction to two formalisms which have been developed to represent incomplete information and derive defeasible conclusions. He specifically highlights approaches which might reduce divergence between formal logic and argumentation theory as accounts of legal reasoning: rigour and controllability, the prime virtue for formal logic, and preservation of the dialectical flexibility of legal and moral argumentation, emphasized by argumentation theorists, are goals which he thinks can both be attained. Here again we see similarities with MacCormick —in particular, where he shows how defeasibility underlies the dialogic nature of legal procedure and has a heuristic function in stimulating the search for new legal arguments to defeat provisional conclusions.

Eric Hilgendorf is concerned with theoretical approaches to argumentation in law. He provides a brief introduction to this and in particular to the discussion in Germany where this approach is particularly strong. He distinguishes two distinct aspects of argumentation. Firstly, arguments can be investigated with respect to consistency and this is the domain of logic. He looks at two prominent German accounts of the logical structure of the application of legal rules —Karl Engisch's and the newer studies of Koch and Rüssman. The second aspect that he discusses is the force of the arguments. This might be termed the problem of justifying normative statements. He tries to refute 'Special Case Thesis', in Robert Alexy's Theory of Legal Argumentation, according to which legal discourse is a special instance of 'general practical discourse'.

Zenon Bankowski provides an analysis of analogical reasoning in law, which, he says, demands an adequate understanding of the universal and the particular. Analogy works in law, as it does in ordinary life, through the idea that the fact that one situation resembles another is important and relevant to our actions. What we require is first of all a base line or point from which we can start and by reference to which we can compare and contrast any particular problem case or situation. Though one can give a complex formalisation of the process of reasoning by analogy in deductive terms, at the basis of analogy is the single instance and it is the 'resemblance' between instances, old and new, which is at the core of analogy. But this is not to say that analogy is just one particular compared with another. All particulars have 'trails of universality'. The notion of sameness and therefore reasoning by analogy is found in a complex interlocking of principles, practices and rules which inform and create the particular instance and *vice versa*. At base this is located in social practice and a particular tradition. So though analogy involves a creative leap which determines that 'this is like that', this leap is domesticated by the tradition and the discourse in which it takes place. In this sense analogy does not provide 'new' answers.

Sean Smith's account of analogical reasoning in law represents the whole process as much more creative. It is a systems-theoretic account of legal reasoning. Common law is reconstructed as a 'recursively closed network of decision making'. This renders it a circular, symmetrical and 'paradoxical' process. For Smith, principles etc. do not found analogical reasoning at all. Analogical reasoning has no rational start, so there can be no basis for the entry of an analogy into the system. It starts from more or less arbitrary distinctions which enter into the system and are somehow 'postponed' or forgotten about. But they generate principles which then find the distinctions in the system and give them a 'rational base'. In this sense the 'paradox' —that the means of justifying the distinction comes from the distinction itself— is hidden. Legal reasoning is explained as the attempt to 'deparadoxify' the paradox, to make it rational —a misplaced hope that it can provide justification for the process of decision-making, by legitimating law beyond the legal system to society as a whole.

Geoffrey Samuel challenges the assumption that legal knowledge is to be found only in propositional rules. Legal reasoning, at least in common law, is presented as an activity which is not merely the application of propositional knowledge —rules— but a mixture of descriptive, inductive and deductive techniques. These techniques, historically, have each been predominant at different stages in the development of law. They are, however, not merely 'past', but to varying degrees are still in operation today. An excessive fixation on the notion of 'rule' obscures this phenomenon. Whether a particular rule is applicable is in part dependent on the formulation of a factual pattern, a case description, which will allow itself to be fitted into the paradigm pattern associated with the rule. As the knowledge relevant to the establishment of these patterns is outside the rule itself, rules are only 'an imperfect means of storing legal knowledge'. In the Roman phrase, they are a *brevis rerum narratio*.

Gregory Pipe outlines a model of common law reasoning, the heart of which is a 'labelling' or naming process: facts are ascribed legal significance by the application of legal labels. It is the jurists' understanding of the concept, which the label represents, that guides their decision —a decision which subsequently has to be justified by providing a insight into this understanding as an explanation. Pipe illustrates how justification does not proceed by providing fixed definitions and examines why this is so. Finally, the implications for 'mechanical decision making' are discussed.

Garrett Barden develops a formalization of the justification of legal decisions, according to which a jural institution generally exhibits the formal structure of a legal person having an entitlement on certain conditions. Conditions and the conditioned are sharply distinguished. The formal expression of the basic form of inference —modus ponens— is *X if C; C; therefore X*. Barden's contribution is a characterization of the legal domain through description of the specific character of the conditioned *X* and the set of conditions *C*. The conditioned *X*, in law, has the internal structure of a three-place relation of entitlement, denoted *RxAy* (*x* is entitled to *A* from *y*). Barden aims to demonstrate that all rules with which the courts are concerned, have this structure; and he proceeds to provide precise meanings for both the notion of 'legal person' (*x* and *y*) and 'entitlement' (*xRy*). He then turns to the nature of the set of conditions *C*. The distinctions Barden makes here, allow him to present a formal analysis of different kinds of novelty in situations of entitlement, and to take further the analysis of both analogical and rule-based reasoning.

Andrew Jones and Marek Sergot make a contribution to a general methodology for the use of deontic logic in the analysis and representation of normative systems. They focus on the rôle of deontic logic in legal knowledge representation and its rôle in systems specification. Deontic logic, they argue, needs to be taken seriously as soon as one is forced to make explicit the distinction between what ought to be the case and what is the case. Deontic logic becomes necessary in representation of the law, when it provides for the legal consequences of unlawful actions. In the context of systems specification, deontic logic might provide a component in a formal language suitable for precise expression of both the specification of an organization and the intended operation of a computer system. If the specification is to make provision for the possibility of violations, i.e. the deviation of actual behaviour from the ideal, then deontic logic is deemed necessary. Jones and Sergot critically to assess views in the AI and Law literature both on when and where deontic logic should be put to use and how this should be done. Their conclusions, finally, deal with a possible development of the theory of normative positions, a theory with relevance to both systems specification and knowledge representation in law.

Joxerramon Bengoetxea looks at the possibility of expert and decision support systems in EC Law, in the context of higher or lower level legal theory. He then re-constructs a model of reasoning and law developed by Jerzy Wróblewski, pointing out the epistemological and phenomenological moments where Artificial Intelligence can provide some help. He is rather sanguine about the possibilities of going far. He lays stress on *decision support*, that is, automated systems which aid the person concerned in not only coming to a decision but also justifying it.

Lilian Edwards relates her experiences in building the Intestate Succession Adviser, a rule-based tutoring aid, which operates in the domain of Scots intestate succession law. Intestate succession suggested itself as suitable for implementation as it seemed semantically unusually clear, while nevertheless being syntactically complex and of social and legal significance. While this initial assessment proved largely correct, problems arose with respect to two less well-documented aspects of legal expert systems design: the need for 'compartmentalization', and issues arising from the pragmatic context in which the legal rules operate. These problems illustrate that interpretation problems occur even in the least ambiguous of domains. Her conclusions are nevertheless tentatively optimistic: though implementing the system demonstrated the many problems of formalizing law, it also revealed that this process might provide a useful source of legal creativity. Two examples illustrate how running the system with unusual sets of facts as input produced unexpected results —results which alert the legal system builder or user to areas of difficulty, and which provide the basis for (human) creation of new rules.

Bob Kowalski investigates parallels between computing and law. He aims to demonstrate that they can be profitably exploited by both sides. He suggests a wide range of possibilities for the transfer of insights, ranging from issues of linguistic style which might provide guidance in the development of a future, single, unified computer language suitable for all areas of computing, to the exchange of techniques both fields need in order to develop, maintain and re- use large, complex bodies of text. His main focus is on similarities between legislation and logic programming. The linguistic style in which legislation is normally written has many similarities with the language of logic programming, but there are a number of ways in which the basic model of logic programming can usefully be extended. In particular, Kowalski discusses the introduction of types, relative clauses, both ordinary negation and negation by failure, integrity constraints, meta-level reasoning and procedural notation. In the reverse direction, he suggests that the linguistic structures of an extended logic programming language might indicate ways of simplifying legal language so as to make it easier to understand.

Sandra Dewitz investigates the possibilities of computerized legal reasoning systems operating in the context of electronic networks. Electronic Data Interchange (EDI) supports the transmission of highly standardized, computer readable business documents over telecommunications networks. Thus the computer itself is the medium through which legally relevant events occur. This allows the possibility of computerized fact-finding, i.e. the 'observation' and 'interpretation' of legal facts —a task which normally must still be performed by humans, and so far is well outside the scope of computer-based legal reasoning. Given a situation consisting of the exchange of EDI documents by certain parties within a certain context (precise conditions are specified by Dewitz) a computerized reasoning system can exploit the nature of EDI documents and document exchange; this, Dewitz argues, can enable the system not only to infer legal consequences from a set of facts, but also, in contrast to standard expert systems where the pre-established and pre-interpreted facts are supplied by the user, to perform identification and interpretation of these facts by itself. There is an important link here with work of MacCormick on law as embodying 'institutional facts', whose presence is recognized on the basis of their constitutive rules. Several contributors point to the minor premise of the legal syllogism, in which the facts are established and subsumed under the antecedent of the major premise, as the one which most stands in need of the human understanding. Sandra Dewitz shows how the computer can play an important part in precisely this area, provided of course that the transactions involved are already being carried out by machine. For these domains, it thus seems feasible to design 'automated legal advisors, acting as a kind of front-line bureaucrat', dedicated to resolving disputes without litigation.

2. RULES AND POLICIES

The aim of the contributors is not only to define the limits of what is theoretically possible and humanly desirable, but also to suggest what may be practically useful, in formalizing legal reasoning, and assisting it with computers.

John Bell argues that the function of legal theory is not just to reproduce what is actually done or believed, but to ensure that legal arguments are the best they can be within a particular legal system. A model of justification, when implemented through a decision support system, can support best practice among lawyers. On the other hand, heuristics looks at the rational processes involved in coming to a decisions. An account of the sources, materials and procedures for arriving at decisions, when implemented through a decision support system, will guide the decision-maker or suggest to him lines of reasoning.

Bell acknowledges the important place of the model of rules in law: it provides standards which restrict, in an agreed manner, discussions about what should be done, and it gives legal certainty, which is itself an important value in the rule of law. But there are other values which the law must also serve, and policy arguments enter as substantive justifications for decisions, which are appealed to when the rules do not provide a clear or an adequate solution. He argues against the view that the regulative function of the law means that it is a self-contained or discrete form of discourse. The purposes of laws have to be taken account of, in the process of interpretation by which a 'normative text' is derived from the physical text. But considerations of policy also move legal reasoning beyond rules, and this imposes constraints on the design of decision support systems. The rôle of such systems could be to direct the legal reasoner as to the determinable standards within which he has to operate, but also to prompt him as to other considerations, even though the result of such prompting will require judgments to be made by the decision-maker himself. Even within these limits there are many degrees of sophistication imaginable in a system, and it merits further research what is possible in practice. On the one hand, a system might be 'dumb', and merely ask the same questions again when it has exhausted the legal sources, or on the other hand, heuristics might be conceivable which make it 'smart', allowing it some adaptation to the case in hand.

'Public policy' is understood by Bell in a wide sense, which includes considerations that some authors (such as Dworkin 1977) would regard as principle and contrast with policy. It is distinguished in very broad terms from 'purely legal' considerations. Public policy, says Bell, makes exceptions to rules, but cannot itself be represented as a rule, because it is a generic heading under which a number of competing values are recognized. Even a single piece of legislation can have diverse objectives, and these have to be given an order of priority. (Sartor later makes the same point, and suggests ways to clarify this by formalization.) The very identification of a legislative purpose is a difficult jurisprudential task. Bell points out that though such considerations are open-ended, they are not completely unpredictable; and he himself give samples of a quite elaborate battery of possible questions of policy, organised in a tree, to which a lawyer could be alerted by a computer system. And it is the latter that might be seen by the computing community as their practically valuable contribution.

Bell shows how policy considerations are not only different in *content* from narrowly legal considerations, but —prima facie— involve a different *form* of argument. The answer they lead to 'depends on a weighing of variables, of seeing how various legs on a stool support the seat, to use Wisdom's analogy' (Wisdom 1953). This immediately raises the question of whether narrowly legal argumentation is not also in this non-deductive form, or equally informal. Pipe's paper later shows how a technical term of law has the 'family resemblance' characteristics found by Wittgenstein in the terms of ordinary language. So it might be argued that legal reasoning in general has the same non-deductive argumentative structure as other kinds of reasoning, well described (in another quotation from Wisdom) as 'a matter of weighing the cumulative effects of one group of severally inconclusive items against the cumulative effects of another group of severally inconclusive items'. This issue of the non-deductive character of legal argument is a recurrent theme in the collection. Of importance at this point is that Bell demonstrates how policy considerations defeat the conclusion which narrowly legal argument —assumed to be rule-based— would otherwise lead to. So he uncovers one important source of a phenomenon in legal reasoning which is then developed in the next two papers, namely *defeasibility*.

Bell's, MacCormick's and Sartor's papers highlight different aspects of defeasibility, all of which have implications for systems development. MacCormick places defeasibility in a jurisprudential context. Sartor demonstrates the demand for non-classical logics of defeasibility which can be employed by computational reasoners. Bell's article exemplifies a different kind of opening for technological inquiry. The sources of defeasibility, as both MacCormick and Sartor point out, are numerous, and can never be fully captured. Legal and jurisprudential inquiry, however, can (1) systematize currently less understood notions like 'public policy', and (2) determine along the way the limitations upon efforts to represent them in a system. These two sorts of information can be of direct utility for expert system design, as they determine both the content of the knowledge which can be provided and the form in which the provision is best made. They help decide whether these aspects of the law to be included in the system's reasoning process, or are better supplied as additional material for further consideration by the user. This kind of work thus complements the development of formalism, in pursuing the goal of building more adequate systems.

3. DEFEASIBILITY AND PRAGMATICS

Defeasibility is not a general logical informality but a specific kind of departure from the standard deductive form of argument. It is found in many kinds of common-sense reasoning as well as in the law, and is represented in formal terms as inferential non-monotonicity.

Neil MacCormick deals with defeasibility as a specifically legal phenomenon whose basis is pragmatic, and which can be expounded in terms of the institutional theory of law which he has developed in earlier writings. 'A legal arrangement or judgment which was initially, or on the face of it, valid, turns out to be open to attack, and under attack to lose its initial validity, or be revealed as never having been valid, despite all appearances.' Like Bell, he thinks that such a possibility allows compromise between 'the need for reasonable security in human plans and the need to uphold principles of deep importance in a given view of socio-legal order'.

He questions the idea of defeasible inference as a logical form. Those who (like Sartor and Kowalski in later papers) are interested in non-monotonic logics, may reply that these have been successfully developed by philosophers and computer scientists (see Ginsberg 1987). However, we should recall the observation of a pioneer in this field, Robert Stalnaker[2],

> The problem is not, how can we define a non-monotonic relation between sets of sentences and the sentences of some language. That is simple enough. The problem is how any such relation could be a consequence relation.

Suppose that we define a relation R such that pRr can be true even though $(p\&q)Rr$ is not true. We have to be able to interpret R as having the properties of 'if ...then...', so that pRr permits inferring r from p. We appreciate the difficulty of this challenge, when we reflect that non-monotonicity has two sides to it, both corresponding to aspects of common-sense reason, both puzzling from the deductivist point of view. An inference is non-monotonic if, although the conclusion r can be inferred from a premise p alone, it *cannot* be inferred from the conjunction $p\&q$. For example, we want to be able to make the following inference:

Tweety is a Bird.

Tweety can fly.

without having in other circumstances to make this one:

Tweety is a bird.
Tweety is an ostrich

Tweety can fly.

But non-monotonicity is misrepresented if this is thought of as showing that the conclusion of r from p, when it is made, is therefore only prima facie or provisional. For then so long as our inferences are non-monotonic, the possibility of their being countered by the arrival of new premises seems to lead to scepticism, the denial that we can ever achieve certainty. Of course it often happens that hypotheses are entertained for the time being and hesitant conclusions are half-drawn, but not all defeasible inferences are like this: for example, there is an important difference in criminal law between a prima facie case (which justifies prosecution) and proof beyond reasonable doubt (which justifies conviction), though the latter as well as the former is defeasible, since new evidence is capable of raising reasonable doubt which did not exist before. The other aspect of non-monotonicity also needs to be emphasized: that although the conclusion *r* cannot be inferred from the conjunction *p&q*, it *can* be inferred from *p* alone.[3] As Sartor points out, 'once pieces of factual and legal information sufficient to ground a certain legal solution have been collected, this solution is not defeated by the mere possibility that further statements are true whose ascertainment would prevent the derivation of that solution'. An inference is not inconclusive simply because it is defeasible (*capable* of being defeated) though indeed it fails if it is *actually* defeated. If it is defeated, we give up the previous conclusion, but we do not conclude that it was previously unjustified. With additional evidence we can be justified in changing our beliefs, but we are not unjustified in holding with confidence any belief which could be changed.

We have to ask whether a logic of non-monotonic inference succeeds in providing for two basic needs of the law, which the legal syllogism purported to satisfy, namely justification and finality in legal decisions. These are not achieved if the most we can say is 'if *p* then *r* —or maybe not', either because the logic does not allow us to draw confident conclusions, or because in doing so it licences credulity. MacCormick does not conclude that this is the most that we can say logically. On the contrary, he argues that the broad view of legal pragmatics he proposes is the proper setting in which to develop the required legal logic for defeasible inference. He recalls how Julius Stone (1964, 1985) objected that the standard lawyers' distinction between a qualification included in a rule and an exception extraneously limiting its application had no foundation in logic, and replies that though that may be true for a simple calculus, it only shows that this is an insufficiently rich logical notation for handling the legal concepts. 'To say there is no logical difference is to invite the challenge: from the point of view of what logic?' And accordingly, Sartor goes on to demonstrate a different logical point of view.

MacCormick's own approach may be summarized under three headings, which relate it to other papers in the collection.

The first might be called the 'epistemology of legal doctrine'. The formulation of the law has to be made in general terms and in discrete propositions, which are always liable to omit reference to some element which is operative in a given case (even though this may figure somewhere else in our account of the legal system). The omission may be by oversight, or for brevity: it may result from the difficulty of arriving at legal knowledge, or from the difficulty of stating it. Geoffrey Samuel (from whom we borrow this use of the term 'epistemology', and the use of the term 'ontology' below) subsequently develops the point that a stated rule is not itself law, but only a summary and incomplete description of law.

The second might be called the 'epistemology of adjudication'. Even though we have already specified, in our statement of the relevant law, both the conditions for making a claim, and the conditions that might defeat it, this does not mean that all these have to be investigated, to arrive at the legal decision of a particular case. Defeasibility in law is related to the allocation of the burden of proof: a defeating condition is seen as one whose negation does not have to be proved by a claimant, but whose negation is open to being refuted by his opponent (thus proving the defeasance). So epistemic concepts of proof and knowledge are built into the analysis of legal reasoning, as they are into the provisions of legal doctrine, and as they have been into some systems of non-monotonic logic, described by Sartor.

The third might be called 'legal ontology'. As MacCormick expresses it, it is related to the institutional theory of the law. On this theory, a background of constitutive conventions sustains the existence of institutional facts. Consider, for example, the institution of marriage. Marriage is a legal status which can be brought into being under complex conditions, its creation is subject to being impeded, and while it is capable of enduring, it is subject to being terminated. (We shall show below how this is related to the 'substantial' aspect of norm-conditions defined in Sartor's paper.)

MacCormick spells out the specific institutional factors and contexts which make defeasibility a pervasive feature of the law. For a typical legal factor is a *power* possessed by some party, subject to the satisfaction of various conditions specifying the qualifications for having and the circumstances for exercizing it; most importantly, it will be subject to compatibility with the powers of other parties. Legal positions are typically relational, with the other end of the relation open. 'With any power, one may always have reason to ask in case of a particular person towards whom a purported exercise of power has been directed whether or not this person is indeed susceptible to this exercise of this power.' Sartor later makes the analogous claim that defeasibility is a relational notion, potentially relating any given norm to countless other norms.

The 'epistemology of legal doctrine' may be contrasted with 'ontology' in that the former is concerned with discovering various elements in the *description* of the legal position, whereas what is now in question is how the legal position is *generated* by the dynamic interaction of institutional forces. Institutions are real elements of the law, and not merely dicta. There is, on the other hand, a link between 'ontology' and the 'epistemology of adjudication'. For legal powers and liabilities are determined as much by what is known or proved, as by what is the case: that is to say, not only our knowledge of these legal facts, but their existence, is so determined. This gives the epistemic factors an essential rôle in legal reasoning which they lack in many other kinds of defeasible reasoning in which they are introduced. Examples of this in statutes are discussed later by Kowalski: for the present, consider an adaptation of his standard example of how a non-monotonic inference is made possible by a combination of object level and meta-level statements:

> A bird flies if it is not shown that it is an ostrich.

Now this must be interpreted with care, to mean something like: If it is not shown that it is an ostrich then you may infer from the fact that it is a bird that it flies. For of course, whether the bird really flies does not depend on whether it is *shown* to be an ostrich but on whether it *is* an ostrich. Understood naïvely, the sentence quoted would represent, not reasoning *about* ostriches, but rather (as an example of the idea that what you don't see isn't so) reasoning *by* ostriches. The legal case is different; for example:

> The defendant is legally liable for the damage
> if it is not shown that he was acting in self-defence.

This means that his liability really does depend, not directly upon what is the case, but upon what is proved.

MacCormick's emphasis on powers is significant in another way. Powers (as in Hohfeld's analysis) are rights which the holder may or may not choose to exercize. They are typical of legal factors in that it is normally up to the beneficiary of such a factor to insist on it, and the legal outcome may be affected by the fact that he does not, even though he could have done. This is another real source of defeasibility in legal argument. A point does not need to be answered if it is not alleged: thus it is not incumbent on the prosecution to disprove every possible defence to the accusation, but only to deal with defences that the accused actually raises. This is true even if, once the defence is raised, it is then for the prosecution to disprove it. Indeed, dialectical aspects combine with epistemic aspects, not only in the procedure of litigation, but in legal transactions generally wherever powers are in play. A debtor's actual obligation to pay depends on the creditor's assertion of his right to payment. The act of assertion, like the existence of knowledge, can itself be a legally operative fact. Performativeness is a pervasive feature of legal utterances, beyond the scope of the more obvious instances. (The theme of performativeness is taken up again, in relation to computer systems in law, by Sandra Dewitz.) This is particularly clear when the law imposes temporal limitations: as MacCormick notes, the fact that the rightful owner did not claim his property before the innocent purchaser bought it from the thief, can mean that it is now too late to do so. We may go on to ask whether the pragmatic character that MacCormick finds in the law, is due to law being a pragmatic discourse, or to law being a discourse with pragmatic subject-matter.[4]

4. FORMALIZING DEFEASIBILITY

Formalizing defeasibility is the goal of Giovanni Sartor's paper, so many of the points raised by Bell and MacCormick return, now in a formal setting. Sartor proposes a logical analysis of defeasibility in legal reasoning, and relates it to the provisions of an actual body of law, the Italian Civil Code. To start with, he accepts the model of a legal norm as a conditional which attaches a legal effect as consequent to an antecedent legal condition. A 'perfect conditional norm' is an (unattainable) theoretical ideal which states a sufficient condition for a legal effect in a total antecedent combining all the relevant provisions made by the law. Within this total antecedent, Sartor distinguishes elements which have to be proved, the *probanda*, and those which have only to remain unrefuted, the *non-refutanda*. The burden of proof for each lies with different parties. The allocation of elements to one category or the other is made by the law on various grounds including grounds of equity and grounds of legal policy.

He shows the epistemic component in legal norms to be of great importance to the law, in that it enables legal consequences to be derived with certainty from factual conditions of uncertainty. The law makes one side or the other the bearer of risk: thus for example a manufacturer is liable for harm caused by his product if he cannot prove that he was not at fault, an accused person whose guilt is in doubt is entitled to an acquittal.

Among the grounds mentioned by Sartor for allocating the burden of proof, we may note one which differs from others in being more directly related to the aim of getting at the truth. It is significantly related to a theoretical interpretation which some have given of non-monotonic inference in terms of autoepistemic logic.[5] On this account, the rationale of being able to infer a conclusion r from a premise p alone, but not from $p\&q$, is that we are sometimes entitled to infer r from the conjunction of p with the fact that p is all we know —i.e., that we know nothing about the status of q; we are so entitled when it is the case that if q were true then we should know it. Legal presumptions sometimes have a similar basis. The onus of proffering evidence of some fact is sometimes placed on one party because the fact in question lies particularly within his knowledge. This does not perhaps altogether justify placing on him the burden of proving it, but it does justify placing on him the burden of raising it or making a prima facie case for it. For if some proposition is such that if it is true then he knows it, then if he does not assert it and testify to it when it is in his interest to do so, it is reasonable to assume that it is not true. This applies, for example, to the question whether someone was acting in self-defence.

Sartor examines the relation between the theoretical distinction of 'probanda' and 'non-refutanda' and a number of other distinctions drawn in the law, such as the distinction between facts which must be proved by the plaintiff and facts which must be proved by the defendant, the distinction between positive and negative facts, and the distinction between rules and exceptions. He discerns two types of conceptualization of the structure of norm antecedents. Some legal distinctions, like his own theoretical distinction, belong to the formal or logical type: they concern conditions for inferring a legal conclusion. Others, in contrast, belong to the substantial type: they concern factors causing a legal effect, and factors preventing the effect: in particular, the distinction in Italian law between *constitutive* facts and *impedient* facts. A substantial distinction is often made the ground for a corresponding distinction concerning the burden of proof, but the connexion between the two distinctions is not analytic. A legal provision (such as article 2697 of the Italian Civil Code, or the similar but more restricted United Kingdom Magistrates Courts Act 1952, s. 81) which makes one depend on the other, is not tautologous.[6] Sartor's view is confirmed by the fact that the law may place the onus differently in relation to the substantial distinction: thus the law sometimes makes rebuttable presumptions in favour of some claim (for example, Italian civil law presumes good faith in a possessor of a thing claiming its fruits, and the English law of tort presumes negligence on the part of the defendant when *res ipsa loquitur*) —so some constitutive facts are made into non-refutanda; conversely, there are criminal offences (in English and American law) where it is for the prosecution to prove that the accused had no lawful excuse for his act —so some exception-negations are made into probanda. The allocation of the burden of proof does not constitute the distinctions on which it relies, since these exist independently and may reflect other values in the background: if the burden is on the defendant charged with murder, who admits the killing, to show that he had some justification or excuse for it, that is because people normally have a right not to be killed; if the burden is on the prosecution to disprove an exculpation offered by the defendant, that is because people normally have a right not to be punished.

Not only the idea that defeasibility involves allocations of the burden of proof, but also the idea of substantial conditions, may be related back to MacCormick's paper. The concepts of 'legal causation' which Sartor cites from Italian law (constitutive, impeding, amending and extinctive facts) fit very well with the institutional theory. One possible way of looking at this theory might be to see it as an extended analogy between the realm of law, and the realm of natural things and states of affairs and their causal interactions. Then, one way of responding to Stone's contention that there is no logical difference (but only a pragmatic one) between the presence of a qualification for the existence of a legal fact, and the absence of a defeating condition, is by examination of a case of natural fact. If a man is served an omelette stuffed with poisonous mushrooms, he may fail to succumb in either of two ways: (1) because he eats only half of it, (2) because though he eats all of it, at the same time he drinks an antidote; and if he does eat all of the omelette, and he succumbs, we say that this is because he ate the omelette and it poisoned him, and not, normally, that it is because he didn't drink an antidote.[7] As Sartor says, the substantial conditions producing a legal effect are the constitutive facts, not these facts together with the absence of impeding facts, though indeed they only cause their effect if impeding facts are not present. Causal laws supply a basis for predictions, but causality is defeasible, since when it is true that A causes B we cannot say simply that whenever A happens then B will happen, but only that A is sufficient to make B happen, *unless something prevents it* (Anscombe 1981). There are reliable causal chains, even if no causal chain is in principle insulated from the possible intrusion of another. Whatever logic is needed to express this, will serve for the law also.

Sartor makes use of the idealization of a ‘perfect conditional norm’, but goes on to explain why this is unrealizable as a basis for legal reasoning. Such norm could only be constructed by synthesizing all relevant norms. But, he argues, these are incapable of being completely determined in advance since they cover an infinity of contingencies. Furthermore, many are conflicting or have the form of rules and exceptions, and cannot simply be put in conjunction —or contradiction would result—, so an order of priority has to be established among them. Comparative judgments have to be made between the diverse interests and values which the law is designed to protect. Even if the perfect norm could be constructed, it would be infinitely complex, and would not provide a foundation for the processes of legal reasoning but would represent their upshot.

The formal outline that Sartor offers fits well with the material on considerations of public policy provided by Bell. This might suggest to us that though the infinity of the task means that it is impossible for the specification of a norm to be exhaustive, it could for practical purposes be made very extensive, and though it would then be extremely complicated, the sort of complication in question is what computers are well suited to handling. But even so, the law thus represented would (as MacCormick points out) be lacking in essential qualities of ‘clarity and cognoscibility’. There would be an impact of computing on the law quite contrary to the clarification and simplification which Kowalski expresses a hope for in his paper.[8] And the practical question would be whether the amount of human labour saved by the use of such a system would be greater than the amount of human labour needed to construct it.

Sartor argues that the application of norms is limited not only by specific exceptions, but by indeterminate evaluative considerations, and he instances ‘self-defence’ and ‘public policy’. This is close to Bell’s contention that ‘public policy’ is not yet another rule but an open-ended generic heading. Sartor’s view, that expounding such terms involves covering indefinitely many unpredictable contingencies, might be queried. For ‘self-defence’ sounds like a single category, even if there are infinitely many means by which, circumstances in which, and harms from which someone may defend himself. Perhaps we should distinguish different ways in which a legal conclusion may be unexpectedly defeated. A further analysis of the ways in which the terms of the law may be unspecific, and in which the situations they have to cover can be novel, is developed by Barden, and we return to this subject below.

Sartor's paper is dealing with two levels of defeasibility. First, there is the defeasibility of a legal judgment about a particular case, which arises from the presence of non-refutanda in the antecedent of the conditional applied to it.[9] This defeasibility is related by Sartor to non-monotonic logics which emphasize the notion of proof. Second, there is the defeasibility of any statement of the law (in the abstract or in application to a particular case) which arises from the possibility that other norms will make exceptions to it.[10] This defeasibility is related by Sartor to non-monotonic logics which emphasize the notion of resolving conflict. Defeasibility in the second sense, he argues, is a relational notion (rather as MacCormick says that powers are relational): it involves the potential encounter between a given norm and other norms. So it seems that the law cannot be thought of as composed of discrete normative atoms. Furthermore, relational defeasibility can affect any norm, and does not define a specific class of norm. So we cannot find here a basis for Dworkin's distinction between rule and principles.

Sartor proposes an analysis which makes possible a modular representation of law in terms of single norms and their relations. He concludes his paper by providing an introduction to two formalisms which have been developed in artificial intelligence to represent incomplete information and derive defeasible conclusions. These go further to bring non-monotonic reasoning back to legal dialectic. The aim is to reconcile formal logic with the theory of argumentation. This can be done because, Sartor says, it is defeasibility that gives legal reasoning the form of a dialogue. In his formalization, legal norms are treated not as axioms for the derivation of conclusions, but as the context in which opposed arguments can be developed and compared. Non-monotonicity that is based on the distinction between probanda and non-refutanda in the antecedent of a norm, is reduced to non-monotonicity that is based on resolving conflicts between norms by an ordering in which one prevails over another. Assuming that all the conditions in the antecedents of any norm are to be probanda, then all non-refutanda can be removed from the antecedent of any norm, and their negations put into the antecedents of other norms which are then ranked as exceptions to the first. So the whole body of law can be broken down into a set of separate conditional norms, with orders of prevalence between them described in meta-statements. These separate norms correspond quite closely to the legislative and judicial texts that state the law clause by clause, and to the successive arguments that might be proffered alternately by one side and the other in a legal debate. The effectiveness of this representation of the law seems to depend on the comprehensiveness and consistency of one global feature, the structure of prevalence-orderings among the norms. If this is not comprehensive, we can still go some way with it. But the possibility that, being built up by pair-wise comparisons, it is not consistent, could be a grave problem. Some of it is presumably given by statutory texts and other legal sources, some is open to decision, and so to argument —but how far can the basis of this be formalized? Furthermore, the various prevalence-relations might be very different things expressed in the same way: special exceptions, more important social values, superior authorities, or simply *stronger arguments*. The analysis, however, aims to represent in an orderly way the structure of legal debate, not to resolve all the issues.

5. LEGAL ARGUMENTATION

The topic of legal argumentation is taken up by Eric Hilgendorf in the next paper. He distinguishes two aspects of argumentation. Arguments can be investigated, firstly, with respect to their consistency, which is checked by logic; and secondly, with respect to their convincing force, which depends on their suitability to the relevant audience. Hilgendorf further distinguishes between the theory of the application of the law, and the theory of the justification of normative statements.

The classical work of Karl Engisch (1943) presents the legal syllogism, by which particular ought-judgments are derived from general ought-judgments, the latter having been obtained by the conversion into propositional form of legal imperatives in statutes and other legal sources. Engisch pays particular attention to the minor premise: subsumption of a case under a norm is based on comparing it with cases which the norm undoubtedly covers. The latter have to be ascertained by interpretation of the norm. But the set of cases that are known instances, that is, the set of cases available for comparison, is extended with each successful subsumption. As every decision contributes to the meaning, this changes continuously, more or less dramatically, according to the cases added. This model aims to describe rules in the German Civil Law tradition; it fits very well with the account given in the following papers by contributors who concentrate on the English Common Law tradition. This seems to point to general facts about law, despite the received idea that there is a great contrast between Civil Law and Common Law systems, based on a contrast between deductive and precedent-following ways of reasoning. Engisch's model is also unifying in another way, in that it assigns to reasoning from cases a clear rôle in the context of rule application. This suggests that the most promising form of computer system would be a hybrid one, combining rule-based and case-based methods — a topic we return to later.

Hilgendorf then considers a more recent formal theory of law-application, the deductive theory of Koch and Rüssman (1982). He criticizes this for including a deontic operator in its notation, while in reality making no substantive use of deontic concepts or systems of deontic logic. Jones and Sergot, later in this volume, make a general point against the unfounded and inoperative introduction of deontic terms.

Hilgendorf then turns to the problem of justifying normative statements in the theory of legal argumentation. He considers in particular the work of Robert Alexy (a member of the Group though not represented in this collection). Alexy's 'Special Case Thesis' (Alexy 1978, 1989), according to which legal discourse is a special instance of 'general practical discourse', in a subtle way both relates law to and distinguishes it from rational argument in general. It is open to criticism from both sides. Bell, in the paper already discussed, objects to the separation of legal discourse as a special form; Hilgendorf, on the other hand, objects that court procedure is subject to constraints which do not merely formalize but are at odds with the principles that have to be respected by non-institutionalized dialectic. He notes in particular the temporal constraints imposed on moves in legal procedure, in which Sartor sees a heuristic value, and in which MacCormick sees an illustration of the pragmatic character of the law.[11]

6. REASONING BY ANALOGY

Zenon Bankowski provides an analysis of analogical reasoning in law, which starts with a model akin to the 'method of similarities' or 'standard case method' discussed by Hilgendorf. He proposes a model of analogical reasoning which depends on the existence of 'base points', cases whose classification is certain for one reason or another. By reference to these we can compare and contrast any particular problem case or situation. In order to make the relevant comparison for deriving a conclusion, it is necessary also to have what we might call (though he does not) 'base lines', that is to say recognized links of 'likeness' between the precedent case and the instant case. As we said above, these 'likenesses' are understandable, according to Bankowski, only in the context of a tradition.

If we offer, in this way, an account of case-based reasoning in law which involves specific characteristics of the law, we have to bear in mind that analogy and case-based reasoning are found in many other fields of inquiry, practical and theoretical, including some that claim universality, such as moral philosophy, and some that are commonly granted to have it, such as mathematics and logic. In mathematics, analogy has a rôle in the discovery of mathematical truths and of mathematical arguments, which precedes the work of formally proving theorems, as was emphasized by Polya (Polya 1954, 1957). In logic, we recognize the validity or invalidity of forms of argument, including deductive arguments, by considering concrete examples, comparing a questionable argument with an analogous one having different subject-matter. Now the 'base points' in Bankowski's account are fixed, in different areas of thought, in different ways: in law principally or typically by the fact that they have been authoritatively decided and so serve as precedents. In mathematics and logic, our knowledge of the base points comes from different sources. It may then be asked whether the 'base lines' are also in some way specific to the area of thought. Is the account of analogy being offered a quite general one? Is it a peculiarity of law that its reasoning depends on tradition, or does the peculiarity of law lie in the particular tradition that it depends on?

Bankowski discusses an analytical model of analogy proposed by Golding (1984), which explains it in terms of the recognition of common features in the cases compared and a rule of inference enabling one to conclude that they must therefore be judged likewise. He challenges Golding's idea that the particularity of the analogy can be dispensed with and the whole argument transposed onto the universal level. There are, however, important aspects of Golding's analysis which also figure in Bankowski's account. Golding's reconstruction of analogical reasoning includes a premise to the effect that the features shared by the cases are relevant to the judgment to be made. And it provides for the inference to be blocked by the presence of countervailing features in a case which distinguish it from the other case. In Bankowski's terms also, the relevance of the resemblances is intrinsic to the analogical thinking: one might say (a point taken up in connexion with Barden's paper below) that the analogy deserves its name because it is not merely a qualitative similarity between the facts of the cases, but a similarity in the relations between the facts and the legal judgments. For Bankowski as much as for Golding, analogy is not simply a brute linking of the cases, but a matter for argument, and counterarguments are also possible. Counterarguments could be distinguished into two kinds: In internal counterarguments, the existence or the strength of the alleged analogical likeness between the cases is denied, or a difference —the contrary of an analogical likeness— is asserted. In external counterarguments, while the first case is granted to be analogous to the second case, it is also shown to be analogous in another way to a third case, in which there has been or ought to be a contrary judgment, so the analogy with this third case either outweighs the former analogy, or defines an exception to its conclusion. (The rule-exception structure in law is not merely a relationship between statutory rules: case-law can equally be a source of exceptions.) In short, analogical reasoning —like the other forms of reasoning discussed in this collection— is defeasible.

This constitutes not only a similarity between case-based reasoning and rule-based reasoning, but confirms the idea that they are intimately linked.

Bankowski's model of analogical reasoning is very akin to the 'standard case method' discussed by Hilgendorf. There is however a significant difference between the use of precedents and the use of standard or typical cases as paradigms. It is typical of general terms of the kind in question that they have clear or central cases for application of the term, and they have a penumbra of doubtful or borderline cases. This picture is due to Wittgenstein; it was presented, within legal theory, by Hart, who held that in the 'open texture' of a term there is a 'hard core' of meaning and a 'penumbra' of doubt, and case-by-case reasoning makes the hard core ever more fixed and certain (Hart 1983). Now it can be as certain that a case is a borderline case for application of the term as it is that a case is a central case. Leading cases in law need not be central ones, and it is not necessary for them to be central for them to play their rôle. For firstly, clear and obvious cases are less likely to be litigated, or, if litigated, reported: it is the difficult ones that are legally more interesting. Secondly, it is the decision of borderline questions that is likely to be most useful for resolving future issues. This is true whether the term to be applied is based on degrees of some one-dimensional resemblance (like hue[12]) or is a family resemblance term based on a network of different points of similarity. This confirms what is also found outside the law, that the best way to discern the threads that make up the fabric of a term, is not to look at the centre of the patch, where they are closely knit, but to examine the frayed edges. For if it is clearer *that* the central cases are instances of the term, it is sometimes clearer *why* the peripheral cases are or are not.[13] The diet of examples offered by the law reports is likely, then, to be rather different from the diet that would be provided by a set of standard cases manufactured as text-book or legislative examples. Of course the fact that a case is borderline makes it the more difficult for the judge who has to decide it, while making his decision more useful for others once he has arrived at it. In short, while cases are decided by comparison, that is not to say that the criterion is degree of similarity to any particular set of cases.

The comparison of cases in law takes many forms, and plays many rôles. Comparison does not always mean that one case is decided on the strength of another one. Sometimes the ground for a decision in one case is a comparison between two others. For it is by putting cases side by side that we can see the pattern which decisions are to follow. We see by virtue of what difference between them, two cases should be decided differently. We see that a difference does not matter, when they should be decided in the same way.[14] Sometimes, by a paradox not unlike the one noted by Smith in the next paper, the point of a case is discerned by comparing its facts with those of another case, and yet it is the first case that is supposed to provide the authority, and this other case is the one that is having to be decided. Thus it was by comparison between *Donoghue* (the snail) and *Grant* (the underpants) that the court got it clear that there was no significant difference between goods to be consumed internally and goods to be worn externally, and thus arrived at the decision of *Grant* itself: *Grant* explained *Donoghue* so that *Donoghue* could decide *Grant*. But this does not make the reasoning viciously circular.

Bankowski's base points are not exclusively precedents or authoritatively decided cases, but include hypothetical cases of whose correct decision the court is otherwise claiming knowledge.[15] Testing general rules, or, by analogical comparison, particular judgements, against hypothetical examples, is a central feature of case-based systems for use in legal argument and elsewhere, notably Kevin Ashley's HYPO (Ashley 1990) and also Lilian Edwards' system described below.

Bankowski offers an example of this which is also of interest as it illustrates another point, that there is case-based reasoning that is not analogical. His example (drawn from the work of MacCormick) is of a case which was decided partly by attending to the unacceptable logical consequences of deciding in the contrary sense. A husband sued for divorce on the grounds of adultery by his wife, she having been artificially inseminated by donor without his consent. The court decided that this did not constitute adultery, on the grounds *inter alia* that if they held that it did they might be forced to hold in a future case that a dead person could commit adultery. The first thing to notice about this case is that the most obvious analogy is directly between artificial insemination and natural adultery, and that the court rejected this. The second thing to notice is that though the reasoning —hypothetical and *reductio*— was from case to case, the cases were not connected by similarity or analogy between different sets of facts, they were the same set of facts in different circumstances, and the judgment about one led to a like judgment about the other by logical consistency. That a dead man cannot commit adultery the court took to be a truth that it needs no authority to establish; that if AID is adultery then a dead man can commit adultery the court took to be a plain inference that does not depend on any drawing of analogy. The court worked with assumptions that enabled it to derive consequences deductively.[16]

This again illustrates how (as in the work of Engisch) case-based and rule-based reasoning can be brought together, and analogy and deductive rule application are related processes. Thus the process of deriving the decision in the instant case from a general rule works through the processes of analogical comparison. Conversely, the process of analogical reasoning can only operate within a network of rules, principles, and deductive reasoning. How far each successful subsumption of a new case extends the rule, depends on how creative the act of comparison is, and how far that is itself a creature of the rules. What this shows is that it is the way in which the comparison is done and the way that it can be integrated into more rule-based reasoning that is important. Bankowski, and Barden (below), represent an attempt to emphasize the rule-based nature of the project, and others in this collection, such as Smith, Pipe and Samuel represent an attempt to emphasize other aspects. If cases and comparison between cases are 'the driving force' even in the application of legal rules, this suggests that computational case-based reasoning is at least well-worth pursuing.

This collection contains no contributions dealing with this paradigm, as the Group did not have the opportunity to go as far into an investigation of this as they originally proposed. Case-Based Reasoning (CBR) as a branch of informatics[17] has its roots in natural language understanding systems. CBR has seen a surge of interest and research effort in a variety of domains, certainly in law, but with prominence far beyond the legal domain.[18] Similarity assessment is crucial to the quality of the system's performance, with regard both to retrieving the most appropriate cases from memory and to achieving a deeper comparison of these cases with the novel case at hand. The quality of the 'matches' the system ascertains between old cases and new directly affects the quality of the system's performance overall.

Comparing cases, as the lawyer will be well aware, is not a trivial task. Samuel gives examples of 'genuine creativity in law' exercised by the lawyer who manages to convince a judicial body that 'ships are like cars' or 'a house is like a bottle of ginger beer'. At first sight, this suggests a flight of fancy, and is apt to leave a sense of puzzlement like that provoked by Lewis Carroll's question 'Why is a raven like a writing-desk?' But as Samuel makes clear, the full structure of the analogy needs to be elaborated. Even if imaginative, these comparisons are not, when examined, unintelligible.[19] As to how 'creative' is the process of analogical reasoning, the contributors differ, and Bankowski is one who, in looking at the application of this form of reasoning in the context of tradition, downplays creativity by presenting this as a key determining factor. But whether or not this is true, a constraining factor seems to be needed. How far can this be provided by rules and how far it is susceptible to a process of automation are questions that need to be addressed. Case comparison cannot be eliminated from the reasoning process. This jurisprudential point of view confirms the judgment in favour of hybrid systems, already formed in discussion of Hilgendorf's paper.

The difficulties involved in matching are given an alternative description in Barden's discussion of the problem of determining 'the rule' from a precedent on the appropriate level and dimension of generality. Of possible rules there are indefinitely many. Barden follows Bankowski's analysis of analogical reasoning, while emphasizing much more than Bankowski does the rôle of an identification of the general rule implicit in the given precedent case. He shows how from a case such as *Donoghue v. Stevenson* can be derived narrower or wider descriptions of the material facts, ranging for example from 'snail in ginger beer' to 'foreign body in consumer good'. He holds that the problem of deciding the relevant description under which the decision of the original case is to be universalized, is jural and not computational, though the computer could be equipped with this description. He sees no theoretical problem about incorporating the result of successfully proposed analogies, but a considerable one over the discovery of new analogies. That Barden's approach is still essentially in terms of rules and universals, might be argued from the other example he discusses, which concerns not more specific and more general descriptions common to cases, but more central and more peripheral species of a genus prescribed in a legal rule. He shows how the constitutional condition for eligibility as President of the United States, 'being a native born citizen of the United States', has application problems of a conceptual character, for example, a person born in a place that is now part of the United States but wasn't at the time of his birth, or a person born in a place such as a U.S. embassy which is part of the national territory by a technical convention of international law.

Barden adds further important points to the discussion of analogy. The example cited above, of narrower or wider generalization, from 'snail in ginger beer' to 'foreign body in consumer good', might suggest a rather simplistic view both of analogical reasoning and of the issues in cases following *Donoghue*. But the real questions come when it has to be decide whether for example a local government surveyor who fails to prevent a builder leaving a structural fault in a house, has the same responsibility towards a purchaser of the house who suffers economic loss, that a manufacturer of ginger beer who fails to prevent a snail getting into a bottle, has towards a consumer of the drink who is made sick. Barden points out that a feature by feature analysis is not the only way, or the most appropriate way, of establishing analogy: 'John buys an orange from Jane' gives an institutional account of certain facts, in terms of which we may compare to it 'Paul buys a car from Priscilla'. But there is not some common feature linking cars and oranges: rather, both can be understood as commodities in the institutional relation of selling and buying. An analysis of feature-by-feature resemblances has its place, but Barden contends that Wittgenstein was mistaken to think it radically opposed to the 'discovery of forms' which it rather supplements. This point relates Barden's account to Samuel's.

For Barden as well as for Samuel and Bankowski, analogy is not just a more or less tenuous similarity. 'Analogy' has a range of senses in philosophical discourse since Aristotle. One view of it (among several expounded in Hesse 1966) is particularly pertinent here. We speak of analogy as opposed to similarity, when the similarity is not qualitative, but between relations. Thus the wheels of a car are analogous to the legs of a horse, not because wheels resemble legs, but because they have a similar structural and functional relation to the whole of which they are parts.[20] Other related aspects of the concept of analogy are brought out by a story cited by Garrett Barden during the Group's discussions. The story is a good example of analogy used to solve a legal problem (and is incidentally of interest as the earliest recorded case on intellectual property). St Columba, while staying in a monastery which owned a valuable manuscript of the Vulgate version of the Bible, at that time the only copy in Ireland, illicitly made his own copy of it, and on being detected, was sued by the monastery, who claimed ownership of the copy. The High King of Ireland decided the case in favour of the plaintiffs, with the dictum 'To each cow her calf, to each book its copy,' i.e. as the owner of a cow owns the calf the cow gives birth to, so the owner of a book owns the copy made from it.[21] An estranged long-term partner is *similar* to an estranged spouse (because as Barden says they have many features in common). On the other hand, a wife who has run off is *analogous* to an escaped whale.[22] Sometimes we speak of analogy rather than similarity when, rather than saying that we find a likeness between X and Y, we say that we liken X to Y: the connexion is in some sense creative, and may be asymmetrical. We decide to base one case on the other. A legal analogy in this sense is appealed to, not so much because our judgment in one case compels by consistency a like judgment in another case, as because it makes it possible: we have to make a judgment in the second case, and we use the first case to supply us with the means of doing so.[23]

It is characteristic of analogy in the senses just considered, that it involves an extension of a judgment to new areas: a point which is also embodied in the concept (going back to Aristotle) of the analogical use of a term. To the extent that legal decisions are based on analogy of this kind, they do indeed seem essentially to involve some kind of extrapolation. Whether computers can be made capable of reasoning of this kind (depending on the area of knowledge in which the reasoning goes on) seems still to be an open question.

A distinction has been drawn above between reasoning with cases and analogical reasoning in the contexts of jurisprudence and philosophy. Likewise, Cognitive Science and Artifical Intelligence contain two distinct bodies of research, one on case-based reasoning, and one on analogical reasoning. (See e.g. Gentner 1989, Kedar-Ceballi 1988, Holyoak and Thagard 1989. For an overview see also Hall 1989.) While the distinction between the two is blurred (for a comparison see Seifert 1989), and to some extent sociological, there is a different emphasis in the two paradigms, to the extent that computational modelling of analogical reasoning has focussed primarily on the aspect that we have highlighted —that is on the role of structural (or relational) correspondences as opposed to mere feature matches. Recent research on similarity within cognitive science, however, has on the basis of experimental results begun to emphasize the rôle of relational and structural correspondence in similarity assessment in general (see in particular Goldstone, Medin and Gentner 1991). And these results seem particularly relevant to an abstract, conceptual domain such as law. Our distinction should thus be read as one based mainly on the source of the comparison (analogy is more encompassing as rules themselves qualify as candidates), rather than a claim about the necessary ingredients for determining the relevant similarity in the case of analogical or case-based reasoning. Relations and structural matches most certainly play an important rôle in case-based reasoning as well.

7. DECISION AND CHANGE

Sean Smith approaches legal reasoning from a distinctive point of view —that of systems theory— but also on the basis of the classical account of legal reasoning offered by E.H. Levi, according to which it is essentially about reasoning by analogy. Smith's account has a number of points of close comparison with Bankowski's, and it also brings to the surface a third major theme of this collection, the sense in which law is an artificial system continually in the course of construction.

Fried (1982, quoted by Bankowski) is another author who has related the analogical character of legal reasoning to the positive nature of legal judgment. Whether they are reasoning from cases or from other legal sources, lawyers must reason about cases, since on any account it is to the decision of cases that their reasoning is finally directed. General and theoretical disciplines such as moral philosophy and economics can never be determinate enough to provide answers to the questions that lawyers must solve. It is the traditional discipline of precedent-based reasoning that fills the gap.[24] Levi (1948, quoted by Smith) argues likewise that principles are on a level of abstraction which means that they cannot generate consistent particular decisions. Legal concepts are developed by analogical reasoning to handle the task. This is also at the heart of Case-Based Reasoning: for example, it is claimed that one of the advantages of CBR is that

> ...many real world domains are so complex that it is either impractical or impossible to specify all the rules involved; a case, however, can still provide a 'solution'; CBR does not require a strong model or deep understanding of the domain...Domains without strong models are domains in which there is *no theory* from which answers to problems can be deduced, or domains where these theories are *partial*. (Hahn, 1993; see also Porter et al 1990, p. 234)

Smith argues that it is in the requirement to make decisions that we find an explanation of the activity of legal reasoning. Legal decisions must not only be made but must be made with justification: however the law, so far from being driven by, generates the justifications with which it makes cases decidable. Well-designed law does this effectively. Legal reasoning, feeding on its own precedents, belongs to a 'recursively closed network of decision making'. It does not legitimize the legal system as a part of the social system generally. This may seem to place Smith in opposition to Bell, in treating law as an autonomous entity; but he argues that the legitimation of the law is best seen as involving the functional differentiation of a system of positive law within a functionally differentiated society.

We have already remarked that, contrary to the view that makes them paradigms in which a rule is implicit, leading cases, or the cases that initiate a new legal concept, need not be central cases of the term whose application they concern. The chronological order of decided cases need not follow the logical order of possible cases.[25] This may be seen as one reason for the phenomenon noted by Smith, that in the history of case-law distinctions are made, then lost sight of, then re-emerge to be combined with others. Judges (both in the common-law tradition and outside it) sometimes like to accompany their decisions with bold general dicta. But it is equally characteristic of them to avoid making any more conceptual commitment than is necessary to decide the case in hand. So the decided case tends to be limited in its implications, because it defines —precisely enough— only a small part of the rule of application of the relevant concept, like an early map showing only a short stretch of the coastline of a largely unexplored continent.

This evidently poses a problem for any system which has to use existing cases as the basis for solving a new case. It may lead to the conclusion that the law, as based on cases, is essentially changeable and fundamentally arbitrary. Standard accounts of Case-Based Reasoning in computer science seem to converge with this view, as well as with the model of analogical reasoning offered by Bankowski. Generally described, CBR systems have some form of storage of past experiences, a 'case memory'. Given a novel case, one or several most similar cases are retrieved from case memory. These provide the basis for the suggested solution. On obtaining feedback on the adequacy of this solution, the novel case is added to memory, if appropriate, thus enabling the system to 'learn'. It should be immediately apparent from this description that the 'solution' offered for a given case is dependent on the set of cases in case memory and thus variable over time. The solutions the system produces have to be checked for their adequacy. A rate of success shows how far the system has acquired the necessary knowledge or understanding. But if the legal system itself is in question, it has to provide its own stock of cases, and can only arrive at the 'correct' answer, to check its suggestion, by the same process whose sufficiency is being checked. Does this make it circular?[26]

Smith follows Levi in seeing the common law as a paradigmatic example of a 'moving classification system'. It is one where 'the classification changes as the classification is made'. As in all recursive systems, the operations —here, decisions— are applied to the results of previous operations. 'The rules change as the rules are applied.' This appears to be not just an empirical observation but a theoretical necessity.

One way of presenting critically the ideas underlying this might be as follows: Suppose we return to Bankowski's model, according to which there are base points, and these are used as standards by comparison with which other cases are decided, leading to the subsumption of these cases under some general term. Then the first query to raise is this: When other cases are included in the term on the strength of their resemblance to these base points, is that because the base points define the meaning of the term or is it that we merely judge them to be instances of the term? If the former, then we can see why a change in the stock of decided cases necessarily changes the meaning of the term. If the latter, then the addition of new cases may or may not change the term, depending on how far they conform to the old cases.

Of course, it may be observed as a matter of fact that as new cases come up the content of a rule tends to drift. This however does not mean that it is impossible in principle to speak of its current sense and range of application. We do observe something that is not just a drift: we also observe the law cautiously progressing. A legal remedy grows, as the scope of conditions for it is progressively enlarged: for example, the liability of the employer, first for torts of the employee committed in the course of his employment for the profit of the employer, then for torts of the employee committed in the course of his employment for his own profit (see Cross 1968, p. 73). Unless we see this as an unfolding of the logical implications of the earlier cases, we are likely to see it as an example of courts pursuing a social policy. Smith's argument, however, is that it can be understood best in terms of the internal dynamics of the legal system given the task of adjudication.

Underlying the claim that the law is always changing, and, if new cases are decided, *must* change, is something like the radical scepticism about the concept of following a rule that has been ascribed to Wittgenstein by Kripke (Kripke 1982), and was expressed by Wittgenstein in the deliberately rhetorical exaggeration 'Every application of every word is arbitrary'. What this is an exaggeration of, is the point that there is only a difference of degree, even if a great difference, between reapplying a term to a new case in the same sense, and applying it to a new case in an extended sense. We may insist that, unless 'novelty' is defined in a certain way, new cases need not change the rule because they may conform to the rule as it was. The problem is that we do not have an independent criterion of what counts as conformity to the rule. For indeed there is a philosophical problem about the application of general terms, which cannot be answered by appealing to the concept of a formulated rule, nor yet by appealing to the concept of standard cases for comparison, since these are equally problematical. This is illustrated by Wittgenstein's example (referred to by Bankowski) of people who continue the series 2, 4, 6, 8... as 98, 100, 104, 108... Neither the formula 'numbers of the form $2n$', nor the initial numbers in the series, 2, 4, 6 and 8, considered as prototypes, even in conjunction with the instruction 'continue in the same way', can determine the generation of the series on the lines that seem natural to us, since the series itself is the criterion of how any of these determining factors are understood. The procedure does not seem to have any external justification. It may appear that all we can ultimately appeal to is the fact of agreement —itself not accidental but the expression of a socially shared practice. The difference between Smith and Bankowski may be over whether this agreement is constructed within the system, or reflects a context of tradition belonging in society as a whole.

Now while this scepticism may be discerned at the root of the idea that the law must continually change, there is a sense in which it is incompatible with it: at least, if what is asserted in effect is that the law may indeed be composed of rules, but of rules that are always changing. For scepticism about rules raises as much doubt about the concept of a difference in a rule as about the concept of identity in a rule. Both assume a fixed criterion of sameness. If you have no way of defining your position at any one time, at least in relation to your position at another time, you cannot say either that you are or that you are not staying still over time: you do not conclude that you are always moving.[27] If change in the law is a replacement of one determinate state of the law by another determinate state of the law, then describing this depends on our being able to say that the law, at one time, is in a determinate state, and to represent this state. There is perhaps another kind of change that the law can undergo, when, from being indeterminate at a certain point, it becomes determinate. The sense in which undecided issues are legally indeterminate, and the sense in which decisions might be thought necessarily to change the law, are discussed in connexion with Barden's paper below. At least we have to distinguish between two senses in which the law may be changed by the decision of a new case. There is the kind of change which came about when it was decided (being previously undecided) that the liability of the manufacturer of ginger beer (in *Donoghue*) implies a like liability for the repairer of a lift (in *Haseldine*); and there is the kind of change which came about when in deciding that it also implied a like liability for the surveyor of a house (in *Dutton*), it was decided that the former exception of real property, based on *Otto* and other cases on which *Otto* was based, no longer held.[28]

Another idea of Wittgenstein's may be cited here, as a possible basis for the view that the law must always be changing. It explains, not the idea that each *application* of a term to a new case involves a somewhat different rule, but rather the idea that it is each *transfer* of a term to a new case by comparison with an established case that involves a somewhat different rule. The relevant Wittgensteinian idea is the concept of a 'family resemblance', which is not just the concept of a set of common features, even with the proviso that a shared feature is understood in terms of a relation of likeness. Items are linked by a family resemblance when any two of them have many features in common, but there need not be any features shared by all of them. So there is a sense in which, when a, b, and c are linked by family resemblance, the likeness between a and b may be a different likeness from the likeness between b and c. The different likenesses build up a family of resemblances because they are linked by overlapping. Furthermore, another item d may be included in the family in virtue of its likeness to b, whereas c is included in virtue of its likeness to a. So here is another basis for the idea that classification by resemblance rests not on a single prototype but on a stock of cases. This reflection bears on the discussion of 'likeness' in Bankowski's paper. However, the point of Wittgenstein's analysis is that a network of multiple resemblances can constitute a single meaning, just as (to use another slightly different analogy of his) a rope is continuous and will bear weight, even though it is composed entirely of shorter overlapping fibres. If F is a family resemblance term whose meaning is given in terms of features $f_1 \dots f_n$, then though all its instances do not have any of the features $f_1 \dots f_n$ in common, they do all have F in common, and may by virtue of F be regarded as all having a common likeness in that respect, and as all being subsumed under a single rule. And the resemblances that unite the family are reciprocal: there are no privileged instances, and every instance depends as much as any other on its links with others, for its inclusion in the classification (see Bambrough 1961).

8. ONTOLOGY AND PATTERN

Samuel's paper brings together the topics of reasoning in accordance with the legal syllogism, and legal reasoning by analogy. He approaches law, considered as an object of legal science, from the point of view of the relation between its epistemology and its ontology. He acknowledges the central rôle of the régime of legal rules and deductive argument, especially in legal systems which have become codified. Comparing the Roman Law and English Common Law systems, he points out that the régime of rules is the end result of an historical development by which a rule of law, which was originally a summary description of the state of the law —not law but a *brevis rerum narratio* of legal decision-making— comes to have a different status as authoritatively constituting this state.

Like Bankowski, Samuel argues that analogical reasoning is original and fundamental, and that when it is subjected to the legal syllogism, by trying to abstract and incorporate in a rule a common property which makes cases analogous, the technique of analogical reasoning is misrepresented, and the reduction to rules is apt to produce something of little practical use for giving right legal answers.

We need what he calls a three-dimensional rather than a two-dimensional model of legal reasoning. Subsuming the facts of a case under the minor premise of the supposed syllogism, alongside another case, actually involves presenting them as displaying a certain isomorphic pattern, and this process cannot be governed by rules. No rule will tell you that the facts of a case are best seen as a contractual relation between two legal subjects, rather than a case of tort, or in some other way. Yet this construction of the case in terms of a certain legal ontology is what is most decisive for the final legal result. The term 'construction' might be used here, not only in its legal sense, but to suggest a comparison with the way the unknown is reduced to the known in a geometrical proof, by introducing a geometrical construction. We might comment, however, that though no one way of seeing a pattern in a case is inevitable, nevertheless not just any pattern can be seen, some constructions will get you nowhere, and a pattern can be argued for as more strongly marked or more instructive than another.

Samuel points out another historical development, by which facts come to be modelled legally in terms of legal objects or entities that then figure in the patterns. One might trace a history of progressive *reification* by which what was, to start with, a set of circumstances in which a remedy is obtainable, is then conceptualized as a wrong that may be suffered, this in turn as a right that may be violated, and this lastly as a piece of incorporeal property. Samuel's point has evident relations to the institutional theory of law, discussed above. Analogy is at work here, in a sense akin to the sense in which analogy is at work in natural science, for example when the effect of the presence of a magnet on the movement of a compass needle is first of all conceptualized as the manifestation of a force exerted by the magnet on the needle, and then this in turn is conceptualized as a field of force attached to and surrounding the magnet, which affects the needle placed within it. In natural science too there can be rival models: combustion as the emission of phlogiston or as the uptake of oxygen, light as waves or as particles.[29] It happens that a single example will serve to illustrate the use of analogies both in science and in law. In physics, 'electricity is like water' —in that it has a force which can cause it to flow— for the purpose of developing the concept of electrical current. In law, 'electricity is like water' — in that it has a normal use but is potentially harmful— for the purpose of applying the rule in *Rylands v. Fletcher*.[30]

We said above that analogy and case-based reasoning are by no means identical. We might now go on to say that not only there is reasoning with cases that is not analogical, but also there is analogical reasoning that is not reasoning with cases. The law often makes use of what might be called 'global' analogies: a whole legal category is compared to another, or constructed on the model of it: thus international treaties are handled on the analogy of contracts between private individuals. This not so much discovering similarities as inventing them, or treating one thing as if it were something else. Analogy here most clearly plays a creative rôle.[31]

The discerning of patterns does not, we would argue, fall outside of reason: but it does perhaps fall outside of rule-based reason, and yet another question is the extent to which it might adequately be modelled by computers. Pattern-matching by computers is a promising area of application of neural networks. (See Barnden and Holyoak, 1994).[32]

9. REMEDIES AND DEFINITIONS

Gregory Pipe begins by insisting that the only justification for the assertion that there exists some legal right is that some remedy is available for failure to respect it. This claim, though controversial, is significantly connected to the question of the specific function of the law in society, raised in different ways by Bell and Smith.[33] The law is not concerned with the broad question what ought to be done, but with the more restricted question what is to be legally enforceable. This gives an edge to the lawyer's task of arriving at decisions by legal problem-solving, which as the previous discussion has shown, plays such a part in shaping the law and in shaping theories about its nature.

Pipe points out that though the idea that the law is concerned with remedies is readily granted in the context of litigation, it must also be recognized as essential to the legal position of a party in a non-litigious situation. This bears on the question of the area of legal activity to which a formal system might be applied. Legal theorists and advocates naturally interest themselves in potentially controversial cases, such as are likely to come to court; much of the analysis of reasoning in the articles discussed so far implicitly reflects the idea that the real life of the law lies at its growth points, as if the rest was dead wood. But there are plenty of clear and easy cases, of more immediate interest to run-of-the-mill legal practitioners and their clients, and it is essential to the law that these should be normal. We need not expect a formalized system necessarily to concentrate on difficult cases, or the kind of legal work that these involve. Pipe suggests in his conclusion that though a formalized system, to which he gives the name 'mechanical jurisprudence', could never be proof against new factors appearing which result in a jurist justifiably deciding differently from the machine, the latter could still be of value as having a low probability of error in practice, since after all human jurists also have a probability of error. (A related point is raised at the end of his paper by Barden.) It is indeed widely supposed in the AI and Law community (most notably in Susskind 1987) that clear cases (in a sense akin to Hart's earlier notion of a 'semantically clear case') can be isolated in some *a priori* way. The papers in this collection show that establishing whether or not a case is clear is always an interpretative problem. There can always be 'new features', and recognizing these is 'hard'; however, the probability of this happening may be low, and thus a system which has no way (through insufficient knowledge) of recognizing novel sources of defeasibility might still be acceptable in practice.

The insistence on remedies determines Pipe's choice of a concept of the law to analyze in detail. He takes the concept of 'consideration' as this figures in the English law of contract. English law (unlike some other systems, such as Scots law) insists on consideration as a condition for the *enforceability* of a promise or agreement.

Consideration as a requirement for a remedy for breach of contract is now such a well-settled label that it can hardly be argued that it is not a necessary condition for contractual validity in law, though of course it is not a sufficient condition. So it appears that a legal rule, the major premise of a legal syllogism (though, as Pipe emphasizes, defeasible in various ways) would undoubtedly include this in its antecedent. Or we might say that there is a legal rule or major premise which specifies a sufficient condition for contractual invalidity, that is, for the *refusal* to grant a remedy for breach of contract. (This might be indefeasible.) At the same time, Pipe points out that this condition, the existence of consideration, is itself incapable of definition. There can very well be cases in which the application of this label is called in question.[34] The problem, once again, is over the minor premise in the argument. Pipe shows by a series of cases how much the concept of consideration has been qualified or —most often— extended to deal with new cases. It appears to be in the state of continual change described by Smith. Pipe himself likens this term —though it is a technical term of the law— to ordinary language terms such as family resemblance terms discussed by Wittgenstein. He brings out a respect in which the problem of defining legal terms such as 'consideration' is indeed analogous to the problem of defining terms in other natural language disciplines and in everyday discourse. If such a term could be defined, it would be defined in other terms which, precisely because of their strict link with the first term, would present the same difficulties of application.

The position in law appears, however, to be even more complicated. For though the term 'consideration' itself may be incapable of definition even in terms of necessary (let alone sufficient) conditions, its function in the law is to form part of the set of necessary or sufficient conditions for another term —contractual validity or contractual invalidity.[35]

The fact that it is very difficult to arrive at a satisfactory definition of a term, and that definitions have had to be revised again and again in the face of counterexamples, does not *in itself* show that the term is indefinable, or that aiming at a formal definition is misconceived. The conclusion may be right, but the argument as it stands is not conclusive. Similar difficulties arise in more formal fields of inquiry, such as mathematics.[36] It has to be shown that legal discourse raises further difficulties of a different nature.

Some of the difficulties the courts have had with the term 'consideration' arise from the fact that they have to make intelligent decisions about when a promise should be enforceable, while at the same time respecting the rule that enforceability entails the existence of consideration. The rule being rigid, it is the application of it that has to be flexible. It is arguable that this has caused a sort of deformation in the concept of consideration, in order to make possible the right decisions. This could be taken as evidence for the claim made by Smith (from a different point of view) that the formal justification of the decision offered by the legal system is a sort of pretence.[37]

There are additional difficulties here, distinct from those concerning the range of application of non-legal terms, which can also come before the courts, for example the question whether a hovercraft is an aeroplane or a boat. The conditions specified by law for the formation of a contract constitute a certain theoretical picture of the nature of contract. This reminds us of the pattern in legal ontology emphasized by Samuel. 'Consideration' is a term of art, an artificial legal concept. The legal history outlined by Pipe shows how the requirement of consideration was used to express the way a contractual obligation is conditional, first upon something done to one's benefit by the other party, then upon the other party's obligation even if not yet discharged, then upon the other party's obligation only if it was itself not pre-existing but reciprocally conditional. The difficulties here are of a kind that would be addressed, for example, by analyzing the concept of contract in terms of deontic logic. That is not to say that they would then disappear, but that they would emerge as theoretical controversies like that over the correct way to handle deontic detachment (see Jones and Sergot). The same difficulties are addressed, and some dealt with in a different way, some dealt with in a similar way, by another system of law which uses a different conceptual scheme.[38]

Among the other complications listed by Pipe is the requirement for any definition to be sufficiently flexible to accommodate different judicial opinions. Disagreement between jurists is something that the law has to try to resolve, as it also resolves other disagreements, but is also something that, on deeply controversial points, it must accept. The ways it has of dealing with a diversity of juridical views are an aspect of the law likely to be important for any formalization of it, and this is a neglected point which merits more attention.

10. JUSTIFICATION AND NOVELTY

Garrett Barden develops and applies a formalization of the justification of legal decisions, treating it as a special case of a model of justification in general. In any domain, he says, a conditioned proposition, X, is justified by a set of conditions, C. He distinguishes ontological and epistemological conditions. In the jural domain, he holds that the conditioned has the internal structure of a three-place relation of entitlement, $RxAy$ (x is entitled to A from y, where x and y are legal persons). He understands 'entitlement' in a sense which includes obligations and liabilities as well as rights —anything that may be due to a person. Many rules are not of this form, but a rule must be of this form to be jural. He argues that, contrary to appearances, legal judgments can always be fitted into this schema. His account means, prima facie, that legal conclusions are propositions capable of truth and falsehood; but he goes on later to qualify this radically.

He then turns to the nature of the set of conditions *C*. In relation to his distinction of ontological and epistemological conditions, he suggests a way of accommodating the possibility that a court is mistaken in its judgment. He also gives an extended analysis of how it can come about that a case and the judgment about it are uncertain or unexpected. He addresses directly the question of what makes a legal position *new* —a concept implicit in much of the discussion in previous contributions. This analysis tackles once again some of the issues discussed, in earlier contributions, under the title of defeasibility, as well as bearing directly on the possible utility of a computerized system as a source of legal guidance. He shows how the stated legal conditions for a judgment may be more or less specific, and how cases may be more or less clear instances of satisfaction of the conditions. There are, he says, three ways in which a case can be juridically novel: in respect of *C*, by presenting a new state of affairs for judicial consideration; in respect of *RxAy*, by involving a new claimed entitlement or a new candidate for legal personality; or in respect of $C \rightarrow RxAy$, by proposing a new relation of conditionality.

This discussion relates to Sartor's contention that the possible defeating conditions for the drawing of a legal conclusion cannot be exhaustively anticipated. Defeasance may be a factual surprise, a conceptual surprise, or a legal surprise. A factual surprise is when some new fact emerges which makes an exception under an already recognized legal heading, as when an old lady recently widowed and claiming her late husband's estate, turns out to have poisoned him with an overdose of nutmeg: this is already covered by Sartor's analysis in terms of 'non-refutanda'. A conceptual surprise is when it is arguable how the given facts are placed in relation to already recognized legal headings, as when a man is charged with impeding the course of justice in that he warned passing motorists to slow down because there was a police speed trap round the next corner, and his defence is that he was preventing the commission of criminal offences. A legal surprise is when some new legal ground for making an exception is successfully argued: for example, when a defendant charged with a crime introduces the novel defence of non-insane automatism.[39] But there is a broad area where it is difficult to say whether the open texture of possible defeating conditions poses questions of fact or of law, or where this issue itself calls for legal decision. Does non-insane automatism really constitute a new legal category, or is it a newly-recognized medical condition which satisfies existing criteria for non-responsibility? It is not clear how far Sartor's ideal 'perfect conditional norm', embodying a complete statement of the law, would have to include specifications covering all the possible factual variations and conceptual complexities. This problem is related to the theoretical question, addressed elsewhere in this book, how far the law is self-contained, and to the practical question, faced by the builder of a system, how far a representation of legal knowledge would have to incorporate a representation of common-sense knowledge about the world (see Haft et al. 1988).

Barden regards the possibility of arguable and still undecided cases as making the law indeterminate —so his position has links with that of Smith. He likens the indeterminacy in question to that ascribed by some philosophers —including himself— to contingent statements about the future. So he contrasts a possible computer system assisting lawyers by anticipation of a court's decision, with a computer system assisting doctors in the making of a medical diagnosis. The ontological conditions for the truth or falsity of the diagnosis already exist, even though the epistemological conditions for affirming or denying it do not. He likens the legal advice, on the other hand, to prediction of the result of a horse-race, which, he says, is not yet true or false. It might be argued against this that, even accepting the general thesis about future contingent statements, legal judgments are different from these also. For when a case eventually comes up for decision, the court can only decide it on the basis of the same sort of considerations that were adduced by the legal adviser —at least, to the extent that the latter fully takes account of the available legal materials for making the decision. There is nothing like the result of the race to decide the question and thus make it a betting issue —at least to the extent that it is considered theoretically possible for the court to make the wrong decision, and for this possibility to be considered in practice by a higher or later court.[40] The logical difference between a system for giving legal advice and a system for medical diagnosis is not just the same as the logical difference between a system for diagnosis and a system for predicting the efficacy or inefficacy, given a certain diagnosis, of a certain course of treatment. Barden concludes, indeed, with a question about the nature of the probability we can ascribe to an opinion about an undecided case, which he contrasts with probabilities capable of being analysed in statistical terms. At the same time he points out that frequency of agreement with the courts is still a reasonable ground for ascribing the first kind of probability —whether to the advice of a human jurist or to that of a machine. In this conclusion he converges also with Pipe.[41]

The indeterminacy of as yet undecided points of law might be likened, we suggest, not so much to that of statements about the future as to that of counterfactual conditionals.[42] In general it need not be true either that if *p* were the case then *q* would be the case, or that if *p* were the case then *not q* would be the case. This is not to say that such hypothetical statements are never true, only that they are not always true. So, arguing along the lines of Smith and Pipe as well as Barden, we might say that sometimes there is not yet any legal truth of the form 'if case *C* came to court, the [right] decision would be *D*'. However, this is not to say that there are never legal truths of this form. To insist that the law is indeterminate wherever an issue has not actually been litigated, would be like saying of some substance that it is not soluble in water, though indeed it has the property that putting it into water causes it to change immediately so that it becomes soluble. A case which is undecided is not therefore undecidable, even in the present state of legal understanding.

11. QUALIFICATION NORMS AND DEONTIC LOGIC

The question of the proper place for deontic modalities in the formal representation of law, is taken up by Andrew Jones and Marek Sergot. MacCormick has offered a jurisprudential account, and Barden a formal account, of legal judgments in *institutional* terms: this endows them with possible deontic import, without making them deontic in themselves. Jones and Sergot return to the question raised by MacCormick and more technically by Sartor, whether the formalization of legal reasoning calls for a logic beyond the standard forms of predicate logic. They also open up further possibilities of connexion and comparison between computer systems and legal systems.

Jones and Sergot note two common but apparently contrary misconceptions about deontic logic in the computer representation of law. The first is, that deontic logic must be used, just because the law is obviously concerned with obligations, rights, and the like. They show how, for many of the purposes a system might be put to, deontic operators are unnecessary, or even when they can be introduced, require only a rudimentary logic. Other contributors such as MacCormick and Kowalski, from jurisprudential and computing points of view respectively, favour on the contrary methods of analysis which in their view effectively bypass the need for explicit deontic operators altogether. Jones and Sergot spell out the circumstances in which it may be necessary to go further.

The second misconception is that systems using deontic logic have already been much developed. They point out that there are actually very few such systems; but they propose a general methodology for progress in this field.

They present a simple but representative example of a set of 'laws', the book-borrowing regulations of a library. First they argue that this could be understood as a specification of how the library system itself should operate. This specification could be met by an utterly reliable set of human protagonists, or by effectively computerizing the library system itself. If we assume that the system works flawlessly, there is no need for a deontic logic. The latter becomes necessary so soon as we envisage the possibility of a violation of one of the norms of the system, especially as an eventuality which the system itself must take account of. For what characterizes deontic logic is the distinction between what ought to be the case and what is the case. And this distinction leads directly to the notorious problems of deontic logic, the Chisholm paradox and related puzzles.[43] These chiefly concern deontic detachment, the rule or rules by which a conditional obligation is derivable as a conclusion from satisfaction of its condition, which is most problematical when the obligation is conditional upon the breach of another obligation. Now violation of a regulation may either occur internally to the system, or may (even more likely) result from extraneous factors which the system has to deal with but over which it has no control; this possibility has to be taken seriously, especially when one regulation precisely concerns the system's response to violation of another regulation. There are all sorts of ways in which even a set of library regulations turns out not to be self-contained and insulated from other concerns, including the provisions of the law at large.

If we understand laws as norms addressed to human agents, it is still possible to separate out the deontic factor (putting it into a separate norm) and consider the laws as primarily 'qualification norms' or definitions of the legal term in the consequent by means of the conditions in the antecedent. Jones and Sergot show how not only the simple example of a library regulation, but also provisions of a statute such as the British Nationality Act, can be understood in this way: the latter as specifying what constitute the qualifications for being a British national. What rights and obligations then accrue can be treated as a separate matter, and is in fact to be found in quite other parts of the law. Likewise, rules based on case-law specify the conditions for the existence of a contract. In effect, this is just the sort of treatment proposed by those other contributors who analyse a law as a conditional attaching a legal consequent to factual conditions. Again, this approach also fits in well with the institutional theory of law.

There are two different ways in which the normative is treated as descriptive: first, when the consequent of a conditional legal norm is taken as the description of what is done, on the assumption that the law is complied with, so the consequent holds ideally; second, when the antecedent of a conditional legal norm is taken as the definition of a legal term in the consequent, so the consequent holds analytically. (In the second case it may be that another legal norm describes the course of action which, according to the law, follows the ascription of this term.) Treating law as either descriptive or definitional and thus avoiding deontic modalities seems to us to be an important point when talking about the social applications of computers and expert systems, and we return to that later in the introduction.

We may also observe a curious feature, in this connexion, of the standard language of legislation in the United Kingdom and other countries. Contrary to what one might expect, language which has a deontic or imperative character on the face of it, is used in precisely those contexts where the possibility of violation is not envisaged; whereas where the possibility of violation is most clearly in question, the language used has on the face of it the character of qualification norms. Thus when a statute such as the British Nationality Act prescribes action by the Secretary of State, it does so in terms of what he shall or shall not do. On the contrary, a typical clause in a criminal statute does not, on the surface, forbid a certain action, but rather declares that any person who does this action is thereby guilty of a certain offence, and is consequently liable on conviction to a certain penalty. The criminal law is an extreme case, in being concerned exclusively with violation. The presumption that the Secretary of State will act in accordance with the law does not necessarily deprive the citizen of recourse to the courts: but the consequence of a successful judicial review is not to punish the Secretary of State, but to bring it about that he does what he ought or, effectively, to achieve the legal result of his doing so. The statute governing his actions could be regarded as a specification of a normally operating administrative system, even when the courts have to be brought in to ensure that it does operate normally. And of course the courts themselves are presumed to know and obey the law (including the law as it particularly governs themselves —for example, the law of judicial procedure) since they are the law's own interpreters and spokesmen. In one respect it might be argued that the above interpretation of statutes governing officials fails to capture an important deontic distinction even in this field, that is, between what, under the statute, the Secretary of State is required to do, and what he is permitted or empowered to do. Earlier analyses of the British Nationality Act (by Sergot and Kowalski) ignored this distinction, in treating 'shall' and 'shall not' as contradictories, whereas in reality they are contraries, since the contradictory of 'shall not' is 'may'. If a statute is a description of what is done if it is fully complied with, how is 'may' expressed in contradistinction to 'shall'?

There is room for questioning here the appropriateness of the term 'definition' as applied to a qualification norm. Is the meaning of the legal term given by the conditions for its application, or by the consequences of its application? Since the point of the norm is to make the connexion between the factual grounds and the legal conclusions, and this connexion is embodied in the legal term, it is difficult to say which pole this term is linked with in meaning.[44] If it is said that the British Nationality Act defines a number of different categories of British national, is that only because there are a number different grounds on which British nationality can be claimed, or because there are also a number of different sets of rights and obligations which may be acquired by one who makes a successful claim to British nationality? The issue is more than verbal. It could give rise to substantive debate on the question of equality of status before the law. How far the qualifying conditions constitute a definition may depend on the deontic modalitics in the law: for example if the Secretary of State is not simply obliged but has some discretion over whether to accord British nationality to one who has the requisite qualifications for claiming it. The issue of definition could also affect the systematic form of representation of the law, even of the single statute. (This is discussed below in relation to Kowalski's paper and Sartor's distinction between exceptions to effects and exceptions to norms.) However, it remains true, as Jones and Sergot point out, that a representation of a statute in a set of qualification norms may be quite adequate for its intended purpose.

They go on to point out that even when the normative components in a law need to be represented, in order to cater for the difference between the actual and the ideal, it can be that no more than a rudimentary deontic logic is required for the purpose in hand. However there can be legal provisions which require a more elaborate analysis, and then some of the trickiest problems of deontic logic become unavoidable.

According to what purpose the representation is to serve, Jones and Sergot propose, in effect, using a predicate logic as long as this remains adequate:

either to describe what happens if everything proceeds as it ought, or to ascribe legal qualifications to facts.[45]

They argue that though limiting the *intended purposes of the system* may very well save its builder from the need to enter the more difficult territories of deontic logic, this cannot so easily be done by limiting the *areas or kinds of law handled*, since even relatively 'easy' or 'self-contained' pieces of law can present the more difficult kinds of deontic situation. In this respect the moral of their investigation is close to that drawn, after a more detailed study of a particular case, by Lilian Edwards.

In conclusion, they suggest a further development, on the lines of the theory of *normative positions*. The forms of representation considered up to this point in their paper, even when they involve deontic operators, still involve only one-place predicates —specifications of the actions or states of single subjects, or impersonal specifications of what should be done or what is legally true. But we often have to deal with a system of relations between subjects, such that the normative position of any one is logically dependent on the normative position of others. As an observation about the law, this brings us back to the contention of MacCormick that the law is typically concerned with powers, and that powers are essentially relational. Jones and Sergot remark on the broader implications of the theory of normative positions, which has its origin in the study of legal relations, but can be applied to diverse types of organization, involving diverse categories of agent —natural persons, corporations, or automatic systems. Thus they outline the broadening context in which, for example, developments will be made on the lines of Sandra Dewitz's paper discussed below. The formalization of law and the development of computers can be expected to proceed in parallel but also to intersect, each making contributions to the other.

A general moral to draw from Jones' and Sergot's paper is that if we are undertaking a formal representation of any piece of law, we have to decide how deep we wish the representation to be. And this decision depends on the purpose that the representation, or the system that contains it, is to serve. Do we want a formal representation which penetrates into the rationale of the legal provisions, the principles underlying the rules?

An example much discussed by the Group, and referred to in several of the papers, will serve to illustrate how a legal provision can be represented formally at different levels. In *Connor*, a widow who had stabbed her husband and thus caused his death, was denied her widow's pension, though her late husband had paid all the due contributions and she would normally have been entitled to it on his decease. This case can be viewed from a number of theoretical and formal points of view. It can be taken as an illustration of how public policy over-rides, in certain cases, legalistic rules (see Bell). It can be taken as an example of the defeasibility of a normal legal conclusion by an unusual condition (see MacCormick). The conflict and ranking of the relevant considerations can represented formally (see Sartor). From all these points of view the defeating circumstance is treated no differently from some other defeating circumstance which does not happen to consist in the violation of a law. But if we go into the deontic complexity of the case, we find, first, that it has features which make it akin to the Chisholm problem, and second, that handling these would make the legal principle of 'not profiting by a wrong' not a material provision of the law but rather a formal aspect of legal inference rooted in deontic logic. The principle means that a fact which is normally a sufficient condition for a right, ceases to be, when the claimant of the right has breached an obligation in bringing the fact about: the fact but for which the claimant would not have the right would not have existed but for the claimant's breach of an obligation, so in some sense it ought not to be that the claimant has the right. This is a crude statement of something which a sophisticated deontic logic would be needed to refine. Such a logic would have to be both deontic and defeasible, and would need to represent the deontic positions of particular agents and claimants.[46]

12. LEGAL THEORY, JUSTIFICATION AND HEURISTICS

Joxerramon Bengoetxea, in the next paper, explores the relations between different levels of legal theory and the problems of designing a knowledge-representation and decision support system for a given area of law. He examines the special difficulties and opportunities presented by a new and growing legal area, the law of the European Communities. After critically reconstructing Jerzy Wróblewski's analytical model of the application of law (Wróblewski 1992), he tries to identify the points at which Artificial Intelligence can provide help in formulating justifications of legal decisions.

Among the levels of legal theory he distinguishes, first, grand legal theory which places law in its social and political context, and establishes the nature of its legitimacy. Existing grand theory is historically tied to the concept of the state, and an appropriate grand theory for EC law still has to be developed. Middle-range theory is concerned with the sources of law, the unit norms that make up a legal system, the conditions of validity of norms, their logical structure, and their systematic relations in institutional categories. At the most concrete level is legal dogmatics, which applies theory to expounding legal doctrine in a particular legal field. One of the incidental virtues of devising an expert system in a restricted area of law is that it makes the background middle-range theory inescapable. Middle-range theory, he argues, is the level most appropriate at present both for the analysis of EC law, and for the development of computerized decision support.

He pays particular attention to the place of legal interpretation in the representation of legal norms —and this relates his paper to Bell's, to the work discussed by Hilgendorf, and to the background work in the Group and elsewhere by MacCormick and Bankowski[47]. In carrying out the task of knowledge representation, informed choices have to be made. It is necessary to decide how closely a computer representation should follow the physical text, both in its content and in the way its materials are divided up; or whether it should embody the results of a particular systematic interpretation of the text; or whether it should propose alternative interpretations marked as being such. These considerations contribute to the difficulty of the task of preparing a computerized system. But at the same time they indicate ways in which the system can assist the lawyer in finding justifications for his decisions. For Bengoetxea, systems that do not, at first blush, appear to play a part in the topics that we are discussing here are very important. For example he places great stress on document retrieval systems, and more generally, on systems which make available to the lawyer the materials that furnish the context of argumentation (whose form is discussed by Sartor). The identification and deployment of source materials (including those background materials which cast light on the policy purposes of legislation) is a far from trivial task.

In general, he sees the rôle of computers as being in the area of legal justification, which (like Bell, Pipe, and other contributors) he contrasts with heuristics. He takes over from Wróblewski a refined and elaborated model of the legal syllogism, and maintains that decision support systems can work within this structure. He recognizes the problems of open texture, defeasibility, and potential conflict of norms, and the occurrence of difficult particular cases for decision, discussed in earlier papers. But he insists that the main difference between clear cases and difficult cases is not that the syllogism only applies in clear cases. The syllogism or logical inference leading to the conclusion holds in both alike: the main difference is that in clear cases the establishment of the partial decisions which figure in the pattern of justification represented in his analytical model, is fairly straightforward and unproblematic from a pragmatic point of view, whereas in difficult cases there are pragmatic difficulties or doubts as to the establishment of any of the partial decisions. In his view, decision support systems can work with a syllogistic structure of justification. Classical formal (monotonic) logic will cover the overall transformation to the conclusion, the underlying structure of justification, and special non-monotonic logics can be devised for the partial decisions

A computerized system can provide decision support in the sense that it provides the justification of a legal decision, which must fit the syllogistic pattern, referring to the material facts and relevant norms. In saying this, he draws attention in effect to a double sense in the expression 'decision support'. For at the same time, a computerized system can provide support in the sense that it assists the human jurist in carrying out this task. He points out that the analytical model of the legal syllogism does not try to capture the process of discovery or heuristic process which actually leads to the decision. Discovery is important, but the aim of the model is rather to control law-applying decisions from a justificatory standpoint. Whatever the cognitive processes which led to the decision, it will only be rationally acceptable if it can be justified according to the model. We may then ask, how far these contentions, true of the theoretical model of justification, are also true of the computerized support systems which are built in accordance with it? We are reminded once again of the contrast between the informal methods of mathematical inquiry described by Polya, and the formal proofs which mathematicians undertake to supply, when they have discovered and established in other ways the theorems that they wish to prove. It is evident that justification and heuristics are not separate matters, but different aspects of the same inquiry. The discovery of proofs is itself a heuristic matter.[48]

Bengoetxea himself points out, as one of the most challenging characteristics of EC law, the specific nature of its heuristics in practice. That is, the need to adopt a comparative law approach at all times. This makes EC law a perfect setting or laboratory for comparative approaches. In order to understand EC law one needs important legal notions developed in a variety of different legal traditions. (This factor complicates and enriches the considerations adduced above by Bankowski and Smith.) 'When interpreting EC law the European Court of Justice does not openly proclaim in the justification of its decisions its use of the comparative method, but the comparison of the different laws of the Member States in order to arrive at interpretative decisions is a constant element of the heuristics of decisionmaking at the Court.' This has radical consequences for the design of expert advisory systems in this area, even though the objective of such systems is formulating justifications.

Bengoetxea suggests that EC Law, because it is a very broad and multifarious field, historically and jurisprudentially novel, serves as a laboratory test case for the use of computers. Lilian Edwards suggests a laboratory test case at the opposite pole: she takes Scots intestate succession law as being an apparently well-established, uncontroversial, selfcontained and unified piece of law, and she relates her experiences in building the Intestate Succession Adviser.

As we said above, while her initial assessment of this piece of law proved largely correct, problems arose with the need to define the area of application of the system and separate it from other areas of the law, and also with the need to take account of the pragmatic context in which the legal rules operate. What she found confirms what is observed by Jones and Sergot even with regard to the extremely simple and restricted example of library regulations. As she says, 'Building a legal decision support system of any kind reveals that the difficulties of legal formalization are not merely philosophical but pragmatic.' And interpretation problems occur even in the least ambiguous of domains. To a great extent, though, it may be observed that the limitations on the system are very much the same in kind and degree as the limitations of, say, a particular statute as applied by administrators and judges. The building of the system draws attention to the limits of its own usability and thus also makes clear the position of this segment of the law.

Lilian Edwards is able to go on to report that the implementation process reveals that attempting to formalize the law is a two-edged sword. A working system has a heuristic function: it can act as a source of legal creativity, by operating as a sort of 'legal fruit machine' to derive from the rules in the domain and possible combinations of facts, a range of legal consequences, predictable or unexpected, desirable or undesirable. She notes that these consequences have higher or lower levels of probability, considered as predictions of how the courts would actually and reasonably decide the cases if they arose. (This relates back to questions raised by Pipe and Barden.) But uncertainty need not be a bad thing, if the purpose of the system is not to replace judges but to serve as a tool for generating arguments, in the hands of advocates in an adversarial system. Thus her system can be used to obtain argumentative materials, whose subsequent handling might be formalized on the lines laid out by Sartor.

Furthermore, a system might —and her system did— generate examples of legal argument for unusual situations of fact, even in a domain which seemed so settled that it had generated only one case of significance in real-life litigation. While some express the fear that a computer system will not be able to anticipate novel problems, it appears on the contrary that a system can go beyond what is actually provided by the case-law. The system can be set to reason as a judge reasons (according to the account given by Bankowski, and discussed above) when he tries a rule for absurdity against hypothetical examples. It is still for the human jurist, of course, to judge whether the consequences of the application of the rule in extreme cases are acceptable, and how the situation is to be dealt with if they are not.

13. ANALOGIES BETWEEN LAW AND COMPUTING

Bob Kowalski finds analogies between law and computing which he regards as potentially enlightening and useful in both areas. Indeed, one could say, broadly, that whereas Sartor proposes to use logic to *describe* legal norms and their relations, and Jones and Sergot propose to develop a logic of deontic terms *symbolically* represented, Kowalski proposes so far as possible to use the characteristics of logic programming to make an *analogue* representation of the law.

He closely examines a number of examples of laws or regulations drafted in natural language, ranging from the British Nationality Act 1981 to a London Underground emergency notice, texts addressed for different purposes to different audiences. He shows how the British statutory draftsman uses an extraordinarily precise and complex form of natural language to make clear the content of and the systematic relations between the provisions of the act. This is where he finds close parallels with logic programming, but also a need to extend the basic model of the latter. He suggests the introduction of type identifiers to handle relative clauses whose subjects are, for example, persons and times, and making a representation not only of facts but also of beliefs. He suggests that non-monotonicity in default rules and rules with exceptions can be handled by exploiting the analogy of *negation as failure*. When 'not *p*' is understood as 'negation as failure', it means (with reference to facts represented in the system) 'it is not shown that *p*'.[49] He shows how the combination of metalanguage with object-language, both in logic programming and in the language of the legislative draftsman, helps to make clear the systematic relations of parts of the law, and facilitates the consistent updating of the system by amendments.

Such techniques enable him, for example, to give a formal representation of aspects of defeasibility that are considered from a pragmatic point of view by MacCormick. When vitiating circumstances are discovered, or arise, to affect some legal arrangement which was established on an assumption of validity, and which would normally persist, they may render the arrangement retrospectively void *ab initio*, or they may render it only subject to cancellation from the date of discovery, or they may be legally too late to affect it. The way the law handles such situations expresses its concern for confidence and stability in the human affairs it governs. Sometimes the law makes subsequent discoveries retrospective in legal effect, sometimes it prefers not to. Legal provisions either way can be catered for by introducing, in the logical representation, a distinction between time when beliefs are held and time when the facts exist.

A question may be raised, how far the logical devices available to Kowalski, are sufficient for handling some of the other complexities of the statutory text, for which the legal draftsman has devices of legal language, and which are handled formally by Sartor. For example, Kowalski considers two subsections from section 40 of the Act, the first of which 40(1) provides that 'subject to the provisions of this section' the Secretary of State may under certain conditions deprive a person of a British citizenship obtained by naturalization; while another 40(5) provides that he shall not deprive such a person 'under this section' except under certain other conditions. He says that 40(1) has the form 'P if Q' while 40(5) has the form '¬P if not R' (where '¬' is classical negation and 'not' is negation by failure); and he shows how with extended logic programs contradiction may be avoided so that 40(5) overrides 40(1). This overriding is expressed in the language of the statute by the words in 40(1) 'subject to the provisions of this section'. But this legal provision actually exhibits an important distinction drawn by Sartor, between exceptions to effects and exceptions to norms. This is captured by the language of the statute with the phrase 'under this section', but it is not clear that it can be captured by Kowalski's analysis. For subsection 40(5) does not provide that (except under the relevant conditions) the Secretary of State may not deprive a person of his citizenship; nor even that (except under the relevant conditions) he may not deprive a person of citizenship acquired by naturalization; but that (except under the relevant conditions) he may not deprive a person of acquired citizenship, *under the power given in section 40* —in particular, subsection 40(1). The Secretary of State is not precluded by this subsection 40(5) from depriving a person of citizenship, without satisfaction of the conditions, under powers given in another section of the

Act or another Act. An exception to an effect is indeed of the form '¬P if S', but an exception to a norm is of the form '¬(P if Q) if S'. One way in which Kowalski might reduce section 40 to the form he gives is by a suitable identification of the consequent of the conditional statements: that is, by putting 'P' not for 'the Secretary of State may deprive a person of his citizenship acquired by naturalization' but for 'the Secretary of State may under section 40 deprive a person of his citizenship acquired by naturalization'. This would be yet a further extension of a device by which consequents are made very specific to the conditions on which they depend. Jones and Sergot use a similar device in distinguishing different categories of citizenship acquired under different titles. Here it goes much further. It may then be necessary to have further propositions in the data-base, expressing the various logical relations between the otherwise opaque contents of the terms 'citizenship', 'citizenship acquired by naturalization', 'deprivation of citizenship', 'citizenship subject to deprivation under section 40' and so forth. The artificiality of the device may not matter for technical purposes, but it may cast doubt on the idea (put forward by Jones and Sergot though not by Kowalski, and discussed further below) that what we have here is a formal expression of 'qualification norms' or 'institutional definitions'. At the same time, Sartor's distinction between exceptions to norms and exceptions to effects seems to cast doubt on the idea of a 'qualification norm' itself.

Those who, like Kowalski, take logic programming as a computing paradigm, tackle the difficult task of reducing knowledge they wish to represent to the canonical form they prefer. Likewise philosophers sometimes have analogous aims — for example, to reduce imperatives to indicatives, so as to make them more amenable to formal treatment, or so as to bring them into conformity with a certain theory of law or morals. From his examination of the example of the London Underground notice, Kowalski finds suggestions of just such a comparison between computing paradigms and jurisprudential analysis. Thus, for

> Please give up this seat if an elderly or handicapped person needs it

he substitutes

> You do a good deed if you give up your seat to a person who needs your seat and is elderly or handicapped.

As he says, the claim that legal imperatives have an explicit or implicit purpose is important in legal philosophy; moreover it underlies the discussion of all aspects of public policy and other values in the formation, interpretation, and application of legal rules, in the papers by Bell and others. The substitution just offered illustrates very well the difficulties that are encountered by a project of eliminating imperatives. If 'Do A!' is regarded by the theory as equivalent to 'If you do A then you get R' (where result R is the achievement of the objective of action), then consider the internally disjunctive command 'Do either A or B!' (= 'I command you to do either A or B'), or alternatively the externally disjunctive command 'Either Do A! or Do B!' (= 'Either I command you to do A or I command you to do B'). Now 'Do either A or B!', on the theory in question, is equivalent to 'If you do either A or B then you get R', which is logically equivalent to 'If you do A then you get R and if you do B then you get R', which on the theory is equivalent to 'Do A! and Do B!' Likewise 'Either Do A! or Do B!', on the theory, is equivalent to 'Either if you do A then you get R or if you do B you get R', which logically implies 'If you do both A and B then you get R', which on the theory is equivalent to 'Do both A and B!' The elementary difference between disjunction and conjunction has disappeared for commands. Kowalski goes on to consider another attempted reduction of the imperative to the indicative —which corresponds to the more standard reduction of the normative offered by Anderson (1967). According to this, 'Do A!' is rendered as 'If you don't do A you get S' where S is a bad thing or 'sanction'. For Kowalski, the 'sanction' is a device for transforming an integrity constraint, so that this serves the purpose of a command to the effect: 'Avoid the sanction and any action which incurs it'. Instead of 'If you don't to A you get S' one could put 'If you do Q then you do A', where 'Q' = 'what is required'. This by contraposition has a similar form to the sanction analysis. 'Q' then does the job that 'R' failed to do. But it is no longer clear that imperatives have been dispensed with. These alternative analyses do not raise the difficulties raised by Kowalski's first analysis, though they are not free from deeper ones.

14. THE PLACE OF COMPUTERS IN SOCIETY

Kowalski's paper also returns us to issues discussed by Bell and others. He points out an analogy between legislation and logic programs in relation to the achievement of their objectives. As programs are written to meet specifications, he says, so laws are drafted to achieve social policies. He suggests that laws like programs might be tested for their adequacy in this respect. We could distinguish here between the more remote or ulterior objectives of a law, the achievement of which can depend on all sorts of extraneous factors, and the proper or immediate objective of a law, which is to achieve a certain *legal* result. This is perhaps closer to the testing of a piece of engineering against specifications, and it is no mean task to show that a law achieves its intended legal result efficiently and effectively. The same holds for other kinds of legal draftsmanship, for example the drafting of a contract by a solicitor, with advice from a barrister, for a client. This point —and the implied analogy between law and engineering— is potentially very significant.[50] It is connected with the other focus of interest in Kowalski's paper, the possible effect of logic on making the law clearer and easier to understand.

The nature of the language used in legal draftsmanship is a question considered also, against a background of concern for the social purposes of law, by Bell in his paper; and Bell prepared other papers for discussion by the Group, on the differences in the legislative styles of different countries, the relation between these differences and differences in judicial practice and expectation, and more generally the relation between legal language and its intended audience. The question was raised whether some styles lend themselves to computer rendering more than others. The detailed rules of British statutes were compared with the broad statements of principle in French legislative text. Bell points out the importance of lawyers' assumptions which can be taken for granted by the legislator trying to convey his intentions. Kowalski emphasizes the democratic requirement of intelligibility to the layman. Considering this issue in connexion with the question of testing law against specifications, we could point out that the ordinary citizen is likely to place conflicting demands on the legal expert. On the one hand the layman wants legal texts that he finds intelligible; on the other hand he wants legal texts that can be relied on to produce the desired results. Different kinds of legal language are better suited to these different purposes. One might compare the different forms of architectural draftsmanship (another area of computer application): a perspective view is intended to convey to the public what a proposed building will look like; a constructional plan, section, or set of details is intended to convey to the builders what they are to make it like. The client will be unhappy to start with if he is only shown working drawings; but he will be unhappy later on if his builder is only supplied with an artist's impression.

This leads us on to a more general question as to the rôle of computers in law and society.

In looking at the function of computers in law and the design of expert systems, the idea of literally intelligent systems or artificial intelligence does not really have to be addressed.[51] The more immediate and practical worry is rather that computers will carry out badly the rôle assigned to them —because of insufficient understanding of the task by the human beings who design them. It is not only computers, but formalization generally, that is likely to be exposed to this criticism. This is seen, for example, in the area of judgments of probability in law. Some particularly crude attempts to introduce mathematical probability into the court room, led critics to object to 'trial by mathematics' (Tribe 1971): but what was really going on was not the misuse of mathematics but the use of bad mathematics.

However the computer is also the object of a different kind of fear. It seems to raise the spectre of a Frankenstein monster somehow taking over. Let us examine this in more detail. We have no problems accepting books in the law. Legal treatises cover the accumulated wisdom of the writer. They do not display just the writer's knowledge but other knowledge as well. They help the reader in giving him or her access to knowledge that they might not have been able to get at personally. Whatever knowledge the book brings, however, we do not worry about it replacing the human being. We feel secure and do not postulate the intelligent book. But we do have this fear with the computer. The machine here is perceived as taking away the task of the lawyer. There is a fear that it will make the lawyer redundant and thus lose some of the essential characteristics of the law. Whereas the book seems to only useful as book-and-lawyer, the computer, we might fear, may one day be able to dispense with the lawyer.

One reason for this is that a book is static, whereas a computer is animated. And yet one could point to more or less formalized or mechanical procedures for taking decisions, that have long since existed in human society. Majority voting, and much besides in the procedure of corporate bodies, is finally a mechanical procedure, even though there is some input of human intelligence.[52]

If we think that the process of law does depend, in part on lawyers, and in part on how our societies are constructed, then how can intelligent machines fit into it? Do we want such a society? We can go further than that. For even if intelligent machines were to be impossible, we might treat expert systems and the like as though they were intelligent. What sort of society do we then create for ourselves? We are led into a sort of science fiction fantasy in which computers gradually take over the world, as mere humans are unable to get in the way and prevent the machine making manifestly bad but not technically 'wrong' decisions.

What rôle, then, *should* computers play in society? Two points of contact between law and computing are (1) where computers are brought to bear on the law, and (2) where the law is brought to bear on computers. (The law of intellectual property in software, of liability in tort for the consequences of computer malfunction, etc., belongs in the latter.) As computers are developed to perform various tasks in society, and as, perhaps, they come to fit more and more the description Aristotle gave to *slaves*, 'speaking tools', the closer these two points may come to convergence. In fact, corporations and other organizations with their artificial decision procedures already loom large in such a position: as legal persons they assume some of the social rôles otherwise occupied by natural persons. With computers we fear that the new slaves may become our new masters.

One way of looking at the rôle of the computer in society is to view the computer as a *social prosthesis*, and to ask where in society we have to place it. This analogy is put forward by Collins (1990). He takes it further, imagining that a human heart can be replaced by an artificial heart. Medical science might not be able to make this a perfect replacement for the human heart. Our body, however, can develop ways of getting round the problems, to enable us to cope with it. The heart might not be able to pump so efficiently, but the body might compensate by producing more red blood cells. This would have the effect of enabling the same amount of oxygen to be pumped round. We would, Collins says, consider this a satisfactory alternative to a human heart even if it did not act exactly as a human heart did. Why? Because the human body would be able to function at least as well as if it had a human heart. This is all that we are interested in and that is all that we would be concerned about. If it did not quite live up to what was expected of it I might adjust my activity in such a way so as I did not notice. I cut out running up hills and to all intents and purposes I have replaced the human heart. The question is can we mimic the inputs and outputs well enough to be able to mimic the performance of the human individual.

It is important, according to Collins, not to apply this analogy by thinking of an artificial brain replacing the real individual human brain. The heart analogy does apply, but in a different way. The computer is a *social* prosthesis. It replaces the human being in the social organism. The question then is whether the intelligent computer can be an acceptable human being within the social organism. If it cannot quite do it, what adjustments does the social organism have to make to make it acceptable? We can make society more or less sensitive to this just as immune-suppressive drug as can make the body less likely reject the artificial heart.

How then should the computer fit into the social organism? What is a computer good at? We are not, according to Collins, wanting it to be 'intelligent'. Collins invites us to consider the Turing Test as originally formulated. In 1950 Alan Turing published a paper in which he proposed an operational definition of the question whether machines could think. This was based on an imitation game where a man and a women are concealed. An interrogator tries to find out which is which by asking them questions which are written on a piece of paper. The answers being handed returned to the interrogator. For the purposes of the game the man agrees to answer as a women while the women answers as herself. Turing suggested that the man be replaced with a machine.

We now ask the question, 'What will happen when a machine takes the part of the [man] in the game?' 'Will the interrogator decide wrongly just as often when the machine is played like this as he does when the game is played between a man and a women?' These questions replace our original question, 'Can machines think?' (Turing, quoted in Collins 1990, p. 181).

What is important here is that the machine has to mimic a man who is imitating a woman. It is far easier to mimic someone pretending to be something that he is not than to mimic what he is. Why? The man will not have to know everything about women for he is only pretending to be one. The knowledge domain of being a woman is infinite, and it would be as impossible for a man to capture that as it would for the computer to capture the whole of law. But pretending to be someone else absolves you from that duty.[53]

Leaving aside the question whether this defines intelligence or not, it gives us a fair idea of what a machine might be good at —the 'fit' into the social organism that we might expect. Machines 'fit' pretty well where they imitate humans imitating machines. The failure might, ironically, be that they turn out to be rather better at it than humans. But we would make allowances, as we did in our heart analogy.

A metaphor we might use is that of 'machine-like behaviour'. Human beings are particularly good at it. Where does it occur? Extreme examples of this can be seen in the military. There, in certain situations, we want soldiers to make automatic responses. The point of the seemingly pointless drill is to get them to do just that. To ensure that soldiers at times obey orders and do certain things without 'thinking about it'. 'Taylorism', that theory of how to run factories, is another example. The splitting of work into smaller units, so that each worker was left with a small repetitive act to do which did not require much though (the conveyor belt principle) worked because the worker was expected to act like a machine. Significantly the word robot comes from the Slavic root for 'work'.

There are which are already existing natural activities, carried out in a regulated manner: as, for example, marching is a regulated form of walking. More significant are those human activities which owe their possibility to being done in a regulated way. Such are counting and calculating. These are mechanical in nature even when done deliberately and intelligently by human beings. Automatic computation by machines then replicates the human moves, following the steps that would be taken by a human being who follows a mechanical procedure. More complicated cases are those human activities in which human skills are combined with the use of machines, as from ancient times in the loom, the potter's wheel, and the abacus. When an artificial human activity is carried out by a device itself invented by humans, artefact consummates artifice.[54]

Computers in law could be seen as taking law further in a direction in which it is already only too apt to go. Law helps to construct the automatic man necessary for the automatic production processes of modern capitalist society. This is not merely Marxist ideology. The significance of it for us can be seen when we look at Weber's explanation for the rise of capitalism. He saw a close connection between the development of a highly rationalised form of legal administration and the development of large industrialized capitalist economies. Here, the predictability and order of the law helped the capitalists in their decision making. At the same time, according to Weber, there occurred increasing use of bureaucracies as institutions for administering work. Here abstract rules are very important since it is they that enable there to be accountability and adequate supervision of the staff at the lower end of the pyramid. For Weber, this was all part of a movement which he called 'rationalisation'. Most attention is paid to maximising efficiency since the most pervasive value is control over the environment and prediction of the future. Just as modern science takes away the magic of the natural world, and its machines make the world rational and predictable, so too does the 'machine' of formal rationality take away the magic from the normative world; it make that world and those subject to it rational and predictable.

On this model, then, one can view legality as a form of machine-like behaviour. We do not want to argue that our problem has been solved, that what is happening is rather than computers being constructed like humans, humans are being constructed like machines! Our problem stems from the view that law is a creative mechanism and that the use of computers stops that creativity. But here our analogy is of some use. For the metaphor of 'machine-like' behaviour is not necessarily negative. In the law it is useful because there we often expect this machine-like response. At least part of the point of law is to create some form of order out of a chaos of particular instances, and, in so doing, create the possibility for prediction. And that in itself is creative. It carves out of the chaotic world an order that we can follow. But this is a particular way of being creative. Our problem is that law is supposed to be creative in that it adjusts to each particular situation, and the machine would negate that. Why would it do so? You cannot explain rules by rules (though see Smith's paper). They infinitely ramify and in the end depend on cultural skills that defy formulation. That is where our understanding of all rules is situated. It is the cultural community that is vital to our knowledge (see Bankowski) and construction of the rules.[55]

15. INSTITUTIONAL FACTS AND ARTIFICIAL REASON

We must be careful not to celebrate creativity or plasticity too far. Everything cannot be infinitely malleable at any time. That goes the way of the anomian moralities where everything depends upon feeling. We need some rules to which we can make automatic responses. We do not want to represent the entire social world. Rather we want to fix it in a particular way to make our social life easier. That is the sense of creativity that we first talked of. We carve out something that we can reply on and do not care if it does not manage to cover our entire social world. One way that the law does this is through the notion of 'institution' and especially the idea, developed by MacCormick and Weinberger of the law being an 'institutional fact'. Several contributors to the volume have touched upon this. Contracts in law, like goals in football, do not exist as 'brute facts' in the world —rather they are constituted by rules. Thus the institution of contract does not exist as a physical object, we know it by understanding the rules that constitute it. The institution of contract is an 'institutional fact' because it cannot be understood without the rules that institute it. In the legal perspective, contracts, wills, trusts etc. have a temporal existence. They are set up by some act or event (institutive rules) and continue until terminated by some other act or event (terminative rules). Once they are in existence there are consequential rules which detail the consequences, in the way of rights, liabilities, powers and duties which arise from the setting up of an instance of any such institution (MacCormick and Weinberger 1986). What is important here, according to MacCormick, is the capacity that these institutions have for creating long term linkages and thus creating what he calls 'diachronic practical information' (or, rather, giving what Weinberger calls 'practical information' a diachronic quality). This becomes relevant when we wish to stabilize the momentary practical information (the information relevant for action at any particular time) that we receive and reduce chance in our acting. Thus the institution of contract will link together the diverse actions of many actors. The facts thus generated will enable practical decisions to be taken on one's activities and enable reasoned long term decisions to be made as to what has to be done.

What happens is that when we enter into an institutional arrangement we are guided along certain pre-determined pathways which the institutional rules lay out for us. This helps us determine our rights and responsibilities and what we have to do, without having to make separate and complicated decisions at each juncture. But it not only gives us this facility, it also enables different people to plan their actions and determine one another's rights and responsibilities.

Sandra Dewitz's design of a system for an electronic contracting network is an example. The system itself would generate the documents. A contract exists as an 'institutional' fact, generated and constituted by interpersonal dealings interpreted under certain rules. But the computation just transforms raw facts into institutional facts according to its program. It does not itself apply a rule. We see here the automatic quality of what happens when we enter the institutional rules of the system. Once there we don't think about it, since the performative network, being the medium through which the acts are performed, can observe acts and record 'successful' on a legal data base. It makes things much more convenient to all parties because this reduces the risk of error and also makes disputes less likely since the institutive rules make things explicit. The 'umbrella contract' pushes 'thinking about it' to the level of institutive rules. As we saw, Jones and Sergot claim that where legislative texts are taken to produce qualification norms, then for practical purposes the deontic modalities can be ignored. If one is going to produce a system which will in fact classify entities in a way in which they ought to be classified, then it is redundant to make it such that it could fail so to classify them when it should. We can design a system that operates according to these specifications in such a way that we can 'force actuality and ideality to coincide'. What we see then is how the normative has become descriptive. The normative world has, in Weberian terms, lost its magic, and become flat and predictable. We can also see something like this working in payroll computers where tax is automatically deducted in accordance with a calculation of the employee's tax liability. Here again normative laws become descriptive, because machines provide for what ought to be, always to be. There is however an override, to slip back into the normative modality through the provision of a system of appeals.

The point of override is important. It is always necessary to know when to stop acting in a machine-like way, though, as we have seen, law's machinelikeness is very important for our social world. But we need the override because we cannot let machine like behaviour take over our world. We might want the world to be predictable but part of being human is that it can also dramatically change.

A way of attempting to achieve that in the context of expert systems is to build in defeasibility. Thus a particular source of defeasibility in law, public policy, provides a set of initial suggestions for the type of support an expert system might provide a user in looking out for crucial factors with a potential to override the default. However, the articles suggest that possible exceptions are not enumerable in advance, simply because they are not known. It is always possible that a new case will exhibit some additional, novel feature that demands an alternative classification. This presents a problem for any computational approach, rule-based, or case-based, or connectionist.[56]

This need not reflect particularly on the use of machines. There is a difference between two kinds of unpredictability: unpredictability of the question, and unpredictability of the answer; between cases we wouldn't have thought of, but when they arise we know what to say about them, and cases where we don't know what to say about them even if we have thought of them. This reminds us of the sort of case that interested Wittgenstein, and is not only connected with defeasibility, but also goes to the roots of the concepts of meaning and understanding: when we asked whether something is covered by what we meant, and we have to confess that we had not considered it, but we are able to say upon consideration that it is, or that it is not. Of course future advances of legal understanding cannot be predicted (if only for the reason given by Popper, that if they were then they would already have occurred). Of course legal computers, as much as legal textbooks, can only represent the actual state of knowledge. We must proceed carefully with the claim that there are things which human jurists can do, but which a machine cannot do —such as resolve new issues when they arise. This leads us to the question how after all the human jurists do it. And there is no knowing what further research in legal philosophy and cognitive science may come up with. There are also things which even a human jurist cannot do. Now if this is not because of limitations on human understanding or on human time and energy, but because of the nature of the subject, then a machine designed to handle the subject must respect the same limitation.

It is at this point that the question becomes more than 'How can automated systems replace the machine-like behaviour of the law?' We have reached the point where we want to move from that mode. We must then turn to look at the way that legal or automated system articulates with other systems in order for it not merely to carry on as before, but to consider and change. If this does not happen, and we do not work on this systemic override, then we might say that the consequence is that we start behaving like machines..[57] It might be said that the consequence of seeing machines as intelligent is that we beget sub-intelligent humans. Our image of ourselves becomes more like a machine. An exaggerated view of the capacities of the machine becomes a reductive view of the nature of human beings

As we have seen, the override can, in some respects, be built into the automated systems and we have seen attempts at that. But in the end what is important here that the automated system must articulate with other non-automated systems. And this is not merely being able to indicate times when it must open out to human lawyers. There creativity is important but, as we have seen, we need to go further than that. We mean here that law become open to the wider world, to other lay inputs, open to other creativities than lawyers' and thus more democratic.

In an exchange famous in English legal history, King James I of England (and VI of Scotland) made the suggestion to his Chief Justice Coke that he as king might preside over his own Courts, to be a check on the law in the last resort. The Chief Justice replied that the King's natural reason —however great his intelligence, general education, and common sense— was not sufficient for the task, which required special training and experience. As he put it, 'the Law is an Artificial Reason'. It is precisely this that might make it susceptible to computer applications. But 'Natural Reason' must have the last word.

NOTES

[1] Particularly relevant is (Bankowski and MacCormick 1989); the general results are published in (MacCormick and Summers 1991).

[2] Robert Stalnaker 'A note on non-monotonic modal logic', presented at the Center for Advanced Study in the Behavioural Sciences, March 1980, much referred to since, and finally published (Stalnaker 1993).

[3] And saying that r can be inferred from p alone, though not from $p\&q$, is not just a concealed way of saying that r can be inferred from p *& not* q.

[4] And it may be noted that the causal rôles of knowledge and assertion are not peculiar to law. For instance, the question whether ginger beer is still pleasant to drink if it contains decomposed snail, may well have a different answer from the question whether it is still pleasant to drink if you know that it contains decomposed snail, or even the question whether it is still pleasant to drink if you have heard it alleged that it contains decomposed snail.

[5] See (Ginsberg 1987).

[6] See (Egglestone 1983) , Ch. 8; also (Healy 1987).

[7] This is not just because it is a negative fact: negative facts *can* have causal efficacy for example, the hole in the bottom causes the boat to sink, starvation causes death, absence makes the heart grow fonder.)

[8] The position might be likened to that in mathematics, where there are proofs, for example of the four-colour theorem, which are so elaborate that they can only be carried out with the help of computers, so they are not perspicuous.

[9] This would be the only defeasibility affecting the application of a perfect conditional norm.

[10] And the statement can always be taken further towards being a perfect conditional norm by adding positive or negative elements to the content of its antecedent.

[11] Argumentation theory, whatever form it takes, has an important rôle in understanding the nature of legal reasoning, as this takes place within the framework of a dialectical procedure. It has also found its way into the area of artificial intelligence and law: we take the opportunity to refer here to the work of Thomas Gordon, who has attempted, on the foundation of Alexy's theory, has attempted to provide a normative formalization and computational model of civil pleading. See (Gordon 1993). The 1994 AAAI Workshop on 'Computational Dialectics' headed by Thomas Gordon and Ron Loui is a tribute to an increasing interest in argumentation and computation.

[12] Around the end of the nineteenth century, the carrying of the red flag in public was forbidden by law in Germany. Some political demonstrators (hoping to evade the law) carried a flag which was a dull pink. The question in court was whether this colour was red.

[13] This explains why the generation of problem cases is a common technique of theory analysis and verification in philosophy as well as in law; it is also one of the uses of a computer system discussed by Lilian Edwards in her paper. Barden suggests, both for reasoning from cases and for reasoning about the interpretation of rules, that a computer system could indicate for the guidance of judges and legal advisers the difference between central, judicially settled instances, and more peripheral, arguable ones. Legal issues might be located on this dimension for the purpose of estimating their susceptibility (1) to decisions with the help of an expert system, (2) to prediction by an expert system of the probable outcome of decision by a judge. Thus a jural condition may have many specifications —but not, he argues, an infinite number— and a decision support system will be more valuable the more peripheral specifications —marked as such— that it contains.

[14] For example, in the case of *Dutton* (discussed by Samuel) the argument did not proceed just by seeing that a house with a structural fault was like a bottle of ginger beer with a snail in it. Multiple issues were dealt with in the case. The defendants argued that liability on the lines of *Donoghue* extended only to physical harm suffered by the plaintiff, and that if he suffered only economic loss then it was not covered. This was countered by considering not one but a pair of hypothetical variants on the instant case, and holding that the argument would lead to an unreasonable distinction between them: if a man suffered injury from a defect in his house then

he could recover, but if he noticed the defect in time to have it corrected at his own expense and thus avoid injury, he could not.

15 This idea is, incidentally, compatible with saying that there is something distinctive about the link between cases involved in lawyers' reasoning from precedents, as opposed to reasoning with examples as it occurs in many disciplines besides law, such as philosophy. For what the court envisages, when it considers a hypothetical case, is often the hypothetical consequences that would follow if a certain decision were taken and subsequently reasoned from *as a precedent*.

16 The argument runs like this: if a wife who is artificially inseminated by donor without her husband's consent thereby commits adultery, then it follows that a dead man can commit adultery. For: (1) if she can be said to commit adultery, then the other party to the transaction —the donor— must also be said to commit adultery. But (2) the donor could be dead by the time of the insemination, and he could not be said to commit adultery by virtue of this use of his donation after his death. This reductio might then be challenged by showing (1) that the consequence does not follow, (2) that the conclusion is not unacceptable. This is when analogy from different cases might come into play. (1) Suppose a wife accuses her husband of adultery, and the fact is that he raped another woman. He can be said to have committed adultery, but his victim cannot. (2) Suppose A mortally wounds B, but then himself dies before B dies. Then after, but only after, his own death, upon the death of B, A can be said to become guilty of murder.

17 For a comprehensive overview see (Slade 1991), (Kolodner 1991), (Kolodner 1992).

18 See for example, (Ashley 1990), (Branting 1991), (Rissland and Skalak 1991). See also related early research by both Rissland and MacCarty.

19 They manifest what Samuel Johnson, writing about the English metaphysical poets, called 'wit': 'Wit... may be more rigorously and philosophically considered as a kind of *concordia discors* ; a combination of dissimilar images, or discovery of occult resemblances in things apparently unlike.' (Johnson, *Life of Cowley*). He cites Donne's comparison, in *A Valediction, forbidding mourning*, of a man that travels and his wife that stays at home, to a pair of compasses.

20 In what may be the root idea of analogy, ratios between numbers, when we say that 6 is to 3 as 4 is to 2, we mean that the relation is similar, not that there is a connexion based on any similarity between 3 and 2 (for indeed one is odd and the other even), and we mean one relation only, since 6 is to 3 as 4 is to 2, as being the double, but not as being the square.

21 The sequel, it is related, was that St Columba refused to accept the court's decision and went to war over the issue.

22 Herman Melville's *Moby Dick*, chapter 43, cites two cases from the English courts around 1800, which the barrister (Erskine) who appeared in both, compared in his pleadings with each other. One was an old form of action (*crim. con.*) by a gentleman whose wife had deserted him or who had had to abandon her, by which he hoped to recover her from another gentleman she now lived with. The other was an action of trover by the crew of a whaling ship from which a whale that they had harpooned had broken free or had had to be cut loose, against the crew of another ship which had subsequently caught the whale; this case was decided on the basis of the customary law of whalers, which distinguished between a 'fast fish', still in the possession of the first to catch it, and a 'loose fish', which has escaped and may now be harpooned by others. The lady in the first case, argued Erskine, was a 'loose fish'.

23 There can be all sorts of reasons why something is easier to explain or to understand in terms of the analogy than when put directly, as when the prophet brought home to King David, by the story of the lamb, the nature of his dealings with Uriah the Hittite.

24 Levi and Fried are describing Common Law systems, but the same point is recognized in apparently very different traditions: thus Portalis in the Preamble to the French *Code Civil* affirmed: 'The skill of the legislator is to discover the principles in each area which most conduce to the common weal; the skill of the judge is to put these principles into action, and to extend them to particular circumstances by wise and reasoned application.'

25 Except in so far as their logical order may go hand in hand with their chronological one, when the concepts of the law are shaped by contingencies of their history.

26 This does not affect the point that a continual provision of new cases is a way of 'teaching' a system, and that a continual checking, against yet further cases, of what the system has 'learned', is a perfectly sound way of ascertaining whether an artificial system has successfully captured the human reasoning it is trying to reproduce.

27 We may indeed say that the law has changed, if the same case is now decided in a different way . But we do not have to say that the law has changed, just because a different case is now decided in the same way. (We appeal here to an unproblematical sense of 'same' and 'different'.)

28 *Dutton v. Bognor Regis U.D.C.* [1972] 1 QB 373; *Otto and Otto v. Bolton & Norris* 1936 2 KB 46; *Cavalier v. Pope* 1906 AC 428.

29 For the use of analogies in science, see (Hesse 1966).

30 English and French writers have been as fond of emphasizing the contrast between each others' styles of thought in physics as in law: see for example the controversy between Pierre Duhem and N.R. Campbell on the relative merits of deductive abstractions and analogical models in scientific theory, and whether theory can be expressed in universal terms without use of the latter, whether the latter are no more than a psychological aid to thought. The controversy is analysed by Mary Hesse (Hesse 1966). To get clearer about the nature of analogy as a help to thought, we might compare the use of Euler circles and Venn diagrams to illustrate logical relations between classes. See (Stenning 1991) who argues (in a context of cognitive science and informatics) that analogy is to be understood as a special case of representation.

31 This does not mean that the analogy is immune from criticism as inapt or misleading. The use of the analogy of contract between private individuals, to model and conceptualize relations between states in international law, is an example of this. This model has been discussed most notably by authors such as (Lauterpacht 1927) and (Raftopoulos 1990), who, while granting its common acceptance, wish to criticize its inadequacy.

32 It is interesting to note recent work on an analogous problem in another field of application than law. Boi Faltings and Peter Struss, editors of *Recent Advances in Qualitative Physics* (Faltings and Struss 1992), observe that in describing and predicting the behaviour of mechanical or biological systems, there is a modelling phase, in which the system must be modelled and described in qualitative terms at the desired level of abstraction and using the appropriate ontology, before the phase at which the relevant general principles of reasoning can be applied. (The general principles in question are quantitative, for example differential equations, handled by computers in a standard way.) The effect of the recent advances dealt with in the book is that it does not treat the modelling phase as informal and entirely dependent on the intellectual skills and intuition of an individual engineer or scientist, but formalizes it, and even provides computer assistance for carrying it out. No doubt there are differences between, for example, a system of pipes conveying liquids in a chemical factory, and a system of rights and obligations in an institution, which make the first more amenable to computerized description than the latter; but the fact that questions of modelling and ontology are involved need not of itself make the problem intractable in principle. Indeed, the theory of normative positions,

adumbrated by Jones and Sergot in their contribution to this collection, is a step in the direction of formalizing legal descriptions and arguments in these terms.

33 It is indicated also ib Lord Atkin's reference to the parable in the case of *Donoghue* (quoted by Bankowski).

34 Bengoetxea later makes an analogous claim that the difficulty of difficult cases does not affect the over-all syllogistic pattern of justification, but the partial decisions that this involves.

35 'Consideration' figures with 'offer and acceptance' or 'agreement', 'intention to create legal relations', etc. The statement of such conditions constitutes what Jones and Sergot later call a 'qualification norm' for the term 'contract'. It should be mentioned here that the inappropriateness of seeking definitions in terms of necessary and sufficient conditions, when legal terms are in question, does not constitute an objection to, though it requires modification of, the idea of 'qualification norms' as establishing a link in *meaning* between a legal term and the factual grounds for applying it. The latter become more like 'criteria' in Wittgenstein's sense. A qualification norm is still 'definitional' in a sense opposed to 'deontic'. And the legal argument is still defeasible at two stages. First, even if the normal conditions, the application of the term 'contract' is still defeasible, for example by mistake, duress, or immorality; and even if the term 'contract' is applicable, there may still be grounds for the court to refuse granting a remedy for breach of contract, for example considerations of equity.

36 A striking and highly representative instance was given by Lakatos (1976). Euler's formula relates the number of vertices, faces, and edges of a polyhedron, and it is accompanied by a proof. But the proof runs into local counterexamples, which mean that it has to be revised, and terms that it uses have themselves to be defined. The formula itself runs into global counterexamples, polyhedrons —strange and unexpected ones— which do not obey the formula; so the term 'polyhedron' has to be defined, and the definition repeatedly elaborated. Though the formulation of a satisfactory definition which will yield the desired formula becomes more and more complicated, we justifiably continue to seek it, and we regard the successive definitions as attempts to capture the concept of polyhedron that we had in mind to start with. Lakatos's book shows mathematicians and scientists that even their disciplines do not conform to a certain theoretical picture of what disciplines, or at least these disciplines, ought to be like. It is often in terms of this picture that the law is compared and contrasted with them, when the question is raised how far it can be formalized, how far it lends itself to reasoning with deductive rules and definitions.

37 There is evidence of this even in the more cautious area of criminal law, in the way English courts reasoned when theft was legally defined as 'taking into one's possession the property of another, with the intention of depriving the owner of it permanently, and without a claim of right made in good faith'. This apparently lucid definition created problems when people were charged with theft who had clearly kept things dishonestly, for example money rightfully payable to someone else and mistakenly delivered to them in a sealed envelope, but there was doubt about whether they satisfied the definition —whether they had *taken* possession, at what point they were *in possession*, whether the intention had *accompanied* the start of possession. One way these difficulties was tackled was to introduce by legislation separate offences, such as embezzlement; another way, was by a noticeable tendency of courts to adjust or even distort the concept of *possession* in order to convict of theft, within the terms of the definition, those who would be classed as thieves in ordinary language and considered by common sense to be deserving of conviction. Theft has now been redefined by statute as 'dishonestly appropriating the property of another': the term 'appropriation' avoids the problems that arose from the conceptual separation of the taking possession and the intending to keep, and the term 'dishonestly' makes the normative factor explicitly present in the antecedent of the legal conditional.

38 For example, similar problems to those over 'consideration' arise for the somewhat different concept of 'cause' in French law. See (Kahn-Freund et al., 1979).

39 This plea is introduced not so much to avoid criminal liability as to avoid the even worse consequences of an acquittal on grounds of insanity: if anything this complication improves the example.

40 Empirical prediction of the behaviour of courts, under the science of jurimetrics, is a different question, answered on the basis of different evidence —though also perhaps amenable to computer treatment. Barden's position does not entail a collapse into American 'legal realism'.

41 One might make use here of a distinction sometimes drawn by lawyers between consequential and circumstantial risks. A consequential risk involves the probability of a future outcome, for example the probability that a woman who now engages in sexual intercourse will become pregnant. A circumstantial risk involves the probability of some already existing state of affairs, for example the probability that a woman to whom a drug is being administered is actually pregnant. One might add a 'conceptual' risk. A rather curious argument has been proffered by some opponents of abortion, that even knowing all the relevant facts we are uncertain whether or not a foetus has the status of a person with rights: there is therefore at least a risk that in carrying out an abortion we are committing murder, and we should avoid this risk. The legal case seems like this last..

42 See the discussion of *realism* about any field of inquiry, in (Dummett 1978).

43 See (Chisholm 1963), (Forrester 1984), (Loewer and Belzer 1983), (Belzer 1987), and generally, (Hilpinen 1970) and (Hilpinen 1981). An example of the Chisholm paradox:

Op : You should go to the party.
$O(p \to q)$: It should be that if you go, you say that you are going.
$\sim p \to O\sim q$: If you do not go, you should not say that you are going.
$\sim p$: You do not go.

From Op and $O(p \to q)$, infer Oq : you should say that you are going to the party.
From $\sim p$ and $\sim p \to O\sim q$, infer $O\sim q$: you should not say that you are going to the party.

So if you should go to the party, but you don't go, then you both should and should not say that you are going.

The other references also present the 'Forrester paradox', the 'Ryekjavic paradox', etc.

44 To take, as usual, an analogy from games: Is the Knave of Clubs defined in terms of the pictorial appearance by which it is recognized, or by the various parts it plays in various games of cards? Is a Knight in chess defined by its equine shape, or by its powers of movement in the game? We are inclined to give contrary answers even in these two similar cases.

45 It may be noted that the device of describing the ideal situation also figures, in a more elaborate form, in the systems of deontic logic developed by Jones in collaboration with Ingmar Pörn, to tackle among other problems the problem of contrary-to-duty obligations. See (Jones and Pörn 1985).

46 The deontic complexity of the case is revealed in the fact that a first attempt to handle it with a crude deontic logic yields ta version of he Chisholm paradox. The case may be represented schematically is follows:

1. If Mr C dies, then it ought to be that Mrs C receives a widow's pension.
2. It ought to be that if Mr C does not die, then Mrs C does not receive a widow's pension.
3. It ought to be that Mrs C does not stab Mr C.
4. If Mrs C stabs Mr C, then he dies.
5. If Mrs C does not stab Mr C, then he does not die.
6. Mrs C stabs Mr C.

The following forms of inference in deontic logic are taken to be valid:

(i) If P, then it ought to be that Q.
P is true.
Therefore, it ought to be that Q.

(ii) If P, then Q.
It ought to be that P.
Therefore, it ought to be that Q.

(iii) It ought to be that if P, then Q.
It ought to be that P.
Therefore, it ought to be that Q.

We also take as valid the normal rule of *modus ponens*, of which (i) is a special case:

If P then Q.
P is true.
Therefore Q.

Now from 4 and 6 it follows (by *modus ponens*) that
7. Mr C dies.
And from 1 and 7 it follows, by virtue of (i), that
8. It ought to be that Mrs C receives a widow's pension.
But from 3 and 5 it follows, by virtue of (ii), that
9. It ought to be that Mr C does not die.
And from 2 and 9 it follows, by virtue of (iii), that
10. It ought to be that Mrs C does not receive a widow's pension.
So (8 and 10) Mrs C ought and ought not to get a widow's pensions.

If, instead of 2, we put
2a. If Mr C does not die, then it ought to be that Mrs C does not receive a widow's pension,
then from 1 and 7 we still get the conclusion that
8. It ought to be that Mrs C receives a widow's pension.
while from 2a and 9 we now get the conclusion
10a. It ought to be that it ought not to be that Mrs C gets a widow's pension.
So (2a and 10a) Mrs C ought to get a widow's pension, but it ought to be that she ought not to.

47 See again (Bankowski and MacCormick 1986) and (MacCormick and Summers 1991).

48 For a discussion of discovery in judicial decision-making, see (Anderson 1992). For further argument on the philosophical importance of heuristics, or the logic of discovery, and of the rôle of computer science in its development, see (Kelly 1988). It may be necessary to mention here that the term 'heuristic' is also used in a peculiar sense within the AI community, to mean a 'rule of thumb' as opposed to an algorithm or rule guaranteed to yield the correct solution: that is not the sense intended here.

49 See (Clark 1978), and for an extension of logic programming to include both negation by failure and classical negation, see (Gelfond and Lifschitz 1990) and (Kowalski and Sadri 1990).

50 For a comparison between precedent-based reasoning in law and precedent-based reasoning in (architectural) design, see the Introduction to (Tzonis and White 1994).

51 See (Sergot, 1990) for a detailed list of some of the ways computers can be used in law, including systems that model the practices of lawyers in a particular area, algorithmic representations of the law in rules, helps in drafting legislation, applications of artificial intelligence techniques, and case-based reasoning.

52 An extreme case of mechanical procedure in law using no living human beings, long before the age of computers, is the famous Roman Law of Citations of A.D. 426: this singled out as authoritative the works of Papinian, Paul, Ulpian, Modestius, and Gaius. Where there was a

conflict, the majority opinion was taken of these, and of further authors cited by them (if the citations were verified); if the votes on the two sides of an issue were equal Papinian had a casting vote.

[53] If I pretend to be a native born inhabitant of Edinburgh, a native born inhabitant we almost always catch me out since there will always be things that I did not know about Edinburgh which I could only have picked up by being there. But it would be much harder for a native born inhabitant to guess who was the impostor and who was pretending to be the impostor. Remember, in the time that Turing was writing, men and women were much more separated socially and it would have been for them much harder to know, one about the other.

[54] It is by no means necessarily true that this diminishes the rôle of human creativity. Operation of a machine, in accordance with a largely predetermined set of instructions following artificial rules and expressed in an abstract notation, can be creative in itself, as well as being an expression of the creativity of others, as is shown by the case of a concert pianist. But we recognise neither their particular area of usefulness nor their danger if we see computers as no more and no less than the latest in the line of keyboard instruments.

[55] Collins gives us an example of a rule in the construction of T lasers: 'Make the lead shorter than 8 inches'. We all understand that. But that is because we all know how to measure. Imagine, however, a society in which there was an élite class of measurers who were the only people who had that knowledge. Thus the criticism that logic programmers, such as Kowalski, do not use lawyers in formulating their texts has a point on this community reference view. For it is lawyers that are the key community and that is where the final understanding and construction will be legal rules will be situated. Indeed studies of legal reasoning show just that. But perhaps Kowalski has a point about democracy.

[56] See (Bechtel and Abrahamsen 1991); for a more technical introduction, (Herts et al., 1991). Neural networks still play a rather limited rôle in the field of AI and Law, but see for instance (Opdorp et al., 1991), (Bouchereau et al., 1991), Bench-Capon 1993), (Groendijk and Oskamp 1993).

[57] Thus small firms in the USA have already started writing manuals using a small vocabulary, etc. —standardizing the English to cut the creativity out.

REFERENCES

Alexy, R. 1978, 1991. *Theorie der juristischen Argumentation. Die Theorie des rationalen Diskurses als Theorie der juristischen Begründung,* Frankfurt/Main, pp. 32, 263.

Alexy, R., 1989. *A Theory of Legal Argumentation. The Theory of Rational Discourse as Theory of Legal Justification,* (trans. by R. Adler and N. MacCormick). Oxford, pp. 15, p. 212.

Anderson, A.R., 1967. 'The formal analysis of normative systems'. In N. Rescher (ed.), *The Logic of Decision and Action,* pp. 147–213. University of Pittsburgh Press.

Anderson, B., 1992. *'Discovery' in Judicial Decision-making,* Ph.D. dissertation, University of Edinburgh.

Anscombe, G.E.M., 1981. 'Causality and Determination', in *Collected Philosophical Papers,* Vol. 2: *Metaphysics and Philosophy of Mind,* Blackwell, Oxford.

Ashley, K., 1990. *Modeling Legal Argument — Reasoning with Cases and Hypotheticals,* MIT Press.

Bambrough, J.R., 1961. 'Universals and Family Resemblances', *Proceedings of the Aristotelian Society,* LXI (1960–61), 207.

Bankowski, Z. and MacCormick, D.N., 1989. 'Some Principles of Statutory Interpretation', in J. van Dunné (ed.) *Legal Reasoning and Statutory Interpretation*, Arnhem: Youda Quint., pp. 41–53.

Barnden, John R., and Holyoak, Keith J., 1994. (Eds.) *Analogical Connections*, Vol. 2 of the series: *Advances in Connectionist and Neural Computation Series*, Ablex, Norwood, NJ.

Bechtel, W., and Abrahamsen, A., 1991. *Connectionism and the Mind*, Basil Blackwell.

Belzer, Marvin, 1987. 'Legal Reasoning in 3-D', in *Proceedings of the First International Conference on Artificial Intelligence and Law*, Boston, Massachusetts.

Bench-Capon, T., 1993. 'Neural Networks and Open-Texture', in *Proceedings of the Fourth International Conference on AI and Law*, Amsterdam, 1993.

Bouchereau, L., Bourcier, D. and Bourgine, P. 1991. 'Extracting Legal Knowledge by Means of a Multi-layer Neural Network', in *Proceedings of the 3rd International Conference on AI and Law*, Oxford 1991.

Branting, K., 1991. *Integrating Rules and Precedents for Classification and Explanation*, Ph.D. dissertation, University of Texas at Austin.

Chisholm, R., 1963. 'Contrary-to-duty Imperatives and Deontic Logic', *Analysis*, 24, pp. 33–36.

Clark, K.L., 1978. 'Negation by failure', in *Logic and databases*, Gallaire, H. and Minker, J. (eds), Plenum Press, pp. 293–322.

Collins, H., 1990 *Artificial Experts*, M.I.T. Press.

Cross, R., 1968. *Precedent in English Law*, Oxford University Press.

Dummet, M., 1978. 'Realism', in *Truth and Other Enigmas*, London.

Dworkin, R., 1977. *Taking Rights Seriously*, London.

Egglestone, R., 1983. *Evidence, Proof and Probability*, (2nd ed.) London.

Engisch, K., 1943. *Logische Studien zur Gesetzesanwendung*, Heidelberg.

Faltings, Boi, and Struss, Peter, 1992. (Eds), *Recent Advances in Qualitative Physics*

Forrester, J.W., 1984. 'Gentle murder, or the adverbial Samaritan,' *Journal of Philosophy*, 81, pp. 193–197.

Fried C, 1982. 'The Artificial Reason of the Law, or: What Lawyers Know', in *Texas Law Review* 60, 1982 pp. 35–58.

Gelfond, M. and Lifschitz, V. 1990: 'Logic programs with classical negation', *Proceedings of the Seventh International Conference on Logic Programming*, MIT Press, pp. 579-597.

Gentner, D. 1989, 'The mechanisms of analogical learning', Chapter 7 of Vosniadou, S. and Ortony, A (eds.) *Similarity and Analogical Reasoning*, Cambridge University press.

Ginsberg, M.L., 1987. (Ed.) *Readings in Nonmonotonic Reasoning*,, Los Altos (Cal.): Morgan Kaufmann.

Golding, M., 1984. *Legal Reasoning*, Borzoi Books, New York.

Goldstone, R.L. and Medin, D.L. and Gentner, D. 1991 'Relational Similarity and the Nonindependence of Features in Similarity Judgements', *Cognitive Psychology*, 23, pp. 222-262.

Gordon, T.F., 1993. 'The Pleadings Game', *Proceedings of the Fourth International Conference on AI and Law*, The Association for Computing Machinery 1993.

Groendijk, C. and Oskamp, A. 1993. 'Case Recognition and Strategy Classification'. In *Proceedings of the Fourth International Conference on AI and Law*, Amsterdam.

Haft, F., Jones, R. and Wetter, Th., 1988. 'A Natural Language Based Legal Expert System for Consultation and Tutoring — The Lex Project', in H. Fiedler, F. Haft, R. Traunmuller (eds.), *Expert Systems in Law: Impacts on Legal Theory and Computer Law*, series *Neue Methoden im Recht* (*NMIR*, vol. 4, pp. 75–98, Tübingen.

Hahn, U., 1993. *Similarity and Case-based Reasoning — A study of Categorization*, M.Sc. Dissertation, University of Edinburgh.

Hall, R.P., 1989. 'Computational approaches to analogical reasoning', *Artificial Intelligence*, 39, pp. 39–120.

Hart , H.L.A., 1983. 'Problems of the Philosophy of Law', in *Essays in Jurisprudence and Philosophy*, Oxford University Press.

Healy, Patrick, 1987. 'Proof and Policy: No Golden Threads', *Criminal Law Review* [1987] pp. 355–366.

Herts, J., Krogh, A. and Palmer, R.G., 1991. *Introduction to the Theory of Neural Computing*, Addison Wesley.

Hesse, M., 1966. *Models and Analogies in Science*, University of Notre Dame Press.

Hilpinen, R., 1970. (Ed.) *Deontic Logic: Introductory and Systematic Readings*, Reidel, Dordrecht.

Hilpinen, R., 1981. (Ed.) *New Studies on Deontic Logic,* Reidel, Dordrecht.

Holyoak, K.J. and Thagard, P., 1989. 'Analogical Mapping by constraint satisfaction', *Cognitive Science*, 13, pp. 295–355

Honoré, A.H., 1986. 'Real Laws', in MacCormick, N. and Birks, P. (eds), *The Legal Mind*, Oxford University Press.

Jones, A.J.I., and Pörn, I., 1985. 'Ideality, Sub-ideality and Deontic Logic.' *Synthese*, 65, pp. 275–290.

Kahn-Freund, O., Lévy, C., and Rudden, B., 1979. *A Source-book on French Law*, Oxford University Press.

Kedar-Ceballi, S. 1988. 'Analogy —from a unified perspective', in, Helman, D.H. (ed.) *Analogical Reasoning*, Kluwer Academic Publishers.

Koch, H. J. & H. Rüssmann, 1982. *Juristische Begründungslehre. Eine Einführung in Grundprobleme der Rechtswissenschaft,* München.

Kolodner, J., 1991. 'Improving Human Decision Making through Case-Based Decision Aiding', *AI Magazine*, pp. 52–68.

Kolodner, J., 1992. 'An Introduction to Case-Based Reasoning', *Artificial Intelligence Review* 6, pp. 3–34.

Kowalski, R.A. 1989: 'The treatment of negation in logic programs for representing legislation', *Proceedings of the Second International Conference on Artificial Intelligence and Law*, pp. 11-15.

Kowalski, R.A. and Sadri, F. 1990, 'Logic programs with exceptions', *Proceedings of the Seventh International Conference on Logic Programming*, MIT Press, pp. 598-613.

Kripke, S., 1982. *Wittgenstein on Rules and Private Language*, Blackwell, Oxford.

Lakatos, I., 1976. *Proof and Refutations*, Cambridge.

Lauterpacht, Hersch, 1927. *Private Law Sources and Analogies of International Law*, Longmans, London.

Levi, E.H., 1948. 'An Introduction to Legal Reasoning', 15 *The University of Chicago Law Review*, pp. 501-574.

Loewer, B. and Belzer, M., 1983. 'Dyadic Deontic Detachment', *Synthese*, 54, pp. 295–318.

MacCormick, D.N., and Summers, R.S., 1991. (Eds.) *Interpreting Statutes: A Comparative Study*, Aldershot 1991.

MacCormick, D.N., and Weinberger, O., 1986. *An Institutional Theory of Law,* Dordrecht..

Opdorp, G.J. v., Walker, R.F., Schrickx, J. A., Groendijk, C. and van den Berg, P.H., 1991. 'Networks at work: a connectionist approach to non-deductive legal reasoning'. In: *Proceedings of the 3rd International Conference on AI and Law*, Oxford 1991.

Polya, G. 1957. *How to Solve It*, Garden City, N.Y., Doubleday Anchor.

Polya, G., 1954. *Induction and Analogy in Mathematics*, Princeton University Press.

Porter, B.W., Bareiss, R, and Holte, R.C., 1990. 'Concept Learning and Heuristic Classification in Weak Theory Domains,' *Artificial Intelligence*, Vol. 45, Nos. 1–2, pp. 229–263.

Raftopoulos, Evangelos, 1990. *The Inadequacy of the Contractual Analogy in the Law of Treaties*, with a preface by Andreas Gasis, Athens: Alkyon, 1990 Publications of the Hellenic Institute of International and Foreign Law.

Rissland, E. and Skalak, D., 1991. 'CABARET: Rule Interpretation in a Hybrid Architecture', *International Journal of Man-Machine Studies*, 34, pp. 839–887.

Seifert, C. 1989. 'Analogy and Case-based Reasoning', in *Proceedings of the 1989 Case Based Reasoning Workshop*, Morgan Kaufman.

Sergot, M., 1990. *The Representation of Law in Computer Programmes: A Survey and Comparison*, Academic Press.
Slade, S., 1991. 'Case-Based Reasoning: A Research Paradigm', *AI Magazine*, pp. 42–55.
Stalnaker, R., [1980] 1993. 'A note on non-monotonic modal logic', *Artificial Intelligence* vol. 64 no 2, pp. 183–196.
Stenning, Keith, 1991. 'Interpreting spatial inclusion as set membership: a case study of analogy at work', *2nd International Colloquium on Cognitive Science*, San Sebastian 1991.
Stone, J., 1964. *Legal System and Lawyers' Reasonings*, Stevens, London.
Stone, J., 1985. *Precedent and Law*, Butterworths, Sydney, 1985.
Susskind, R., 1987. *Expert Systems in Law*, Oxford University Press.
Tribe, L., 1971. 'Trial by Mathematics', 84 *Harvard Law Review*, p. 1329.
Tzonis, A and White, I., 1994. *Automation Based Creative Design*, Elsevier, Amsterdam.
Wisdom, J., 1953. *Philosophy and Psychoanalysis*, Blackwell, Oxford, p. 157.
Wróblewski, J., 1992. *The Judicial Application of Law* (*Sadowe Stosowania Prawa*), trans. & ed. by Zenon Bankowski and Neil MacCormick, Kluwer.

(For Zenon Bankowski)
Faculty of Law
University of Edinburgh
Scotland

(For Ian White)
St John's College
Cambridge

(For Ulrike Hahn)
Centre for Cognitive Science
University of Edinburgh
Scotland

JOHN BELL

POLICY ARGUMENTS AND LEGAL REASONING

There are a number of appropriate objects of legal research in the area of computers and the law. This paper studies an aspect of legal justification, 'policy arguments', which introduce a wider range of considerations than those found in the posited sources of law. It looks at arguments which are, or ought to be, acceptable justifications for a legal decision or solution, i.e. the regulative ideals which are accepted in a legal community. The function of legal theory is not just to reproduce what is actually done or believed, but to point out inadequacies and inconsistencies in arguments to ensure that legal reasoning is the best it can be within a particular legal system. Implemented through a decision support system, a model of justification can support best practice among lawyers.

By contrast, heuristics, the logic of discovery, looks at the rational processes involved in coming to a decision. It studies the sources for decisions, the material on which they are based, and the routines for the practice of decision-making. Implemented in a computer programme, the decision-maker is guided as to the appropriate steps and considerations involved in the legal decision. These can be relevant whether the decision-making itself is a matter of authoritative fiat or whether it is a process of rational persuasion. This applies even if the best reconstruction of the decision-making process is to talk of 'understanding' (Barden n.d.), 'insight' (Lonergan 1957), or 'seeing relevance' (Martino n.d.) in the way certain facts relate to legal rules. Other papers in this collection, notably those of Bengoetxea, Samuel and Barden, touch on these issues.

Of course, there is an important relationship between the two. A decision will be difficult to justify if it has not been arrived at by a rational procedure for considering the relevant features. But the importance of looking at justifications is to establish the regulative ideals which control the process by which a decision is reached. It may well be that the moment of 'understanding' or 'insight' cannot be captured or reproduced through logical modelling. All the same, by being required to provide justifications which are adequately persuasive, the decision-maker is constrained to check his or her solution against an external standard and, possibly, revise it in the light of what is found.

Z. Bankowski et al. (eds.), Informatics and the Foundations of Legal Reasoning, 73–97.

1. POLICY ARGUMENTS IN A RULE-BASED SYSTEM

In terms of a model of legal justification, I think it is still appropriate to conceive of law in many ways on a model of rules. Law does serve to provide precise instructions about what individuals and officials are expected to do. Of course, there are other, very valuable, ways of seeing how the law operates which would limit the importance of the model of rules as a description of the function of law in society. But, as a model of the discourse of legal justification, the model of rules retains an important place, and this is of some comfort to those attempting to design computer-based decision support systems. All the same, even within this limited sphere, the model needs significant modifications. One feature which has to be taken into account is the way in which arguments about the function of law, or 'policy arguments', are used in the process of generating and interpreting legal rules. Such arguments seem to go beyond the realm of law and greatly reduce the possibility of a useful decision support system for legal justification.

1.1. The practice of rules

If we assume a society composed of individuals with different skills and aspirations, then, even if they share a religious or political beliefs, they will still need some common set of prescribed standards or guides to behaviour to provide a settled basis for social existence, a common reference point for making decisions. Enacting texts or having standards declared by a judge are social practices by which such common standards are given a determinate, canonical form. The textual form is meant to encapsulate the essential points of the rules laid down in society.

The social importance of these rules is to restrict the discussion about what should be done. The very function of law is to reduce the complexity of social problems by treating them in a more manageable way (Luhmann 1967). Within a set of specified value premises, handled by specific procedures, certain problems can be more easily resolved. Of course, this does not remove dispute about the design of the system, but once it is set up, the social problem can be resolved in a manageable fashion.

For instance, take the law on strikes. We might dispute whether workers should be free to strike, whether public services such as railways must be kept running, whether collective bargaining is an appropriate social process, and so on. Once we have a set of legal rules about procedures for calling strikes, about the liability of unions, about how to handled complaints about breaches of the rules, then the character of the social dispute is changed. The legal game (as opposed to the political or social game) is a debate about whether these rules have been complied with: has there been a ballot? did everyone have a chance to cast a vote? were there irregularities in the ballot question? and so on. The social questions don't go away, but there is a forum for channelling energies into perhaps artificial, but certainly more manageable issues. For a start, the interests of the beleaguered passengers are ignored.

In the terminology of Atiyah and Summers, law provides a series of 'formal' reasons for decision, appealing to established rules and other standards, which obviate the need for discussion of the substantive reasons which make one solution preferable to another (Atiyah and Summers 1987). The solution may be imperfect from an absolute view, but it does have some benefits. All the same, the substantive justifications for the system and its rules do not disappear from view altogether. It is simply that they do not have to be referred to in all cases. But it is precisely in policy arguments that they re-emerge for consideration.

1.2. The problem of policy arguments

Policy arguments may be defined as substantive justifications for decisions to which judges appeal when the standards and rules of the legal system do not provide a clear resolution of a dispute. In contrast to authority reasons which appeal to clear rules and principles of the legal system, policy arguments appeal to the values which justify a choice of an appropriate rule.[1] Now such an exercise would seem to take us into the realms of non-legal arguments, or at least would place us in an overlap between legal and other spheres of discourse.

Policy arguments are offered as justifications for various interpretations of legal texts. Rarely can the law be conceived of as providing no possible solution at all. Whether by analogy or by direct appeal to a legal rule or principle, several competing, and legally plausible, solutions will be offered in a hard case, which build on established legal standards. Policy arguments are offered as reasons for preferring one solution over another. Some take the view that policy arguments are specific non-legal arguments introduced into the legal discourse. My own view would be that such a radical separation of legal and non-legal discourses is unhelpful to an understanding of law.

1.3. In what way is law self-contained?

If the social function of law is to reduce social complexity and produce some form of social consensus by an objective process of social decision-making, then it might seem appropriate to see law as a closed and discrete field of discourse. Such a discrete character can be envisioned, as by Kelsen, simply in terms of a system of validity, without any systematization and distinctiveness in content. But this will merely produce a system which is logically open to substantive reasons drawn from outside (Tamello 1959, Kelsen 1990). Those who wish to argue that legal reasoning can remain significantly discrete have to argue for a distinguishable systematic content, or at least for some radical transformation of the 'non-legal' material when it becomes part of the law.[2] Furthermore, to justify legal reasoning as a specific discourse, it must impose some logical, not merely rhetorical, constraints on argument (Weinberger 1972).

For Alexy, the rules of rationality in legal reasoning do not exclude arguments of fairness or social utility, but they have to be integrated into an answer from the legal point of view. The 'special case thesis' that he proposes suggests that legal arguments have a claim to correctness which is not absolute, but is merely relative to the standards of a particular legal system:

> [T]he claim to correctness is indeed also raised in legal discourse, but this claim, unlike that in general practical discourse, is not concerned with the absolute rationality of the normative statement in question, but only with showing that it can be rationally justified within the framework of the validly prevailing legal order (Alexy 1989).

In this way, the claim to correctness departs from given legal premisses, but not all the steps in the legal argument are fixed in advance. Indeed, because not all the rules of legal discourse can be satisfied in a precise manner, there is always room for disagreement on results.

> Nevertheless, as an element of legal reasoning, general reasoning takes place under conditions which considerably increase its determinative capability, not least in virtue of the institutionalization of legal discourse...(Alexy 1989, p. 288.)

A degree of transformation takes place through the requirements of legal reasoning, but to a great extent, the framework which Alexy outlines simply excludes possible reasons for justifying a decision, rather than attempting to establish a radically distinctive set of arguments.

Indeed, even those who view law as a total system do not suggest it has clear answers to all problems. For Canaris (Canaris 1964), law is seen as a system of norms with various levels of indeterminacy: at the level of specific provisions, in the objectives of the law, or in legal principles. The apparent 'gaps' in legal provisions are filled by the use of various intra-systemic techniques, such as analogy or appeal to the *ratio iuris*. Dworkin's suggestion that law is a matter of interpretation explains this idea perhaps in clearer language (Dworkin 1986). In this, Dworkin argues that, when faced with a hard case, one where the legal rules do not generate a clear result, the judge resorts to higher-level legal values called principles and resolves conflicts between these on the basis of 'integrity', giving effect to the solution which is most consistent with a proper understanding of the political values underlying the legal system as a whole.

> Judges...decide hard cases by trying to find, in some set of coherent principles about people's rights and duties, the best constructive interpretation of the political structure and legal doctrine of their community...It will include convictions about both fit and justification. Convictions about fit will provide a rough threshold requirement that an interpretation of some part of the law must meet if it is to be eligible at all...anyone who accepts law as integrity must accept that the political history of his community will sometimes check his other political convictions in his overall interpretative judgment...Thus he must choose between eligible interpretations by asking which shows the community's structure of institutions and decisions —its public standards as a whole— in a better light from the standpoint of political morality...[T]he different aspects or dimensions of fit and substance, and the different aspects of substance are in the last analysis all responsive to [the judge's] political judgment. (Dworkin 1986, pp. 245–58.)

The connection between legal and non-legal argument is that the latter provides justifications for one interpretation of the law, rather than another. For Dworkin, arguments of social or political policy are properly considered as legal arguments (Dworkin 1986, pp. 258–60). In other words, in order to achieve the right legal answer, the lawyer has to have regard to social and political arguments as part of the legal argument. The law does not run out, but its empire stretches beyond many conventional source-based definitions of what is law, and it becomes thereby rather diffuse. (Cf. Raz 1979).

It is not clear that these efforts are particularly helpful to a project which seeks to examine the place of computer-based decision support systems. To be sure, any well-found legal justification may have to include the wider considerations which Dworkin specifies. But I would agree with Zippelius that the systematic unity of the law is only a 'projected unity, only an attempted constructive proposal, which stands under the threat of modification at any time, should the results of individual searches require this, and which cannot be transformed into a procrustean bed of concrete knowledge' (Zippelius 1977). It is something which is difficult to establish in advance of solving a particular issue.

Any artificial reasoning process is necessarily limited to reasoning from established posited sources where the drawing of inferences from legal sources can be formalized to some extent. The wide scope of 'legal reasoning' which Dworkin gives does confer political legitimacy on certain kinds of judicial debates, but is of little help in helping us identify the reproducible specific character of legal reasoning. Furthermore, by stressing constructive interpretation, it tends to underplay the place which such source-based reasoning plays in legal life, and thus the scope for any form of artificial intelligence system.

I would maintain that there are some solutions to legal problems which can be justified satisfactorily simply in terms of the clear meaning of legal texts, but there are also interpretations of the law which require, partly or wholly, broader justifications. All the same, the law is not self-serving, but has to relate to the social order. As Corsale suggests:

> The legal order is thus, concretely, the explicitation of the social ideology of the group to which it refers, in the sense that the norms serve to define specific models of behaviour in harmony and in function of general goals presided over by the social ideology (Corsale 1970).

Law tries to offer as clear and narrowly defined set of issues as possible, while serving its social purposes. As a result internally satisfactory readings of the law remains open to the judgment of wider considerations. In such a setting policy arguments might be considered as 'non-legal' in that they are not directly based on formal sources of law, but relate these to other considerations.

1.4. What are policy arguments?

Legal rules are not written in an exhaustive fashion. Much has to be left as undetermined or understood. Three features of what is understood command our attention. The first is the purpose of the rule: what policies it is to further? The second is the relationship of the rule to other legal standards: how are the policies of the rule to relate to other policies which the law is pursuing? Thirdly, there are considerations about the function of law: how do the law's policies fit other social objectives? The concept of 'policy' is often used to describe any of these in legal discourse, but it is worthwhile being more precise, if we are to construct a framework in which decision-support systems will be able to operate effectively.

1.4.1. Policy and arguments about the purpose of the rule. Rules are adopted to achieve certain social or political objectives. These reasons for rules are obviously relevant to how they are to be interpreted in cases of doubt. Most legal systems adopt some form of 'teleological' or 'purposive' construction of legal texts, even if this requires you to read words into them (see e.g. Cross 1987). Such an approach requires the lawyer to use judgment to decide which solution would best achieve the objective or policy of the legislation. The solution is justified not so much because of the wording of the text, but because of the instrumental judgment made about how to further the policy of the legislation. The legal text provides incomplete instructions as to how this is to be done, and the reasoning of the judge or lawyer is substantive in much the same way as the reasoning of the person who made the law in the first place, though the lawyer may have less scope to achieve other objectives. Scope for substantive reasoning is important when a piece of legislation has more than one objective. For instance, rent restriction legislation is mainly to protect tenants, but it may contain provisions enabling a landlord to repossess property if he wishes to use it for the benefit of himself or a member of his family. Now how do you interpret such a provision about repossession? Do you give effect to the main purpose of the legislation as a whole or to the purposes of the exception in favour of the landlord?[3] The lawyer is left to achieve a suitable balance between these purposes, and to justify his order of priorities.

Such policy reasoning may well be specifically invited by the legal rule itself. Standards of variable content, such as 'reasonableness', 'fairness', and the like invite the lawyer to develop the policy of the legislation as time goes on. They decide whether it is socially desirable that surveyors can exclude liability to house-purchasers when they make a survey for the benefit of the mortgage lender, or whether such exclusions are proper in contracts for the sale of vegetable seeds.[4] The arguments needed to decide whether the exclusions are 'reasonable' require the lawyer to consider the ease for one party to take out insurance, the character of the risk, the skills of the person relying on the statement of the surveyor or the quality of the seeds, and so on. What the legislator has done is to delegate the development of the rather broad objective of providing protection to consumers against unfair terms to the judges who decide on an *ad hoc* basis as cases arise. The 'policy or purpose of a statute' does not pose the same problems as 'policy arguments' properly so-called, since it provides a legal solution which can be justified simply by appeal to legal sources without the need to demonstrate that the solution is otherwise meritorious or socially beneficial.[5] By creating appropriate retrieval systems, the texts which identify the purpose of legislation can be made available to those applying it and reasoning from the legislation and the purposes thus identified can frequently be fairly self-contained.

1.4.2. Policies relating the rule to other legal values. Not everything can be stated in legal texts or judgments, even if they are as long as they are in England. The connections between legal provisions have to be determined at a later stage by legal interpretation. This requires some form of priority to be assigned between legal values on the basis of the consequences of different solutions, or on the basis of consistency and coherence with the rest of the law. Such consequentialist justifications are akin to what the non-lawyer would use as a basis for decisions.

One could isolate a number of legal values relevant to legal decisions, which are frequently referred to by lawyers as 'policy arguments'. For example, legal fairness requires both fair procedure and observance of principles such as 'no man may profit from his own wrong', '*fraus omnia corrumpit*' and so on.[6] Legal rights are obvious values to bring into consideration in Western societies. They suffer firstly from the need for definition and secondly from the need for weighing. It is all very well to assert that we believe in the right to property. But what does that involve? If I fly over your house at an altitude of 200m, or if I turn my neighbouring house into a brothel, have I violated your rights to property? What kinds of interference are prohibited by such a right? Again, constitutional values are obviously connected in that they will include some fundamental rights. There will be other constitutional considerations as well, such as the separation of powers, and the like. These will produce general principles which have to be balanced against the specific objectives of a rule. Third party interests are often marginalized in the classical inter partes legal dispute. All the same, these may have a bearing on the decision to be taken, and the interests of third parties introduce a new set of consequences not specifically catered for in the legal rule.[7] Established legal values may also have an impact on the interpretation of legal rules. Thus the right to strike might be limited by the principle of maintaining continuity in public services.[8] There are numerous other such principles. In addition, although interaction between different legal orders is determined to a greater or lesser extent in different legal systems, it may be necessary for lawyers to decide more precisely how to reconcile domestic law with international law, treaty obligations, European Community law or federal law.[9]

All these legal values are stated at such a level of abstractness as to require judgment as to their meaning and importance in relation to the objectives of a specific legal rule. Both interpretation and reconciliation require significant argument which will take account of non-legal expectations. For the most part, however, these arguments are really posited principles of the legal system and could be mapped relatively easily for the purposes of a decision support system.

1.4.3. Policies related to the function of the law. If one of the functions of the law is to conform to social objectives and meet expectations in the community, then it can be expected that in situations of legal unclarity, reference will be made to how a legal solution can best fit those objectives. Traditionally, legal systems invoke a number of considerations which are the classical terrain for 'policy arguments'. A number of established categories of such policy arguments exist.

(i) Protecting legal institutions may require a restriction in the number of cases brought, to prevent a flood of litigation on one area which will hamper the performance of the courts in many areas.[10] The reputation of the courts may require that the courts do not make judgments in areas of high political controversy. (ii) Protecting social institutions may require that the courts penalize those who seek to undermine governmental institutions and processes, e.g. by corrupt practices or by hampering their effective operation.[11] The social institutions will mainly be governmental, but could also include institutions like the family or organized religion. (iii) Public order is an obvious value for the law to promote. This will include the prevention of public disorder and the investigation and prevention of crime, and national security.[12] Here the lawyer may either make his own assessment or, more frequently, defer to the assessment made by another competent instance, e.g. government ministers or the police. (iv) Good morals are social values which the law may wish to endorse, even in the absence of a specific text, e.g. by invalidating contracts for sexual immorality. (See Treitel 1986, pp. 337–8). (v) Social utility may restrict the normal application of legal rules. Thus, where one landowner uses his property for recreational purposes which interferes with the enjoyment of his neighbour's land, the utility to the wider community of those recreational purposes may be relevant in deciding whether the interference with the neighbour's property rights should be tolerated.[13] (vi) Justiciability: judges need to decide whether they are competent to make decisions on certain issues. In some areas, the courts will make their own policy judgments, in others they exercise minimal scrutiny (i.e. intervene only where there is manifest unreasonableness or lack of proportionality between ends and means), or accept the decision of the other bodies, whether in government or in relation to decisions of professional and sporting organizations, parents, and so on. Such attitudes are justified by the social function of law in the particular area, and also by the degree of social controversy surrounding an issue.[14]

Such policy considerations look beyond legal texts to the wider function of law. They require almost an outsider's view of what the law should be doing, though their frequent use in law makes them predictable and contained aspects of legal discourse. All the same, it is always possible that there will be novel perspectives about what law ought to be doing which are less statable in advance, and more closely relate legal and non-legal argument. It is this third category of argument which might best be described as policy arguments.

2. THE PLACE OF POLICY ARGUMENTS IN LEGAL REASONING

Stated in such a way, it is clear that policy arguments are best seen as meta-arguments about the function of law, rather than just simply as introducing considerations which the legal texts have ignored or expressed inadequately. They offer a scheme of interpretation for reading the legal texts. To understand their rôle in legal argument, it is necessary to look more generally at the interpretative process.

2.1. Settling the physical text

The first problem in the process of legal interpretation is the need to collate the text fully so as to produce a complete canonical text —a text which contains all the words from which the normative content of the text is to be derived.

2.1.1. Collation and drafting style. Legal texts come in different forms. In some, as with a Code, the relevant provisions are meant to be included within it and related to each other in a systematic way. But in many other cases the compilation of the text is more difficult. For instance, French statutes rarely contain a list of the provisions repealed, whereas this is commonly done in the UK. Again, attempts are frequently made to provide a fully redrafted text for amended provisions, so mechanical difficulties in collating the canonical version of the text are rare, but do exist. In 1991, legislation on trades union immunity involves reading together provisions in Acts of Parliament passed in 1974, 1976, 1980, 1982, 1985, 1988 and 1990. Equally in France, I observed a proposed amendment to the Postal Code which produced six diverging versions of the newly amended article from different members of the Conseil d'Etat. Their solution was to have a full, authoritative version included in the proposed bill! In the absence of a consolidated text, the reader has to engage in a creative act of construction to build the physical text which serves as the basis for further interpretation and application.

Assigning definitions to key terms in the legislation is in the UK, more than France, a mechanical exercise. The statute itself will frequently provide definitions. But definitions may be provided in two other ways: by inference from the confrontation of provisions within the statute as a whole, or by reference to external knowledge about the context of legal provisions and social activities involved. In general, inference from the text is given priority over external definition by cross-reference.

2.1.2. The rôle of inference in establishing the text. Inference typically involves the application of ordinary rules of grammar. Does one expression usually give rise to the inference of another? Internal consistency within a text may suggest that an inference is justified.[15] Legal texts are not drafted to produce a complete and comprehensible set of instructions without further processing. Most officials, citizens and lawyers applying the text resort to secondary literature for clarification and precision —be this in ministerial circulars or practitioners' commentaries. The function of decision support systems is primarily to make available the text and the supporting secondary literature is produced, rather than for illustrating and implementing this secondary literature. Given differences in drafting style, the procedures and sources to make available the background material and the full text may vary from one legal system to another, but this is not a considerable impediment to the use of similar technology at least within systems of the European Communities.

2.1.3. The place of external reference. Reference to matters defined outside the legal text to be interpreted is frequent. Some concepts are simply of ordinary common sense, common edge, or contemporary values, such as 'advertisement' or 'dishonest'. Others are more technical, such as the issue of who is a 'controlling officer' or 'organ or representative' of a firm, which requires definition from outside the statute by reference to the statutes of the firm itself or general principles of company law. But, of course, this will lead to other interpretive questions. For instance, is the 'controlling officer' of a company defined by the nature of the office held, or in terms of the operational structure of the firm in question?[16] But it may be only when we understand the purpose of corporate liability that can we begin to make a sensible stab at a definition.[17]

2.2. The normative text as interpretation

The above illustrations demonstrate that the line between mechanical compilation of a text and giving sense to it is really a continuum requiring interpretation at all stages, even though in the former the leads may have been given in the text itself. But as Barden states (Barden, n.d.), there is a necessary transformation between the rule on paper and the operative rule.

It is a commonplace among much contemporary writing that the legal text is a product of interpretation in that its meaning requires an act of will or judgment. I have been suggesting here that this applies almost as much to the construction of the canonical text (what are the words to be interpreted?) as it does to the normative text (what rules are laid down by the canonical text?).

Any legal tradition has certain routines, such as conventions and practices of statutory drafting, which offer certain rather mechanical processes which lawyers can follow in deciding the content of a statute, and thereby reduce the scope for divergence in interpretation. These may include various values assumed as a background to the text to be interpreted which represent the 'other legal values' which mentioned earlier in 1.4.2.

2.2.1. Lawyers' assumptions and presumptions. In addition to routines, a legal community will operate with certain assumptions in its approach to legal texts, especially statutes. These may be linguistic, e.g. assuming that terminology in a text will be consistent, and that the provisions of the statute are both coherent among themselves and in relation to other similar rules within the legal system.

There may be also be certain policy presumptions adopted in case of doubt, such as against changing the previous law, against taxation, or in favour of the liberty of the subject. Established public policies might also be considered as policy presumptions of this kind. These assumptions are based on what statutes normally do or what they ought to do constitutionally. Such assumptions may be justified by the interpretation given to provisions of the constitution, e.g. on the division of lawmaking power between Parliament and other lawmakers, or just on the normal practices of the legislature. Both are what a good lawyer knows, but are not necessarily formalized in the legal system, and certainly not in the same way. What appears under 'presumptions of interpretation' in an English book on statutory interpretation, will appear in France under the constitutional rules governing the required content of *loi*, as opposed to executive legislation by way of *règlement*. In the end, these constitute conventions of legal discourse.

2.2.2. The accepted legal context. Over and above these, there will be accepted judgments of relevant legal principles. By this I mean that a statute will be taken to integrate into certain established rules and principles. Thus a planning statute will be assumed to integrate into the corpus of law on land use and environmental law, but not, say, into the law on local taxation or local government finance, or even agriculture or education.[18] Although some of these ideas will be spelled out in the purpose of the legislation itself, this will not necessarily be the case. The issue of carry over from one set of legal ideas or concepts to another is a matter of controversy: see *Fisher v. Bell*[19], where the issue whether 'offers for sale' in a criminal statute should be treated as importing the distinction made in contract law between an 'offer' and an 'invitation to treat'.

2.2.3. Summary. The process of interpretation is summarized in the following figures:

(a) Practices and routines to establish the canonical text.

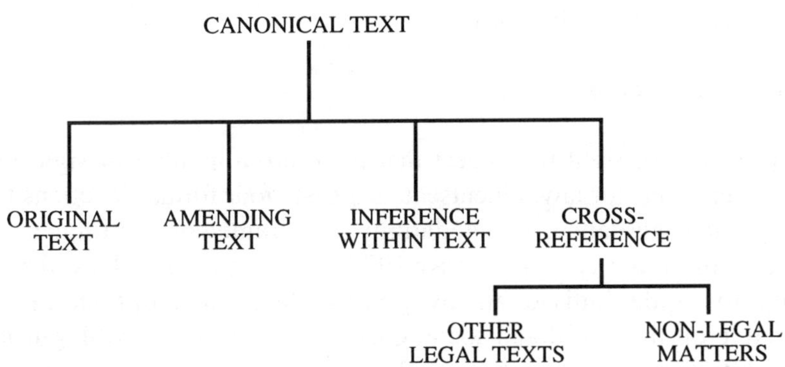

(b) Establishing the normative text.

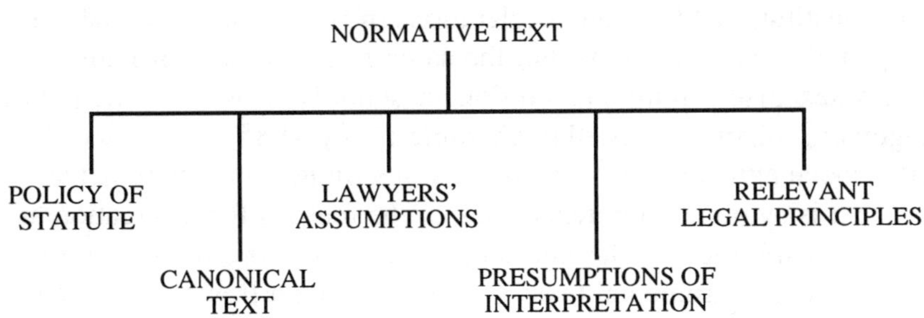

2.2.4. The place of policy in interpretation. If the process of interpretation needs to draw on so many sources in order to provide grounded interpretations, what is the place of policy? I would suggest that policy justifies the choices and priorities assigned to the various sources in the interpretive process. It is not so much an additional source, as a way of seeing the product of law in terms of its overall social function. Whereas the various assumptions of other legal values represent other forms of posited sources from which legal argument is drawn, policy arguments about the function of law are much more involved in encouraging forms of insight into the content of law.

3. THE FUNCTIONS OF LAW

What is most important is that law operates within certain expectations as to its social functions. It is expected in some ways to be a technical and restricted form of discourse. All the same, there may be proper debate as to the formal or substantive functions which the law plays, and it is here that policy arguments have their origin.

3.1. Formal Functions

Indeed, it may be right to suggest that there are a number of significantly different functions for law. Fikentscher suggests four formal functions for the law: (i) value-guidance; (ii) updating; (iii) framework-setting; and (iv) delegation of authority (Fikentscher 1977). In setting out values, the law is seeking to guide individuals by getting them to adopt an exclusive perspective on the world and social conduct —to take everything from the legal point of view. But such an exclusive approach depends on how legal values expressed in legal texts are related to non-legal values. For instance, some legal texts should be seen as symbolic of a social tradition (Perry 1984). Constitutional texts and declarations of rights are notoriously open to such symbolic interpretations, but the same might be said of legislation on race and sex discrimination, religion in schools, worker participation in management, or on strikes (though some (Grey 1985) would see them as specific social agreements to be enforced in a limited and instrumental way). Where text is symbolic, reference back to the reasons for its creation and its sources of inspiration in the non-legal world are more obviously required than with more instrumental texts. Equally, setting a framework, such as by laying down general clauses or open-ended standards for judicial decision-making, is an invitation to make use of values which are not closely defined by the law, but which are constrained by the context in which they are used. The judge has to decide what is fair and just in all the circumstances in distributing property on divorce, but always within the context of various procedures and general policy directives. The fourth function shades into this in that the more there is latitude within the framework, the more there is really a delegation of decision-making. This occurs frequently in the enforcement of pollution legislation, where the powers of inspectors really function as a delegation of authority to take steps by enforcement or bargaining in the shadow of enforcement to achieve some general policy goals.

In many ways, the formal character of a text follows from its substantive functions. We choose certain forms of text to fit its social function. But once the form of the text is understood, then the appropriateness of policy or other arguments is more easily appreciated.

3.2. Substantive Functions

Substantive functions of the law can be both general, e.g. to require a wrongdoer to pay compensation for harm caused, and specific, e.g. not to require compensation to be paid for what is done in judicial proceedings. Functions, like legal principles, provide reasons and orientations for the operation of legal rules. Unlike principles, they are more amorphous in content and difficult to weigh. They are pointers to where the law should be going, rather than relatively precise objectives. As such, they offer perspectives on what the law is doing.

To the extent that these substantive functions can be specified, and where the law is fundamentally instrumental in its formal function, then I would suggest that some reference to them can be built into a computer-based decision support system. Where the formal function of the law is more symbolic and the substantive functions are more diffuse or general, then it will be more difficult to provide a useful prompt to the decision-maker.

This suggestion about the possible systematisation of some features of policy arguments within law will be shown by reference to the notion of 'public policy'.[20]

3.3. Public policy and the substantive functions of law

Public policy is difficult to define. In broad terms, it consists of functions which lawyers believe the law should serve, but which are not typically formulated in a text. They form part of the 'lawyers' assumptions' against which a text is read. A good example is *R. v. Registrar General, ex p. Smith.*[21] Section 51 of the Adoption Act 1976 provides:

> [T]he Registrar General shall on application made in the prescribed manner by an adopted person a record of whose birth is kept by the Registrar General and who has attained the age of 18 years supply to that person on payment of the prescribed fee (if any) such information as is necessary to enable that person to obtain a certified copy of the record of his birth.

Smith was such a person, but the Registrar General refused to give him the necessary information because he was a patient in a secure mental hospital (Broadmoor), having been convicted, inter alia, of the manslaughter of a cellmate whom he mistook for his foster mother. The Registrar was afraid that Smith would use the actual record of his birth to trace his real mother and perhaps to do violence to her. The Divisional Court had no difficulty in upholding the decision of the Registrar General. The statutory right was effectively denied where there was a real risk that it would be used for future criminality. To treat the right as absolute would outrage the public. It did not matter that there was no precedent for the Registrar General's argument.

The operation of public policy is a compromise between various values which the law has to serve. As Treitel remarks, 'The present attitude of the courts represents a compromise between the flexibility inherent in the notion of public policy and the need for certainty in commercial affairs' (Treitel 1986, p. 367). Legal certainty is an important value in the rule of law. It enables people to predict with a fair degree of accuracy the way in which the law will impinge on the activities which they wish to undertake. But it is only a formal value, since it requires merely that the law be specific, coherent, set out in advance, with sufficient clarity to guide individuals before disputes arise which may have to be resolved in court. Ease of administration would also point in this direction. Reduction in discretion in the hands of administrators will help to contain the need for such officials, the speed with which they can work, and the kind of accountability they have to give to the clients of the system. Both values move the law in the direction of routinised, bureaucratic administration, and this provides also for consistency and equal treatment.

But there are other values which the law must also further. Most notable among these are fairness, the reflection of public values, and social control, and they all feature in 'public policy'.

Fairness needs little comment; it is obvious that a system which appeals to 'justice' as its reason for existence should seek to achieve results which are fair. In the area of restraint of trade, restraints both during and after employment contained in contracts between employers and employees are struck down really because the bargaining power of the former is too great and the terms are not a fair compromise between the interests of the parties.[22] Whatever the parties may have freely agreed, it is not appropriate for the law to endorse what they have done. For the most part, however, in the area of voluntary arrangements, the law is content to ensure procedural fairness in the way an agreement was reached (i.e. the absence of duress or fraud), rather than to look at the substantive outcome of an agreement.

Law states not only the limits of individual action, but also public values. To disapprove of conduct communicates the values of society and tries to elicit support for the law among the public in general. The concern of the judges in *R. v. Registrar General, ex p. Smith* was to keep the law in touch with what they took to be the expectations of the community in the prevention of crime, when they refused a person access to the name of his natural parent where there was a serious likelihood that he would then commit serious violence against her. That judges wish to consider themselves spokespersons for social consensus is not doubted, though their ability to achieve this may well be doubted. (See Bell 1983, pp. 10–17 and ch. 7.) Equally, the law is perceived (by lawyers at least) as a neutral backbone of social stability, a reflection of the values of society.

Specific legal rules are meant to exhibit this feature. In another place, I have summarised the established heads of public policy as preventing harm to governmental institutions (e.g. by 'treating' electors), protecting recourse to judicial institutions, protecting the institution of the family, protecting economic institutions, protecting constitutional values (e.g. the freedom of the individual), preventing infringement of good morals (e.g. by contracts involving prostitution), and preventing fraud. (See Bell 1991). Over time, such heads have become fairly precise, though they are open to development to meet changing circumstances, but such a breach of legal certainty does note really impede the rule of law. Law exists, to quote Honoré (1977), to reinforce people's reasons for conformity to certain standards. To perform this task, it must be able to react not only against the law being used as an instrument of unfairness, but also when the use of law runs counter to other cherished beliefs in the community. In this way, conformity to public (better, 'institutional') values may be more important than simple conformity to rules.

Social control is also an objective achieved through public policy, which exists as a corrective to specific rules. Like discretions within the operations of rule-structured systems such as social security, public policy allows officials to deal with facts which are either unforeseen or difficult to calculate. The officials are enabled to keep control over the conduct of individuals, where results, or merely the purposes of individuals are undesirable. Law creates a system of authorization for official action, rather than just dictating what officials must do.

In protecting social institutions, judges are concerned to ensure that rights and freedoms do not harm society as a whole. Judges and other officials need freedom to exercise control in order to preserve the system as a whole. To that extent, interventions cannot be totally predictable, and the courts need to be able to look beyond form to substance and motives.

The judicial function reflects the complexity of what is required from law as a social institution. Judges are focal decision-makers in the western legal tradition, whether in the common law or in the civil law. Although the bureaucratic, rule-based model is more officially enshrined in the civil law, there is much left for decision by judges in practice, and public policy provides an important juncture at which the rôles of judges and legislators interact. Although judges and commentators are keen to indicate the lack of identity between the rôles of the two, there is an important overlap. Perhaps the best expression of the difference is given by (Malaurie 1953): that legislators can decide on the basis of political opportunism, while judges must try to base themselves on something more permanent and stable. The line between the two ideas is, however, very fluid and imprecise.

The kind of judicial rôle in question is seen by the desire to base decisions on objective evidence of public benefit or harm determined by other institutions or, failing that, by legal tradition. (See Bell 1991, pp 175-6.) Published reports of independent committees, judicial precedents, or even, in some cases, current government policy, may all provide the kind of objective evidence on which judges prefer to rely. Judges are unwilling to have their decisions characterised as idiosyncratic (any more, for that matter, than are legislators). The susceptibility of the judiciary to criticism in this regard is an important feature in encouraging them to work with fairly well-established standards of public policy.

4. PUBLIC POLICY IN A DECISION SUPPORT SYSTEM

Two issues arise for consideration from what has gone before. The first is a narrow concern for the extent and manner of dealing with public policy within a decision support system. The second, wider issue concerns the function of law and the implications this has for the analysis of legal reasoning as a whole.

How should the problem of public policy be handled in a decision support system?

In formal terms, public policy appears as an exception to the *prima facie* rights or obligations which can be derived from a statute or contract. But it is not easily formulated as an excepting condition because the exception is not of the same genre as the rule. Whereas the statutory conditions for obtaining widow's allowance can be set out in rule form, the exception of public policy cannot, because it is not reducible to a simple set of rules.[23] Public policy appeals to a set of general values. It is not so much a standard in its own right, of the kind studied by Gaudemet and Teubner (Gaudemet 1972, Teubner 1971), as a framework within which a number of competing values are related to one another. There are importantly predictable elements within the general rubric of 'public policy', in that fairly precise heads of public policy can be identified, but they involve a number of complex relationships between values. Even the apparently straightforward idea that 'no person shall profit from their own wrong' requires an assessment of what kind of wrong has been done (a crime alone will not suffice), how far granting a right or benefit will be reprehensible, and whether there are countervailing considerations, such as in the case of motor insurance contracts. The kind of reasoning used in reaching conclusions on such issues as whether 'no person shall profit from their own wrong' applies is not easily reduced to terms of formal logic. The answer depends on a weighing of variables, of seeing how various legs on a stool support the seat, to use Wisdom's analogy (Wisdom 1953).

Given that character of the legal reasoning involved, the involvement of public policy is difficult to introduce simply into a decision support system. Potentially, public policy may occur as an exception to any *prima facie* legal solution. The assessment of its relevance to a particular situation must be made by the user guided by the system itself. What the system must be content to do is to alert the user to the possible defeasibility of the solution offered by the expert system, and to suggest steps in determining whether the defeasibility conditions of public policy are met.

One approach would be to follow the logic of legal reasoners in such cases, while recognising that legal reasoning here is typically a matter of legal 'common sense', rather than well-articulated judgments.

There are, it seems to me, a number of basic questions (Level 1) which may alert the legal reasoner to the potential application of public policy, and then further, more detailed questions (Level 2), which might help guide its actual application (Level 3).

Level 1 questions relate to the various functions of the law and invite the reasoner to consider whether these perspectives are relevant to the inquiry he or she is making. Once a decision has been made here, then more precise answers can be sought at lower levels.

Level 1. Among the leading candidates for inclusion at this level are:

(a) Might the right or obligation which is sought to be enforced be considered as infringing the purpose of a statute whose provisions would normally apply to the situation under consideration?

(b) Has the right or obligation claimed arisen in a suspect (illegal or immoral) way?

(c) Might enforcing the right or obligation be considered to cause harm to the normal functioning of government or the political process?

(d) Might enforcing the right or obligation be considered to interfere with the normal administration of justice?

(e) Might enforcing the right or obligation be considered to affect adversely normal family life?

(f) Might the enforcement of the right or obligation be considered to infringe conventional views on sexual morality or fair dealing?

(g) Might the obligations or rights created interfere with the normal operation of a competitive market in the goods or services to which the agreement relates?

Subsequent levels would then offer more precise questions. For example, on question (e), there might be levels as follows:

Level 2. Among the questions on family life might feature the following:

(a) Do the obligations imposed restrict the freedom of a person to choose whether to marry or to choose their marital partner?

(b) Is one of the parties seeking to derive financial gain from the choice by another of their marital partner?

(c) Are any obligations imposed which affect the usual rights of a parent or parents in relation to their children?

(d) Do the obligations or rights created affect the welfare of a child?

Level 3. Should answers at Level 2 be positive, further questions might be posed to obtain a balancing judgment on the values at stake. For instance, the following:

(a) What is the strength of the evidence that the obligations will affect family life detrimentally?

- (i) is there an official report demonstrating this?
- (ii) can an analogy be drawn with statutes which consider such activity harmful?
- (iii) is there any judicial precedent which has found or suggested that such a harm exists?
- (iv) is there any other evidence which might be adduced to demonstrate the harm?

(b) What are the advantages which can be demonstrated to flow from enforcing the obligation?

- (i) which arise from the specific arrangement to the person imposing the obligation, the person on whom it is imposed, to third parties, or to the community at large?
- (ii) which arise more generally from permitting a large area to freedom of contract or disposal of one's property?

(c) Is the judgment whether the advantages outweigh the disadvantages one which it is appropriate for legal institutions to make (as opposed, for example, to leaving the matter for resolution by the legislature)?

(d) If legal institutions can make such judgments, are the disadvantages in (a) sufficiently serious to displace the normal legal validity of the arrangement creating the obligation in question?

Even if such an array of questions can be formulated, it must be recognised that public policy is not capable of complete axiomatisation. Not only cannot a complete list of applicable axioms be drawn up, the list would be complex in the weight assigned to the various variables. The goal of simplicity in axioms cannot be met fully.

Furthermore, the justifications offered for public policy judgments are often not found in precise sources. There may be reports, precedents or analogies with statutes. All the same, the weight assigned to material in each source varies significantly from topic to topic. In addition, there will always be the possible recourse to more intuitive judgments which have no specific source. It is part of the non-deductive character of public policy judgments that they remain primarily in the area of evaluation in terms of local priorities, rather than grander systematisation. This is not to deny the rationality of the judgments made, merely to indicate the difficulties in reducing the whole approach to a single grand system of axioms announced in advance.

5. CONCLUSION: AN INSTITUTIONALISED RULE OF LAW

Public policy offers an illustration of the way legal systems, even formalist ones like the English and French, operate by conferring on those who have to implement the legal system the task of integrating specific rules with broad statements of social objectives. However much the idea of hard-and-fast rules may dominate legal thinking, this more wide-ranging set of values cannot be ignored, and this says much about our ideas of legality and the rule of law.

Legal certainty is an important value in the rule of law. It enables people to predict with a fair degree of accuracy the way in which the law will impinge on the activities which they wish to undertake. This value is met by a (theoretically) programmable set of rules and exceptions and moves in the direction of routinised, bureaucratic administration. But there are other values which the law must also further. Most notable among these are fairness, the reflection of public values, and social control.

In order that these other values can be a common basis in a heterogeneous society, it may be that they have to be institutionalised through law. Within the institutional framework of law, otherwise pertinent questions can be ignored or downplayed. To achieve this significant elements of public policy become reduced to a set of rather conservative values which are taken to be agreed in society, whether this is in fact true or not. This is an important lesson to draw from those who have stressed this institutional character of law, and the formalism of legal reasons which is linked to it. (See especially MacCormick and Weinberger 1986). The institutional character of law in itself provides a form of stability and certainty which constrains and legitimates power. Precise rules and other standards have an important rôle within such an institutional setting. But public policy illustrates ways in which the functions of the institution of law may feature more directly in the way decisions are taken according to law. It acts as a kind of 'safety valve' concept in the implementation of more precise legal standards. It may be used in a rather tentative and pragmatic way, but this is not a failure of approach, merely a reflection of the rather diverse circumstances in which it may be appropriate to use it. The rule of law is served in such a context by requiring that justifications be given for the solutions reached to show that they fit coherently with the underlying purposes of the legal system. It may be that the various values expressed in doctrines of public policy are more ideal than actual in the current state of the law, as, indeed, are ideas of integrity and coherence. But such an ideal aspect to law is important as a regulative device within the institution of law. It encourages decision-makers to make the law more fully fit the ideal. In this way public policy as an expression of the ideal functions of the legal system relates to the idea of public policy as a framework for decision-making. The rule of law requires reasons to be given for the exercise of power, even if that exercise is not predictable in advance.

The rôle of the decision support system is primarily to identify and prompt the legal reasoner as to the determinable standards with which he or she has to operate. The variety of the elements of law which is demonstrated by the idea of policy arguments simply shows that the results of an analysis of legal rules is potentially defeasible once the functions of the rules are taken into account. The legal reasoner, though perhaps not the decision support system, has to be aware of this possibility. All the same, the decision support system can hope to be somewhat more complete than simply reproducing the model of legal rules. It can be designed to prompt the reasoner as to other features in the legal system, although the results of such prompting will require complex and controversial judgments to be made by the decision-maker himself or herself.

NOTES

1 (Bell 1983) pp. 22–23. See also (Summers 1978). One might want to suggest with Lord Simon of Glaisdale that they are 'considerations of social interests beyond the purely legal which call for the modification of a normal legal rule' (*D v. NSPCC* [1978] AC 171, 235.) Cf also (Tate 1959): 'Policy considerations I define ... as those based upon social or practical or equitable reasons why a court should decide a present controversy in a given manner; as contrasted with purely "legal" or logomachical arguments based upon the wording of a statute or the holding of a precedent and reasoning therefrom.' However this introduces a distinction between 'legal' and 'non legal' reasons which is not particularly helpful for our purposes. Suffice it to say that policy arguments lie at the intersection between legal and non-legal discourses about the resolution of a problem, and the content of both types of discourse at this point is substantially the same.

2 In this context, I would suggest that an 'autopoietic' perspective merely confirms the view that law is open to external influences in a significant manner. As Luhmann suggests, there may be some form of factorising of external perspectives in order to fit within the law, but this does not mean that law is not significantly shaped by external objectives. (Luhmann 1990) As with Dworkin, this simply suggests that there must be a minimum 'threshold of fit' before a policy perspective will be eligible for application, and that, when it is applied, it will provide exclusionary justifications for legal decisions.

3 *Pocock v. Steel* [1985] 1 WLR 229; Cross p. 191.

4 *Smith v. Eric Bush* [1989] 2 WLR 790, HL; *Mitchell v. Finney Lock Seeds* [1983] 2 AC 803, both on the 'reasonableness' provision of the Unfair Contract Terms Act 1977.

5 Here I take the view that to apply the purposes and principles underlying a particular provision is to apply thc provision itself: cf. Art. 5, lid. 2, Nieuw B.W. ('Toepassing van rechtsbeginselen die aan wetsvoorschriften ten grondslag liggen, geldt als toepassing van die voorschriften.')

[6] See, e.g. *R v. Chief Adjudication Officer, ex p Connor* [1981] QB 758: a woman cannot claim a widow's allowance if she was criminally responsible for her husband's death.

[7] See for example *Miller v. Jackson* [1977] QB 966: the interests of the cricket-going public taken into account when deciding whether to prevent a cricket club from continuing its games, even though they interfered with the use and enjoyment of a neighbour's land.

[8] CE 7.7.1950, *Dehaene,* JCP 1950 II 5681 conclusions Gazier, where it is stated 'Sirs, it is the less strictly legal, but more pressing and altogether more difficult, considerations which will determine your choice.' He then relies on arguments about the authority and continuity of government, the effect of public and private sector strikes, the efficacy of the legal system if it went against common opinion, the importance of the work done by the civil servants in question, and the role of courts, legislature and the administration in deciding the social policy in this area.

[9] For example, the relationship between national law and directives of the EEC has arisen recently in England and France: *Duke v. GEC Reliance* [1988] 1 All ER 626; *Factortame Ltd v. Transport Secretary* [1991] 1 All ER 70; CE Ass 3.2.1989, *Cie Alitalia*, AJDA 1989, 387.

[10] See *Rondel v. Worsley* [1969] 1 AC 191: the immunity of barristers for actions in the conduct of litigation prevents a flood of cases by disgruntled clients, and protects the authority of judicial decisions.

[11] *Parkinson v. College of Ambulance Ltd* [1925] 2 KB 1.

[12] See e.g. *Moss v. Maclachan* [1985] IRLR 76: in the absence of a text, the police were authorized to stop strikers heading for an illegal picket: Generally, (Bell 1991).

[13] *Dunton v. Dover DC* (1978) 76 LGR 87.

[14] Compare *Duport Steels Ltd v. Sirs* [1980] 1 WLR 142 (industrial relations) with *Gillick v. West Norfolk AHA* [1985] 3 All ER 402 (prescribing the contraceptive pill to girls under the age of consent without their parents' knowledge), *O'Reilly v. Mackman* [1983] 2 AC 237 (the creation of a distinction between procedures in public law and those in private law) and *Mareva Compania Naviera v. International Bulkcarriers* [1980] 1 All ER 213n (the creation of new procedural remedies).

[15] See *Dixon v. BBC* [1979] 2 All ER 112 cf. *BBC v. Ioannou* [1975] QB 781.

[16] *Tesco v. Nattrass* [1972] AC 153.

[17] Thus we might refer here to the ministerial memorandum accompanying the French criminal code which states as one of the reasons for the criminal liability of the corporation: 'Furthermore, the decision which is at the origin of the offence is taken by company organs themselves, which determine the industrial, commercial or social policy of the enterprise.'

[18] *Darlassis v. Minister of Education* (1954) 52 LGR 304; *Stringer v. Minister of Housing & Local Government* [1970] 1 WLR 1281.

[19] [1961] 1 QB 394.

[20] For further elaboration of this notion, see (Bell 1991).

[21] [1990] 2 All ER 170. See further (Bell 1991) and *R v. Chief Adjudication Officer, ex p Connor* [1981] QB 758, above note 6.

[22] *O'Sullivan v. Management Agency & Music Ltd* [1985] QB 428.

[23] See *R v. Chief Adjudication Officer, ex p Connor* [1981] QB 758, supra note 6.

REFERENCES

Alexy, R., 1989. *A Theory of Legal Argumentation* (trans. & ed. R. Adler and N. MacCormick), Oxford, p 220.

Atiyah, P.S. and R.B. Summers, 1987. *Form and Substance in Anglo-American Law*, Oxford, pp 23–25.

Barden, G., n.d. Working papers contributed to the ESPRIT Group.

Bell, J., 1983. *Policy Arguments in Judicial Decisions*, Oxford.

Bell, J., 1991. 'Conceptions of Public Policy', in P. Cane & J. Stapleton (eds), *Essays for Patrick Atiyah* , Oxford.

Canaris, C.-W., 1964. *Die Feststellung von Lücken im Gesetz*, Berlin, pp. 97–100.

Corsale, M., 1970. *La certezza del diritto*, Milan, p. 124.

Cross, R., 1987. *Cross on Statutory Interpretation* (2nd edn by J. Bell & G. Engle), London, pp. 17–19.

Dworkin, R. 1986. *Law's Empire*, London

Fikentscher, W., 1977. *Methoden des Rechts*, Tubingen, IV, pp. 303–8.

Gaudemet, Y., 1972. *Le juge administratif et la technique du standard,* Paris.

Grey, T.C., 1985. 'The Constitution as Scripture', 37 *Stanford L Rev.,* 1.

Honoré, Tony, 1977. 'Real Laws', in P.M.S. Hacker and J. Raz (eds.), *Law, Morality and Society*, Oxford, p. 118.

Kelsen, H., 1990. 'On the theory of interpretation', 10 *Legal Studies* ,p. 127.

Lonergan, B.F.J., 1957. *Insight: A Study of Human Understanding*, London.

Luhmann, N., 1967. 'Positives Recht und Ideologie', 53 *ARSP* pp. 531, 565.

Luhmann, N., 1990.*Essays on Self-Reference*, New York; pp 238–9.

MacCormick, D., and O. Weinberger, 1986. *An Institutional Theory of Law* Dordrecht.

Malaurie, P., 1953. *Ordre public et 'public policy'*, Reims, pp. 66–8.

Martino, A.A., n.d. Working papers contributed to the ESPRIT Group.

Perry, M.J. 1984. 'The Authority of Text, Tradition, and Reason: A Theory of Constitutional Interpretation', 58 *S. Calif. L Rev.* pp. 552, 559 & 564.

Raz, J., 1979. *The Authority of Law*, Oxford, ch 3.

Summers, R.S., 1978. 'Two Types of Substantive Reasons: The Core of a Theory of Common Law Justification', 63 *Cornell L Rev.* 707, 716–25.

Tamello, A., 1959. 'On the Logical Openness of Legal Orders', 8 *American Journal of Comparative Law* p. 187.

Tate, A., 1959. '"Policy" in Judicial Decisions', 20 *Louisiana Law Rev.* 62

Teubner, G., 1971. *Standards und Direktiven in Generalklauseln*, Frankfurt.

Treitel, G.H., 1986. *The Law of Contract* (7th edn), London.

Weinberger, O., 1972. 'Fundamental Problems of the Theory of Legal Reasoning' 58 *ARSP* 305, 331–3.

Wisdom, J., 1953. *Philosophy and Psychoanalysis*, Blackwell, Oxford.

Zippelius, R., 1977. *Das Wesen des Rechts* (4th edn), Munich, p. 190.

Faculty of Law
University of Leeds
England

NEIL MACCORMICK

DEFEASIBILITY IN LAW AND LOGIC

Defeasibility is a concept of interest to lawyers and to logicians. Sometimes legal arrangements are said to be defeasible in the sense that they can be upset or set aside despite an initial appearance of validity and durability. In logic, ways are sought to handle cases of inference or entailment where the connection between condition and consequence is less watertight than that required by classical logic(s). And then the talk is of 'defeasible logic'. Debate at the junction between law and logic, especially debate on the harnessing of information technology, expert systems and the like to legal work, seems specially apt for inquiring into defeasibility as, perhaps, a concept of joint interest to lawyers and logicians.

1. EXPLICIT AND IMPLICIT DEFEASIBILITY IN LAW

The idea of the 'defeasibility' of legal concepts has been on the go at least since the time of H. L. A. Hart's early essay on 'The Ascription of Responsibility and Rights' (Hart 1948–9), subsequently disowned by its author (Hart 1968), but later rehabilitated by G. P. Baker (Baker 1977). For my own part, I put up a perhaps similar idea (without at the time noticing the similarity) in 1973 in 'Law as Institutional Fact' (MacCormick 1973). There, I suggested that when we contemplate our best attempts to formulate 'institutive' and 'terminative' rules for legal institutions like contract or trust or marriage or rights of testate or intestate succession, we have to note that the conditions a given rule-formulation states to be required for the establishment of a particular concrete instance of an institution (or 'arrangement', see MacCormick 1988) of that type ought really to be envisaged as no more than 'ordinarily necessary and presumptively sufficient' conditions of the relevant legal consequence(s).

The point about defeasibility is that every appearance of validity may attach to some arrangement set up under legal rules or some legal state of affairs ostensibly arising from some set of rules and events: and yet it can happen that this arrangement or 'institutional fact' is subject to some kind of invalidating intervention. That which was initially, or on the face of it, valid turns out to be open to attack, and under attack to lose its initial validity, or be revealed as never having been valid, despite all appearances. That is, the arrangement (or whatever) in question is defeasible, and invalidating events bring about its defeasance.

Z. Bankowski et al. (eds.), Informatics and the Foundations of Legal Reasoning, 99–117.

The easiest case of this to imagine is that of what we might call 'express defeasibility'. As an example, one might think of a rule about a right *R*, where the rule expressly states the positive conditions for the vesting of *R* in an appropriate person, but also expressly makes this subject to some exception or proviso. So the formulation of the conditions in relation to *R* is in such terms as 'if conditions c_1, c_2, c_3 are satisfied then *R* vests in *A* as against *B*, but not if *B* shows that exceptional condition e_1 exists'.

The point of this formulation has to do with the pragmatics of right-claims and right-enjoyment. Under it, all *A* need do to establish a good claim to the subject matter of *R* is satisfy, or show to be satisfied, c_1, c_2 and c_3. Under the rule as formulated, it is not up to *A* to show that the situation is not exceptional. It is up to the other interested party, *B*, to show that the case is exceptional in that e_1 exists. By so doing, *B* defeats *A*'s otherwise good claim. Any assertion by *A* of a claim to the right (or its subject matter) on the footing of c_1, c_2 and c_3 is defeasible, and will be defeated if *B* can indeed show or prove that e_1. Where there is no dispute, *A*'s confidence in his claim, or in secure enjoyment of the right or its subject matter, depends on B's being unable to show or to prove that e_1. For total security, it must actually not be the case that e_1.

For example, *A*'s claim to the proceeds of an insurance policy is usually made out by *A*'s showing the insurers that the contingency has occurred against which insurance was taken out. It is not up to *A* to show the absence of every possible vitiating circumstance that might defeat his entitlement to the insurance payment. Again, there are cases where defeasance of a right depends on *B*'s taking timely action. If *A* fraudulently purchases goods from *B*, for example, by giving a dud cheque under a false name, *A* acquires a voidable title to the goods, and can pass the title to a third party unless *B* in the meantime takes appropriate steps to rescind the transaction. So long as *A* retains the goods unsold, *A*'s title is a defeasible one, and effectual rescission by *B* defeats it. An innocent third party who purchased from *B* after rescission would in turn have only a defeasible title, pending recovery of the goods by *B*. There may be many other examples of express defeasibility in this sense. Still, it does not seem that what is here called 'express defeasibility', important though it is, exhausts the idea, or perhaps even captures its most interesting cases. Indeed, if I am right in thinking that the express formulations of institutive rules of legal institutions are always properly regarded as stating only 'ordinarily necessary and presumptively sufficient' conditions for the arrangements they regulate, implicit defeasibility afflicts all instances of legal institutions. Even in cases of express defeasibility, there may be possibilities of implicit defeasibility over and above the explicit conditions of defeasance.

The reason for this is easy to state when one contemplates the reality of a concrete legal system. It is necessary to consider how the principles and implicit values of such a system interact with the more specific provisions one lays down, or can lay down, in explicit rules. Well-known examples of this are found in the cases from many jurisdictions dealing with the problem of the murderous legatee. The one who kills the testator to accelerate succession to the promised legacy then finds that the anticipated right of succession under the will is defeated by the principle that the law should not enable persons to profit from their own crimes. Of course, the case-law in respect of wills is now so well settled that it can be taken as constituting a settled rule in the given context; prima facie rights of succession under a formally valid will do not avail in favour of a legatee who has unlawfully killed the testator.[1]

It remains the case, however, that the underlying principle extends more broadly than the particular rule I just formulated, and can in appropriate settings lead to new understandings of different legal rules. A recent illustration makes this vivid. In *R. v National Insurance Commissioner ex p. Connor*[2], a woman had applied for a widow's pension on the ground that her husband was dead, and she therefore a widow. In fact, she satisfied all the explicit statutory conditions of entitlement to a widow's allowance, for her husband had died and his national insurance contribution record satisfied the stated conditions. The alert clerk to whom application was initially made, however, recognised the widow in this case as one who had been widowed by her own hand, through accidentally stabbing her husband with a carving knife during a quarrel. In consequence, she had been convicted of the manslaughter of her late husband. The clerk refused to make payment and in due course this refusal was upheld by the National Insurance Commissioner, and then by the Divisional Court on an application for review. The principle that the law will not uphold rights arising directly out of criminal misconduct was held to apply to the pension statute as well as to other sorts of entitlement arising on death. Although the principle does not automatically disqualify, but requires judicial scrutiny of all the circumstances of a particular unlawful killing, the Lord Chief Justice and his brethren held that the unlawful killing in this case did have the effect of defeating the statutory right that had ostensibly vested in the widow, and that she had claimed in all honest conviction of her right to the widow's allowance. So the established legal principle here constitutes an unstated exception to the express statutory conditions for vesting of a right, an exception which itself requires an exercise of discretionary judgment by a deciding official or judge.[3]

Should it be said in this case that the right proved defeasible? Or that there never was a right in the first place? Is it just a case where the widow claimed that to which she had no right, for all that she and her advisers honestly thought she was entitled to it? Was the claim defeated because the right never existed (despite appearances) or was there here a right that proved defeasible and was defeated? The conceptualization proposed here opts for denial that the claimed right actually exists. It seems better to conceptualise this in terms of defeasance (or defeat) not of a right itself but of the claim made to the right. The claim is put forward on (and would be justified by) what turns out to be an inadequate or incomplete understanding of the legal conditions for acquisition or enjoyment of the right. In the given instance, the misunderstanding involved treating the express satisfactory conditions as themselves not only necessary (which indeed they are) but also sufficient for acquisition of the right conferred by statute.

The 'right' is, after all, a theoretical object, an institutional fact. Such facts exists only where there is perfect and undefeated satisfaction of all conditions (the implicit as well as the explicit) actually required in a given case. It is the ascription of a right, or the asserting of a claim to it (or to what one purports to be entitled by the right, e.g., payment of a widow's allowance), that can be defeated, not the right itself. So it is not after all the *concept* that is defeasible, but some formulated statement of conditions for instantiating the concept in given cases, or some assertion, ascription or claim based on a certain understanding of those conditions. It is easy to see why legal doctrine may express itself in defeasible formulations of relevant legal rules. For almost any right or other legal institution there may well be certain exceptional or abnormal conditions whose presence will vitiate the vesting of a right, but their very abnormality makes it unfruitful to state the necessity for the absence of those conditions in every formulation of the right. Even the draftsman responsible for statutory formulations of the conditions for vesting of rights of given types is subject to constraint on the exceptions and provisos which can practicably be made explicit in the legislative formulation of such matters. Conversely, it is equally easy to see how a citizen or even the legal adviser can perceive a claim as sufficiently justified when all express statutory or doctrinally stated conditions are shown to be met in a given case. Yet there is the risk of a trumping of what is expressly stated in law by recourse to what is deemed implicit albeit unstated (at least, unstated in the given context).[4]

The present view of defeasibility connects with a related view about one omnipresent problem concerning the formulation or articulation of the law. The problem is in one aspect that of limits to accuracy or exhaustiveness in statements of the law, and in another aspect that of the reliability with which one can draw inferences from the express statements in which law is formulated. Law has to be stated in general terms, yet conditions formulated generally are always capable of omitting reference to some element which can turn out to be the key operative fact in a given case. The difficulty concerns the multiplicity of possible conditions which may arise from the interaction of different parts of the law with each other and the interaction of explicitly enacted rules, or doctrinally formulated restatements of rules, with principles and values in the manner indicated. Notoriously, it would be extremely difficult, perhaps impossible, and for sure the enemy of any kind of clarity or cognoscibility in law, to attempt a formulation of every conceivable precondition of validity in every statement of every rule. So general formulations of rights are apt to leave many background conditions unstated, especially those which arise only in rather exceptional cases. The presence of unstated elements appears to be a general feature of law, albeit different legal systems take different characteristic lines on the degree to which statutory draftsmanship should tend towards completeness in each statutory formulation, rather than giving broader allowance to a reading of statutes in the light of their whole systemic context.

In any system, those who formulate rules for widows' pensions are unlikely to focus their (or our) attention particularly on the comparatively rare instances of widowhood that occasioned by the wrongful killing of the widow's deceased husband. Their characteristically more concise general statements of rights are thus subject to defeasance when the exceptional cases do turn up. Exceptions occur whenever a situation arises in which the particular events in issue bring into operation some legal principle or value of sufficient importance to override the presumptive sufficiency of the conditions stated expressly as conditions for the vesting of the right. The special situation activates some background factor which exceptionally vitiates the vesting of a right that would otherwise be unproblematic. The general statement of the right is adequate if it stipulates what is necessary and sufficient for establishing the right in the common run of cases, subject to any express exceptions or provisos for regularly occurring and readily foreseeable (or doctrinally well-documented or case-law established) defeating factors. But the operation of background principles can be seen as raising the possibility of rather open-ended exceptions in cases of an exceptional or unusual sort.

One feature identified in the earlier discussion of express defeasibility remains highly significant in relation to implicit defeasibility. For again the pragmatic aspect looms large. It can hardly be the case that a party relying on the explicitly stated (even if only presumptive) conditions of the rules as legislatively or doctrinally stated, with or without a case-law gloss, has normally first to imagine and then to disprove all possible legally defeating conditions that might afflict some arrangement or right in which that party is interested. It must be up to some other interested party to raise a relevant and effective challenge. Defeasibility again finds its explanation in the pragmatics of legal practice. Where a claim is made with some *prima facie* justification in law, it is up to the one who challenges the claim to show what is wrong with it in the context, wrong enough for it to be defeated when all things are considered.

A different example drawn from the common law may help to fortify the point proposed about the pragmatics of assertions or claims of right. Let us consider the common law of evidence, in particular the doctrine which differentiates between qualifications upon an entitlement and exceptions to it. If *A* has a right upon certain conditions but subject to a certain (negative) qualification, then *A* bears the burden of proving that all its conditions are met, and this includes proving the absence of any qualifying circumstances. If, however, *A* has a right under certain conditions, but the vesting of the right is expressedly subject to a certain exception, then the evidentiary burden shifts to the other interested party or parties to show that the exception does obtain.

So a shipowner who shows that a chartered ship has been sunk can claim a right to be exempted from liability under the charterparty. For the contract is terminated by frustration through the loss of the ship. But there is a rule that frustration must not be self-induced. If non-self-inducement is properly taken to be a qualification intrinsic to the concept of frustration, this will leave the onus on the shipowner to show that the ship's loss (e.g. by torpedoing in wartime) was not due to faulty navigation. But if self-induced loss counts as an exception to the normal rule of frustration through loss of the ship, then it will be the charterer who bears the burden of proving that there was some fault on the shipowner's (or the master's or crew's) part. It will not be for the shipowner to disprove such fault.[5]

There is on this point an argument by the late Julius Stone which, if sound, would undercut the present thesis in relation to this very example. Stone finds here one of his 'legal categories of illusory reference'.[6] So far from neatly exemplifying the presence or absence of express defeasibility, he challenges the roots of this difference or alleged difference between a qualification included in a rule and an exception extraneously limiting its application. He argues that there is no logical difference between 'for all x, if x is F and x is not G, then x is H' and 'for all x, if x is F then x is H, but not if x is G'. So legal qualifications and exceptions are logically indistinguishable; accordingly, says Stone, there can be no logical justification for the differential burden of proof which the law proclaims to be dependent on exactly this differentiation. The practice of differential allocation of burdens of proof cannot be logically compelled by a difference in different kinds of fact. For they do not differ logically. There must be some other explanation for it altogether. A difference justified (if at all) on some other ground is being dressed up as depending on the (after all bogus) logic of 'qualification' versus 'exception'.

There is an important point here (though not as convincing in relation to his concrete examples as Stone claimed[7]). A truth-functional logic that allows only of conjunction ('and'), disjunction ('or'), negation ('not') and material implication ('if... then...') does indeed lack the capacity to handle the distinction we are dealing with. This is (*inter alia*) because it has to treat 'but' as simply a form of 'and'. For such a logic, qualification and exception are indistinguishable, as Stone says. But this does not mean that the distinction is for all purposes an illusory one. As we have seen, there is a real and important difference located in the pragmatics of legislation, doctrinal rule formulation, and claim-making in particular cases. This is in a way acknowledged by Stone, in so far as he accounts for the use of the 'categories of illusory reference' in terms of the pragmatic development of the common law by the judiciary. Judges, he says, can by the use of these categories achieve the reality of legal change and development while preserving the illusion of timeless continuity in the common law. Yet it does not defeat the present argument, but reinforces it.

No doubt it is true that in such an area as this, the vagueness or malleability of law-formulations, whether in statute, or case-law, in doctrine, or in contractual documents, create scope for judicial discretion in the way indicated by Stone; we shall look further into this in a moment. But it must also be said that the broader view of legal pragmatics here proposed gives a more complete account of the phenomenon, and shows why in its proper setting the difference between qualification and exception is far from illusory. That it would be so in the context of a purely truth-functional propositional calculus merely shows that this would be an insufficiently rich logical notation in which to handle concepts like conjunction, qualification, and exception in law. To say there is no logical difference is to invite the challenge: from the point of view of what logic? Only if the qualification/exception doctrine is interpreted in particular logical terms is it an identity masquerading as a distinction. But in the present argument, the difference is real. This difference, like other cases of defeasibility, ought primarily to be understood in terms of pragmatics. So if a rule is formulated in the terms that a right vests on conditions c_1, c_2, c_3, but this is subject to exceptions in case e_1, e_2, ... , we are to take that express formulation as one conventionally used to signal one allocation of the burden of proof, while the other formulation, in terms of positive and (qualificative) negative conditions of vesting signal the opposite allocation. Where a formulation is vague on this point, the issue is how best to interpret it in the light of an underlying rationale for the distinction. For the issue is (as much as anything else) which type of formulation to choose.

The present suggestion is that fair allowance ought to be made for the difference between what it is reasonable to formulate as the ordinarily necessary and presumptively sufficient conditions of some legal entitlement, and rather exceptional or unusual conditions which another interested party may be able to adduce as objections to finally granting the entitlement. Such latter conditions are then more properly treated as defeating conditions than as ordinary (negative or qualificative) conditions of vesting in the first place. The particular example can best be handled in terms of the general account developed here of defeasibility as a concept belonging to legal pragmatics. What logical calculus or notation would be needed to model this, e.g. for the purposes of developing legal expert systems or other intelligent knowledge-based systems, is a question that can be set aside for the moment. Suffice it to say that there seems no reason to assume that one could not devise a sufficiently enriched logic to handle all this.

2. PRAGMATICS AND REALISM

What has been said so far, although claiming a base in pragmatics, might be criticised as far from pragmatic enough. Considered in the perspective of what Robert Summers has dubbed 'pragmatic instrumentalism'[8], or more particularly in the perspective of legal realists of the stripe of Oliver Wendell Holmes, Jr[9], the present account may be though much too accommodating to shadowy 'institutional facts' behind the plain facts of how the law is actually administered. In 'The Path of Law' (Holmes 1920), Holmes delivered a broadside against any ontological assumptions about legal rights and duties. Such terms were of value solely in the context of predictions about what the courts would order people to do or desist from doing under sanction of some punishment or enforceable civil remedy. There was in his view a risk of metaphysical or moral confusion if people imagined the law conjuring into existence shadowy objects such as rights or duties independently of what one could count on the courts and judges actually doing.

Some will say that just such a metaphysical conclusion befogs the present paper on account of its postulation of rights as existing in law independently of claims made about them, and as that which lies behind the (justified) judicial upholding of claims by appropriate remedial decrees and orders. Coupled with this could well come an objection to the idea about the conditions of implicit defeasance as these were sketched above. For the idea was developed that there might be objectively be principles and values of a system which, rightly weighted and weighed, intervene so as genuinely to defeat a legislative or case-law or doctrinal statement of conditions for a right, or an individual's claim to a right in a given case. Surely, it will be insisted, the moment of defeat is not the occurrence or presence of supposedly objective defeating factors. The moment of defeat is that at which a court holds that despite appearances some claim made by somebody is an unsound one. And, just as Stone argued, this is a matter more of judicial policy-making and principle-expounding than of some objective pre-existing legal state of existence or non-existence of a right. Rights only do exist when voluntarily respected or judicially upheld given an absence of voluntary respect. There is no point in any other way of speaking about rights. Entities should not be needlessly multiplied.

Pursued rigorously, this line of objections would lead not to a rejection of the idea that defeasibility is all about pragmatics. It would say that it is exactly about pragmatics, but above all the pragmatics of law-enforcement. You can think yourself as secure as you like in some legal arrangement or legal advantage, but your ultimate security lies in judicial enforcement and nothing else. What the courts will in fact uphold for you is the sum total of your patrimony or aggregate of rights; you may think or hope you have more, but such thoughts or hopes are defeasible. The source and meaning of defeasibility can be traced simply to the insecure predictability of the judicial decision in difficult cases. Defeasance occurs when a court upsets expectations, as courts are always capable of doing. Defeasibility is simply the possibility of such defeasance. Express defeasibility is simply defeasibility that is strongly predictable in the light of statute or case-law.

Further strength to this general line of argument may be derived from the fact that in at least some circumstances of defeasibility, such as those noted above in *Connor's* case, the principle whose application generates the exception has been interpreted in the case-law as requiring in each case of unlawful killing a judgment as to the degree of heinousness and culpability, so as to determine whether the case requires defeasance of the *prima facie* right or not. Even apart from this, the weighing of principles and values against express rules with a view to determining whether they support an exception is clearly a matter of judgment on any view. Discretion of some sort[10] is involved here. The only open question is whether this imports a purely subjective judicial choice, or a judgment involving in-principle objective factors. The best answer seems to be that there are objective factors here, but they are necessarily mediated through judicial subjectivity. The process is one of determination[11], not of deduction.

In any event, the difficulties of a predictive rather than a normative interpretation of legal categories have been sufficiently often explored to require no restatement here. The normative interpretation is to be preferred, even when we write in allowance for the necessity of judicial intervention is some types of case. A right is what legally ought to be (and thus probably will be) upheld by the courts, or what will *justifiably* be upheld by the courts; defeasibility concerns legally justifiable exceptions to ordinarily necessary and presumptively sufficient conditions; exceptions which ought to be made when the question is put to a court. This normative interpretation as developed here depends on a theory of legal institutions, and particularly on the conception of legal powers developed therein. To this I now turn.

3. POWERS AND DEFEASIBILITY

It is an obvious and important proposition that law has as much to do with enabling as with obligating. In large part, H.L.A. Hart's *The Concept of Law* (Hart 1961) is an exploration of the theoretical significance of this truth. Law gives powers as well as duties, and these can be powers exercizable in a private capacity, as in contracting a marriage, forming a partnership, making a will, buying and selling stocks and shares, or in a public capacity, as in voting upon legislation, judging a lawsuit, issuing a notice of demand for the payment of taxes, granting planning permission for property development under a zoning law, issuing payment of a social security benefit.

This aspect of law can be envisaged as involving a legally conferred capability to alter the legal situations or relationships of legal persons. Powers in law in their simplest form are powers to vary in some way the incidence of duties or claim-rights or liberties: for example, by consenting to take part in a boxing match with *B*, *A* (validly) waives the right not to be assaulted by *B* (so far as concerns those forms of physical attack allowable under the rules of boxing). But vastly more complex powers can also be envisaged, including power to confer, vary, or restrict powers and cognate relations as well as powers to confer, vary, or restrict duties and rights.

Powers are thus conceived as conferred by legal rules which guide both conduct and judgment of it by differentiating valid and invalid results of acts performed with a view (actual or imputed) to bringing about certain legal consequences which would not otherwise obtain. Valid exercises of power are effective in changing the legal situation in some way, and indeed they often bring about complex sets or series of changes. Whatever reason one has for bringing about such changes, these are reasons to observe the law's requirements for validity; hence such requirements are in the Kantian sense hypothetical in character. Public powers are, however, quite often subject to a categorical duty of exercising them in certain circumstances, e.g., when a valid request or complaint of some kind is made through some person's exercise of private power.

A complete understanding of any particular power (and, generalising, an adequate understanding of the concept 'power' in its normative sense) depends on adequate awareness of the whole range of circumstances required for validly exercising power. The conditions of legal enablement are always in some measure complex, and in each case must cover the following points:

(a) Which person or persons, having
(b) what general capacity or particular position or appointment,
(c) subject to what required circumstances, and
(d) in the absence of what vitiating circumstances or factors,
(e) by what if any special procedures or formalities, and
(f) by what act
(g) in respect of what if any other persons
(h) having what general capacity
(i) can constitute a valid instance of what legal institution?

The concept of an institution in point (i) here is very important. Powers are powers validly to bring about some arrangement, some new constellation of legal relationships. Particular arrangements are instances of general abstract 'institutions' of law, such as marriage, contract, trust, property transfer, incorporation of a company, or such as statute, judgment, tax assessment, planning permission. Particular arrangements, as instances of such institutions, endure in time from the moment of their valid establishment until some later date when they are terminated either by a further exercise of power or by some other legally stipulated event (for example, somebody's death). During their valid existence (and sometimes even after it) they function as the conditions of other ulterior legal consequences, including duties and rights of particular persons or persons in general, and also various forms of power. This accounts for the way in which valid exercises of power amount to effectual changes in legal relationships, or the legal state of affairs viewed nonrelationally .

Points (a) and (b) draw attention to the qualifications required for having and exercising any legal power. Private powers depend upon general characteristics of persons (such as age, soundness of mind, gender, citizenship) summarised in terms of 'capacity' —contractual capacity, capacity for marriage etc. Where a substantial range of capacities is dependent on the possession of certain personal or ascribed characteristics, the possession of these characteristics is conceptualized as the holding of a particular 'legal status'. Public powers depend on the holding of particular positions or special competences by election or appointment.

Points (c) and (d) draw attention to the way in which powers may be exercizable only given the presence of certain conditions, and their exercise may still be defeated or vitiated by the presence of adverse circumstances such as mistake, intoxication or duress, or bribery or bias in the case of public powers. The idea of defeasibility seems to have its most particular application here, so this is a topic to which I shall return in full detail shortly.

Points (e) and (f) draw attention to the fact that exercising a power requires the performance of some act, possibly attended by some solemnities or formalities of procedure or execution. Points (g) and (h) draw attention to something particularly important in the case of private powers, namely that it is common for such powers to be exercizable only in respect of other persons who themselves have appropriate capacity, and who often indeed have a reciprocal power, that of acceptance or rejection of an arrangement proposed by the first party's initial power-exercising act: for example, where *A*'s offer of marriage or of some other contractual terms must be matched by *B*'s acceptance of the offer on the same terms. Where there is both valid offer and valid acceptance, the joint act of the parties is effectual to set up validly the arrangement in question.

This draws attention to the question whether or when powers should be considered relationally or as having some form of 'correlative'. As we have just seen, certain private powers are clearly relational in the strong sense that their full exercise requires the consensual or reciprocal interaction of two or more parties, all having requisite capacities. On the other hand, public powers of a law-making kind do not characteristically require any such consensual or reciprocal interaction, and are thus not relational in the strong sense. Still, it can always be a question whether a particular person is or is not subject to a particular power exercizable by another. Perhaps a police officer purports to arrest a person who has refused to give certain information requested by the officer. Or, more spectacularly, a federal judge purports to issue an order to the president requiring that certain tapes in the president's possession be surrendered to the court. In each case it is a question whether the given purported exercise of power is indeed valid against that other person in the given circumstances. Another like question is whether a legislature whose powers of legislating are subject to defined limits can validly pass legislation to ban or restrict abortions, or indeed to remove restrictions on them.

On this account, since power-exercising acts purport to change the legal position in some way, and since this must affect some person in some way, there is always a relational aspect to the exercise of power. For it is always open to question which persons can legally have their legal situations altered in the given way by that act of that power-holder. Whereas Hohfeld used the term 'liability' to denote exposure to the valid exercise of a certain power (Hohfeld 1913), I should be inclined to favour a less misleading terminology, and have suggested as a rival term 'susceptibility'.

It is, in any event, clearly not necessary always to treat all powers relationally; only the above-noted strongly relational private powers and others like them have to be so treated for all purposes. But for any power, there can be some circumstances when a relational view of it is apt. With any power, one may always have reason to ask in case of a particular person towards whom a purported exercise of power has been directed whether or not this person is indeed susceptible to this exercise of this power. And on a certain widely held conception of fairness, any such party affected should be given the opportunity to raise any grounds of objection to the exercise of power that he or she thinks provable and appropriate to defeat the effectiveness in law of the purported exercise of power in the given case.

This observation brings us back to the point about vitiating conditions that defeat the validity of an otherwise proper exercise of a power. Points (c) and

(d) on the above list of matters to be determined for the full specification of a power were:

> (c) subject to what required circumstances, and
> (d) in the absence of what vitiating circumstances.

As we have seen, the exercise of a power requires there to be a person with appropriate capacity or competence performing a specified act in a specified form (procedure), but in addition there have to be appropriate background circumstances, such as prior possession of a property right one proposes to transfer, or the giving of due notice, e.g. in the case of marriage, or having an appropriate intention, e.g. intention to create legal relations (contract), intention to create an irrevocable trust (trust), or the like; such 'positive' conditions are within the knowledge and, to a degree, the control of the party who seeks to exercise a power. To some extent they contrast with the 'negative' conditions envisaged in (d), circumstances which must be absent for the valid exercise of power, circumstances whose presence vitiates the otherwise valid exercise of power, such as mistake (error) of one or both parties, or fraud, or unintended contravention of some collateral provision of the law, or illegal or immoral purpose of one or both parties. As the earlier mentioned case of *Connor* reminds us, this kind of vitiating factor may depend upon a background principle of law, not necessarily on an explicit rule or explicit condition or exception specified in a rule-formulation. Characteristically, such vitiating factors are often of a sort which lie outside the control, and perhaps even the knowledge or reasonably discoverable knowledge, of the person who exercises the power. Difficulties of a similar sort might affect questions of capacity both of the power-exercizer and of the other party in case of a strictly bilateral power. So whenever a person acts with a view to exercising a certain power, though he or she (and his or her legal advisers) can take all possible steps to secure regularity in matters within his or her own control or knowledge, and can exercise considerable diligence to check on the absence of vitiating circumstances, yet even so there remains some risk, often only the faintest risk, that events as they unfold will reveal some defect such that the ostensibly valid exercise of power has been defective, and hence either a nullity *ab initio* or nullifiable (voidable) in its effects as from the moment of discovery of the defects or some earlier or later date determined by appropriate legal provisions.

This is a pointed illustration of what gives the idea of defeasibility its practical importance. There is doubtless a strictly theoretical point of view, expressive of a simply ontological concern with law and legal institutions, from which all putative or purported rights and arrangements in law either have perfect and valid existence or do not (or are already subject to valid nullification on appropriate application). But in the practical world of the persons who seek to act within and under the law, this viewpoint is normally unavailable in pure form. People act with limitations of available information and foresight, both as to matters of fact and as to questions of law of the kind which demand careful and reflective deliberation on issues of legal principle. They do, and they have to, take a great deal upon trust. The practical human view of the world is not *sub specie aeternitatis* but moment by moment, becoming aware of events as they unfold, and responding as best one can in the light of current information and deliberation.

As I have pointed out elsewhere[12], the virtue of legal institutions and legal arrangements is that they procure a certain degree of through-time stability in one's normative position. A common aim of many power-exercising acts is to achieve arrangements with this kind of transtemporal security. To reflect on defeasibility is to be reminded of the other side of that coin. However hard one tries, there is always a risk of disappointment, of failure.

Nevertheless, it remains in general true in legal practice that someone who relies on the validity of arrangements made through the exercise of power is able to trust in their presumptive validity on account of the satisfaction of positive conditions about capacity, background circumstances and formality. Unless objection is raised, and unless the objector can establish by appropriate proof that there was/is a vitiating factor present, the arrangements will stand (and, quite often, ulterior arrangements subsequently made in good faith relying on the validity of the prior arrangement will not be vitiated by a discovered defect of the prior arrangement). Pragmatically, defeasibility puts the question over to the 'other side'. This is the law's compromise between the need for reasonable security in human plans and the need to uphold principles of deep importance in a given view of socio-legal order. There is no standing presumption that existing arrangements violate principles, but there is always some possibility of challenge in case they do.

4. DEFEASIBILITY AND LOGICAL INFERENCE

I have stressed the pragmatic character of legal defeasibility, and with reason. For there have been attempts to import the idea of defeasibility directly into logic, through the idea of implication. Defeasible implication is a weaker, challengeable, version of implication, by contrast with material implication as it is commonly understood. The difficulty, however, is that 'defeasible implication' does not seem to do the kind of work we ask of 'implication' in a logical setting. In a simple-minded way, I take it that the difficulty arises in relation to *modus ponens*. Given the premises that '*p* implies *q*' and '*p*', it follows (of course) that '*q*'. But if the major premiss is only that '*p* defeasibly implies *q*', our conclusion will only be that '*q* or not-*q*', and since that is a tautology we did not need our defeasible inference to discover it.

But of course defeasible reasoning does not mean just to tell us that *q* or not–*q*. What it means to say is that *q* will obtain except in rather exceptional circumstances, which would have to be specially proven, this proof cancelling the initial supposition that *q*. To handle this formally, we should need to devise a way of symbolising: '*q*, but exceptionally not-*q* if special reasons are shown'. Defeasible reasoning is about what you should be able to put your shirt on, provided you keep your eye open for the exceptional case. It has more to do with (prudent) propositional attitudes than with propositions. In short, on the present understanding of defeasibility, it is not strictly implication that is defeasible. Rather, the conclusion of an argument is defeasible given suitable presentation and proof of defeating circumstances. Alternatively, some formulations of legal rules have to be understood as statements of ordinarily necessary and presumptively sufficient conditions for a legal consequence, so that allowance must be made for unstated exceptions upon appropriate intervention and proof by an interested party. Where legal generalisations are thus understood as defeasible, it does not need to be supposed that the conclusions they warrant (when taken with other appropriate premises) emerge from some sort of defeasible or second-rate implication or entailment. The point is rather that the conclusion is not legally final or conclusive in itself, but subject to exceptional negation in situations of the kind we have explored. It is only when a potentially defeasible conclusion is actually unchallenged, or undefeated despite challenge, that it is proper for the conclusion in question to be put into effect as a matter of law. What is needed from the logicians seems to be a formal system that can cater for challenges, or excepting provisions of the appropriate pragmatic character (involving both argumentative and evidentiary burdens). This would seem to me better to capture the true character of legal defeasibility than attempted dilutions of the character of implication in its logical setting.

This has a certain obvious importance for AI applications in the legal domain. There are no doubt several possible ways of logically modelling the conception of defeasibility developed in this paper, any one of which could be of use in the design of usable legal expert systems. It is beyond my skill and knowledge to develop such models myself. Perhaps a way to handle the matter would be to mark in some way any proposition whose formulation seems to leave it open to the possibility of defeasance. In respect of each such proposition, it would be desirable to have available an open-ended check-list of generic conditions capable of vitiating the exercise of a relevant power, the vesting of a relevant right, or the establishment or termination of a given institutional arrangement, or whatever. This would give a basis for testing any weak points in a chain of reasoning, and thus of establishing in normal situations an at least guarded confidence in one's conclusions. No doubt the open-ended character of defeasibility, related to the omnipresence of the unforeseen in human experience, and to the ever-open possibility of judicial development of legal principles and values in the light of the accidents thrown up by life and litigation, will always defy final and absolute confidence in any human inference or arrangement. But it is often possible to establish a position of assurance beyond reasonable doubt. The more thorough one's checklists and one's checking, the less reasonable any surviving doubt.

I conclude that defeasibility is a highly important feature of legal reasoning. By and large, even statutory provisions (and *a fortiori* case-law propositions) are usable in practical legal reasoning only subject to rational reconstruction. Moreover, any reasonable approach to systemic interpretation of enacted statutes will also treat legislative formulations as effectively defeasible since only providing presumptively sufficient or necessary conditions as to whatever is enacted. This is an essential feature of a rational legislative-and-interpretative practice, for otherwise statutes will fail to chime with important principles and values of established law. Hence defeasibility has an omnipresent importance. Hence any formulation of legal provisions by way of doctrine, or of litigious argument, or as part of the knowledge base of an expert system, is likely to be defeasible in some circumstances. To find some way of handling this logically would be a precondition for any satisfactory development of expert systems or other artificial intelligence applications in law. The notion of 'defeasible implication' in itself seems a flawed one. But it is hoped that these reflections on legal defeasibility may be of help in pressing forward with work on the concept of defeasibility in logic.

NOTES

[1] See *Riggs v Palmer* 115 N.Y. 506; 22 N.E. 188 (1889), and cf. in the U.K., *Cleaver v. Mutual Reserve Fund Life Association* [1892] 1 Q.B. 147; *Re Crippen* [1911] P. 108; *Smith* 1979 S.L.T. (Sh Ct).

[2] [1981] All E.R., 770.

[3] See now the Forfeiture Act 1982, the first two sections of which add to the partly discretionary 'forfeiture rule' a judicial discretion to mitigate the effects of forfeiture in appropriate cases; so now forfeiture itself is explicitly defeasible.

[4] Cf (Wróblewski 1991).

[5] See the *Joseph Constantine* case, [1942] A.C. 154.

[6] See (Stone, 1985), pp. 61–77, esp. at 68–73, and compare the earlier (Stone, 1964).

[7] My doubts about Stone's analysis of the *Constantine* case were stated in (MacCormick, 1978) pp. 145–6; his brisk reply is at (Stone, 1985) pp. 4–6, and p. 79, fn. 32.

[8] See (Summers, 1982).

[9] (Holmes, 1920) contains at pp. 168–76 a counterblast to any ideas of rights as objects subsisting apart from predictions of what courts will do in certain circumstances.

[10] For discussion of different senses of —or analyses of— discretion, see (Dworkin, 1978) pp. 31–39; but cf. (MacCormick, 1978) pp. 264–5, and (MacCormick, 1981) ch. 7.

[11] This Thomistic idea of *determinatio* or 'determination', I derive from John Finnis. See, e.g., (Finnis [1985] 1987) also (Finnis, 1992).

[12] Cf. (MacCormick, 1988), and compare, on the idea of a 'normativist' theory of institutions, (MacCormick & Weinberger, 1986).

REFERENCES

Baker, G.P., 1977. 'Defeasibility and Meaning', in *Law, Morality and Society*, P.M.S. Hacker and J. Raz (eds.), Clarendon Press, Oxford, pp 26-57.

Dworkin, R., 1978. *Taking Rights Seriously,* (rev. edn.) Duckworth, London, pp 31-39

Finnis, J., 1992. 'Natural Law and Legal Reasoning' in *Natural Law Theory: Contemporary Essays*, R. George (ed.), Clarendon Press, Oxford.

Finnis, J., [1985] 1987. 'The Critical Legal Studies Movement', *American Journal of Jurisprudence* 30 pp. 21-42 at 40–42; repr. in *Oxford Essays in Jurisprudence: Third Series*, J.Eekelaar and J.Bell (eds.) Clarendon Press, Oxford, pp. 144–65 at 163–5,

Hart, H.L.A., 1948. 'The Ascription of Responsibility and Rights', *Proceedings of the Aristotelian Society* 49, (1948–49) pp. 171–94

Hart, H.L.A., 1961. *The Concept of Law*, Clarendon Press, Oxford.

Hart, H.L.A., 1968. *Punishment and Responsibility*, Clarendon Press, Oxford, Preface.

Hohfeld, W.N., 1913. 'Fundamental Legal Conceptions as Applied in Judicial Reasoning', *Yale Law Journal*, 23, pp. 16–59.

Holmes, O.W., Jr., 1920. 'The Path of the Law', in O.W. Holmes, *Collected Legal Papers*, Constable and Co., London, pp. 167–202

MacCormick, N., 1973. 'Law as Institutional Fact', *Edinburgh University Inaugural Lecture* No 52, Edinburgh University Press; reprinted (1974). *Law Quarterly Review* 90, pp. 102–29.

MacCormick, N., 1978. *Legal Reasoning and Legal Theory,* Oxford, Clarendon Press, 1978

MacCormick, N., 1981. *H.L.A. Hart*, Edward Arnold, London, ch 7.

MacCormick, N., 1988. 'Institutions, Arrangements, and Practical Information', *Ratio Juris*, vol. I, no. 1.

MacCormick, N., and O. Weinberger, 1986. *An Institutional Theory of Law,* Dordrecht.

Stone, J., 1964. *Legal System and Lawyers' Reasonings*, Stevens, London.

Stone, J., 1985. *Precedent and Law*, Butterworths, Sydney, 1985.

Summers, R., 1982. *Instrumentalism and American Legal Theory*, Cornell University Press, Ithaca N.Y.

Wróblewski, J. 1991. 'On the Unstated in Law: Implicit Presuppositions and Conventions', in *Controversies about Law's Ontology*, P. Amselek and N. MacCormick (eds), Edinburgh University Press.

Faculty of Law
University of Edinburgh
Scotland

GIOVANNI SARTOR

DEFEASIBILITY IN LEGAL REASONING

This paper proposes a logical analysis of defeasibility in legal reasoning.

First the traditional conception of the legal norm as a conditional statement subordinating a legal effect to a total legal antecedent —representing a sufficient condition— is considered.

Then, two categories of elements occurring in total legal antecedents are distinguished, the elements to be proved (shortened into '*probanda*') and the antecedents not to be refuted (shortened into '*non-refutanda*'). The ascertainment of the *probanda* is necessary to derive the legal effect: those who are interested in deriving the effect have the onus of ascertaining those elements. The ascertainment of the *non-refutanda* is not necessary for this purpose: he who is interested in impeding the derivation of the effect has the onus of refuting them. The distinction between *probanda* and *non-refutanda* corresponds to the combination of rules and exceptions.

This fundamental logical structure of legal knowledge is related to the defeasibility of legal reasoning, which can be conceptualized as non-monotonicity: the consequences derivable from a set of legal and factual premises can be invalidated by further information (able to contradict a *non-refutandum* or to satisfy the condition of an exception).

Defeasibility is the basis of the dialectical character of legal procedures and has a heuristic function: the attempt to defeat provisional conclusions stimulates the search for new knowledge. It has, therefore, a fundamental rôle in legal reasoning, and especially in judicial reasoning. Moreover, the notion of defeasibility puts into question the distinction between rules and principles.

Only recently has non-monotonic reasoning been treated by means of logical methods: artificial intelligence has developed a number of formalisms to represent incomplete information and derive defeasible conclusions. Some of these methods, which will be discussed in Section 4, are especially interesting for legal theory since they might settle the conflict between the two 'logics' of moral and legal reasoning: symbolic (formal) logic and the theory of argumentation. In fact, they can satisfy both the aspiration to rigour and controllability, which has motivated the legal application of symbolic logic, and the need to preserve the dialectical flexibility of legal and moral reasoning, which is emphasised, on the other hand, by the theories of argumentation.

Z. Bankowski et al. (eds.), Informatics and the Foundations of Legal Reasoning, 119–157.

1. CONDITIONAL NORMS

Legal norms, or at least most of them, have a conditional structure: they subordinate a legal effect to a legal condition.

By *legal effect, sensu largo*, we mean every qualification established by a legal norm: the ascription of deontic or normative modalities (obligations, permissions, rights, powers ...), but also of status (such as the qualities of citizen, parent, spouse ...), professional titles (doctor, judge, barrister, professor ...), other legal qualities of persons (incapable, deprived of civil rights, bankrupt, habitual criminal ...) and things (personal property, real property, public domain ...).

By *legal condition, sensu largo,* we mean any condition to which a legal effect is subject.

We call *perfect conditional norms* those norms connecting a legal effect to a sufficient condition, that we call *total antecedent*. Usually, the statements contained in legal texts do not express perfect conditional norms. As will emerge from the examples illustrated in the following, such norms can be constructed only by combining, or putting into relation, many legal statements, and their complete formulation constitutes an ideal objective that can never be perfectly fulfilled. Nevertheless, it is opportune to start our discussion from consideration of the logical structure of perfect conditional norms. Further on, we will see how perfect conditional norms can be translated into combinations of rules and exceptions.

The most direct formalisation of a conditional norm is obtained through a conditional statement (an implication): the consequent of that statement indicates the legal effect established by the norm; the antecedent, the total legal condition to which the effect is subordinated. Here we only consider norms whose effect can be represented as a literal[1], and whose condition can be represented as a conjunction of literals that we will call *elements of the antecedent*, or simply *elements.* Therefore, the norms here considered seem *prima facie* susceptible of being formalised as conditional statements of the type[2]

$$E \text{ IF } A_1 \text{ AND } \ldots \text{ AND } A_n$$

where E is the legal effect and $A_1, \ldots, A_n$ are the elements of the total antecedent.

This representation —a legal effect is subordinated to a sufficient condition, constituted by a conjunction of literals— corresponds to the formalisation usually proposed by legal theory and legal logic, but does not capture a fundamental aspect of the content of perfect conditional norms:

it does not explicate the use of those norms in the derivation of legal conclusions.

In fact, the law confers on certain authorities —in particular, the judges— the power to establish authoritatively the solution of legal conflicts. The judges must ascertain the legal situation existing between the parties and decree the result of the ascertainment with a decision that prevails over the existing legal situation, if contrasting with it. It is true that the ascertainment of every legal effect must be accomplished (or at least justified) through the law, that is by applying legal norms to the facts of the facts of the case.[3] Nevertheless, for the judges to declare a certain legal effect, the ascertainment of all elements of a total legal condition producing the effect is not necessary. The judge has the duty to consider a total legal condition satisfied, and therefore its effect ascertained, whenever:

1. some elements of those legal conditions —which we call *elements to be proved* (abbreviated as *probanda*)— are ascertained;
2. the complements[4] of any of the other elements of the legal condition —which we call *elements not to be refuted* (abbreviated as *non-refutanda*)— are not ascertained.

To say that a literal L occurs as *non-refutandum* in a legal condition, amounts to affirming that, for the satisfaction of that legal condition, it is not necessary that L is ascertained, it suffices that L is not refuted, i.e., that its complement $\overline{L}$ is not ascertained (ascertaining $\overline{L}$ means to refute L). Each perfect conditional norm has therefore the following structure:

$$E \text{ IF } A_1 \text{ AND } \dots \text{ AND } A_i \text{ AND } \langle A_j \rangle \text{ AND } \dots \text{ AND } \langle A_N \rangle$$

where the $A_1, \dots, A_i$ are *probanda* (elements to be ascertained, for the legal condition to be satisfied) and the $\langle A_j \rangle, \dots, \langle A_N \rangle$ are *non-refutanda* (elements not to be refuted, for the legal condition to be satisfied): the quality of *non-refutandum* is indicated by the symbols $\langle\ \rangle$.

The division of the elements of the antecedent into the two categories just defined determines the rôle of each element in the derivation —or, rather, in the justification— of the effect of the norm. In fact, the derivation of a legal effect can be considered justified, in a certain justification context, if the effect is the consequent of a norm (accepted in that context), whose antecedent is satisfied. And a norm condition must be considered satisfied if every *probandum* contained in that norm antecedent has been derived in the accepted justification context, and no *non-refutandum* included in that antecedent has been refuted.

The distinction between *probanda* and *non-refutanda* concerns all elements specified in a norm antecedent, not only the facts to be empirically evidenced, but also those elements not needing to be evidenced (being accepted by the other party, or not contested, or notorious), and those elements which express legal qualifications. The latter cannot be the object of direct empirical evidence —legal effects are not empirical realities— but are to be derived using legal norms as inference rules. The relevance of the distinction between *probanda* and *non-refutanda* for the evidential aspects is, indeed, just a reflection of the rôle played by this distinction in the derivation of legal conclusions.

This distinction does not coincide with the rule excluding *non liquet* decisions —the principle according to which the judge, when the antecedent giving the condition for the right of the plaintiff is not satisfied, must reject the claim, and deny the existence of that right.

In fact, the rule excluding *non liquet* decisions only indicates the decision to be adopted when the antecedent giving the condition for the right of the plaintiff is not satisfied, but does not establish when this antecedent is to be considered satisfied. This is precisely what is provided by the distinction between *probanda* and *non-refutanda*. This distinction would be relevant also in legal systems where the judge, when the norm antecedent was not satisfied, simply had to bring the procedure to an end without taking a decision. It would then be the criterion for the choice between two alternatives: (a) a judgement in favour of the plaintiff and (b) a *non liquet* decision.

The prohibition of a *non liquet* decision transforms the contents of the (b) alternative into a decision in favour of the defendant, but does not modify the criteria for the choice between (a) and (b), and the categorisation here advanced concerns precisely those criteria.

2. ELEMENTS TO BE ASCERTAINED (*PROBANDA*) AND ELEMENTS NOT TO BE REFUTED (*NON-REFUTANDA*)

The division of the elements of each total antecedent into *probanda* and *non-refutanda* is the tool for achieving different legal-political purposes: (a) reconciling the legal protection of opposed interests, (b) simplifying the proof of complex norm conditions and realising a certain equilibrium between the parties, (c) granting particular protection to certain legal positions.

(a) A legal consequence constitutes the solution that the legislator has considered normally adequate for the situations in which certain typical elements are present. Nevertheless, the same legislator may recognise that further circumstances require diverse solutions, even in presence of the typical elements. The typical elements grounding a certain legal effect are normally, but not necessarily, capable of producing the legal effect. For the effect to be realised, the absence of every circumstance capable of preventing its realisation is also needed: the complement $\overline{C}$ of every impedient circumstance C ($\overline{C}$ denotes the absence of C) must occur in the total antecedent, besides the typical elements. If the judge were to derive a legal effect only when all the elements of a total antecedent are ascertained —both the typical facts and the complements of every impeding circumstance— it would be practically impossible for the plaintiff to obtain a favourable decision: he would lose in all cases of uncertainty concerning any elements of the total antecedent upon which the claimed legal effect depends. Therefore, only the facts normally able to ground the effect are *probanda*, while the complements of the fact able to prevent the realisation of the effect are *non-refutanda*. This means that the effect can be derived when all typical elements are ascertained, provided that no impeding circumstance is also ascertained.

(b) In some cases, the proof of certain elements of the total antecedent upon which a legal effect is conditioned is particularly difficult for the person interested in deriving that effect. This happens especially when those elements come within the other party's sphere of influence and there is an imbalance of power and knowledge. The legislator can qualify those facts as *non-refutanda* to improve the trial position of the weaker party, so achieving a substantial equality.

(c) In particular contexts, substantial legal positions are granted a special protection by qualifying as *non-refutanda* some elements of the total antecedent upon which the realisation of those positions depends.

2.1. Probanda and non-refutanda: criteria for the distinction

Legal language does not have terms to directly express the general distinction between *probanda* and *non-refutanda*. This distinction is associated, instead, with various pairs of opposite terms, used by legal doctrine in different contexts. In particular, we can recall the following dichotomies: constitutive *vs.* impedient facts; non presumed *vs.* presumed facts; facts to be proved *vs.* facts for which there must not be proof to the contrary; facts about which the onus of proof is on the plaintiff *vs.* facts about which the onus of proof is on the defendant.

2.1.1. Constitutive vs. impedient facts: Usually, it is affirmed that in Italian law[5] the fundamental criterion for alloting the onus of the proof is laid down in Art. 2697 of the Civil Code:[6]

Art. 2697 (*Onus of proof*). Any person who wishes to have a right recognized before the courts must prove the facts constituting the grounds for it. Any person who raises an objection about the ineffectiveness of these facts, or objects that the right has been modified or is extinct must prove the facts on which the objection is based.

The facts representing the grounds (the justification) of the legal effect, and therefore constituting or causing it (as efficient causes), are called *constitutive facts* (in Italian, *fatti costitutivi*). Constitutive facts represent the substantial ground of the legal effect: they are the events or states which realise the connections of interests the law wants to be regulated by the effect. Usually, they must be ascertained if the judge is to find the legal effect which is the object of the claim. In other words, constitutive facts are *probanda*.

The *impedient facts* (in Italian, *fatti impeditivi*) are those capable of preventing the realisation of the effect, although the constitutive facts are present. The *impedient facts* are events or circumstances that, even when the constitutive fact are present, amount to a total situation, a global connection of interests in which the effect is judged inappropriate, even though a partial aspect of that situation can be represented by the constitutive facts. So, for example, one who intentionally causes unjust damage (constitutive fact) is under the obligation to compensate that damage (legal effect), but the obligation disappears in cases of self defence (impedient fact).

Impedient facts must, as a rule, be ascertained, for an exception to be accepted and consequently for the claim to establish a certain legal effect to be rejected. In other words, the complement $\overline{F}$ of each impedient fact F is a *non-refutandum* in the antecedent of the norm establishing the impeded effect. (To say that a fact $\overline{F}$ is a *non-refutandum* in the antecedent of a norm means exactly that when F is ascertained, then the effect of the norm cannot be derived).[7]

Therefore, if a legal effect E is caused by the constitutive facts

$$F_1^C, \dots, F_m^C$$

and its realisation is hindered by the impedient facts

$$F_1^I, \dots, F_n^I$$

then the norm establishing the effect can be usually represented as follows:

$$E \text{ IF } F_1^C \text{ AND} \ldots \text{AND } F_i^C \text{ AND } \left\langle \overline{F_1^I} \right\rangle \text{ AND} \ldots \text{AND} \left\langle \overline{F_j^I} \right\rangle$$

Identifying constitutive facts requires a teleological analysis, intended to establish which elements, among those conditioning the legal effect, represent the ground, the substantial justification of the effect. This analysis, nevertheless, may avail itself of textual arguments.

Prima facie, the facts specified in the principal proposition of the provision establishing a certain legal effect (which may be expressed in a categorical or hypothetical form), have the rôle of constitutive facts. On the other hand, the facts specified in exceptive propositions —governed by conjunctions such as 'unless', 'save that', 'except that', etc.— have *prima facie* the rôle of impedient facts. For example, in art. 1481 of the Italian Civil Code—

Art. 1481 (*Danger of revendication*). The buyer can suspend payment of the price when he has reason to fear that the thing or part of it could be reclaimed by a third party, unless the seller provides suitable guarantees.

—only the danger of the revendication claim is constitutive for the right to suspend payment. The giving of the guarantees by the seller, indicated by the locution 'unless the seller provides suitable guarantees', prevents the right to suspend payment arising, and therefore the seller's not giving guarantees must be qualified as *non-refutandum* (it is not necessary that the buyer should prove the lack of guarantees, to support his right to suspend payment, but when the guarantee is ascertained, the right fails).

In other cases, impedient facts are specified in statements separate from the proposition expressing the general rule, statements that are called *exceptions*, and which derogate from the general rule, given certain conditions.

We can assimilate to the impedient facts, the *amending* or *extinctive* facts, i.e., those facts determining the modification of the legal effect (e.g., a partial payment reduces the right to a credit), or its elimination (e.g., a total payment extinguishes that right). Amending and extinctive facts are usually specified in separate norms, which qualify those facts as the causes of the modification or the elimination of the effect. For example:

Art. 1236 (*Declaration of remission of the debt*) The declaration of the creditor of remission of the debt extinguishes the obligation when the debtor is notified ...

2.1.2. Presumed vs. non presumed facts: The partitioning of the elements of the norm antecedent into *probanda* and *non-refutanda* does not always respect the rule just illustrated, that is, the principle according to which constitutive facts are *probanda* while the complements of impedient facts are *non-refutanda.* In fact, the law —having regard to difficulties of proof, inequalities in power, or other factors— often intervenes with specific norms that make a different qualification of the elements in the norm antecedent, derogating from that principle.

In such cases it is said that the fact —which would be considered as *probandum* according to the principle, but which is instead qualified by the law as *non-refutandum*— is 'presumed' (for the derivation of the legal effect). This terminology is adopted, sometimes, by the same legislator as in the examples above. Example:

Art. 1148 (*Acquisition of the fruits*). The holder in good faith of a thing makes its fruits his own.
Art. 1147 (*Possession of good faith*) ... Good faith is presumed.

Qualifying an element A_i as presumed, for the derivation of a legal effect E, means to establish that, for E to be derived, A_i does not need to be ascertained, it suffices that $\overline{A_i}$ is not ascertained. Thus the combination of the two norms set out above can be represented as follows:

x acquires the property of *y* IF
x is the holder of a thing *c* AND
c has produced the fruit *f* AND
⟨*x* is in good faith⟩.

The ambiguity of the term 'presumption' should be stressed. We consider here only the so-called rebuttable presumption (*praesumptio juris tantum*), which we must distinguish both from the presumption of fact (*praesumptio hominis*) and from the irrebuttable presumption (*praesumptio juris et de jure*).

A *presumption of fact* is a judicial inference based on circumstantial evidence and on probable rules of experience. On the other hand, in rebuttable presumptions, by qualifying a fact as presumed the law neither makes an inference of that fact nor orders it to be made. Rather, it prescribes that the legal conclusion must be derived even if the presumed fact is not ascertained, so long as the complement of the latter is not ascertained either (cf. Sacco 1957, 407 ff).

We have an *irrebuttable presumption* when the law, after having established the consequences of a certain fact, also intends to allow the same consequences to be produced by a different fact. So, using a synthetic formulation[8], it says that the first fact is presumed (or is understood as verified) when the second is proved. Since the law intends to equate the two facts, the proof that the presumed fact has not occurred is irrelevant, once the other has been proved. On the other hand, in *rebuttable* presumptions, the proof of the complement of the presumed fact (that is, the proof that the presumed fact has not occurred) prevents the legal effect from being drawn.

2.1.3. Facts to be proved vs. facts of which there must not be contrary proof. In other cases, the law distinguishes explicitly between fact to be proved and fact to which contrary proof must not be given (for deriving a certain legal effect). Obviously, the former are *probanda*, while the latter are *non-refutanda* .

For example, art. 2051 Italian Civil Code lays down that it is not necessary to prove fault to show the liability of the receiver for damage caused by things in safe-keeping. Liability is excluded only if lack of fault (a fortuitous case) is proved:

Art. 2051 (*Damage caused by things in custody*). A person is liable for damage caused by things in his custody except where he shows evidence of a fortuitous case.

This prescription could be represented as follows:

x is responsible for the damage d IF
x has in custody the thing c AND
c has caused d AND
$\langle x$ was at fault$\rangle$.

The statement $\langle x$ was at fault$\rangle$ is a *non-refutandum* in the antecedent establishing the liability of the receiver, and this means precisely that the receiver is always liable for the damage caused by the thing under custody, with the exception of the cases in which his fault is refuted, i.e., the cases in which he is proved not to be at fault.

On the other hand, art. 1189 Italian Civil Code specifies that, in the norm concerning payment to an apparent creditor, good faith is not a *non-refutandum* (as in art. 1147-1148, above quoted), but a *probandum:*

Art. 1189 (*Payment to the apparent creditor*). The debtor who pays the person appearing legitimated by univocal circumstances is freed from the debt if he proves to be in good faith.

This last prescription can, therefore, be formalized as follows:

x is freed from its debt d IF
x has paid d to y AND
y appeared to be legitimated AND
x was in good faith.

2.1.4. Facts for which the onus of the proof is on the plaintiff vs. facts for which the onus of the proof is on the defendant. The distinction between probanda and non-refutanda is connected, especially in civil law, with the division of the onus of the proof between the plaintiff, concerned that the judge should finds a certain legal effect (for example, the right to compensation), and the defendant, concerned that the same effect should not be found.

The plaintiff bears the risk of the non-ascertainment of the *probanda* conditioning the legal effect: if those facts are not proved, the effect cannot be derived and the plaintiff has to lose. In this sense, the plaintiff has the onus of proving the *probanda*. Considering that an element is to be considered as proved not only when it has been empirically evidenced, but also when it is admitted, not contested, notorious, or derived from ascertained facts by virtue of legal rules, the plaintiff interested in deriving the effect of a norm has the onus of evidencing a set of facts sufficient to derive all *probanda* (not ascertained in other ways) occurring in the antecedent of that norm.

On the other hand, the defendant bears the risk of the failure to prove the *non-refutanda* occurring in the same antecedent: if all *probanda* are ascertained and no *non-refutandum* is disproved, the legal effect must be derived, and the defendant has to lose. In this sense, the defendant bears the onus of proving (*rectius*, the onus of disproving) the *non-refutanda.*

Therefore, when a special provision qualifies as *non-refutandum* an element that should be considered *probandum* by the general principle of art. 2697 Italian Civil Code (or qualifies as *probandum* an element to be considered *non-refutandum*), this provision is said to invert or shift the onus of proof. In fact, if an element A_i is qualified as *non-refutandum*, then the plaintiff can obtain the declaration of the corresponding legal effect without A_i being ascertained, while the defendant has the onus of refuting A_i (of proving $\overline{A_i}$) to block the derivation of the effect. On the other hand, if an element A_j is qualified as *probandum,* then the defendant can obtain the rejection of the plaintiff's claim without refuting A_j while the plaintiff has the onus of getting A_j ascertained.

2.1.5. Positive vs. negative facts. A total antecedent, as we have seen, is a conjunction of elements, and each element is a positive literal (an atomic formula), or a negative literal (the negation of an atomic formula). Therefore we can correspondingly distinguish positive and negative antecedents.

Usually, positive elements are *probanda.* In fact, they represent the events and the conditions that substantially ground (constitute) the legal effect, and consequently, by art. 2697 Italian Civil Code (or by the corresponding principle of 'legal logic'), they must be ascertained for the effect to be derived.

Negative elements, on the other hand, are usually *non-refutanda.* They represent the negation of impedient facts, which, again by art. 2697, must be ascertained for the derivation of the effect to be blocked.

Therefore, as a rule, negative facts do not have to be ascertained for the effect to be derived (*negativa non sunt probanda*): it is sufficient that the complementary positive facts (the impedient facts) are not ascertained. For example, according to art. 2043 Italian Civil Code[9], to show that a person is liable for damages he has intentionally caused it is not necessary to show the lack of justification causes (self defence, state of necessity, ...). Nevertheless, if the existence of one of such causes is shown, liability fails. The total antecedent of tort liability could therefore be represented as follows:

> *x* is liable for the damage *d* caused by the fact *f* IF
>
> *x* has brought about the fact *f* AND
>
> the fact *f* has caused the wrongful damage *d* AND
>
> *x* was at fault for the fact *f* AND
>
> ⟨*x* has NOT brought about the fact *f* by self defense⟩ AND
>
> ⟨*x* has NOT brought about the fact *f* because of a state of necessity⟩ AND
>
> ⟨*x* was NOT incapable during the *f* ⟩ AND
>
> .
>
> .
>
> .

The rule establishing that negative facts are *non-refutanda* can have exceptions, as in the following example, where a negative *probandum* occurs:

Art. 2033 (*Undue Payment*). He who has effected a payment that was not due has the right to claim back what he has paid.

> *x* has the right to claim back *y* IF
>
> *x* has effected the payment of *y* AND
>
> *y* was NOT due.

The rules qualifying positive facts as *probanda* usually operate by establishing presumptions or inversions of the onus of the proof. Thus, in the above proposed formalisation of art. 1147–1149 and 2051 Italian Civil Code, the good faith of the holder, and the fault of the receiver are positive *non-refutanda.*

2.2. Non-refutanda and uncertainty

Legal decision must normally be based on incomplete information, since the facts to be judged are situations of events in the past upon which limited knowledge is available.

By distinguishing *probanda* and *non-refutanda*, law establishes the consequence of uncertainty: if an element A_i is uncertain (neither A_i nor $\overline{A_i}$ has been ascertained) the norm antecedents in which A_i is *probandum* are not satisfied, while norm antecedents in which A_i is *non-refutandum* are satisfied (as far as A_i is concerned).

This phenomenon has an enormous importance in legal practice. For example, a recent directive of the European Community concerning consumer protection has introduced into the Italian legal system an inversion of the onus of proof concerning the manufacturer's fault, by qualifying as *non-refutandum* the fault of the manufacturer, it formerly being a *probandum.* The norm

> *x* is liable for the damage *d* IF
> *x* has produced the product *p* AND
> *p* has caused the unjust damage *d* AND
> *x* was at fault.

has been replaced by the norm

> *x* is liable for the damage *d* IF
> *x* has produced the product *p* AND
> *p* has caused the unjust damage *d* AND
> ⟨*x* was at fault⟩.

Because of the new qualification of the element '*x* was at fault', when no certainty is reached about the fault of the manufacturer (neither fault nor no-fault is ascertained), the manufacturer must now be held liable, while before he was free from liability.

2.3. *Rules and exceptions*

The term exception denotes two related structures of legal language:

— *The exception-fact*, that is the fact whose ascertainment blocks the derivation of a certain legal effect. Each complement of a *non-refutandum* included in the antecedent conditioning the effect represents, in this sense, an exception.

— *The exception-provision*, that is a norm able to block the application of another norm, even when the antecedent of this latter norm is satisfied. In the exception-provision, the exception-fact becomes the condition of a separate norm, prevailing over the rule, and blocking its application when the exception-fact is satisfied.

The law often uses the technique of the combination of rules and exception-provisions (to which we will refer, from now on, simply as 'exceptions'), to express complex regulations, which reconcile opposite interests. We can distinguish two types of exceptions:

(a) *Exceptions to norms.* The exception provides that a particular normative statement, unambiguously identified, does not apply in a given situation. Example (from law 27 July 1978, n. 392, regulating the leasing of urban properties):

Art. 34. In the case where a lease relating to a property coming within the provisions of Art. 27 has been terminated ... the lessee has the right to an indemnity ...

Art. 35. The provisions of the previous article do not apply to the termination of leases concerning properties used for carrying out activities not involving direct contact with the public ...

(b) *Exceptions to legal effects.* The exception establishes that, in a certain situation, a particular legal qualification does not occur, is excluded. In that situation the application of all norms prescribing the involved qualification is blocked. For example, art. 2044 Italian Civil Code, by stating that

Art. 2044 (*Self defence*) Anyone who causes damage by defending himself or others is not liable

makes an exception to all provisions establishing liability, i.e., blocks the application of all those norms.

The logical treatment of exceptions is problematic since exceptions seem to include two aspects:

— A content in the object language (i.e., at the same level of the rule derogated by the exception): the exception is a conditional statement whose effect is the negation of the effect of the rule (exception to legal effects), or to the rule itself (exceptions to norms).

— A meta-linguistic content: the exception has precedence over the rule, and thus blocks the application of the rule when it is in conflict with the exception itself.

Because of the object level content, rule and exception are potentially contradictory. The contradiction obtains when both the antecedents of the rule and of the exception are satisfied. The contradiction can be solved, nevertheless, thanks to the meta-language content of exception, i.e., because the exception prevails over the rule.

Let us consider, for example, the following formalisation of art. 2043 and art. 2047 Italian Civil Code.

r_1: *x* is liable for the damage *d* derived from the fact *f* IF
x has brought about *f* by fault AND
f has caused the unjust damage *d*.

e_1: *x* is NOT liable for the damage *d* derived from the fact *f* IF
x has brought about *f* in self defence.

Let us suppose the following case: Mary, during a quarrel with her husband Mark, has defended herself by throwing at him a valuable piece of pottery, belonging to Mark's collection.

f_1 : *Mary* has brought about *DishThrow* by fault.
f_2 : *DishThrow* has caused the unjust damage *DishBreak.*
f_3 : *Mary* has brought about *DishThrow* in self defence.

The set containing the rule r_1, the exception e_1, and the facts f_1, f_2 and f_3, is logically contradictory: from this set it is possible to derive both statements

Mary is liable for the damage *DishBreak* derived
from the fact *DishThrow*

and

Mary is NOT liable for the damage *DishBreak* derived
from the fact *DishThrow*.

The contradiction is to be solved by giving priority to the exception, i.e., by deriving only the effect established by the exception. If the rule establishes the legal effect E while the exception prescribes $\overline{E}$, and the conditions of both rule and exception are satisfied, only $\overline{E}$ must be derived.

There is a strict connection between norms whose condition contains *non-refutanda* and the combinations of rules and exceptions. Each combination of rules and exceptions can be translated into an equivalent set of norms whose condition contains *non-refutanda,* and *vice versa.*

For this purpose, it is sufficient to insert the complement of the condition of the exception into the antecedent of the rule (for an exception to effects, this insertion must be carried out for all rules whose effect is contradicted by the exception), and qualify that complement as a *non-refutandum*. A rule such as

$$r: \quad E \text{ IF } A_1^r \text{ AND ... AND } A_n^r$$

and an exception

$$e: \quad \overline{E} \text{ IF } A^e$$

correspond to the statements

$$E \text{ if } A_1^r \text{ AND ... AND } A_n^r \text{ AND } \left\langle \overline{A^e} \right\rangle$$

$$\overline{E} \text{ IF } A^e$$

The rule and the exception of the preceding example can therefore be translated into:

x is liable for the damage *d* derived from the fact *f* IF
x has brought about *f* by fault AND
f has caused the unjust damage *d* AND
⟨*x* has NOT brought about *f* in self defence⟩.

x is NOT liable for the damage *d* derived from the fact *f* IF
x has brought about *f* in self defence.

This translation is correct, in the sense that a legal effect is derivable from the translation exactly in those cases in which the effect would be derivable from the corresponding combination of rule and exceptions. (For a discussion concerning the representation of rules and exceptions, cf. Sartor 1991.) Usually in legal theory a different, and fundamentally erroneous, treatment of exceptions is proposed. The fusion of the rule

$$r: \quad E \text{ if } A_1^r \text{ and ... and } A_n^r$$

and the exception

$$e: \overline{E} \text{ if } \mathrm{A}^e$$

is said to produce the statements

$$E \text{ if } A_1^r \text{ and ... and } A_n^r \text{ and } \overline{A^e}$$

$$\overline{E} \text{ if } A^e$$

In the first of those statements, which corresponds to the old rules, the complement of the condition of the exception has been inserted, without qualifying it as *non-refutandum*. This translation in our example would give the following result:

> *x* is liable for the damage *d* derived from the fact *f* IF
> *x* has brought about *f* by fault AND
> *f* has caused the unjust damage *d* AND
> *x* has NOT brought about *f* in self defence.
>
> *x* is NOT liable for the damage *d* derived from the fact *f* IF
> *x* has brought about *f* in self defence.

It is easy to see that this formalisation is not equivalent to the above combination of rule and exception. The combination of rule and exception allows Mary's liability to be derived even when there is no information about the existence (or the inexistence) of a situation of self defence, while the statements just indicated allow this conclusion to be derived only when the premises set contains the assertion that the fact has not been brought about in self defence.

In general, classical logic is inadequate to express combinations of rules and exceptions, since it only offers the choice between:

(a) the formulation

> E IF A^r
> NOT E IF A^e

that leads to a contradiction (from which *sequitur quodlibet*) when both the antecedents A^r of the rule and A^e of the exception are satisfied, and

(b) the formulation

> E IF A^r AND $\overline{A^e}$
> NOT E IF A^e

from which nothing is derivable when the condition of the rule is satisfied but we have no information concerning the condition of the exception.

2.4. Nonmonotonic reasoning in law

A piece of reasoning is called *monotonic* when it satisfies the following condition: if it derives a consequence C from a premises set Π_1, then it also derives C from every super-set Π_2 of Π_1, (from every set Π obtained by adding to Π_1 further premises). Logical deduction is typically monotonic: no logical consequence gets lost by adding to the premises.

A reasoning model not satisfying the monotonicity condition is called non-monotonic. In non-monotonic reasoning a statement Π derivable from Π_1 may not be derivable from the set Π_2, obtained by adding further premises to Π_1. Norms containing *non-refutanda* and combinations of rules and exceptions determine non-monotonic inferences.

In the case of norms whose antecedent contains *non-refutanda*, non-monotonicity occurs whenever we pass from a premises set satisfying all *probanda*, and not disproving any *non-refutandum*, to a larger premises set in which a *non-refutandum* is disproved.

Let us assume, for example, the following conditional norm:

> x is liable for the damage d derived from the fact f IF
> x has brought about f by fault AND
> f has caused the unjust damage d AND
> $\langle x$ has NOT brought about f in self defence$\rangle$

with the facts:

> f_1: *Mary* has brought about *DishThrow* by fault.
> f_2: *DishThrow* has caused the unjust damage *DishBreak*.

From these premises we can derive the conclusion that Mary is liable. Nevertheless, if the further premise

> f_3: *Mary* has brought about *DishThrow* in self defence.

is added, the conclusion that Mary is liable is no longer derivable since the complement of the *non-refutandum*

> $\langle$*Mary* has NOT brought about *DishThrow* in self defence$\rangle$

becomes ascertained, and therefore the condition of the norm is no longer satisfied.

In combinations of rules and exception, non-monotonicity is realised when a set of premises Π_1 satisfying only the condition of the rule is transformed into a larger set Π_2 satisfying both the condition of the rule and the condition of the exception. In this case the conflict with the exception prevents the derivation of the effect of the rule, although the condition of the rule is satisfied.

Let us assume, for example, the rule and the exception above:

r_1 : *x* is liable for the damage *d* derived from the fact *f* IF
x has brought about *f* by fault AND
f has caused the unjust damage *d*

e_1 : *x* is NOT liable for the damage *d* derived from the fact *f* IF
x has brought about *f* in self defence

and moreover the facts

f_1 : *Mary* has brought about *DishThrow* by fault
f_2 : *DishThrow* has caused the unjust damage *DishBreak*.

Given these premises, only the condition of the rule is satisfied, so that the consequence established by the rule for the facts of the case can be derived (Mary is liable). Nevertheless, if we add the premise

f_3 : *Mary* has brought about *DishThrow* in self defence

the antecedent of the exception is also satisfied. We can therefore derive the consequence established by the exception (Mary is not liable), while the consequence of the rule, being contradicted by the exception, must be retracted.

Antecedents of exceptions have a particular rôle in legal disputes. To discredit a legal conclusion, it is not always necessary to attack the premises of the argument grounding that conclusion, but it can be sufficient to adduce further facts: if the complement of a *non-refutandum* (or the condition of an exception) is ascertained, then the inference based on a norm containing the *non-refutandum* (or on the rule contradicted by the exception) is defeated, and the conclusions already derived must be retracted.

2.5. *Substantial and logical aspects in the structure of norm antecedents*

Our discussion so far has pointed out some aspects of norm antecedents concerning the substantial relation between factual situations and legal effects, and other aspects of norm antecedents concerning the logical structure upon which the derivation of legal consequences is based.

The distinction between constitutive and impedient facts falls within the first type of conceptualization. As we have seen, constitutive facts are able to cause a legal effect since they realise the substantial situation that the effect is intended to regulate (the situation in which the effect appears the most adequate legal solution); impedient facts are capable of preventing the realisation of the effect since they give the comprehensive situation a characterisation excluding the effect (i.e., a characterisation making the effect fail even in presence of the constitutive facts).

The distinction here proposed between *probanda* and *non-refutanda* concerns, on the other hand, the logical-normative structure of total antecedents, i.e. the linguistic structure upon which the derivation of the legal effect depends: *probanda* must be ascertained and *non-refutanda* must not be refuted for the conditioned effect to be derived.

We can therefore contrast the substantial efficacy of an element, understood as its ability to determine the realisation of a certain legal effect, with its formal-logical efficacy, understood as its ability to ground the derivation of that effect.

Between the two aspects just indicated there is a dynamic connexion:

— The substantial evaluation of the elements of the norm condition can be translated into the determination of their logical efficacy (and therefore into the linguistic structures, formal or informal, in which this efficacy is expressed): as stated by art. 2697 Italian Civil Code, constitutive facts are usually *probanda*, and the complements of impedient facts are usually *non-refutanda.*

— The substantial relevance of the elements in the antecedent can be established by reference to the linguistic structures in which those elements occur: the propositions governed by 'unless', 'except that', etc., usually introduce impedient facts, while the norms denying the effect or stating the inapplicability of other norms constitute exceptions (whose antecedent expresses an impedient fact).

The two aspects, nevertheless, cannot be considered equivalent, unless the provision of art. 2697 is deprived of any meaning: if constitutive facts meant simply *facts to be proved*, then in stating that constitutive facts have to be proved that provision would only repeat that the facts to be proved are exactly the facts that must be proved.

The 'substantial' distinction between constitutive facts and (complements of) impedient facts originates from the fact that the same concrete situation can exhibit several conflicting interests, all protected by the law. This plurality of interests is reflected in the possibility of ascribing to one and the same concrete fact a multiplicity of legal and moral qualifications: for example, a contract of employment imposing the accessory obligation to engage in certain political, religious, or sexual activities represents the exercise of contractual autonomy, but also a violation of personal liberty; the killing of the assaulter is a homicide, but also the defence of the life of the assaulted person; the act of a soldier disobeying an order violates military discipline, but may protect fundamental constitutional values. In such cases we must distinguish the different, and possibly incompatible, *prima facie* evaluations of the relevant situation —each one separately considering certain aspects of that situation— and the overall judgement resulting from the comparison and balancing of all those evaluations.[10]

The division of the element of total antecedents into *probanda* and *non-refutanda*, and the combination of rules and exceptions, are, on the other hand, normative structures that allow us to derive legal conclusions conciliating those interests, reflecting their comparative evaluation.

The distinction between the substantial and the logical structure of norm antecedents allows us to express two notions of 'partial legal antecedent' (or 'legal antecedent' *tout court*), understood as the set of elements that determine a legal effect:[11]

— From a substantial point of view, a legal antecedent is composed only of the constitutive fact, i.e., the facts able to cause a legal effect subject to the condition that no impedient fact exists.
— Under a formal-logical point of view, on the other hand, a legal antecedent is constituted only by the set of the *probanda* contained in the total antecedent of the norm establishing the effect, i.e., by the facts whose ascertainment compels us to derive the effect subject to the condition that there is no *non-refutandum* included in the same total antecedent whose complement is ascertained.

From the substantial point of view, the relation of 'legal causality' between norm condition and legal effect is a relationship of adequacy (and, therefore, of motivation, if we go back to a will establishing the effect), while from the formal point of view it is a relationship of defeasible derivability.

It is up to the interpreter, when the legislator has not made explicit provision (requiring the proof of certain elements, and the lack of proof to the contrary for other elements, stating rules derogated by exceptions, etc.), to evaluate the legal relevance of the elements in the norm antecedent and translate this evaluation into logical normative structures. Usually, evaluations of the substantial interests and logical structures coincide: as specified by article 2697, the elements determining a legal effect (constitutive facts) justify the derivation of that effect (are *probanda*), while those elements expressing a prevailing opposite interest (impedient fact) block that derivation (are complements of *non-refutanda*). We must however consider specific prescriptions establishing presumptions or inversions of the onus of the proof: to facilitate the proof, or to protect certain substantial legal situations, the logical structure of certain antecedents can diverge from the evaluations underlying the distinction between constitutive and impedient facts.

The relation between substantial interests and linguistic structures also explains the contrast between two notions of impedient fact advanced in Italian legal doctrine: the concept of impedient fact as a purely negative element, i.e., an element that it is not necessary to prove in order to derive the effect, but whose ascertainment blocks that derivation, and the concept of impedient fact as a positive element, that is as a force pushing toward a legal solution incompatible with the effect of the constitutive facts. Clearly, the negative concept expresses the logical aspect, while the positive concept expresses the substantial aspect.

3. NON-MONOTONIC REASONING AND DEFEASIBILITY IN LAW

In the previous pages we have illustrated some normative structures —*non-refutanda* and combinations of rules and exceptions— grounding non-monotonic inferences.

These structures indicate a model of defeasible inference, in which legal reasoning derives conclusions susceptible of being defeated by further information. The formal models of defeasible legal reasoning require new logical tools.

3.1. Non-monotonic logics

Classical logic deduces consequences implied by some set of premises, consequences necessarily true when all those premises are true and therefore not defeated by further information. Therefore, it is unable to deal with defeasibility: it cannot express the normative structures grounding defeasibility and cannot perform the inferences required by these structures. In fact, a conditional norm expressed in classical logic cannot have any other structure than

$$E \text{ IF } A_1 \text{ AND } \ldots \text{ AND } A_n$$

where all $A_1, \ldots, A_n$ are *probanda*.

The effect is not deducible until all elements of the antecedent are ascertained, and, once the effect is deduced, further information cannot defeat its derivation. It is not possible to represent norms whose condition contains *non-refutanda*, nor is it possible to represent combinations of rules and exceptions.

Although not reducible to classical logic, defeasible reasoning may nevertheless be 'logical' in the sense of being rigorous and controllable. A number of non-monotonic formalisms —the so called *non-monotonic logics*[12]— effectively reconcile defeasible reasoning with logical rigour, and so allow us to avoid the dilemma that induced Hart to disown his own work on defeasibility (Hart [1949] 1964) to support a 'rationalistic' model of law and of legal reasoning.

Non-monotonic logics, instead, propose provisional conclusions justified by the totality of the available premises.

These logics present, therefore, two related aspects:

—*Defeasibility*. By adding new information to a premises set Π_1, a new set Π_2 can be obtained from which some consequences of Π_1 are no longer derivable.

—*Global reasoning procedures*. To derive a conclusion C from a premises set Π it is not sufficient to isolate a subset Γ of Π, from which C is derivable. We also need to check that Π does not include further information external to Γ which defeats the derivation of C.

Some non-monotonic logics put the accent on the notion of onus of proof, representing defeasible statements as rules whose antecedent contains *non-refutanda.* Every such rule is destined to remain non-applied whenever the complement of a *non-refutandum* is shown.[13]

Other non-monotonic logics, instead, put the accent on the notion of conflict (inconsistency), representing defeasible statements as rules that may run up against exceptions (or, more generally, against statements endowed with superior strength).[14]

3.2. Interest evaluations and non-monotonic logics

The legal application of non-monotonic logics (like any other formal methods) presupposes a fundamental operation that remains outside the logical apparatus: the interpretation of the legal texts and the formulation of the result of the interpretation in precise syntactic structures, expressed in a univocal language.

In particular, as we have seen, the determination of the logical structure of normative antecedents (and the co-ordination of rules and exceptions) is connected to the assessment of the substantial structure of those antecedents: the constitutive facts become *probanda*, while complements of the impedient facts are represented by *non-refutanda* (the complements of the impedient facts considered as the antecedents of exceptions).

The law is not always unequivocal in ascribing the qualifications of 'constitutive' and 'impedient' facts, and does not always determine precisely the relevant events and circumstances. An exhaustive statutory specification of impedient facts would presuppose the exact identification of all circumstances capable of rendering legally unacceptable, in any future case whatever , the legal solution provided by a general norm. For these purposes we should have to: (a) identify precisely, in descriptive terms, the set of situations involving legally relevant interests incompatible with the effect of the norm, and (b) establish under what conditions those interests must prevail over that norm.

This is clearly impossible because of the limits to our knowledge of future situations and of the indeterminacy of our purposes. Therefore the application of each norm is limited, not only by specific exceptions, but also by indeterminate and estimated provisions, making it possible to take account of needs conflicting with the interests protected by the norm. (It is not significant, for the purpose considered here, whether those provisions have been stated by the legislator, formulated by legal doctrine or decided by the judiciary). This is the function of grounds of justification such as self defence or a state of necessity, and of causes of contract invalidity such as the violation of public morality or of public order.[15]

Faced by a concrete case satisfying the antecedent of a rule, but including legally relevant aspects opposing the application of the rule, the interpreter, having to decide whether the rule should prevail or not, can extend the available legal premises by the specification of a general 'principle' —a specification that should be applicable to the facts of the case (for example, if the contract in question concerns the exercise of prostitution, we must establish that such contracts violate public morality)— and qualify the specification of the principle as an exception to the rule. The specification of the principle and its qualification as an exception presuppose a comparative evaluation of the interest protected by the norm and of the interest expressed in the specification of the principle —an evaluation that gives precedence to the latter.

A comparative evaluation is also required, in default of a clear legislative indication, to establish preference relations between specific norms.

3.3. The heuristic function of defeasibility

Legal conclusions derived by means of non-monotonic inferences can be defeated by further information. This however does not rule out legal certainty, understood as a relative predictability and controllability of legal decisions. In many concrete cases just one legally relevant aspect emerges, or the conflict between different aspects can be solved by the priority criteria provided by the legal system.

Moreover, once pieces of factual and legal information sufficient to ground a certain legal solution have been collected, this solution is not defeated by the mere possibility that further statements are true whose ascertainment would prevent the derivation of that solution. For this purpose explicit and accepted information is required: the decision concluding a legal proceeding must be justified (and can therefore be checked) only on the basis of the knowledge collected in the preceding phases, and further information capable of invalidating the content of that decision is usually no longer admissible after the adoption of the decision.[16]

The possibility of deriving defeasible legal conclusions, and the existence of time limits beyond which defeating factors cannot be alleged, are important stimuli for legal discussion: they induce the interested party to provide within the time-limits all new information that may be capable of defeating the derivation of undesired legal conclusions. This holds not only for the facts of the case, but also for normative information: although it is presumed that 'the judge knows the law' (*jura novit curia*), the party who would lose given only the elements that have emerged at a certain stage of the suit, has an interest in drawing the attention of the judge to the exceptions capable of invalidating conclusions provisionally reached. Non-monotonicity therefore plays a heuristic function both in the ascertainment of the facts of the case and in identifying the applicable norms.

3.4. Defeasibility and the distinction between rules and principles

From our discussion it emerges that defeasibility is a technique used by the law to tackle cases in which norms (or legally relevant interests) clash with one another.

Defeasibility appears therefore to be a relational notion: it concerns each single norm only when this norm is considered in connection with other norms and interests and, therefore, in relation to the totality of the legal system.

This implies that defeasibility cannot represent the specific difference identifying a determined category of norms, giving to those norms a peculiar logical status. This is the thesis that has, however, been put forward by Dworkin (1977, pp. 24ff), who seems to ground precisely on defeasibility the logical distinction between two types of norms, which he calls respectively *rules* and *principles*. This author, after affirming that 'the difference between legal principles and legal rules is a logical distinction', specifies this difference as follows:

> Rules are applicable in an all-or-nothing fashion. If the facts a rule stipulates are fixed, then either the rule is valid, in which case the answer it supplies must be accepted, or it is not, in which case it contributes nothing to the decision. ... The rule might have exceptions, but if it does then it is inaccurate and incomplete to state the rule so simply, without enumerating the exceptions. ... [Principles] do not set out legal consequences that follow automatically when the conditions provided are met...

The counter-instances of a principle cannot be treated as exceptions,

> because we could not hope to capture these counter-instances simply by a more extended statement of the principle.

A principle continues to be valid even if it does not prevail under certain circumstances.

In law (as in morality) it impossible to find 'rules' such as those described by Dworkin. Perfect conditional norms (i.e., prescriptions providing for a legal effect subject to a sufficient condition), from whose examination our discussion started, are not linguistic structures concretely existing in the legal world. Those norms represent the ideal result of the synthesis of connected norms[17], and, more generally, of the co-ordination of incompatible legally relevant aspects, on the basis of comparative evaluations. For no norm is it possible to provide an exhaustive list of its impedient facts (nor therefore an exhaustive list of the *non-refutanda* that are conditions for the derivation of the effect of the norm), without using vague evaluative formulations (notions such as self defence, state of necessity, public morality, public order, etc.), which only refer to open classes of exceptions, each postulating an *ad hoc* comparative evaluation.

Therefore, the rewriting of the legal system in the form of a set of perfect conditional norms could never be completed. In any case the resulting formulations would be extremely complex —there would be an infinite number of prescriptions, each of them with an endless antecedent; they would be difficult to modify —the introduction of an exception would require the modification of thc antecedents of all norms incompatible with the exceptions, and each new norm would have to contain the complements of the antecedents of all incompatible prevailing norms, and the complements of all situations expressing legally superior incompatible interests; and they would be extremely uncertain —uncertainty concerning the perfect conditional norm would be the sum of the uncertainties concerning all conflicts that had to be resolved in formulating its total antecedent. It must therefore be admitted that

> in the actual state of legal language ... the specific norms in which a positive legal system is practically and historically articulated are not separate and well-insulated atoms nor can they be considered as complete totalities, sufficient to determine their effect. (Falzea [1965] 1985, p. 306).

Every norm possesses the characteristics Dworkin attributes to principles: it is defeasible in a set of circumstances not abstractly predetermined, and remains valid even if contradicted by prevailing norms in particular cases. No norm is applicable exactly to a set of well-defined cases, since defeasibility is a relational notion, and even when a norm is clearly expressed, indeterminacy concerning its relation with other norms and, more generally, its positions in the whole legal system may become relevant (cf. Raz 1972; Alexy 1981, 72ff).

Therefore, the distinction between rules and principles, if grounded upon defeasibility, is not a division between categories of norms with different logical structures, but, at most, an empirical distinction and a difference of degree, depending on the level of prevalence of features which every norm possesses to a certain extent: we can say only that a norm is a 'rule' to the extent that its antecedent contains precise descriptive terms, and its priority (its relative importance) in regard to other norms is exactly determined, and that it is a 'principle' to the extent that its antecedent contains imprecise or evaluational terms, and its priority is indeterminate.

4. LOGICS FOR NON-MONOTONIC REASONING

Here we present two non-monotonic logics: the first formalises the notion of *non-refutandum* in meta-logics, the latter treats the rule-exception relation in a logic for legal argumentation.

4.1. Meta-logic

Non-monotonic reasoning can be treated with a logical language amalgamating object language and metalanguage (cf. Kowalski and Bowen 1982), namely a language that can refer both to extra-linguistic objects and to its own syntactical features, and in particular to the derivability relation defined over itself.

Every *non-refutandum* ⟨*A*⟩ can thus be translated into the metalanguage expression '$\overline{A}$ is not derivable in Π', where Π is the set of the available premises. In other words, *non-refutanda* are interpreted as statements whose complement must not be derivable from the current set of factual and legal assumptions (the justification context).

In this interpretation, the rule establishing that a contract is valid, under the condition that it does not result void or voidable, could be expressed as follows:

> *x* is a valid contract IF
>
> *x* is a contract AND
>
> '*x* is void' is NOT derivable in Π AND
>
> '*x* is voidable' is NOT derivable in Π.

where Π contains all statements that can legitimately be used to ground the conclusion that the contract is valid, i.e., in a judicial proceeding, the legal norms applicable to the case and the ascertained facts. The use of such meta-statements (which mention the theory to which they belong and the derivability relation defined over that theory) poses interesting theoretical problems (in relation to Gödel's well-known theorems), but does not compromise the possibility of performing logical inferences, even automatic ones (cf. Kowalski and Bowen 1982). Reasoning using 'amalgamated' theories is non-monotonic, since by adding new axioms to the theory, the theory itself, and therefore the meaning of meta-statements, is changed. Consequently, in the extended theory some previously derivable consequences may fail.

For example, from the premises set Π containing the rule above and the fact

> *Sale*1 is a contract

we can derive that *Sale*1 is a valid contract. The antecedent of the rule is satisfied (in P we can derive that *Sale*1 is a contract, while we cannot show that *Sale*1 is void or voidable), and therefore the consequent can be obtained by *modus ponens*. If we add the fact

> *Sale*1 is void

the condition of the rule is no longer satisfied (in Π we can now show that *Sale*1 is void), and therefore we can no longer derive the consequent of the rule.

4.2. A formal model of legal argumentation

The formalisation of the notion of argumentation will allow us to bring non-monotonic reasoning back into legal dialectic. On this view, every set of legal 'reasons', i.e., every set of premises upon which a legal decision can be grounded —statutory, judicial, doctrinal provisions, factual assertions, etc.— represents, not a set of logical axioms —an axiomatic base— but rather the context in which opposed arguments can be developed and compared.

The model here proposed (already introduced in Sartor 1992, 1993) is inspired by the formal theories of argumentation developed by Simari and Loui (1990) and Prakken (1991, 1992). This model exhibits the advantages of logics for defeasible reasoning based upon the notion of conflict, which obtain non-monotonic reasoning by solving explicit conflicts between contradictory premises.

The advantages are as follows:

(a) Emphasis is put on the substantial foundation of legal defeasibility, that is the opposition of incompatible legally relevant interests. Each of those interests is considered in a distinct norm, and in cases of conflict only the stronger of those norms (the one protecting the interest prevailing in the examined situation) will be applied.

(b) It is possible to realise representations of legal knowledge that are simpler, more modular, and nearer to natural language. In particular, rules bearing on complex situation can be formulated in distinct norms, each treating a separate aspect (interest) emerging in those situations.

(c) The explicit representation of rules and exceptions allows a dynamic adaptation of the normative systems. The exceptions already in force prevail over the rules subsequently introduced in the normative system, while new exceptions also limit the rules already in force.

Moreover, the formalisation of the notion of argumentation allows us to treat not only normative conflicts whose outcome is pre-established (combinations of rules and exceptions) but also situations of uncertainty (conflicts between norms having the same importance): as well as a reasoning procedure to develop strong arguments, which positively justify their conclusion, we shall define a procedure to develop weak arguments, which ground merely defensible conclusions. Finally, this reasoning model not only leads to intuitively satisfying conclusions, but also grounds those conclusions by rendering explicit the connection between the favourable and contrary arguments.

Let us represent legal norms as simple inference rules[18] of the type:

R: E IF A_1 AND … AND A_n

where R is the rule name, E is the legal effect (a literal), and the elements $A_1,\ldots, A_n$ are literals (all those elements are *probanda*). Here is an example

r_1: x is liable for the damage d derived from the fact f IF
x has brought about f by fault AND
f has caused the unjust damage d.

The prevalence relations between norms are represented by meta-statements such as:

n_1 prevails over n_2.

The language can express conflicting norms. In particular, an exception to a legal effect is a norm denying a legal conclusion and prevailing over the norms establishing that conclusion (or over some of those norms). The following statements express respectively the linguistic and meta-linguistic aspect of such an exception:

e_1: x is NOT liable for the damage d derived from the fact f IF
x was incapable during f;
e_1 prevails over r_1.

It is also possible to formulate norms stating the inapplicability of other norms (exceptions to norms). For example, the following norm is a second level exception, excluding the applicability of exception e_1 in case of culpable incapability:

e_{e_1}: NOT applicable($e_1(x, f)$) IF
x was culpably incapable during f;

e_{e_1} prevails over e_1.[19]

Exceptions allow us to eliminate from norm antecedents all elements not to be refuted: every *non-refutandum* specified in the antecedent of a norm is translated into a separate exception subordinating the inapplicability of the norm to the complement of that *non-refutandum*. For example, the norm:

> x is NOT liable for the damage d derived from the fact f IF
> x was incapable during f;
> $\langle x$ was NOT culpably incapable during $f \rangle$

corresponds to the combination of exceptions e_1 and e_{e_1}, with the above stated preference relation.

An *argument* for a legal conclusion c is a non-redundant set of rules and facts from which c is derivable. A literal p is *derivable* with an argument A iff A contains a norm n: p IF q and further premises (norms or facts) which allow the condition q of that norm to be derived. An argument can therefore include partial arguments, which establish intermediary conclusions, necessary for reaching the final conclusion. Let any argument included in an argument A be called a *subargument* of A.

A *counterargument* to an argument A_1 is an argument A_2 that directly attacks A_1 (it contradicts the conclusion of A_1 or it denies the applicability of the rule establishing that conclusion) or directly attacks a subargument of A_1 (it contradicts the conclusion of that subargument or denies the applicability of the corresponding rule).

When an argument A_1 is attacked by a counterargument A_2, it is necessary to compare the strength of the argument (or the subargument) directly attacked and the strength of the corresponding counterargument. For this purpose we must compare the norm r_1 in which A_1 (or the subargument of A_1) culminates and the norm r_2 in which A_2 culminates. The comparison can give three results:

— If r_2 prevails over r_1, then A_1 is defeated, under the condition that A_2 is not defeated by contrary arguments. A defeated argument cannot ground valid legal conclusions.
— If neither of the two norms prevails over the other, then A_1 is merely defensible, always under the condition that neither A_1 nor A_2 is defeated by contrary arguments. A merely defensible argument is not sufficient to ground its conclusion, but must nevertheless be considered: it indicates an undecided case, whose solution requires additional criteria.
— If r_1 prevails over r_2, then A_1 has passed the test, and its conclusion is certain (justified) always under the condition that A_1 is not defeated by other arguments.

Let us now consider an example illustrating the expressive capacity of the language just introduced and the flexibility of the corresponding inferential model (for a complete formal definition, cf. Sartor 1993).

Let us assume that Mary wants compensation from John, saying that he crashed into her fence with his motor-cycle. Here are the rules to be applied (these rules are the formalisation of art. 2043, 2048, 2046 of the Italian Civil Code):

r_1: x is liable for the damage d derived from the fact f IF
x has brought about f by fault AND
f has caused the unjust damage d ;

r_2: x is liable for the damage d derived from the fact f IF
x is a parent of y AND
y is liable for the damage d derived from the fact f;

e_{r_2}: NOT applicable($r_2(x, y, f, d)$) IF
x could NOT prevent his son y
from bringing about the fact f;

e_1: x is NOT liable for the damage d derived from the fact f IF
x was not capable during f;

e_{e_1}: NOT applicable($e_1(x, f)$) IF
x was culpably incapable during f.

The proposed representation is quite near to the language of the Italian Civil Code: the main difference consists in the fact that the elements expressed as *non-refutanda* in the norms of the code have been transformed into explicit exceptions. Let exceptions to a legal effect prevail over the norms establishing that effects (e_1 prevails over the rules r_1 and r_2) and exceptions to specific norms prevail over the norms to which they refer (e_{r_2} prevails over r_2, and e_{e_1} prevails over e_1). Let us finally assume the following facts:

f_1: *John* brought about culpably the harmful fact *FenceCrash*;
f_2: *FenceCrash* has caused the unjust damage *FenceBreak*;
f_3: *Mark* is a parent of *John.*

Given those facts, Mark appears liable for the damage caused by John (since the antecedents of both rules and of no exceptions, are satisfied). The set of the now available premises $\{r_1, r_2, e_{r_2}, e_1, e_{e_1}, f_1, f_2, f_3\}$ offers a strong argument for the liability of both John and Mark.

The argument for John's liability is the following. $A_1 = \{f_1, f_2, r_1(John, FenceCrash, FenceBreak)\}$, where $r_1(John, FenceCrash, FenceBreak)$ denotes the instance (concretization) of norm r_1 concerning the individuals (subjects, objects, events) whose names are between the parentheses.[20] A_1 includes, in other words, the following set of norms and facts:

$A_1 = \{ r_1(John, FenceCrash, FenceBreak)$:
John is liable for the damage *FenceBreak* derived from the fact *FenceCrash* IF
John has brought about *FenceCrash* by fault AND
FenceCrash has caused the unjust damage *FenceBreak* ;
f_1: *John* has brought about *FenceCrash* by fault;
f_2: *FenceCrash* has caused the unjust damage *FenceBreak*.$\}$

The argument A_2 for Mark's liability is obtained by adding to the A_1 the fact f_3 and the instance of rule r_2 concerning the individuals *Mark, John, FenceCrash, FenceBreak*. Therefore, A_1 is a subargument of A_2.

Mark can free himself from the liability by satisfying the antecedent of an exception. For example, if he proves that John was incapable at the moment of the accident:

f_4: *John* was incapable during *FenceCrash.*

John's liability fails (here the reasoning is non-monotonic) because of the first exception, and consequently, Mark's liability fails also.

In fact, thanks to f_4 it is now possible to develop a counterargument A_3 defeating both A_1 and A_2:

$A_3 = \{ e_1(John, FenceCrash, FenceBreak)$:
John is NOT liable for the damage *FenceBreak* derived from the fact *FenceCrash* IF
John was NOT capable during *FenceCrash*;
f_4: *John* was NOT capable during *FenceCrash*$\}$.

The conclusion of A_3 (the non-liability of John) derived by means of the exception e_1 contradicts the conclusion A_1 (his liability) derived by means of the rule r_1. Exception e_1 prevails over rule r_1 and consequently A_1 is directly defeated. Also A_2, which includes A_1, is defeated: A_3 prevents the derivation of John's liability and so prevents a necessary precondition of the liability of John's father.

Let us now assume that Mary proves that John's liability was due to his fault (his incapability derived from the his state of drunkenness), so that the following fact is inserted in the premises set of the decision:

f_5: *John* was incapable by fault during *FenceCrash.*

Thanks to f_5 it becomes impossible to contest either A_3 or its counter-argument A_4:

A_4 = {e_{e_1} (*John*, *FenceCrash*):
NOT applicable(e_1(*John*, *FenceCrash*)) IF
John was culpably incapable during *FenceCrash*;
f_5: *John* was culpably incapable during *FenceCrash*}.

A_4 defeats A_3 and consequently A_3 is no longer able to oppose A_1 and A_2, and these last arguments regain their validity and once again ground their conclusions, i.e., the liability of John and Mark. Let us now assume that Mark affirms that he could not prevent John's action, since he did his best to bring up his son well, and he also specifically warned him on the consequences of alcohol. He affirms the following rule and fact:

r_3: *x* could NOT prevent his son *y*
from bringing about the fact *f* IF
x has brought *y* up well;
f_6: *Mark* has brought *John* up well.

In the normative context so obtained Mark's liability fails, while John's liability remains. In fact, A_1 (concerning John) is not attacked by any valid counterargument, while A_2 (concerning Mark) is defeated by the following counterargument A_5:

A_5 = {e_{r_2}: NOT applicable(r_2(*Mark*, *John*, *FenceCrash*, *FenceBreak*)) IF
Mark could NOT prevent his son *John*
from bringing about the fact *FenceCrash*;
r_3: *x* could NOT prevent his son *y*
from bringing about the fact *FenceCrash* IF
x has brought *y* up well;
f_6: *Mark* has brought *John* up well}.

A_5 defeats A_2 (since e_{r_2} prevails over r_3) and therefore frees Mark from any liability.

Mary does not question that Mark has given a good upbringing to his son. Nevertheless, she affirms that only a specific hindrance to control John justifies the statement that Mark could not prevent the fact, and denies that such a hindrance exists in the concrete case.

r_4: *x* could prevent his son *y* from bringing about the fact *f* IF
x was able to control *y;*

f_7: *Mark* was able to control *John.*

These additional premises allow us to develop the following counter-argument A_6, that attacks A_5:

$A_6 = \{r_4$: *Mark* could prevent his son *John*
from bringing about the fact *FenceCrash* IF
Mark was able to control *John;*

f_7: *Mark* was able to control *John*$\}$.

Let us assume that no element emerges allowing r_4 to prevail over r_3 or *vice versa*: In this case, we must conclude that arguments A_5 and A_6 —which contradict each other and have the same 'strength'— are both dubious (merely defensible). We must therefore conclude that Mark's liability (grounded on A_2), being contested with a dubious argument (A_5), is itself dubious.

The judge cannot come to a halt in face of uncertainty: a decision must still be taken. Neither can he arbitrarily adopt the conclusion suggested by one of the alternative arguments: this would violate the universalizability principle, since different cases could be solved differently on the basis of the same premises, choosing now the one, now the other argument (cf. Alexy 1978, 278 ff).

The justification context of the decision must be extended with additional premises allowing us to conclude, e.g., that r_4 prevails over r_3. Obviously, in this case A_6 would defeat A_5, so that A_2, freed from that counterargument, would recover its validity, and Mark would be liable again.

These additional premises, like any substantial evaluation, cannot be provided by any formal method: it is up to the lawyer to assess the legal relevance of the different aspects of the situation. What is required from legal logic, and what traditional logics are unable to offer, is the capacity to dynamically determine the conclusions deriving from the changing context of choices, evaluations, and assumptions upon which legal arguments are based. The approach illustrated here models the evolution of those conclusions as the adduced premises change, and so allows fundamental aspects of legal reasoning —the dialectic contrast of opposing theses and points of view— to be represented without giving up logical rigour.

Formal methods for non-monotonic reasoning have a special relevance, not only for legal informatics —which initiated their application in law (cf. Gordon 1988; Prakken 1992; Sartor 1991, 1992)— but also for legal theory.

In particular, the formalisation of the notion of argumentation allows us to reconcile the two logics of legal reasoning, formal logic and the theory of argumentation, which for a long time have been developing separately, in a state of mutual incomprehension, if not in an open clash:

— The scholars following a logical approach have given priority to the search for correctness, checkability, and certainty of legal reasoning, and have therefore underlined the lack of rigour and determinacy of the theories of argumentation.
— The theorists of argumentation, on the other hand, have stressed aspects such as the conflict of opinions, the evaluation of alternatives, and rational choice, and have therefore condemned symbolic logic for its incapacity to tackle these fundamental aspects of moral and legal reasoning.

By extending formal methods outside the domain of deduction we can overcome the false alternative between logic and argumentation, preserving logical rigour and emphasising the factors of dialectical conflict —and therefore of choice and evaluation— which characterise legal and moral reasoning.

NOTES

1 Let us call any atomic formula and any negation of an atomic formula a *literal*. In particular, let us call atomic formulae (for example 'x is a parent of y') *positive literals* , and let us call the negations of atomic formulae (for example 'x is *not* a parent of y') *negative literals*. We can assume here that any legal effect is a literal, since we do not consider the logical representation of normative positions (in particular, of deontic qualification), but only examine the relation between normative antecedents and legal effects.

2 In the usual logical formalism, such norms would be expressed in the syntax

$$\forall x_1 \ldots \forall x_i (E \leftarrow A_1 \wedge \ldots \wedge A_n)$$

where $x_1, \ldots, x_m$ are the free variables in $E, A_1, \ldots, A_n$, and $\forall$ is the universal quantifier 'for every'. We prefer to use a more intuitive language, which employs, instead of the usual logical connectives $\neg$ $\wedge$ $\vee$ $\leftarrow$, the expressions NOT, AND, OR, IF, and leaves universal quantifiers implicit. Therefore, we read open formulae (i.e., those formulae containing free variables) as the universal closures obtained by universally quantifying all free variables occurring in those formulae.

3 'Art. 113 Italian Code of Civil Procedure (*Decision according to the law*). In deciding the case, the judge must follow the legal norms, unless the law gives him the power to decide according to equity.'

4 The negative literal NOT *B* (for example, '*x* is NOT a parent of *y*') is the complement of the positive literal *B* ('*x* is a parent of *y*'), and *vice versa*. The complement of a literal *L* is indicated as $\overline{L}$.

5 All following examples, unless otherwise specified, are taken from the Italian Civil Code.

6 It is well known that in other legal systems, as in the German one, there is no explicit prescription corresponding to art. 2697 of the Italian Civil Code, but the rule established by that norm is accepted as a general principle of 'legal logic' (cf. Patti 1987, p. 8 ff).

7 Italian legal doctrine sometimes qualifies the complements of impedient facts as presuppositions ('presupposti'), to mean that those elements are not to be included in the efficient causes of the legal effect —represented by the constitutive facts— since they only determine the historical–environmental situation in which constitutive facts can operate.

8 And taking account of historical and ideological considerations.

9 'Art. 2043 (*Tort compensation*). Any intentional or negligent act, causing unjust damage to other persons, places anyone who who performs that act under a duty to pay compensation for damages.'

10 This aspect is well conceptualized by W.D. Ross (1930, 1939), who introduces the notion of *prima facie duty*: 'I suggest "*prima facie* duty" or "conditional duty" as a brief way of referring to the characteristic (quite distinct from that of being a proper duty) which an act has, in virtue of being of a certain kind (e.g., the keeping of a promise), of being an act that would be a duty proper if it were not at the same time of another kind which is morally significant' (Ross 1930, p. 19). According to this author 'Moral intuitions are not principles by the immediate application of which our duty in particular circumstances can be deduced. They state [...] *prima facie* obligations. [...] We are *not* obliged to do that which is only *prima facie* obligatory. We are only bound to do that act whose *prima facie* obligatoriness in those respects in which it is prima facie obligatory most outweighs its *prima facie* disobligatoriness in those aspects in which it is *prima facie* disobligatory' (Ross 1939, pp. 84-85).

11 In Italian legal doctrine the expression *fattispecie* is normally used to express exactly this notion of legal antecedent, and this is the case also for the German word *Tatbestand.*

12 Nonmonotonic formalisms can be called *logics* (in a wide sense), although they authorise non-logically-valid inference, since they provide rigorous language, precise inferential procedures, and are often also given logical semantics. Many non-monotonic logics have been developed in artificial intelligence, the discipline purporting to realise computer systems able to perform (or simulate) intelligent behaviour.

13 Among non-monotonic logics based on the notion of *non-refutandum*, the following may be recalled: meta-logics (cf. Kowalski and Bowen 1982), autoepistemic logic (cf. Moore 1986, 1988), default logic (cf. Reiter [1980] 1987; Reiter and Criscuolo[1981] 1987), circumscription (cf. McCarthy [1980] 1987).

14 Among the logics obtaining non-monotonicity through conflict, we may refer to the following: abduction (cf. Peirce [1931] 1984, and in computer science, Poole 1987), belief revision (cf. Alchourrón and Makinson 1981, 1982; Alchourrón, Gärdenfors, and Makinson 1985; Gärdenfors 1988); some conditional logics (Delgrande 1988); the formal model of argumentation (Simari and Loui 1992, Prakken 1992, Sartor 1993).

15 The impossibility of formulating indefeasible universal statements has specific reasons in morality and in law (concrete cases can express incompatible moral and legal requirements), but

empirical rules also are defeasible. Any empirical rule —for example 'birds fly'— can be transformed into a universal statement only by integrating it with an endless sequence of specifications (or qualifications): a bird flies under the condition that it is not a penguin, it is not an ostrich, it has wings, it has feathers, it is alive, etc. As McCarthy (1969) observes:

(a) it is impossible to produce an exhaustive listing of all the qualifications necessary to transform a *defeasible* rule into a universally valid statement;

(b) even if all (or most) of those specifications were rendered explicit, it would be impossible, or too onerous, to verify in every concrete case the existence of all the specifications.

Nonmonotonic logics allow us to face problem (b): they offer inference methods to derive conclusions by means of the general rules, but allow us to retract those conclusions whenever one of the necessary qualification fails. On the other hand, problem (a), i.e., the need for an exhaustive specification of all relevant qualifications, cannot be solved with logical tools. This is true for both empirical and legal rules.

[16] Except where there is the possibility, in the limits established by the law, of starting a new procedure (or a further phase of the already existing procedure) intended to obtain a new decision modifying or substituting the preceding one. The connection between certainty and limits in the use of new information can also be seen in 'preclusion' or 'barring' in legal proceedings.

[17] Let us recall that rule and exception can be rendered consistent by inserting the complement of the antecedent of the exception, qualified as *non-refutandum,* in the antecedent of the rule.

[18] In qualifying legal norms as inference rules we intend to affirm that they must be used only 'forwards': we can derive the effect of the norm when the antecedent is satisfied (*modus ponens*) but we cannot derive the negation of the antecedent by assuming that the legal consequence does not obtain (*modus tollens*). The interpretation of conditional statements as inference rules is adopted in default logic (cf. Reiter [1980] 1987), but this notion has been informally discussed long ago in theories of ethical and legal reasoning (cf. Toulmin 1958).

[19] In Sartor (1993) this language (with the corresponding inferential procedures) is extended so that defeasible meta-conditionals concerning preference relations between norms can also be formulated.

[20] The statement r_1 (*John, FenceCrash, FenceBreak*) is the result of substituting for the variables *x*, *f*, and *d*, occurring in the rule r_1, the constants *John, FenceCrash,* and *FenceBreak.*

REFERENCES

Alchourrón, C.E., and D. Makinson. 1981. 'Hierarchies of Regulations and Their Logic.' In *New Studies on Deontic Logic,* edited by R. Hilpinen, 123–148. Dordrecht: Reidel.

Alchourrón, C.E., and D. Makinson. 1982. 'On the Logic of Theory Change: Contraction Functions and their Associated Revision Functions.' *Theoria* 48 (1): 14–37.

Alchourrón, C.E., and D. Makinson. 1985. 'On the Logic of Theory Change: Safe Contractions.' *Studia Logica* 44: 405-422

Alchourrón, C.E., P. Gärdenfors, and D. Makinson. 1985. 'On the Logic of Theory Change: Partial Meet Functions for Contractions and Revisions.' *Journal of Symbolic Logic* 50: 510–530.

Alexy, R. 1978. *Theorie der juristischen Argumentation.* Frankfurt: Suhrkamp.

Alexy, R. 1981. 'Zum Begriff des Rechtsprinzip.' *Rechtstheorie.* Beiheft 1: 59–87.

Baker, G.P. 1977. 'Defeasibility and Meaning.' In *Law, Morality, and Society: Essays in Honour of H.L.A. Hart*, edited by P.M.S. Hacker and J. Raz. Oxford: Clarendon Press.

Brewka, G. 1991. *Nonmonotonic Reasoning. Logical Foundations of Commonsense.* Cambridge: Cambridge. University Press.

Delgrande J.P. 1988. 'An Approach to Default Reasoning Based on a First-Order Conditional Logic: Revised Report.' *Artificial Intelligence* 36: 63–90.

Dworkin R.M. 1977. *Taking Rights Seriously.* London: Duckworth.

Falzea, A. [1965] 1985. 'Efficacia giuridica.' In *Voci di teoria generale del diritto*, 239–432. Milano: Giuffrè. First published in *Enciclopedia del diritto* 16: 432–509.

Gärdenfors, P. 1988. *Knowledge in Flux.* Cambridge (Massachusetts): MIT Press.

Gordon, T.F. 1989. 'Issue Spotting in a System for Searching Interpretation Spaces.' In *The Second International Conference on Artificial Intelligence and Law: Proceedings of the Conference*, 157–164. New York: ACM Press.

Hart, H.L.A., 1948. 'The Ascription of Responsibility and Rights', *Proceedings of the Aristotelian Society* 49, (1948–49), pp. 171–94

Jones, A.J., and I. Pörn. 1991. *DEO'91: First International Workshop on Deontic Logic in Computer Science, Amsterdam, The Netherlands, December 11–13, 1991, Proceedings*, 232–247. Amsterdam: Vrjie Universiteit.

McCarthy, J. [1980] 1987. 'Circumscription —A form of Non-Monotonic Reasoning'. In: *Readings in Nonmonotonic Reasoning*, edited by M.L. Ginsberg, pp. 145–151. Los Altos (Cal.): Morgan Kaufmann. First published in *Artificial Intelligence* 13: 27–39.

McCarthy, J., and P. Hayes. [1969] 1981. 'Some Philosophical Problems of Artificial Intelligence'. In *Readings in Artificial Intelligence*, edited by B.J. Webber and N.J. Nilsson, pp. 431–450. Los Altos (California): Morgan Kaufmann. First published in *Machine Intelligence 4*, edited by B. Melzer and D. Michie, pp. 463–502. Edinburgh: Edinburgh University Press.

Moore, R.C. [1984] 1987. 'Possible-world Semantic for Autoepistemic Logic'. In *Readings in Nonmonotonic Reasoning*, edited by M.L. Ginsberg, 137–142. Los Altos (Cal.): Morgan Kaufmann. First published in Proceedings *1984 Non-monotonic Reasoning Workshop*, New Palz (New York): American Association for Artificial Intelligence.

Moore, R.C. [1985] 1987. 'Semantical Considerations on Nonmonotonic Logic'. In *Readings in Nonmonotonic Reasoning*, edited by M.L. Ginsberg, pp. 127–136. Los Altos (Cal.): Morgan Kaufmann. First published in *Artificial Intelligence* 25: 79–94.

Patti, S. 1987. *Prove. Disposizioni generali.* Bologna: Zanichelli, Foro italiano: Roma.

Peirce, C.S. 1931. *Collected Papers.* Cambridge (Massachusetts): The Belknap Press of Harvard University Press.

Perelman, C. 1979. *Logique juridique. Nouvelle rhétorique.* Paris: Dalloz. 2nd edition.

Poole, D.L. 1988. 'A Logical Framework for Default Reasoning,' *Artificial Intelligence.* 36: pp. 27–47.

Pollock, J.L. 1987. 'Defeasible Reasoning', *Cognitive Science* 11: 481–518.

Prakken, H. 1991. *A Formal Theory about Preferring the Most Specific Argument.* Rapport nr. IR-259. Amsterdam: Vrije Universiteit, Faculteit der Wiskunde en Informatica.

Prakken, H., 1992. *Logical Tools for Modelling Legal Arguments.* Amsterdam: Prakken.

Raz, J., 1972. 'Legal Principles and the Limits of Law', *Yale Law Journal*, 81: 823.

Reiter, R. [1980] 1987. 'A Logic for Default Reasoning'. In *Readings in Nonmonotonic Reasoning*, edited by M.L. Ginsberg, 68–93. Los Altos (Cal.): Morgan Kaufmann. First published in *Artificial Intelligence* 13: 81–132.

Reiter, R., and G. Criscuolo. [1981] 1987. 'On interacting defaults'. In *Readings in Nonmonotonic Reasoning*, edited by M.L. Ginsberg, 94–100. Los Altos (Cal.): Morgan Kaufmann. First published in *Proceedings of the Seventh International Joint Conference on Artificial Intelligence* — IJCAI 1981, 270-276. Vancouver.

Ross, W.D. 1930. *The Right and the Good.* Oxford: Clarendon Press.

Ross, W.D. 1939. *Foundations of Ethics.* Oxford: Clarendon Press.

Sacco, R. 1957. 'Presunzione, natura costitutiva od impeditiva del fatto, onere della prova (aspetti diversi di un fenomeno unico o fenomeni autonomi)', *Rivista di diritto civile* 3: 399–423.

Sartor, G. 1991. 'The Structure of Legal Norms and Nonmonotonic Reasoning in Law'. In *The Third International Conference on Artificial Intelligence & Law: Proceedings of the Conference*, 155–164. New York: ACM Press.

Sartor, G. 1992. 'Normative Conflicts in Legal Reasoning'. *Artificial Intelligence and Law*. 1: 209–235.

Sartor, G. 1993. 'A Simple Computational Model for Nonmonotonic and Adversarial Legal Reasoning'. In *The Fourth International Conference on Artificial Intelligence and Law. Proceedings of the Conference*. New York: ACM Press.

Searle, J.R. 1978. 'Prima Facie Obligations', in *Practical Reasoning*, edited by J. Raz, 81–90. Oxford: Oxford University Press.

Simari, G.R., and R.P. Loui, 1992. 'A Mathematical Treatment of Defeasible Reasoning and its Implementation'. *Artificial Intelligence* 53: 125–157.

Toulmin, S. 1958. *The Uses of Argument*, Cambridge University Press.

CIRFID
Faculty of Law
University of Bologna
Italy

ERIC HILGENDORF

ON SOME PROBLEMS OF THE THEORY OF LEGAL ARGUMENTATION[1]

1. INTRODUCTION

The Theory of Legal Argumentation as it is discussed today in Germany may be characterized as an adoption of analytical philosophy and critical theory in the domain of basic research in jurisprudence. It is well known that the relationship between philosophy and jurisprudence has at all times been very difficult. Jurists tend to repel influences from philosophy whereas philosophers usually are very glad if they are adopted by legal science or even by the judicature. Important adoption processes of this kind in our century in Germany are neokantianism, neohegelianism and phenomenology, *materiale Wertethik,* and hermeneutics. It is since the mid-seventies that analytical philosophy and critical theory have been exercising a growing influence on basic research in German legal science.

Ulfrid Neumann has undertaken the effort of surveying some of the relevant works and of listing their main theses (Neumann 1986). Neumann believes that he has found in the term 'argumentation' a common denominator of the works surveyed by him. He presents three factors as essential: attempts to develop a general theory of argumentation; recent discussions on the problem of the application of the law; and the rediscovery of the topic of 'argumentation' in moral philosophy (Neumann 1986, p. 2).

The general theory of argumentation Neumann is referring to is the German variant of what is known as 'informal logic' or 'practical reasoning' in Great Britain and the United States or as 'nouvelle rhétorique' in France and Belgium. Every now and then we find the denomination 'dialectic' as well. The term 'argumentation theory', however, seems to be relatively young.[2] All the proponents of a general argumentation theory seem to have the idea in common that formal logic is insufficient for the analysis of argumentation in natural language. We can easily agree with that. However, there are doubts as to how a 'general argumentation theory' could contribute to changing this state of affairs. As far as I know, no representative of this discipline has succeeded in shaping the tasks and aims of his or her field of research into a brief yet expressive formula. I therefore propose to rely on those authors who want to practise the general theory of argumentation as applied logic. Proceeding in this way seems even more plausible if we bring

Z. Bankowski et al. (eds.), *Informatics and the Foundations of Legal Reasoning,* 159–176.

the history of the general argumentation theory back to our minds. The analysis of mistakes in argumentation has always been an integral part of formal logic. It is only in the seventies of our century that the character of the argumentation theory changed, at least in Germany. 'Argumentation' now became an emotion-rousing keyword of numerous disciplines and scientific approaches, as in linguistics for instance, where a rather widely understood 'pragmatism' could be established, or in moral philosophy, where the 'theory of discourse' presented itself as a new cognitive ethics. These young approaches were markedly interdisciplinary, they were hostile to empiricism and tended to mix up scientific analyses with political and general moral viewpoints. Thus they managed to attract far more attention than is usually accorded to new scientific developments.

That jurists, too, besides their other activities, are arguing, is not a discovery of Legal Argumentation Theory. There are also quite a few older monographs on 'Law and Linguistics'.[3] But it was 'Legal Argumentation Theory' which for the first time put argumentation into the centre of its investigations. The practicability of these new approaches in jurisprudence has, however, been disputed from the beginning.[4]

In further discussions quite different aspects became prominent, for instance a descriptively orientated comparison of arguments in various fields of law, the adoption and critical reflection of contemporary philosophy and theory of science, or a 'theory of action' politically understood and extremely critical with regard to the judiciary. Ulfrid Neumann distinguishes between a logical-analytical approach to the legal theory of argumentation, a topic-rhetorical one, and finally one concerned with the theory of discourse. We have to add what he calls the analysis of judicial opinions, and 'complex models' of legal argumentation: the last group obviously has to be understood as a remainder category (Neumann 1986, pp. v–vii).

I believe that Neumann's categories are a very useful working basis. However, it is clear that classification into one or the other category will very often cause problems. We can state without exaggerating that the contributions to the *leitmotiv* 'argumentation' coming from legal theory and legal philosophy comprehend almost as wide a spectrum as the general argumentation theory does. Without much hesitation Legal Argumentation Theory has assumed approaches and fragments of theory from moral and social philosophy, from linguistics, and from logic, and has tried to make them usable for old problems of legal methodology and legal philosophy, such as, for instance, the relationship between legal norm and judge, or the problem of the 'good law'. We therefore agree with Neumann that we have to ascribe to legal argumentation theory a great number of approaches in part highly heterogeneous, and that 'theory of legal argumentation' does not mean 'a certain orientation but a certain problematic field in legal philosophy' (Neumann 1986, p. 2).

In order to bring some primitive structure into this amorphous field of research, I suggest the following distinctions:

Argumentation can be investigated in two respects. The first one deals with the consistency of argumentation. It is the rôle of logic to check consistency, for only logic can ensure that from true premisses true conclusions are drawn. The consistency of argumentation does not depend on the agreement of an audience. A precondition of the logical analysis is the elucidation of argumentation structures. Logical mistakes will spoil the consistency of an argumentation context. They form a first group of mistakes in argumentation.

The second respect in which argumentation can be analysed concerns the plausibility and convincing force of the arguments proposed. Plausibility and convincing force depend on the relevant audience; consistent arguments will be particularly effective most of the time, but this is not always true. The investigation of factors influencing the plausibility and convincing force of arguments is an empirical task. The use of methods unsuited to the case at issue forms the second group of mistakes in argumentation.

Many more practically oriented presentations investigate the subject 'argumentation' in both respects, putting more or less emphasis on the one or the other. At the *Tübinger Verhandlungsseminar*[5] ('The Tübingen Seminar on Negotiation') for instance, the leitmotiv *Strukturdenken* ('structural thinking') and hence logical analysis plays the most important part. However, a sharp distinction between logical und empirical questions is not necessary in these practically oriented workshops. More disturbing to me is the blurring of this distinction in numerous more theoretical investigations which deal with legal argumentation as a subject of basic legal research. In addition to the blurring of logical and empirical aspects, very often descriptive and normative points of view are confused, although it should be clear for jurists —at least if they are engaged in basic legal research— that it is one thing to ask how an argumentation actually takes place and another to ask how it should take place. Very often this sort of confusion is hidden behind the formula 'rational argumentation'.

We have asserted above that the modern legal argumentation theory in Germany could be understood as being an adoption of analytical philosophy and critical theory in the domain of basic research in jurisprudence. It is mainly analytical philosophy which has influenced teachings on the application of the law (see Section 2), whereas critical theory, and in this context primarily the so-called theory of discourse, has been discussed in connection with the old problem of the justification of normative statements (see Section 3).

2. THE THEORY OF THE APPLICATION OF THE LAW

2.1. The traditional understanding of being subjected to the law

According to Article 20 paragraph 3 *Grundgesetz* (Constitution of the Federal Republic of Germany), the executive power and the judiciary are subject to legislation and the rule of law (*Gesetz und Recht*). This is to protect every citizen from any illegitimate state intervention in his personal sphere of liberty. The traditional answer of German jurists to the question as to the nature of this subjection refers to a relationship of logical deduction: a judicial sentence should be presentable in the form of a syllogism, law being the first premiss, description of the case the second, and the sentence the conclusion. According to Wieacker (1967) this concept of application of the law spread in Europe from the sixteenth century onwards. The judicial syllogism, however, was quite early attacked, for instance in our century by the *Freirechtsbewegung* and by representatives of legal hermeneutics. Regina Ogorek (Ogorek 1986) has ascertained that in the section of legal theory which treated the canons of legal interpretation the idea of a mechanically logical adjudication can only be discerned as being at the most a marginal appearance at the beginning of the century, a late consequence of the codification movement, so to speak. Her report reveals that in the old yet still topical dispute on the relationship between legal norm and judge, incorrect empirical-historical theses were too often taken as premisses and consequently positions were attacked which actually never had been held in this sense.

A classical study of the application of German law is the work of Karl Engisch (Engisch 1943). Engisch's investigations are divided into three parts. In the first one he treats the logical structure of the deductive justification model. It is identified as a *modus ponens.* In the next step, Engisch turns to the major premiss, the general 'ought-proposition' *(Sollenssatz)* as derived from the law. However, most of his investigation is dedicated to the minor premiss, where Engisch distinguishes between three aspects: subsumption, establishing the facts of the case, and the logical interrelationship between establishing the facts and subsumption.

According to Engisch, the aim of all legal application processes is the finding of concrete legal 'ought-judgements' (*Sollensurteile*) (Engisch 1943, p. 2). These can be expressed positively as well as negatively. The ought-judgement is truth-valued and is in that way distinct from an imperative which cannot be qualified as being 'true' but only as being 'just' or 'sufficient to a given purpose'. Codified norms represent state imperatives. In order to derive truth-valued particular ought-judgements, they have to be turned into general ought-judgements. Thus the place of the legal imperative:

> Whoever has killed a person with intent and wilfully, etc., is liable to be punished as murderer and to be sentenced to death

will be taken by the truth-valued judgement:

> According to German Criminal Law, whoever has killed a person with intent and wilfully, etc., is liable to be punished as murderer and to be sentenced to death.

After legal imperatives are transformed into general propositions, the logical structure of the application of law can be represented as a syllogism.

Engisch pays great attention to the ascertaining of the minor premiss of the judicial syllogism. He defines subsumption as the assignment of the particular case at issue to the class of cases covered by the statute (Engisch 1943, p. 23). To subsume a single case under the legal elements of a norm means nothing else in principle but that we compare the new case with those cases that are undoubtedly addressed and dealt with by the norm (Engisch 1943, p. 26). Thus the central element of application of the law is comparison with regard to similarities.

To ascertain those cases undoubtedly addressed by the norm is the task of interpretation. So in the law-application process interpretation precedes subsumption. The category of cases comprised by the legal norm is of course extended by each successful subsumption. Past subsumptions have therefore to be taken into account when interpreting. The way in which the legal elements of a norm are expressed linguistically has no impact on the logical structure of the subsumption. We can say the same with regard to the selection of the interpretation method. The deciding authority on the comparison of the single case to be subsumed and the cases comprised by the norm is our 'sense of right and wrong' (*Rechtsgefühl*). This, however, falls within the scope of empirical psychology and not in that of legal theory.

For Engisch, a particular problem for the logical analysis of law-application is that the similarity of the case being subsumed to the cases ascertained by interpretation as being comprised by the norm, can only be construed in 'some single respects' and only 'to a certain extent' (Engisch 1943, p. 30). Engisch stresses the fact that the points of comparison are not to be considered as being unchangeable, but they are fixed by the legislature or depend on the interests of the legal practitioner. Still, the central element of all application of the law is the comparison in respect of similarities between the cases undoubtedly comprised by the norm and the new case to be judged. Engisch's reconstruction of the law-application process is still, I think, the most lucid and useful of its kind. (See Appendix.)

2.2. The justification model of Koch and Rüssmann

The most interesting attempt, to date, at more precisely defining the idea of justifying judgements deductively, was made by Hans-Joachim Koch and Helmut Rüssmann (Koch and Rüssmann 1982). They mainly introduce two ideas. The first one proposes to apply formal deontic logics, the second one to take some findings of modern philosophy of language into account.

They render the deductive model in the following way (*op. cit.* p. 56):

$$(x)\ (Tx \leftrightarrow O(R(x)))$$
$$(x)\ (M_1 x \leftrightarrow Tx)$$
$$(x)\ (M_2 x \leftrightarrow M_1 x)$$
$$.$$
$$.$$
$$.$$
$$(x)\ (Sx \leftrightarrow M_n x)$$
$$Sa$$
$$O\ (R(a))$$

M_1 to M_n (M for '*Merkmal*') are to symbolize the process of interpretation of a legal concept, S (for '*Sachverhalt*')$\leftrightarrow M_n x$ shows the end of the interpretation process.

Koch and Rüssmann label the logic they used 'deontic logic', and in their deductive justification model they use the deontic operator 'O' for symbolizing the relevant legal consequence. However, it is clear that many typical features of deontic logic are missing. This is not true as regards their commitment to a logic of norms —they consider propositions such as '$O(R(x))$' as truth-valued— for most deontic logicians today prefer proceeding this way to using a logic of imperatives. But they make no use of the otherwise usual interdefinability of deontic operators. More precisely, they do introduce these rules but they do not make use of them in their model of deductive justification of legal judgements. Thus we have to ask whether a deontic logic is necessary at all for the reconstruction of the law-application process or whether the traditional predicate logic would not suffice, and by an application of Ockham's razor the manifold problems of deontic logic would be excluded.

In the analysis of Koch and Rüssmann, the proposition '$O(R(x))$' is never broken up into its elements. They rather treat the deontic operator 'O' and the proposition '$R(x)$' as a single entity all the time. We have seen then that they do not apply the sign 'O' in its usual function as a deontic operator, but rather they want to make clear that '$R(x)$' is expressing a legal consequence, that is to say an originally prescriptive sentence, which for the purpose of reconstructing the law-application process was transformed into a descriptive sentence.

This use of the sign 'O' does not turn the logic used into a deontic logic. It is, rather, the well known and for present purposes unproblematic predicate logic. Predicate logic is rich enough to reconstruct the process of law application in the way proposed by Engisch and more precisely defined by Koch and Rüssmann. Therefore Engisch was right to do without any norm-logic investigations in his work.

Furthermore, the assumptions in the philosophy of language that Koch and Rüssmann are taking as a basis for their model are not uncontestable. The sub-disciplines of linguistics that are most interesting —especially for jurists— i.e. semantics and pragmatics, have not yet been advanced to a point where they could reach even a relatively firm consensus on what basic questions have to be dealt with. Often, the so-called 'pragmatics' above all seems still to remain in a pre-scientific philosophical state. Terms such as 'discourse', 'communication', etc., point to another problem of pragmatics as science, i.e. the risk that some authors might try to reach a broader audience by using linguistics as camouflage for their personal beliefs of what the true, the good and the beautiful are.

Koch and Rüssmann believe it is possible to advance discussion on the judicial activity which is usually called 'interpretation' by introducing Carnap's pair of terms 'intension' and 'extension'. In order to strengthen their position they discuss numerous theses in the philosophy of language which originated in semantics and pragmatics. But by going greatly beyond what has been ventured so far in German legal theory, they render their position more vulnerable than it would have been without this excursus. We should not be surprised if their representation has been the object of crude criticism. For instance, Dietrich Busse, a linguist closely attached to

Friedrich Müller's *Strukturierenden Rechtslehre,* has attacked their attempts to refine the deductive model. Busse reproaches them for operating with an essentialist notion of meaning which would give to meanings features proper to facts, i.e. the ontological status of platonic entities (Busse 1989, p. 99). However, this charge is completely incorrect. Contrary to Busse's reproach, Koch and Rüssmann expressly refuse to accept a rigid relationship between the language-symbol and the object of reference in extra-linguistic reality. They maintain that the qualities expressed by a language-symbol depend on the language conventions within a community: 'There is no true, specific, or natural meaning of an expression independent from convention.' (Koch and Rüssmann 1982, p. 7).

We may even advance another argument against Busse. The word 'meaning' itself is a term in language; the meaning of 'meaning' consequently will have to be defined. Definitions, however, are not true or false but fit or unfit for a given purpose. Legal methodology bases its efforts of legal interpretation and of respecting the requirement of subjection to the law, on the objective of ascertaining the possibilities and the conditions of subordinating the executive and the judiciary to legislation. It therefore is not only possible but even wise for legal science to assign other contents to 'meaning' than those assigned either by an empirical linguistics or even by some speculative and moralising version of 'pragmatics'. Busse's objection that the method of intension and extension would still not describe any meanings (op. cit. p. 98) therefore completely misses the point. What is crucial is the question whether the notion of 'meaning' proposed by Koch and Rüssmann can be applied profitably in jurisprudence, rather than the question whether they follow the notion of meaning favoured by Busse. The intension/ extension couple which they draw from modern logical semantics, is therefore likely to be quite a useful basis for judicial activity if we do not burden it with disputes that have nothing to do with legal theory but should rather be taken care of by linguists doing fundamental research.

3. THE PROBLEM OF JUSTIFICATION OF NORMATIVE STATEMENTS IN THE THEORY OF LEGAL ARGUMENTATION

3.1. The Special Case Thesis

'Justice and morality' is a classical topic of philosophy of law. Robert Alexy has taken it up in his rightfully highly praised *Theory of Legal Argumentation* and has defined a 'Special Case Thesis' according to which legal 'discourse' is a special case of 'general practical discourse' (Alexy 1978, Alexy 1989). On the basis of this thesis Alexy believes himself justified in recommending the use of the so-called 'ethics of discourse', moral-philosophical proposals associated with the Frankfurt School, within the law-application process and for the operation of a possible justification of normative statements. Alexy belongs among Germany's leading legal theorists today. He has set up new standards of clarity and precision. Criticising him on some of his points of view is not to belittle his achievements, but rather to proceed on the path he has opened for German legal theorists, i.e. to adopt the methods and insights of analytical philosophy to problems of law and its application.

In the old dispute between ethical cognitivism and ethical non-cognitivism, the discourse ethicians, with Karl Otto Apel and Jürgen Habermas taking the lead, have assumed a rather surprising position. Non-cognitivists believe that all attempts made so far to give morals a basis by scientific means have failed. That is why we would have to accept for the time being that ultimate values cannot be attained by cognition; according to non-cognitivists we will have to avow these values, i.e. have to make a choice. Non-cognitivists require that we engage in debate on moral questions and in particular on 'ultimate values' *(letzte Werte).* As these values are a matter of personal choice in the end, it is necessary to unveil the different positions, to discuss diverging opinions and to look out for a practical consensus. According to this viewpoint nobody commands a privileged access to the knowledge of what is morally right. This viewpoint prevailed on the Continent after World War II. Outside religious circles there then remained only the so-called Frankfurt School, besides some scattered adherents to the *materiale Wertethik,* who avowed ethical cognitivism. However, the position of the former Frankfurt School was anything but clear, for problems of justification were hardly dealt with, on account of their belief in a philosophy of history inspired by Marx and Hegel.

Jürgen Habermas, main protagonist of the younger generation of the Frankfurt School, has given up philosophy of history and has put the philosophy of language in its place. He argues on the basis of theses put forward by Karl-Otto Apel, who called them 'transcendental-pragmatic'.[6] Here I should like to draw attention to one peculiarity of these proposals:

In discourse ethics, cognitivist and non-cognitivist viewpoints are linked by maintaining the demand for argumentation and consent and by claiming at the same time that this position was not entailed by the experience that all moral-philosophical 'attempts at ultimate justification' *(Letztbegründungs-*

versuche) had failed (see Apel 1973). Hence, the commitment to argumentation and consent is not, according to a discourse-theoretical viewpoint, an expression of the insight that we cannot attain ethical knowledge but itself represents ethical knowledge in a cognitive sense, which is allegedly founded on the structures of language.

Now back to Alexy. He summarizes his Special Case Thesis as follows:

> Legal discourse is a special case of general practical discourse on the grounds that:
> (1) legal discussions are concerned with practical questions [...]
> (2) these questions are discussed under the claim to correctness [... and] because legal discussions
> (3) do take place under constraints [...] (Alexy 1978, pp. 37, 262ff; Alexy 1989, pp. 15, 212ff)

Alexy obviously means by general practical discourse a discussion where practical questions are involved and are being discussed under the claim to correctness. Legal discourse is also qualified by those features but it takes place —and this is the characteristic factor— within a framework of limiting conditions, such as , for instance, the fact of being subjected to the law.

Is he here concerned with definitions or with empirical statements about what jurists do? This is one of the core problems of Alexy's Special Case Thesis. Alexy does not deal with this question explicitly. However, we can conclude from what he says that at least his representation of the general discourse must be a definition. For the sake of argumentation I will use the terminology proposed by Alexy in the following and will examine somewhat closer the three objections to the Special Case Thesis that he makes himself.

Alexy admits the first objection, which states that legal discussions do not involve practical questions, insofar as he admits that 'there are many discussions relating to legal questions which are concerned not with substantiating normative statements but rather with the establishment of facts.' Alexy mentions in this respect investigations in legal history, sociology of law, and legal theory, descriptions of valid law, and predictions of future judicial behaviour. He continues by saying that on the other hand there exists legal reasoning, both in legal practice and in the realm of legal science, which intends to solve practical questions, and that in both fields it plays a central rôle. Alexy is obviously talking about the justification of normative statements. Questions like this do indeed appear in moral philosophy as well as in the legal context. So far Alexy's argument holds good.

Alexy considers the statement that in legal discourses no claim is made to 'correctness' as another possible objection against the Special Case Thesis. He does in fact believe himself that the claim of 'legal discourses' to correctness is different from that of 'general practical discourse', yet to his mind this difference is of no relevance to the Special Case Thesis:

There is no claim that the normative statement asserted, proposed, or pronounced in judgements is absolutely rational, but only a claim that it can be rationally justified within the framework of the prevailing legal order. (Alexy 1978, p. 264; Alexy 1989, p. 214).

In fact, we usually demand of moral philosophers as well as of jurists that they should not be satisfied by mere statements but that they try to justify these statements 'rationally'. Unfortunately, no accord has been reached so far as to which justification was to be considered as 'rational' and hence 'correct'. Terms such as 'rationality' and 'correctness' are therefore extremely vague. It is only due to the vagueness of Alexy's core terms that his Special Case Thesis seems to be plausible so far.

The last objection discussed by Alexy proposes that it is impossible to consider legal discussions as 'discourses' because of the constraints which govern those discussions. In order to evaluate this objection we will have to clarify first what actually is meant by the term 'discourse'. So far it has been used synonymously with 'discussion'. Jürgen Habermas has defined the term 'discourse' as a form of communication characterized by argumentation, where claims which have become problematic are made the subject-matter and are scrutinized as to their soundness (Habermas 1973, Habermas 1984). Alexy obviously follows this definition (Alexy 1978, p. 139ff; Alexy 1989, pp. 105ff). For him the decisive point seems to be that discourses are any form of discussion which are to a certain extent free of limitations. Because of the ampleness of this requirement Alexy can easily call discussions in legal science 'discourses'.

However, it obviously seems very difficult to qualify court hearings, such as criminal proceedings for instance, as 'discourse' in the sense mentioned above. Neumann is right when he points both at the judge's rôle as master of proceedings and at the advocate's primary purpose of reaching a favourable outcome, which means that the arguments advanced are of a strategic nature (Neumann 1986, p. 85). Even Habermas, to start with, had on these grounds considered judicial proceedings as being not a discourse but a strategic undertaking (Habermas 1971). Alexy, too, gives a particular intermediate position to judicial proceedings which does not allow their simple categorization as discourse, while insisting that they cannot be theoretically understood without reference to the concept of discourse. We can object, however, that a process could very well be 'understood theoretically' by *contrasting* it with the discourse definition. But Alexy's aim is to defend his Special Case Thesis. He therefore has to try to subsume even criminal proceedings under the discourse definition. Alexy manages by simply neglecting the constraints of the court proceedings: according to his viewpoint, both the parties, as well as the judge, claim to be arguing 'rationally' as they

> claim to speak in such a way that every rational person would have to agree with their viewpoint. They at least purport to be making arguments such that they would gain assent under ideal conditions. Discourse theory is thus not only suited to the theoretical understanding of the reasoning involved, it is necessary to understanding it. (Alexy 1978, p. 271; Alexy 1989, p. 219).

The attempt to surpass Habermas on discourse-theoretical grounds[7] does have its cost, however: the only content remaining in the Special Case Thesis is the statement that argumentation in the legal context, too, claims to be 'rational'. As such a claim is probably almost always connected with the putting-forward of an argument, the Special Case Thesis becomes trivial.

The *prima facie* plausibility of the Special Case Thesis, then, is due to the vagueness of Alexy's terminology, especially with regard to the terms 'rational' and 'correct'. Every now and then Alexy gives the impression that his theses are merely based on apt terminological definitions. He does not seem to notice that his Special Case Thesis would then become analytical. In other passages he applies the Special Case Thesis to actual conditions, such as in legal science or in the court proceedings. In order to comprehend even criminal proceedings as a special case of the 'general practical discourse', Alexy deems it sufficient to state the 'claim to correctness' as a common feature of practical discourses, which, according to his viewpoint, is always proposed in all proceedings of this kind. In this case the Special Case Thesis does not become trivial just because it is analytical but rather because it hardly excludes anything any more.

3.2. The rules of argumentation

Alexy also tries to develop rules of argumentation which, according to him, are appropriate to governing general practical and legal discourses. This attempt may be criticized in two respects. First of all, the basis on which Alexy founds his rules is questionable. Are they reasons which are 'ultimately justified' *(letztbegründet)* in the sense of transcendental pragmatism (Apel)? Or is he talking about moral knowledge in the cognitive sense just as Jürgen Habermas did with regard to the rules of the ideal speech situation? Is the justification of Alexy's rules goal-oriented? Or are they, finally, proposals springing from personal preferences of the author that we may equally accept or reject?

A second point giving grounds for criticism is the fact that even the best-founded rules will manage to discipline actual practical argumentation only if they are stated in a way which allows the possibility of adhering to them. Rules which are formulated so widely that they do not prohibit anything or so narrowly that it is impossible to follow them cannot fulfil their task.

The foundation of Alexy's rules is a question of moral philosophy.[8] I suggest that neither Apel nor Habermas have succeeded in uncovering a path leading to moral knowledge. Hence Alexy's rules do not have the cognitivist foundation that they are alleged to have. We can therefore ask what grounds there are for adhering to them. A strong argument in favour of Alexy would be if we could easily and entirely direct actual argumentation —for instance in jurisprudence— with the help of his canon of rules. But is this possible? Let us consider one example.

Alexy's rules (2.1) to (2.3) say:

> (2.1) Everyone who can speak may take part in discourse.
>
> (2.2) (a) Everyone may problematize any assertion.
>
> (b) Everyone may introduce any assertion into the discourse.
>
> (c) Everyone may express his or her attitudes, wishes, and needs.
>
> (2.3) No speaker may be prevented from exercising the rights laid down in (2.1) and (2.2) by any kind of coercion internal or external to the discourse.
>
> (Alexy 1978, p. 240; Alexy 1989, p. 193)

These rules are quite obviously not practicable. If we applied them literally all orderly discussion would break down. Alexy, too, is aware of the problem. However, he believes he is able to defend his rules: their function as a positive criterion might cause problems, but functioning as a negative criterion they could be effective:

> Justificatory arguments which would not be accepted when (2.1)–(2.3) (including the additional rules of discourse) were satisfied, are to be regarded as invalid. (Alexy 1978, p. 240; Alexy 1989, p. 193)

The question is how Alexy will know at what time the negative criterion is satisfied. Rules (2.1) and (2.2) are formulated without any time index; we might have to understand rule (2.3) even in such a way that it explicitly excluded any temporal limitation of the discourse. Discourses then have to be continued infinitely in principle, according to Alexy. We may assume —on the basis that rules (2.1) and (2.2) are satisfied— that reasons which were not accepted until time T suddenly will be accepted at time T' just because new points are introduced in the discussion. It is therefore impossible to consider the non-acceptance of reasons by parties in the discourse in the ideal speech situation as definitive. This is why non-acceptance cannot be a usable criterion for the soundness of a justification. It is only from the viewpoint of the Day of Last Judgement that we might draw a different conclusion.

I finally would like to consider a particular example of a rule of Alexy for legal discourse. All legal professionals very soon find by experience that the traditional canons of interpretation —i.e. interpretation according to the literal sense, the systematical context, the historical context, and the general intention and purpose of the legal norm— may lead to differing results. Discussions have been going on for a long time now as to whether a ranking order could be established among the canons.[9] Alexy's rule of discourse refers to this discussion when it says:

> Arguments which give expression to a link with the actual words of the law, or the will of the historical legislator, take precedence over other arguments, unless rational grounds can be cited for granting precedence to the other arguments. (Alexy 1978, p. 305; Alexy 1989, p. 248)

With the help of this rule on allocating the burden of argumentation Alexy wants to ensure subjection to the prevailing legal order. This approach respecting the rule of law does undoubtedly deserve our agreement. Unfortunately though, Alexy does not explain what he will do when the law in force conflicts with discourse-theoretical insights into the 'structure of language'. This possibility cannot be precluded right from the start. Probably the saving clause: 'unless rational grounds can be cited for granting precedence to the other arguments', added by Alexy as a precaution, would have to come into play. However, there is a certain problem linked to this clause, and Alexy recognizes it, too: the clause is only usable if he makes clear what is meant by 'rational grounds'.

Alexy writes:

> Those grounds alone are rational which can be justified in a rational juristic discussion. (Alexy 1978, p. 305; Alexy 1989, p. 249)

This statement, however, is obviously circular, for Alexy defines 'rational' legal discussion itself as that governed by the rules of discourse. We can therefore raise considerable doubts about these rules.

Of course this is not the end of the theory of legal argumentation. Yet it does not seem possible to found such a theory on the philosophy of language with reference to Habermas or Apel as authority. I believe that not only in the analysis of legal argumentation but also in moral philosophy a sceptical approach committed to lucidity and intellectual probity can provide a sounder basis than a mysterious 'rationality' allegedly founded on the structures of language.

APPENDIX[10]

Today, we generally acknowledge that the legal practitioner will never find the solution of his or her problem solely by proceeding deductively, i.e. deducing it from a legal norm. In every application of the law there is a moment of decision. (This was stated very clearly by Kelsen 1960.) This, of course, is of great importance with regard to the use of computers in jurisprudence. Modern legal rhetoric has taken on the task of structuring the decision process and of making it verifiable intersubjectively. It thereby relies on methods which may be briefly referred to as 'Structural Reasoning' (*Strukturdenken*) and 'Standard Case Method' (*Normalfallmethode*).

The formation of legal students in Germany is still imbued by the basic idea of becoming a judge. Hence, the most important activity of the legal student is the interpretation of texts; he or she has to comply with the canons of interpretation which were established by von Savigny more than 150 years ago (Savigny 1840). As a first rule of interpretation the beginner has to learn about the so-called 'grammatical method'. According to this rule, the legal practitioner has to use the literal sense of the words of the legal norm at issue as a starting point, he or she may not at any rate infringe on the limits set up by the literal sense of the norm when deciding a case. However, the *communis opinio* admits that in many cases the grammatical method does not lead to an unequivocal solution. In one of its first decisions, the German *Bundesgerichtshof*, for instance, had to deal with the question whether spraying someone with hydrochloric acid had to be qualified as 'use of a dangerous tool' in the sense of the norm §223a German Criminal Code. (See *Bundesgerichtshof* n.d.) The analysis of the literal meaning of 'dangerous tool' does obviously not lead to a definite solution. The legal practitioner rather has to look out for some other criteria.

The prevailing opinion within methodology holds that the intention of the legislator is a crucial criterion for a correct decision. This is also called the 'historical method of interpretation'. However, considering the great number of those participating in the process of legislation today, the historical method has to cope with the very difficult problem of deciding whose motives are to be decisive for the interpretation of the norm. We may think of the motives of the members of parliament who have passed the legal norm at issue, or the ideas of the government officials who were in charge of elaborating and drawing up the norm. It is a matter of fact that even within a single group various motives can be found. Hence, the historical method of interpretation in most cases is not able to reach an unequivocal result.

With these problems in mind we must not be astonished if modern discussions on methodology refer to the systematics of the legal norms, using it as a third rule of interpretation. The norm, it is said, has to be construed in such a way that it will fit into the systematical order of the law, and even into the whole comprehensive legal order. Accordingly, ambiguous terms have to be construed identically wherever they may be employed in legal codifications. The goal of this so-called 'systematical rule of interpretation', in the end, is to assure consistency. However, the problem of 'systematic interpretation' is notorious: the legislator is not bound to employ certain terms in different codes in the same sense. It is even possible that within one code of legal norms the same term is used in different senses. There is for instance the noun 'intent' (*Absicht*) and the adjective 'intentional' (*absichtlich*) which are used in various articles of the German Criminal Code. However, legal dogmatists agree to interpret this term sometimes in the sense of 'desire to attain a certain end' (*zielgerichtetes Wollen*) and in some other cases 'foresight of the inevitable consequences' (*sicheres Wissen*). (For further details see Jescheck 1988.) Hence, neither the systematical method of interpretation is obviously able to reach an unequivocal solution in all cases.

The prevailing opinion proposes as a last and at the same time most important method of interpretation the so-called 'teleological method of interpretation'. According to this rule the legal practitioner should use the 'general intention and purpose' of the statute as a guideline and stick to the interpretation which complies most with the 'general purpose and intent' of the norm. At first sight this seems to be the most plausible idea. Nevertheless, after some deeper reflection we come to ask who or what will determine 'purpose and intent'. It is obviously not the intention of the legislator which becomes relevant here, otherwise the 'teleological interpretation' would be identical with arguments based on the history of the legal norm. However, if we refer to the intention of the legal practitioner as authority, we are giving him complete liberty to determine what the 'general purpose and intent' of the statute is; in this case the teleological interpretation will be of no help in the search of a correct decision.

Taking this dilemma into account, numerous authors have claimed the existence of an 'objective intent of the legal norm' which may divert from the ideas of the legislators as well as from those of the practitioners. (See, for instance, Larenz 1991, p. 333 ff.) This view, however, mistakes the grammar of the word 'intention': according to contemporary linguistic usage only living beings may have intentions, and letters on paper cannot —they can at most be the expression of a human will. A supposed 'objective intention of the norm' therefore does not exist, and we may cast grave doubts on the teleological method of interpretation as a whole. It may be added in this context that the methods of interpretation mentioned are not usable for computer programming either.

We consequently would prefer another method of law application, a method which often is called 'method of comparison with regard to similarities' (*Ahnlichkeitsvergleich*) or 'Standard Case Method' (*Normalfallmethode*). The most important preparatory work has been furnished by Karl Engisch (Engisch 1943). The essentials of the new method are as follows (for details see also Haft 1990):

If the legal practitioner is confronted with the question whether or not a problematic case can be subsumed under a legal norm, he or she has to examine as a first step what cases are comprised beyond doubt by the norm. This examination and ascertainment of the 'Standard Cases' may proceed on the basis of ordinary understanding. 'Standard Cases' of a 'dangerous tool' according to § 223a German Criminal Code would for instance be a knife or a revolver. In a second step, the legal practitioner has to extract the structures of the case at issue as precisely as possible (structural reasoning). Sketches can be of valuable help in this process. (See the examples given in Haft 1990, p. 90f.) Now we compare the case at issue with the standard cases as to relevant similarities. If they are comparable, then the case at issue can be subsumed under the norm, if they are not are comparable, the subsumption must fail and the legal norm is not applicable to this case.

The crucial question now obviously is to know which aspects of the standard cases and the case at issue have to be taken into account for the comparison. All conceivable cases are similar in some respects and in some they differ. When searching for the relevant points of comparison the practitioner should therefore, as a guideline, look at the purpose intended by the legislator during the process of drawing up the statute. If this is impossible, he or she may select the relevant aspects himself or herself, although he is not supposed to proceed arbitrarily but has to adhere to the intention of the statute according to his or her understanding of it. It is important to oblige the practitioner to present and explain in any case the aspects on which he or she has based his or her comparison. By using clear and well-structured arguments the practitioner solicits the acceptance of the persons involved. This, too, is an application of a well-understood 'rhetoric'.

In this way the process of the application of law may be presented much more clearly than by the mysterious techniques of traditional methodology. With regard to the simulation of the law application process by computers, the question arises as to how the comparison or the analogy could be picked up precisely. Some attempts were made in the course of the LEX Project. On this, see (Haft, Jones and Wetter 1988) and (Philipps 1991). However, we have to admit that legal informatics is still far from being able to furnish practical results in this area.

NOTES

[1] Abstract of (Hilgendorf 1991) translated by Mirjam Rieker, Tübingen.

[2] Cf. the list of titles in (Barth & Martens 1982).

[3] For example: (Horn 1966), (Podlech 1976), (Rieser 1976), (Garstka 1979).

[4] Cf. (Koch 1977), (Esser 1979).

[5] See the anthology (Gottwald and Haft 1987).

[6] For a further discussion of discourse ethics see (Hilgendorf 1991).

[7] Today, Habermas follows Alexy's propositions, cf. (Habermas 1987).

[8] See (Hilgendorf 1991) for possible answers to these questions.

[9] See, for instance, (Larenz 1991, pp. 343–346).

[10] From 'Legal Rhetoric between *Structural Reasoning* and *Standard Case Method*', by F. Haft, M. Gerblinger and E. Hilgendorf.

REFERENCES

Alexy, R. 1978, 1991. *Theorie der juristischen Argumentation. Die Theorie des rationalen Diskurses als Theorie der juristischen Begründung,* Frankfurt/Main, pp. 32, 263.

Alexy, R., 1989. *A Theory of Legal Argumentation. The Theory of Rational Discourse as Theory of Legal Justification,* (trans. by R. Adler and N. MacCormick). Oxford, pp. 15, p. 212.

Apel, K.O., 1973. 'Das Apriori der Kommunikationsgemeinschaft und die Grundlagen der Ethik. Zum Problem einer rationalen Begründung der Ethik im Zeitalter der Wissenschaft' in Karl Otto Apel, *Transformation der Philosophie,* vol. 2, *Das Apriori der Kommunikationsgemeinschaft,* Frankfurt/Main 1973, pp. 358, 359, 435, 412 f.

Barth, E. M., and Martens, J. L., 1982. (eds.), *Argumentation: Approaches to Theory Formation. Containing the Contributions to the Groningen Conference on the Theory of Argumentation, October 1978,* Amsterdam, pp. 295–328.

Bundesgerichtshof, n.d. *Entscheidungen des Bundesgerichtshofs in Strafsachen (BGHSt)* [Collection of criminal cases decided by the Highest German Federal Court of Justice] vol. 1, p. 1 ff.

Busse, D., 1989. 'Was ist die Bedeutung eines Gesetzestextes? Sprachwissenschaftliche Argumente im Methodenstreit der juristischen Auslegungslehre —linguistisch gesehen' in F. Müller (ed.), *Untersuchungen zur Rechtslinguistik. Interdisziplinäre Studien zu praktischer Semantik und strukturierender Rechtslehre in Grundfragen der juristischen Methodik,* Berlin, pp. 93–148.

Engisch, K., 1943. *Logische Studien zur Gesetzesanwendung,* Heidelberg.

Esser, J., 1979. *Juristisches Argumentieren im Wandel des Rechtsfindungskonzeptes unseres Jahrhunderts,* Heidelberg, p. 12.

Garstka, H., 1979. 'Zum Beitrag der Linguistik zur rechtswissenschaftlichen Forschung', *Rechtstheorie* 10, pp. 92–102.

Gottwald, W. and F. Haft, 1987. *Verhandeln und Vergleichen als juristische Fertigkeiten,* Tübingen.

Habermas, J., 1971. 'Theorie der Gesellschaft oder Sozialtechnologie? Eine Auseinandersetzung mit Niklas Luhmann' in J. Habermas, N. Luhmann, *Theorie der Gesellschaft oder Sozialtechnologie — Was leistet die Systemforschung?* Frankfurt/Main, pp. 142–290 (200f).

Habermas, J., 1973. 'Wahrheitstheorien' in *Wirklichkeit und Reflexion. Festschrift für Walter Schulz,* H. von Fahrenbach (ed.), Pfullingen, pp. 211–265 (214).

Habermas, J., 1983. 'Diskursethik — Notizen zu einem Begründungsprogramm' in J. Habermas, *Moralbewußtsein und kommunikatives Handeln,* Frankfurt/Main, pp. 53–125 (1 10).
Habermas, J., 1984. *Vorstudien und Ergänzungen zur Theorie des kommunikativen Handelns,* Frankfurt/Main, pp.127–183 (130).
Habermas, J., 1987. *Theorie des kommunikativen Handelns*, vol. 1: *Handlungsrationalität und gesellschaftliche Rationalisierung*, Frankfurt/Main, p. 62 fn 63.
Haft F., 1990. *Juristische Rhetorik*, Freiburg, München.
Haft, F., Jones, R. and Wetter, Th., 1988. 'A Natural Language Based Legal Expert System for Consultation and Tutoring — The Lex Project', in H. Fiedler, F. Haft, R. Traunmuller (eds.), *Expert Systems in Law: Impacts on Legal Theory and Computer Law*, series *Neue Methoden im Recht* (*NMIR*, vol. 4, pp. 75–98, Tübingen.
Hilgendorf, E., 1991. *Argumentation in der Jurisprudenz. Zur Rezeption von analytischer Philosophie und kritischer Theorie in der Grundlagenforschung der Jurisprudenz, (Schriften zur Rechtstheorie,* vol. 146) Berlin.
Horn, D., 1966. *Rechtssprache und Kommunikation. Grundlegung einer semantischen Kommunikationstheorie,* Berlin.
Jescheck, H.H., 1988. Lehrbuch des Strafrechts. Allgemeiner Teil, Berlin, p. 267ff.
Kelsen, H, 1960. *Reine Rechtslehre*, Vienna, pp. 346–354.
Koch, H. J. and H. Rüssmann, 1982. *Juristische Begründungslehre. Eine Einführung in Grundprobleme der Rechtswissenschaft,* München.
Koch, H. J., 1977. 'Ansätze zu einer juristischen Argumentationstheorie?' in *Archiv für Rechts- und Sozialphilosophie (ARSP)* 63, pp. 355–377.
Larenz, K., 1991. *Methodenlehre der Rechtswissenschaft,* Berlin.
Neumann, U., 1986. *Juristische Argumentationslehre*, Darmstadt.
Ogorek, R., 1986. *Richterkonig oder Subsumtionsautomat? Zur Justiztheorie im 19. Jahrhundert,* Frankfurt am Main, p. 368.
Philipps, L., 1991. 'Analogie und Computer', in R. Alexy, R. Dreier and U. Neumann (eds.), *Rechts- und Sozialphilosophie in Deutschland heute. Beiträge zur Standortbestimmung*, supplement No. 44 to *Archiv für Rechts- und Sozialphilosophie*, Stuttgart, pp. 275–286.
Podlech, A., 1976. 'Rechtslinguistik', in D. Grimm (ed.), *Rechtswissenschaft und Nachbarwissenschaften, vol.* 2, München, pp. 104–116.
Rieser, H., 1976. 'Sprachwissenschaft und Rechtstheorie', in D. Grimm (ed.), *Rechtswissenschaft und Nachbarwissenschaften,* vol. 2, München, pp. 117–142.
Savigny, F.C. von, 1840. *System des heutigen römischen Rechts*, vol. 1, Berlin, pp. 206–221.
Wieacker, F., 1967. *Privatrechtsgeschichte der Neuzeit unter besonderer Berücksichtigung der deutschen Entwicklung,* Göttingen, p. 188.

Faculty of Law
University of Tübingen
Germany

ZENON BANKOWSKI

ANALOGICAL REASONING AND LEGAL INSTITUTIONS

I start by looking at what is involved in moving from a snail in a ginger beer bottle, through sulphites in underpants and antimony sulphide in manganese, to a lift in a shaft. Lawyers from the Anglo-Saxon jurisdictions will recognise these facts as coming from cases in the law of delict or tort and they will recognise that I am starting with the famous case of *Donoghue v. Stevenson*. Here it was held that Mrs Donoghue, who was made ill by starting to drink, in a café, a bottle of ginger beer in which she claimed there had been a decomposing snail, had a remedy in negligence against the manufacturer with whom she had no contractual relation. Lord Atkin said:

> A manufacturer of products, which he sells in such a form as to show that he intends them to reach the ultimate consumer in the form in which they left him with no reasonable possibility of intermediate examination, and with the knowledge that the absence of reasonable care in the preparation of putting up the products will result in an injury to the consumer's life or property, owes a duty of care to the consumer to take reasonable care. ([1932] A.C. at 599)

The next situation concerns an Australian doctor who bought some underpants in which the manufacturer had negligently left iron sulphites during the washing process. Grant bought them and contracted dermatitis from which he was severely ill. He sued the manufacturer.

> If the foregoing are the essential features of Donoghue's case they are also to be found, in their Lordships judgement, in the present case. The presence of the deleterious chemical in the pants, due to negligence in manufacture, was a hidden and latent defect, just as much as the remains of the snail in the opaque bottle: it could not be detected by any examination that could reasonably be made.....It was argued, but perhaps not very strongly, that Donoghue's case was a case of food or drink to be consumed internally whereas the pants were to be worn externally. No distinction, however, can be logically drawn for this purpose between a noxious thing taken internally and a noxious thing applied externally. (Lord Wright in *Grant v. Australian Knitting Mills* [1936] A.C. 35)

The third case, *Kubach v. Holland* [1937] 3 All E.R. 907 is rather more complicated. Here a school teacher bought from the second defendant some manganese dioxide which was in fact that and a quantity of antimony sulphide. This had in turn been bought from a third party but the invoice stated that the goods 'must be examined and tested by user before use'. This was not told to the teacher and neither he nor the second defendant did so. There was an explosion in the class. In an action by a schoolgirl injured in

Z. Bankowski et al. (eds.), *Informatics and the Foundations of Legal Reasoning*, 177–190.

the blast the second defendant was held liable but the original manufacturer was judged not liable. Lord Hewart CJ, having discussed Donoghue, said:

The case which is there contemplated is, I think, in essential respects the opposite of the present case. The manganese dioxide which the third party ought to have supplied here to the second defendants might have been sold for a variety of purposes....It was common ground that a very simple test, if it had been carried out, as the third party's invoice prescribed, and as the first defendant was not warned, would immediately have exhibited the fact that antimony sulphide had erroneously been made up and delivered as manganese dioxide.

In *Haseldine v. Daw and Son Ltd.* [1941] 3 All E.R. 156. Haseldine was injured by a lift in a block of flats. This had just been serviced by a company, A.& P. Steven Ltd., who had a contract to service the lift and report any problems to the owners of the block of flats. This they did negligently and did not give a report to the owners. Goddard L.J. said

If there was any doubt about the governing principle of *M'Alister (or Donoghue) v. Stevenson*, Lord Wright has dissipated it. The manufacturer was held liable not because he was interested in his product being used as it left the factory but because he had no reason to contemplate an examination by the retailer or ultimate user before use. On what sound principle then, can the case of a repairer be distinguished from that of the maker of an article? Of course, the doctrine does not apply to the repairer of any article any more than to its manufacture. If I order my tailor to make me a suit, or a watchmaker to repair my watch, no one would suppose that anyone but myself was going to use the suit or watch. If the tailor left a large needle in the lining, and it injured a person to whom at some time I lent the coat, I should think that the latter could not recover against the tailor. The relationship would be altogether too remote...The case of a lift repairer, however, is very different. A lift in a block of flats is there to be used by the owner and his servants, the tenants and their servants, and all persons resorting thereto on lawful business. Blocks of flats and offices are frequently owned by limited companies, who would be contracting parties with the lift engineers. In a such a case, the employer would be the one 'person' who could by no possibility use the lift. If the repairers do their work carelessly or fail to report a damage of which, as experts, they ought to be aware, I cannot see why the principle of *M'Alister (or Donoghue)* should not apply to them.

Looking at these cases and the reasoning that is employed in them we can see that the analogical reasoning used in the law seems to be a version of the reasoning by analogy that we use in our everyday lives. What we require is a first of all a base line or point from which we can start and by reference to which we can compare and contrast any particular problem case or situation. In this instance we can see that the base point here is a 'manufacturer of products, which he sells in such a form as to show that he intends them to reach the ultimate consumer in the form in which they left him with no reasonable possibility of intermediate examination'. We can see constant reference to it in the other cases and it is their implicit similarity or dissimilarity to that case that is important. Thus the 'deleterious chemical in pants, due to negligence in manufacture, was a hidden and latent defect just as much as the remains of the snail in the opaque bottle'; in *Donoghue* it was a 'case of food and drink to be consumed internally whereas the pants were to be worn externally'. In *Haseldine* it was a repairer rather than a manufacturer. In *Kubach* there was a possibility of examination which was not afforded in the other cases. But it is not just a retelling of the similarities and dissimilarities of the factual circumstances that are important but also a judgement of which factual similarities are important and which factual dissimilarities are to be ignored. Thus 'on what sound principle can the case of a repairer be distinguished from that of a manufacturer?' and no distinction can be drawn between 'a noxious thing taken internally and a noxious thing applied externally'. The fact that a schoolgirl was injured by a latent defect in a good supplied by a manufacturer was not the same because there was, between the manufacturer and schoolgirl, as it were, the possibility of the very examination which the manufacturer advised.

So we look for a base point, one where the correctness of a decision can be established, and then look to the similarities and differences with other cases. At this stage a decision is made depending upon the importance and relevance that we ascribe to the differences and similarities. How is this to be selected? If we look at common law systems at least, one can see that the doctrine of precedent or *stare decisis* provides the institutional setting for analogical reasoning. In the idea that courts should follow past relevant decisions of appropriate courts in the hierarchy, we not only get the keystone of analogical reasoning —like should be treated alike— but also a natural base point, that previous decisions of an appropriate court in the hierarchy are to be taken as authoritative, i.e. is correct. This might be called the system's central idea of justice, if not a central idea of justice in general. But all this still rests on whether we can give some content to this way of looking at things. As Hart (1961) says,

> 'Treat like cases alike and different cases differently' is a central element in the idea of justice, it is by itself incomplete and until supplemented, cannot afford any determinate guide to conduct ....[U]ntil it is established what resemblances and differences are relevant, 'Treat like cases alike' must remain an empty form. To fill it we must know when, for the purposes in hand, cases are regarded as alike and what differences are relevant. (p. 155)

We can give a more formal account of the type of reasoning involved here thus. The base case has facts Á, Ã, S, as does the problem case. We can therefore make the decision because there is a rule that says, 'whenever facts Á, Ã, S, decide X'. But there is a problem here for it depends upon the assumption that all cases that are alike have facts in common and that these correspond to legal rules. If we take the examples with which I began my paper, then we can see that on one view of it the cases do not really have that many facts in common at all. Thus the snail in the ginger beer bottle which features in our base line case does not appear in any of the other cases; lifts and underpants also seem unique to their particular cases. Chemicals appear in at least two of the cases but they do not correspond to any legal rule. This would seem to imply the unique particularity of each case. But we did, in our discussion, see other facts that were in common. Thus there were latent defects, articles bought by third parties and this can correspond, with same emendations to a legal rule of the type formulated in *Donoghue v. Stevenson.*

A manufacturer of products, which he sells in such a form as to show that he intends them to reach the ultimate consumer in the form in which they left him with no reasonable possibility of intermediate examination, and with the knowledge that the absence of reasonable care in the preparation of putting up the products will result in an injury to the consumer's life or property, owes a duty of care to the consumer to take reasonable care. ([1932] A.C. at 59)

But this leaves us with some problems. First of all it seems to imply the unique particularity of every case which would make analogy impossible. We can make these facts more abstract and thus more general, an 'ultimate consumer' instead of an 'a lady of a certain age', a 'manufacturer' instead of a ginger beer maker. But in doing this we are having regard 'for the purposes in hand' what cases are to be seen as similar and what different. This implies that these fact categories do not correspond to legal rules but that they are constituted by them. It is the universal rule that is important and not the actual facts of the case. Thus we talk of the 'facts' of *Donoghue v. Stevenson* but we almost always use the principle that I have quoted above and indeed used as at least part of the 'facts' of the case. But if this is the case then we do not really need the facts of the case at all and we can dispense with analogies and work with the rule in deductive form. Thus the examples of analogical reasoning that I shown above are merely deductions from the original rule set out in *Donoghue*.

This does not capture the flavour of reasoning in the common law. There certainly is deduction, but the case by case method does seem somewhat different from that and particular facts of particular cases are important. As Detmold (1984) says, (p. 179):

The first function of a judicial precedent is to stand as an example. The example is the decision of the case and the particulars on which it is based. There is a temptation to think that one reads a law report merely to learn of the (universal) properties and relations that obtained in the facts of the case with a view to constructing an appropriate norm; that one's interest in and knowledge of the particulars is irrelevant. But this is a mistake. One can know particulars as well by reading as by seeing, touching and hearing .....And since it is particulars that give the intrinsically practical response which constitutes reasons, it is to the particulars of the precedent that I must attend if I am to learn the practical business of judging hard cases....The weight of reasons is unstatable. If I am to learn how to weigh reasons in law cases it can only be from the example of precedent cases. Thus does institutional history educate.

Detmold puts an extreme form of this view of particularity, holding that it is the facts of a practical case and nothing else that gives me a reason for deciding it one way or another. But, he goes on to say, the weighing of particular facts implies comparison and, though they are unique, the weighing can only be done by virtue of their attached universals. We weigh particulars with certain universals 'particularily attached'. Thus, even for Detmold, what is important in common law reasoning are both facts and universals and it is to the relationship between 'institutional history educating us' and rules that we must look to get some answer to the problem. Here we can see the general problem of the universal and the particular, how far does our reasoning depend upon the unique individual case and how far does it depend upon general and universal rules or principles drawn therefrom and the relation between these. This is often expressed in terms of the conflict between substantive and legal justice but I want to put it in this more abstract way because, as I will point out at the end of my paper, it is the relationship of the universal and particular that is the key question not just in legal reasoning but in political and social arrangements in general.

Golding (1984) puts forward a more complex formalisation which might be able to encompass both the particular facts and the universal rules. He suggests that analogical reasoning might be reconstructed as follows:

1. X has characteristics Á, Ã;
2. Y has characteristics Á, Ã;
3. X has characteristic S;
4. Á, Ã are S-relevant characteristics;
5. Unless there are countervailing characteristics Y has S;
6. There are no countervailing characteristics;
7. Y has S.

Let us see how Golding's formalisation would work with our examples:

1. A provider of ginger beer is one who produces a product which is intended (i) to reach the ultimate consumer (ii) in such a form as to leave him with no reasonable possibility of intermediate examination.
2. A provider of a lift is one who produces a product which is intended (i) to reach the ultimate consumer (ii) in such a form as to leave him with no reasonable possibility of intermediate examination.
3. A provider of ginger beer is one who (iii) owes a duty of reasonable care to that consumer notwithstanding the lack of contractual relationship.
4. Being the provider of a product which is one which (i) is intended to reach the ultimate consumer (ii) in such a form as to leave him with no reasonable possibility of intermediate examination is relevant to (iii) owing a duty of reasonable care to that consumer notwithstanding the lack of contractual relationship.

5. Unless there are other countervailing characteristics the provider of a lift is one who (iii) owes a duty of reasonable care to that consumer notwithstanding the lack of contractual relationship.

6. There are no countervailing characteristics.

7. The provider of a lift is one who (iii) owes a duty of reasonable care to that consumer notwithstanding the lack of contractual relationship.

8. A. & P. Steven Ltd is the provider of a lift.

9. A. & P. Steven Ltd owes a duty of care notwithstanding the lack of contractual relationship.

The above can be taken as describing how *Haseldine v. Daw* was decided by analogy with *Donoghue v. Stevenson*. Let us now look at same of the ways that we might want to challenge the result. It was argued in that case that

6. There was a countervailing characteristic here in that A. & P. Steven Ltd was a repairer.

How does one argue for this? We can see this by looking at how the argument was defeated in this case. It was rejected in effect by another argument from analogy which said that though the first two premises should read

1. A provider of ginger beer is one who produces a product (O) of which he is the manufacturer and which is intended (i) to reach the ultimate consumer (ii) in such a form as to leave him with no reasonable possibility of intermediate examination.

2. A provider of lift is one who produces a product (OO) of which he is the repairer and which is intended (i) to reach the ultimate consumer (ii) in such a form as to leave him with no reasonable possibility of intermediate examination.

We can say that characteristic OO is not a countervailing characteristic because it is analogous to characteristic O. Thus the distinction between a repairer and a manufacturer is not a relevant distinction for the purposes of owing a duty of care. And we can show this by another argument from analogy which enumerates characteristics of a manufacturer and repairer.

But other forms of reasoning came into play also. Thus premise 3 was a problem when *Donoghue* was first of all being decided: was a provider of ginger beer one who owes a duty of reasonable care to that consumer notwithstanding the lack of contractual relationship? Now this might be solved by other forms of legal reasoning, such as reasoning from principles, consequences and rules. What is important here is whether the analogy is relevant or not. We might argue that being the provider of a product which is one which (i) is intended to reach the ultimate consumer (ii) in such a form as to leave him with no reasonable possibility of intermediate examination is *not* relevant to (iii) owing a duty of reasonable care to that consumer notwithstanding the lack of contractual relationship.

Here is the key point in the argument, for it is here that we must decide whether to apply the analogy or not. The way we do this, it is argued, is by claiming that we apply the analogy if the consequences are good or if it instantiates a good principle etc. But this would have the effect, as we noted above, of dispensing with the analogy altogether and working from the consequences of the particular situation or the principles involved. This is not the case for the following reasons. Firstly, when arguing as to the relevance of an analogy what we are often saying is that the analogy is not perfect and that the resemblance, if we look deeper, is not really there. Thus when we looked at the provider of ginger beer and the 'provider' of a lift we saw that there was an argument that claimed that this was a superficial resemblance and that if we looked deeper we could see that this was not the case because one was a 'repairer' and the other a manufacturer'. In that case the argument did not work. However we can see haw the form of the argument here is still one of analogy by way of refining a seeming 'brute fact' into more characteristics to see whether there really is a resemblance. What is at stake here is the bruteness of the particular fact or situation. If we do not find it brute enough then we can 'split the atom' and get down to characteristics where we do or do not see analogy and similarity. This is not merely a sort of inductive exercise, enumerating more and more characteristics in order to get a true resemblance, rather it is the quality of the resemblance that we are looking for. Obviously, at all these levels, differing forms of reasoning take place. So our unhappiness at a certain level of 'bruteness' can stem from our views of the relevant rules of law or consequentialist or principled reasoning. But this does not displace analogical reasoning for it is quite often a way of showing a deeper resemblance. And so analogical reasoning is not displaced by the other forms of reasoning but rather they co-exist in an interlocking mixture. To the claim that the principle has priority over the analogy we may say that if you do not know how to answer the particular case you will not know the principle. Consequentialist reasoning, as put forward by MacCormick, claims, *inter alia*, that sometimes in a hard case you find your answer by looking to the consequences or implications of the instant case and then answering a hypothetical case based upon it. It has been argued that if you can do that then why bother with the hypothetical case. The hypothetical case is important—because we know the answer, for whatever reason, to that and from there we can work back by analogy. However, does this not appear like our earlier formalisation of the analogical argument namely; the base case has facts Á, Ã, S, as does the problem case therefore make the decision because there is a rule that says, 'whenever facts Á, Ã, S, decide X'? And if this is the case it follows that we fall into the analogous trap of not needing the analogy since we can work deductively from the rule. Again this is not really the case for it is the analogy that gives us the answer and the rule or principle that enables us to make sense of the analogy. Perhaps the rule or principle will enable us to go on to construct other analogies but only in so far as we do not find an analogy that will alter that rule or principle. Rather like the series 2, 4, 6, 8, 10 where we know that the principle is +2 until we find that the next number is 14. At the base of this form of legal reasoning then is the single instance, the legal analogy, even though it functions within an interlocking network of reasons, principles and rules. This view of it seems to me to fit the institutional framework and tradition of the common law with its insistence on arguing through the cases and *stare decisis*. But if somewhere at the bottom of all this is the single instance, the analogy, and this depends, as we saw, upon the quality of the resemblance, then how are we to judge that quality? Though we are in a network of interlocking reasons and principles which all help to create the notion of 'sameness', at the bottom of all of this there is still same characteristic which we say is just the 'same' as another. How do we know this? Hume thinks that the argument by analogy and therefore precedent works through the faculty of imagination. There is no matter of fact outside of the practice of legal reasoning and the body of the law that enables us to say that the one case is like the other. For Hume, what allows us to make these judgements is not what he would call reason but rather the faculty of the imagination. This is not to be seen as merely a 'brute fact' about human psychology but rather same social fact about humans or a society in general (see Postema 1987). What this means is that imagination is something that can only work within the context of a social practice. Thus the judgments of analogy are not idiosyncratic and objective for they take place with a strategic social context. Thus we may say, by analogy from Wittgenstein, that there is no private reference to the idea of 'sameness, nothing that is our own to which no one else has logical access to. 'Same' is a public concept which makes sense only within the context of a particular language and form of life. Thus we do not understand the 'same' by adding any new facts but, by looking at it from within a context and tradition, we make valid and rational choices (See Kripke 1982). It is within the context of this legal tradition then, with its interlocking network of principles, rules etc. that we find the conditions for making valid assertions of analogy and disanalogy. Analogy is at base a social concept.

What is the 'tradition' or context wherein the analogy that I am talking about finds its social base? Martin Krygier (Krygier 1986) has a useful analysis of what 'tradition' might mean here. He claims that traditions have three main elements which are pastness, authoritative presence, and an element of social transmission. What do these mean?

(i) *Pastness* — A tradition sees the past as important for every tradition is made up of elements from the real or imagined past. You cannot start a tradition intentionally *de novo* What is important here is the institutionalisation of past maintenance; the legal past is made important to the legal present by the practices, *inter alia*, of recording certain writings, giving authoritative status to some, ranking them in ways that can be understood by initiates but might seem mystical to the 'rational' outsider etc. This gives the legal past power in the legal present. Arguments are expected to be justified in terms of past traditions and arguments. But that is not to say, however, that the past becomes a dead hand upon the present for it is a matter of interpretation of the past and, as the hermeneutic tradition shows us, that is not fixed. What is important is justifying a present decision by emphasising and showing its continuity with the past.

(ii) *Authoritative presence* — This follows on from the above point. The past is not simply part of the law's history, rather it is a recognised part of its present. Douglas Hay (1984) argues that 'thinking like a lawyer' involves what historians might call 'presentism', —'the fallacy of working from present concerns to past origins is anathema to historians, but necessarily half the lawyer's method'. As Maitland said 'What is required of the practising lawyer is not, save in the rarest cases, a knowledge of medieval law, but rather a knowledge of medieval law as interpreted by modern courts to suit modern facts' (Fisher p.491). In other words, for the lawyer, as opposed to the historian, Whig history is something to be welcomed. The legal history of a particular doctrine or principle as it is excavated by the practising lawyer is something different as looked at by a historian. The former is a participant in the tradition the latter need not be and, insofar as he is a historian, will not be. But one can go further than this and say that an analogous thing can be said about the future. For analogy often works not only by looking at past analogies, authoritative or otherwise, but by constructing possible future ones which might also help in testing possible answers to the problem case. Thus in *Maclennan v. Maclennan* 1958 S.C. 105 where the question was could the husband be granted a divorce on the grounds of his wife's adultery, the adultery consisting in her having artificial insemination by donor (AID) without his consent. Here, it was held that this did not constitute adultery on the grounds, *inter alia*, that if it was held that it could they might be forced, in a future case, to hold that a dead person could commit adultery. What happens here is that, as it were, a future hypothetical precedent is created in order to show the validity or otherwise of the present decision. Precedent, and therefore analogy, can thus work backwards as well as forwards. The difference is one of weight or, as Dworkin (1986) says, gravitational force. The past has more than the future. But what is important to note here is how the future cooperates with the past in solving the problems of the present. The future is just as much the future in the present as the past is the past in the present.

(iii) *Transmission* — There need also to be means of transmitting the past over the generations. This means that tradition is a social thing, not something for individuals alone. The means of transmission and those entrusted with it will play a crucial part in determining the form of that tradition. Tradition where the transmission is entrusted to a caste of experts will be different from those where it is entrusted to a single sacred book available to all. One has only to contrast the Roman Catholic church with its emphasis on the 'teaching authority of the church', i.e. the hierarchy, and the Protestant tradition with its emphasis on the sole authority of the Bible. Why have tradition and why have a legal tradition? One answer is that we cannot start afresh each time. As Karl Popper said when speaking of science, 'If we start afresh, then, when we die, we shall be about as far as Adam and Eve were when they died (or, if you prefer, as far as Neanderthal Man)' (1969 p.126). We cannot operate in a vacuum. We cannot, as revolutions often have, start from a 'year one' and create a totally new society without reference at all to the old. We cannot effect even more minor social reforms *de novo* ignoring the social and economic context that the solution has to be placed in. moral philosophy and economic theory can never be determinate enough to give answers to all the problems that lawyers must solve. They must go back to tradition.

> So what is it that lawyers know that philosophers and economists do not? The answer is simple: the law. There really is a distinct and special subject matter for our profession. And there is a distinct method... It is the method of analogy and precedent... The discipline of analogy fills in the gaps left by more general theory, gaps which must be filled because choices must be made and action taken. (Fried 1982, p.57)

This is also supported by many views of legal reasoning that ultimately base the acceptability and rationality of legal reasoning on the fact that it takes place within a particular audience or group and it is only because of the cohesiveness of the groups that choices which might seem arbitrary do not become so. Thus John Bell (1986) shows how the constraints within which legal reasoning operates are defined not merely by the logical structure of the logical procedures adopted for performing the task but also by the socially developed criteria of what is acceptable. Canons of acceptable argument embrace both rules defining the logical character of legal discourse and standards of acceptability developed by the principal group within the audience to which reasons are addressed. Rationality, predictability and accountability work within this mode. Thus there is an interlocking network of reasons, principles, rules, standards, analogies which go to make up the tradition and quite often the process of justifying a decision at law will be a mixture of articulated and unarticulated arguments and assumptions which constitute the tradition and thus give coherence and rationality to it. Here is also where legal scientists can play an important part for they can make clear the interrelations and coherences in the tradition which the practitioners might just know. It is this knowing how of the practitioner which comes through socialisation, a knowledge of the correct answer without necessarily being well versed in the structure of the argument, which is often evidence of a tradition. Their work in doing this adds to and affects the tradition. But one must be careful not to assume that it is these principles of coherence etc. that give the theory of the tradition. They are rather part of the form of life of that tradition, instantiating and presupposing the moral values of that form. As Nigel Simmonds puts it:

> Legal and political theories are not descriptions of brute fact. Nor are they merely postulated ideals or aspirations. Theories reflect and are reflected in our social relationships. And the historical development of our social life is itself a part of the intellectual evolution of our ideas. ... And if understanding a moral or political concept is a matter of understanding the 'form of life' to which it belongs, an articulation of this or that conception may well require attention to its history. Moral and political values thus cannot and should not be discussed in isolation from the institutions and social c histories that shape them. (Simmonds, 1984 p.13)

We have so far seen how analogical reasoning works in the context of a tradition, which is to say an institution held together by history and argument and their dialectical interplay. Thus the law can only develop within the context of its own tradition. There is no reference outside of the tradition. It is in this way that the version of the 'right answer thesis' used by Dworkin in *Law's Empire* can be understood. Dworkin there claims that the right answer is one that is acceptable within the tradition, it makes no sense to ask whether this answer is *really* right. But this seems to lessen the scope for the innovative effect of analogical reasoning within the law since, for any analogy properly to work it must be subsumed within the tradition of the law. So we cannot learn anything new by analogy for the similarity always exists within the tradition and we find that we knew it all along. We cannot make great leaps of the imagination. At the base of the system of reasoning I have been describing lies the ineffable, the creative leap of the imagination 'This is like *that*'. But this is domesticated within the tradition or discourse and so loses its capacity to surprise, radically to change direction, to transcend. One can see examples of this in the law where parables are used as analogies by the judges and transform the fierce messages they contain into doctrines of the common law. Thus the parable of the good Samaritan in *Donoghue*.

> The rule that you are to love your neighbour becomes in law: You must not injure your neighbour, and the lawyer's question: Who is my neighbour? receives a restricted reply. You must take reasonable care to avoid acts or omissions which you can reasonably foresee would be likely to injure your neighbour. Who then, in law, is my neighbour? The answer seems to me to be persons who are so closely and directly affected by my act that I ought reasonably to have them in contemplation as being so affected when I am directing my mind to the acts or omissions which are called in question. This appears to me to be the doctrine in *Heaven v. Pender* as laid dawn by Lord Esher.

Commenting on this dictum in *Home Office v. Dorset Yacht Company* [1970] 2 All ER at 310 Viscount Dilhorne said,

> Lord Atkin's answer to the question 'Who, then, in law is my neighbour? while very relevant to determine to whom a duty of care is owed, cannot determine, in my opinion, the question whether a duty of care exists.

Or as Lord Diplock said in the same case,

> The very parable of the good Samaritan which was evoked by Lord Atkin in *Donoghue v. Stevenson* illustrates, in the conduct of the priest and of the Levite who passed by on the other side, an omission which was likely to have as its reasonable and probable consequence damage to the health of the victim of the thieves, but for which the priest and the Levite would have incurred no civil liability in English law. Examples could be multiplied... one need not warn him of a risk of physical danger to which he is about to expose himself unless there is some special relationship between one and him such as that of occupier of land and visitor; one may watch one's neighbours goods being ruined by a thunderstorm although the slightest effort one one's part could protect them from the rain and one may do so with impunity unless there is some relationship between one and him such as that of bailor and bailee. (p.326)

In the case of *Race Relations Board v. Charter* [1972] 1 All ER 556, an Indian who was an active Conservative and member of the local association applied for membership of the local conservative club and was turned down by reason of his colour. It was held that club was concerned with providing facilities to a section of the public since the members of the club were themselves constituted a section of the public since they were not numerically negligible and the quality that distinguished them from the public at large, that they were conservatives, was essentially impersonal. This being so discrimination contrary to the Race Relations Act had occurred. The question in this case was whether the East Ham Conservative Club was a genuine private club, thus not 'providing facilities to a section of the public' and thus in the position of a private householder. The parable of the guests at the wedding feast is used as an analogy to help us understand what 'public' means.

The guests bidden to supper in the parable did not seek to obtain or use their hosts food and drink, still less did those who on his instructions were compelled to come in from the highways and hedges. Even if those who came in at his first invitation or later under that compulsion were the public or a section of the public....they were not seeking but sought. That is one reason why a private householder may still lawfully turn a person from his house on grounds of race or colour or national or ethnic origins. (per Stephenson LJ 565).

We do not see the Kingdom of Heaven here, rather a careful discussion of the what counts as our private lives for the purposes of the Race Relations Act. A parable of openness becomes an analogy of closure. This is not to say that within the tradition analogy does not produce rich and new solutions. But the solution we get to is one which in a sense we already knew. For the tradition can be viewed as timeless in the sense that past present and future are all involved in different ways and with different weights in any decision and so the decision is always already there. It is this, rather than a natural law theory, that, it seems to me, is implied when it is claimed Dworkin assumes that law is 'discovered'.

What we have been looking at up till now is how analogy works as a mode of reasoning employed by judges and how, ultimately, it cannot tell us anything new because it is always locked into a discourse and a tradition. In this ending however, further questions are inevitably raised. Surely traditions develop and change beyond all recognition? Cannot we see this in history? Are there forms of reasoning based on analogy, employing perhaps allegory or metaphor, that enable us to move beyond a tradition and to import and export ideas between traditions? Are there institutions that serve as bridges to other traditions or that can be seen as windows from the one into the other? Or is it the case that we are all immutably locked into our traditions and discourses with no real way out? I finish then, with a quotation from Kafka who raises, appropriately enough, these questions in a metaphorical and allegorical way (Kafka, 1946):

Many people complain that the words of the wise men are always only parables but cannot be used in daily life, and this after all is all we have. When the wise man says: Go over', he does not mean that we should go over to the other side, which we could do if it were worth it. He means same mythical Beyond, something that we do not know and that he cannot describe in any more detail and that cannot help us here. All these parables really say is that what cannot be grasped cannot be grasped and we knew that anyway. The things that concern us in our daily lives are different.

One man said: What's stopping you? If you were to follow the parables you would became parables yourselves and thus be freed from the troubles of daily life.

The second said: 'I bet that that's a parable too.'

The first said: 'You won!'

The second said: 'But unfortunately only in the parable.'

The first said: 'No, in reality: you lost in the parable.'

REFERENCES

Bell, J. 1986. 'The Acceptability of Legal Argument' in *The Legal Mind,* (eds) MacCormick, D.N., and Birks, P., Oxford University Press, Oxford; pp. 44–65.

Detmold, M.J., 1984. *The Unity of Law and Morality,* Routledge and Kegan Paul, London.

Dworkin, R., 1986. *Law's Empire*, Fontana, London.

Fisher, H. (ed) *The Collected Papers of Frederic William Maitland,* Cambridge University Press, Cambridge.

Fried C, 1982. 'The Artificial Reason of the Law, or: What Lawyers Know', in *Texas Law Review* 60, 1982 pp. 35–58.

Golding, M., 1984. *Legal Reasoning*, Borzoi Books, New York.

Hart, H. L. A., 1961. *The Concept of Law*, The Clarendon Press, Oxford.

Hay, D., 1984. 'The Criminal Prosecution in England and its Historians', *Modern Law Review* 1984 pp. 1–29

Kafka, F., 1946. 'Von den Gleichnissen' in Brod, M. (ed), *Beschreibung eines Kampfes, Novellen, Skizzen, Aphorismen aus dem Nachlaß* , Fischer Verlag, Frankfurt am Main.

Kripke, S., 1982. *Wittgenstein on Rules and Private Language*, Blackwell, Oxford

Krygier, M., 1986. 'Law as Tradition', in *Journal of Law and Philosophy,* 1986, pp. 237-262.

Popper, K., 1969. 'Towards a Rational Theory of Tradition' in *Conjectures and Refutations*, Routledge and Kegan Paul, London

Postema, G., 1987. 'The Roots of Our Notion of Precedent' in Goldstein, L. (ed) *Precedent in Law* , Clarendon Press, Oxford.

Simmonds, N., 1984. *The Decline of Juridical Reason,* Manchester University Press, Manchester.

Faculty of Law
University of Edinburgh
Scotland

S.C. SMITH

THE REDUNDANCY OF REASONING

It is often complained that legal reasoning occupies a more or less redundant position within systems-theoretical accounts of law. This is a position I have little trouble with. Indeed, in this paper I argue that the distance systems theory takes to justification within the legal system should be considered one of its most attractive features. A central distinction is made between the decisions or primary operations of the legal system which change its state, and observations (primarily those used in legal reasoning) which are directed at changing its state. From here, systems theory reverses the usual order of things. Rather than decisions being explained in terms of observations, which is central to the whole method of persuasion in reasoning, systems theory attempts to explain legal reasoning in relation to the process of decision-making within the legal system.

I first of all try to reconstruct the common law as a recursively closed network of decision-making. This is seen as a circular, symmetrical, and indeed paradoxical process. Legal reasoning is then explained as the attempt to render this symmetry asymmetrical, to 'deparadoxify' (to use an ugly word) the paradox. This can be done in (at least) two ways. The first is to build redundancies (this time in its information-theoretical sense) or a memory within the system to which the operations of the system can then become oriented. The second is to externalise the paradox by reference to values. Systems theory is then in a position to distinguish these as cases of internal and external reference. They can also be explained in functional terms as attempts to deflate and inflate the symbolic medium of the legal system. If it has a preference at all, it would be to support the deflation of the legal system. But again, this follows from the attempt to see legal reasoning within the context of the legal system as a whole, where it is seen as compensating for the inflationary pressures caused, e.g., by legislation.

Finally, we should ask what it is that gives rise to the redundancy complaint. I argue that it is a misplaced hope in the rôle of legal reasoning in legitimating the legal system beyond the legal system to society as a whole. Once again, I take sides with systems theory. Legitimation, both factually and normatively, is better seen as a product of the differentiation of the legal system as a system of positive law within a functionally differentiated society. In short, we can and do tolerate bad law now because we can make it better law in the future.

Z. Bankowski et al. (eds.), Informatics and the Foundations of Legal Reasoning, 191–204.

1. LEVI'S ACCOUNT OF LAW

There can be few better accounts of law from a systems theoretical perspective than E. H. Levi's 'An Introduction to Legal Reasoning' (Levi, 1948). That it is not also written in the language of systems theory is scarcely relevant. It begins with the early history of the common law in the United States of America, and describes its gradual transformation in a period of increased travel and trade. What is important is the mechanism of this transformation. Levi traces the expansion of *danger* as a legal category, the increasing penetration of risk consciousness, and the circulation of such ideas in and out of the legal system. But what makes this happen is law as process, as demonstrated by the common law's seemingly infinite capacity to reproduce itself —the iterative generation of cases out of cases. When it is said that the legal system is closed, nothing more is meant than that each new decision must have a footing in prior decisions of the system. And far from being eclipsed by the greater use of statute law, case law becomes an indispensable partner in the allocation of jurisdictions and of liabilities. In short, it is an attempt to locate the position of law, and in particular the common law, in the transition to modernity.

2. DISTINCTIONS

The subtlety with which lawyers are able to draw distinctions between cases has, by now, passed into the folklore of the common law. However, it must be doubtful whether from that position we can win a good understanding of how distinctions work. The mechanisms of legal reasoning, Levi warns, 'should not be concealed by their pretence' (*op. cit.*, p. 501). And this pretence is built into the presuppositions of lawyering, the commitment to providing reasons, or at least criteria for what are to count as good reasons, and the representation of such reasons as being authorised by particular texts. Rather, Levi goes behind this pretence to try and uncover the 'lower level' (*op. cit.*, p. 507) operations of the common law process itself. Working with an evolutionary perspective, he stresses the contingency of change, how the legal system fumbles its way in an environment which is in principle inaccessible to it and can only be reconstructed using its own categories, its own distinctions. Using distinctions, the legal system can break up the 'seamless web' of decisions based on decisions, construct lines of argument, trends and patterns of development. Distinctions are the tool with which the common law observes everything, including itself. Levi's analysis is shown to best effect in his discussion of the distinction between things that are dangerous and those that are not dangerous, its pathology in early nineteenth century English law and the later common law of the United States. But it is just here that we find the core problem of legal reasoning. How can the common law observe itself? How can it introduce distinctions into a system which 'has no beginning and no end'? How can it gain a footing in the common law at all, unless paradoxically as a distinction which is somehow not a distinction. The answer George Spencer Brown gives in his book *Laws of Form* (Spencer Brown 1969) is that a system can only start in a more or less arbitrary fashion. Hence, the command with which his calculus opens —'Draw a distinction!'

Let us begin with Levi and the case of *Dixon v. Bell.*[1] The plaintiff's son suffered severe facial injuries when a loaded gun exploded in his face. The defendant's thirteen or fourteen year-old servant had been playing with the gun during the course of fetching it for her master. Now this case, as we shall see, was later taken to be the precedent or leading case controlling liability for dangerous articles. But however this may be in retrospect, it cannot have been so at the time the decision was made. This is the paradox with which Spencer Brown's *Laws of Form* is concerned. *Dixon v. Bell* may well have 'drawn a distinction' —that between things 'inherently' dangerous, and things which may become so as a result of some latent defect— but it could not have observed that distinction at the same time as having introduced it. As Levi says, 'Lord Ellenborough attempted no classification of dangerous articles. He was content to describe the gun "as by this want of care ... left in a state capable of doing mischief".' (*Op. cit.*, p. 508). In other words, he was content merely to indicate 'something mischievous through want of care'. I suppose he could have also taken time within the same case to indicate the precise distinction on which this finding was based. But such a procedure would have carried its own risks. In going beyond what is required for a decision, the judge assumes greater responsibility than he needs to and indeed than is perhaps appropriate. Indeed, the common law system itself has well-known safeguards against this. There is a limit to what cases can stand as authority for. And even if Lord Ellenborough had tried to go beyond this, it may well become interpreted as obiter in subsequent cases. However, having introduced the distinction, it now had to be abandoned to observation by other plaintiffs in other cases.

This happened in *Langridge v. Levy.*[2] Again, a loaded gun was involved. But this time one that was so badly made that it blew up in the hands of the plaintiff. Counsel for the defendant pointed to a distinction between things 'immediately dangerous or mischievous by the act of the defendant' and 'such as may become so by some further act to be done to it' (*op. cit.*, p. 508). However, the court rejected any such distinction (Lord Ellenborough's caution was hardly misplaced, then!), finding nevertheless for the plaintiff on other grounds —fraud (because the defendant knew the gun was defective), and a suggestion of direct dealing (because while not sold to the plaintiff he knew it was to be used by him). So the additional step of articulating the distinction was not necessary in order to decide the case. Although observed in argument, it has not yet acquired orientation value within the system.

Nor indeed was it of any use in *Winterbottom v. Wright.*[3] It is important to note here that, during this period when no distinction has yet been settled, the indication of 'things of a dangerous nature' is held fixed, while the other side of the distinction, the context in which the indication is made, is being changed. Winterbottom did not involve anything such as a loaded gun which might 'become dangerous' if a 'further act' such as playing with it or accidentally setting it off is done. This case involved a coachman suing the manufacturer of the coach for injuries suffered when he was thrown from his seat. The latent defect in the manufacturer of the coach required some distinction between 'things of a dangerous nature and those which might become so if improperly constructed', which as Levi is careful to tell us 'need not be the same as requiring a further act to be done to make it dangerous' (*op. cit.*, p. 509). So even this subtle shifting of the distinction is not yet enough to persuade the court to orient the operations of the legal system to it.

However, in *Longmeid v. Holliday*[4] the distinction between things in their nature dangerous and those which become so through some latent defect finally wins code value within the legal system. Patent dangers are illegal: they give rise to liability. Latent dangers are legal: they give rise to no liability. The one distinction is superimposed on the other. Or in the more precise language of Spencer Brown, the distinction between patent and latent dangers re-enters the legal system. It now has orientation value. It can be used to guide further operations of the system. Spencer Brown's concept of re-entry is introduced in order to deal with the paradox of observation which we began with. How can a system observe itself? All observation requires the use of a distinction. But which? A further distinction would be needed in order to answer this question —one which, obviously, is not yet available to us. Spencer Brown's suggestion is to postpone the paradox until the system has become more complex, otherwise the system could not even get started. So we 'draw a distinction'. And through repeated observations of the distinction it can, in time, acquire orientation value through re-entry. It is important to stress this word 'postpone'. Re-entry cannot 'solve' the paradox, it merely disguises it. The re-entered distinction is treated as the same as the distinction with which the system started —which it both is, and isn't! This should be clear from the discussion of the inherently dangerous/not inherently dangerous distinction. The concept of dangerous things is treated as fixed and unchanging. But as the discussion of *Winterbottom* showed, the context or precise nature of the distinction is constantly shifting. *Longmeid* involved a defective lamp, 'Holliday's Patent Lamp', which, while bearing the defendant's name, was in fact pieced together by others from parts he had purchased. The plaintiff was the wife of the purchaser and could not, therefore, sue on the contract. However, Holliday did not know of the defect and so there was no fraud such as had been established in *Langridge*. Since this was a latent defect, it was much more like the defective carriage in *Winterbottom* and the defendant escaped liability.

> And it may be the same when any one delivers to another without notice an instrument in its nature dangerous, ... as a loaded gun which he himself loaded, ... A very strong case to that effect is *Dixon v. Bell.* But it would be going much too far to say that so much care is required in the ordinary intercourse of life between one individual and another, that, if a machine not in itself dangerous —a carriage, for instance— but which might become so by a latent defect entirely unknown, although discoverable by the exercise of ordinary care, should be lent or given by one person. even by the person who manufactured it, to another, the former should be answerable to the latter for a subsequent damage accruing by the use of it. (*Op. cit.* p. 510, quoting Parke, B. @ 755)

That the court expressly relied on *Dixon v. Bell* makes it clear that it was the distinction as introduced in that case that is now being cited as authority. But the implicit reference to *Winterbottom* makes it equally clear that it is not the same distinction, but is the distinction 'as developed' in subsequent cases. And indeed this additional distinction (!) between explicit and implicit case reference tells us how to reconstruct the history of these cases. The 'authority' is *Dixon*. The 'development' is *Winterbottom*. The *Longmeid* case, therefore, represents the re-entry of the distinction between patent and latent dangers in the legal system.

The next phase can be described as one in which this distinction becomes condensed and confirmed during its application in United States law. Both operations are inextricably interwoven in reasoning by analogy. In condensation, 'different' cases are treated as identical. *Thomas v. Winchester*[5] involved a mislabelled poison. This was held to be sufficiently like the case of the loaded gun in *Dixon*. And being 'imminently dangerous', it was quite unlike the defective wagon in *Winterbottom*. A defective hair wash, too, came to be seen as immanently dangerous. But not a weak balance wheel for a circular saw. This was more like the case of the defective wagon.

Note that it is both sides of the distinction that are being condensed. The loaded gun serves as the type case for patent dangers —the defective wagon for latent dangers. Commenting on the inclusion of a defective scaffold in the imminently dangerous category, Levi comments that nevertheless 'the court followed tradition in announcing that a defective carriage would be out' (*op. cit.*, p. 512). As for confirmation, this is merely the reverse side of condensation. Not only are different cases treated as identical, but the same distinction gains in authority from its repeated application in different cases. It gets confirmed. As it moves from case to case, it gets applied in new contexts and acquires additional meaning. In calling an exploding coffee urn dangerous, a New York court took the trouble to try and account for this additional meaning. 'Given an "inherently dangerous" article, the court explained, a manufacturer becomes liable for negligent construction which, when added to its inherent characteristics, makes it "imminently dangerous".' (*Op. cit.*, p. 513) All clear? Even the confirmations, it seems, can get condensed. But this is not all. The final phase in the history of the dangerous things concept can be illustrated with Spencer Brown's notion of 'crossing'. In fact we have already witnessed several crossings in the second phase. Already, the re-entry of the distinction has rendered the initial paradox harmless. It has turned it into a contradiction. The two sides of the distinction are internally related as opposites. A single operation of negation is necessary in order to 'cross' from one side to the other. And in the drawing of distinctions, such crossings are being made routinely. The case is not like a defective wagon. Therefore, it must be more like the loaded gun! But all of this happens within a distinction to either side of which the assignation of code values legal and illegal has become relatively stabilised. What we are now faced with is a crossing of the code values themselves. In *MacPherson v. Buick*[6], what had been the exception was now the rule. Where the manufacturer had once not been liable unless it could be shown that the thing was imminently dangerous, he was now liable in principle unless he could show that there was no reasonable expectation of danger.

I think it is Levi who has identified what we can call, using the language of self-referential systems theory, 'recursivity', the repeated application of operations to the results of previous identical operations. (See Luhmann, 1990, p. 276). For Levi, the common law is a paradigmatic example of a 'moving classification system'. It is one where 'the classification changes as the classification is made'. As in all recursive systems, the operations —here, decisions— are applied to the results of previous operations. 'The rules change as the rules are applied.' (*Op. cit.*, p. 503.) Levi beautifully sums up this view of the common law process as follows:

> In the long run a circular motion can be seen. The first stage is the creation of the legal concept which is built up as cases are compared. The period is one in which the court fumbles for a phrase. Several phrases may be tried out; the misuse or misunderstanding of words itself may have an effect. The concept sounds like another, and the jump to the second is made. The second stage is the period when the concept is more or less fixed, although reasoning by example continues to classify items inside and outside the concept. The third stage is the breakdown of the concept, as reasoning by example has move so far ahead as to make it clear that the suggestive influence of the word is no longer desired. (*Op. cit.*, p. 506)

With this notion of 'jumping' from step to step, Levi is identifying the operative level of the system. But, as he goes on to say, this process is 'likely to make judges and lawyers feel uncomfortable'!

3. CONDENSATION AND CONFIRMATION IN A LEGAL SYSTEM

Why? Because it runs 'contrary to the pretence of the system'. Far from describing the contingency of the system, lawyers try to show how a decision is necessarily required by the strength of their reasoning. They do not display the system's hesitant, faltering steps, but construct unilinear 'trends' or 'patterns' of development. They give the system a history. It is precisely this which the operation of re-entry achieves in the legal system. It is one way of neutralising the paradox of the legal system.

We can see this in the way, for example, *Dixon v. Bell* is cited as authority in the *Longmeid* case. Suddenly, the distinction between dangerous and non-dangerous articles has a history, a pedigree. And the court is left with the difficult task of explaining away *Winterbottom*, a task which is helped by referring to it only indirectly. Similarly, in *MacPherson v. Buick*, Judge Cardozo is faced with the task of re-working the relevant historical boundaries. No longer is *Dixon v. Bell* the real ancestor of the distinction. Rather, 'the foundations of this branch of the law ... were laid in *Thomas v. Winchester*'. It was obviously thought necessary to provide a genuinely American authority for the distinction rather than an English one. But it is also because Judge Cardozo felt, in a case involving a defective motor car, that he had to distance himself from unhelpful authorities involving defective wagons. '[P]recedents drawn from the days of travel by stagecoach do not fit the conditions of travel today', he said. It is not just *Winterbottom* that is ruled out, then, but also the earlier case of *Dixon*. The history has to be re-written.

In order to see how this happens, we must take a closer look at condensation and confirmation in the common law. The key thing to note is that these are not separate operations but separate ways of looking at the same operation —they occur simultaneously. We have already discussed how, when an indication is made, it is not possible, simultaneously, to indicate the distinction with which it is made. And I argued that it followed from this that such distinctions can only be observed and handled within a system. Now I want to say that it is just because of this inability to indicate the operative distinction that it is left more or less unarticulated, as a context. When the indication gets repeated, then, it is not always possible to check that the context remains the same. Indeed, strictly speaking it will always be different. However, this difference, the confirmation, remains latent. Meanwhile, the condensation can become symbolised in maxims such as 'treat like cases alike'. What was once a paradox, is now a harmless tautology. A tautology, of course, which needs to be 'unfolded' through time, through building up chains of cases. This is redundancy in the sense given to it by information theory, that is, the attempt to reduce the element of surprise in the system. The redundancy of reasoning is the attempt to convince that a particular decision is compelled by the history of the system.

4. ANALOGICAL REASONING AND SYSTEMS THEORY

But for Levi, reasoning is redundant in a second, less technical sense. It can be mere 'window-dressing' (*op. cit.*, p. 507). It is so when it attempts to 'soar above the cases and to find some great overall rule which can classify the cases as though the pattern were really not a changing one' (*op. cit.*, p. 510). What is the difference between this and reasoning by analogy? In both cases, there is an attempt to represent a pattern of cases. But in reasoning by analogy, the reference is to the history of the system. It is a case of internal reference. With principles, there is a reference to some value or set of values. It is a case of external reference. From a systems theoretical perspective, both represent attempts to handle the constitutive paradox of the legal system.

But Levi wants to go further than this. He wants to be able to say that legal reasoning is really about reasoning by analogy. Analogical reasoning closely tracks the circular, adaptive mechanism of the common law described earlier. Levi's argument seems to be that references to principles or over-arching rules operate on a different level. Now what would it mean to say that they operate on a different level? One possibility is that they can only ever capture in a static form what is a dynamic process. Coming very much after the fact, the lower level operations of the system may already have moved on. 'Rationalisations are always post-rationalisations.' Levi suggests as much in his analysis of the dangerous things concept. Only during the period of consolidation and confirmation are there 'the inevitable attempts to soar above the cases' (*op. cit.*, p. 510). But at the same time, this period prepares the ground for the dramatic switching from a situation of no liability to one of liability for latent defects. This occurs in *Macpherson*, only one year after quite the opposite has been stated with equal certainty by the same Court of Appeals. Moreover, whether or not *Macpherson* brought the law into line with 'social considerations' as was often claimed, 'it did not', Levi warns, 'remove the necessity for deciding cases' (*op. cit.*, p. 517).

So this is one possibility. Closely linked to it is a second possibility. Levi dislikes principles because they are articulated at such a high level of abstraction that they cannot generate decisions. They do not lend themselves to specific if-then statements, but have to be weighed. A principle can be used to justify one thing on one occasion and quite the contrary on another occasion. Think of the Supreme Court's decisions on abortion over the last twenty years. As Levi says, the Constitution 'permits the court to be inconsistent' (*op. cit.*, p. 506). Quite a bit of work has to be done, then, to move from a principle to a particular decision, and this makes legal reasoning both more important and more fragile.

A third possibility, again slightly different, is that principles operate on a different level because, in Spencer Brown's words, they cannot re-enter the operative level, that is acquire orientation value within the system. But this is clearly false. Writing in 1948, Levi could not be expected to have predicted the inflation of tort claims that has occurred since then both in Britain and the United States. But it has become clear that principles such as those announced in *Macpherson v. Buick* and *Donoghue v. Stevenson*[7] can have expansionary or inflationary effects on the number of tort cases that can be successfully brought under the rubric of such principles. Secondly, it is clear that principles can work a profound transformation of the law, which could be called the positivization of case law. By referring to principles, it is possible to shorten the reference to cases, to the history of the law. As in the abortion example, it is possible to decide inconsistently over a relatively short space of time. Who would have thought that the decision in *Anns v. London Borough of Merton*[8] could be overruled so soon after it was made? So while principles may indeed operate at a higher level, they are not so lofty that they cannot be re-introduced within the legal system. It is tempting to think that they cannot work a re-entry, because they are not framed as a distinction but as an identity. But is it not precisely this that makes them more capable of re-entry than the distinction itself, firstly because an identity is easier to handle than a distinction, and secondly because it effectively disguises the paradox of the system.

So my reading of systems theory would not go all the way with Levi and argue for the redundancy of principles. Rather, it would see internal reference and external reference as complementary ways of handling the paradox of the system. In systems-theoretical terms we can call informational redundancy or internal reference a deflation of the symbolic medium of law and external reference its inflation. What we can say is that only if a system has achieved sufficient complexity, only if there is already enough redundancy in the system, can any variety or inflation be introduced. These modes of reasoning need not be seen as antithetical.

But at this point, it seems to me, the perspective of systems theory would try to locate the function of legal reasoning within the context of the legal system as a whole. Here, there is a good argument on functionalist grounds for saying that redundancy and variety have become institutionally differentiated within legal systems. Innovation is the function of the legislature. Redundancy is the function of the courts. Together they are 'cooperative law-making bodies' (*op. cit.*, p. 523). Failure to appreciate this can be dangerous. On the one hand, if courts are 'active' then it can be argued that legislation is not needed because the courts will later come to a more appropriate interpretation. Conversely, if legislative provisions can be interpreted away, it is not to be expected that the legislature will ever act. Either way, the result is legislative inertia. 'The legislation needs judicial consistency' (*op. cit.*, p. 523). Put differently, the legal system works better as a functionally differentiated system, and if courts and legislatures can appreciate the restrictive rôle they have within the system.

5. THE RÔLE OF LAW IN SOCIETY

So systems theory reverses our perspective. Put crudely, it is not so much that good reasons require certain decisions, but that the decisional structure of the law dictates a certain style of reasoning. It gives a particular account of reasoning as taking place within the context of the common law process, and of the common law process within the legal system as a whole. But these comments seem to me to be the least important contribution that systems theory has to make. Systems theory compels us to look at the rôle of law in society and therefore, here, the rôle of common law and legal reasoning in society. By way of conclusion, I want to tentatively explore these questions.

For Levi, it is the common law as a system of decisions that provides the key to legitimation. Throughout his essay, he dramatically underplays the significance of legal reasoning. Indeed, at all points he is at pains to stress the contingency of the system and the occasionally pathetic attempts of lawyers in trying to close that gap. This is what he has to say about *Macpherson*:

> As was to be expected, counsel for the plaintiff urged that an automobile was 'dangerous to a high degree'. It was, in fact, similar to a locomotive. It was much more like a locomotive than like a wagon. 'The machine is a fair rival for the Empire Express,' he said. (*Op. cit.* p. 514.)

And so on. Now to some extent, we have been able to explain this sort of reasoning within the context of the common law and the legal system. The perspective here is the internal differentiation of the legal system. We can explain reasoning as required by the doctrine of dictum, as an attempt to internalise or externalise the constitutive paradox of the law, as an attempt to fill the gap opened up between rules and principles, between programmes and the code. But none of this warrants conclusions concerning external differentiation, the differentiation of the legal system within society. To this extent, systems theory runs quite counter to the whole tradition within discourse ethics and argumentation theory, as I understand it. From this latter perspective, the reference to values and justifications within the legal system is interpreted in a quite different way. It is taken as evidence of the incomplete differentiation of the legal system, that it is not just a system of positive law composed of decisions, but has a footing in a cluster of shared values. All systems, it is argued, ultimately have their roots in such values. It follows that legal reasoning is important not because it is caught up in resolving the internal paradoxes of the system, but because it ultimately provides the link between law and community, between system and lifeworld.

I am not at all convinced by this line of reasoning. Firstly, I think there is good evidence that courts do resolve paradoxes, and I think Levi's article shows us where to look for it. Secondly, I suspect that this distinction between law and community, expert and lay, is just another way of resolving the paradox. But here, rather than being in the temporal dimension through creating a history, it is in the social dimension. The paradox is split into two and communicated to different actors. Neither side can hear the message communicated to the other, and the paradox does not 'arise'. In the words of one author, the law creates an 'acoustic separation'. Thirdly, the question for systems theory now becomes whether this is a good way of solving the paradox, and to ask whether there are not better ways. It does not seem to me that the reference to values is going to be helpful to the arguments discourse theorists want to make. This is because, while values appear to be connected to the social dimension, providing the link they want to see between law and community, ultimately they are and cannot help being bound up with the distinct temporal dimension of the law. As I mentioned earlier, the reference to values in tort law has become a method of re-organising the relevant history of the law. It allows courts to depart from prior decisions and behave inconsistently. This, it seems to me, can only frustrate the hopes of discourse theory. They could try and argue that this temporal re-organisation is required to better integrate the legal system with the temporal demands of other systems. But this, frankly, must appear implausible to anyone acquainted with the recent history of, say, tort law. The law and the economy do not tell the same time.

Has systems theory got any better suggestions? Again, Levi's article shows us the way. Legitimation does not come through legal reasoning but through legal process. It is law as system, precisely what is usually thought to be in need of legitimation, that legitimizes itself. Here, we have to be careful to avoid the orthodox interpretations of Levi's article. Usually, he is seen as providing an account of law changing in response to social forces outside the law. Passages such as the following are emphasised:

> Reasoning by example shows the decisive rôle which the common ideas of the society and the distinctions made by experts can have in shaping the law. The movement of common or expert concepts into the law may be followed. The concept is suggested in arguing difference or similarity in a brief, but it wins no approval from the court. The idea achieves standing in society. It is suggested again to a court. The court this time reinterprets the prior case and in doing so adopts the rejected idea. (*Op. cit.* p. 504.)

And this is even exploited to lend support to the famous 'relitigation thesis', namely that the likelihood of an idea influencing the law varies directly with the number of times it is litigated before the courts. Where Levi slipped up is only in failing to show which ideas, which forces determine the development of the law. According to the economic version of the relitigation thesis, this can easily be amended by showing that rules that are inefficient are more likely to be (re-)litigated, and through this mechanism the common law tends towards efficiency.

But I want to argue that this represents a complete misunderstanding of Levi's article. What is seen as an obvious weakness —the failure to identify any specific external mechanism— is in fact its strength. Indeed, it is Levi's thesis. What he is arguing is that just because the common law is closed to any one specific external force, it can become open to any. And it is this which legitimates the common law. Here are the lines which immediately follow the previous quotation:

In subsequent cases, the idea is given further definition and is tied to other ideas which have been accepted by the courts. It is now no longer the idea which was commonly held in the society. It becomes modified in subsequent cases.

This should serve to correct the above highly selective reading. What Levi is saying is that there is no simple exchange of ideas between law and its environment. Any idea has to be read together with the past and future decisions of the system which give it its legal sense. In this sense the law is a closed system. There is an aspect of this process which legitimates the system to its immediate participants. The litigants have 'participated in the law making. They are bound by something which they helped to make' (*op. cit.*, p. 504). Moreover, the parties 'bring into the law the common ideas of the society'. But we must remember that the system is designed to deal with controversy. 'The effort to find complete agreement before the institution goes to work is meaningless' (*op. cit.*, p. 574). And ideas that fail today, 'will have their day again. This is what makes the hearing fair...' (*op. cit.*, p. 504).

What is important is not so much the substantive value of the ideas themselves, but the institution of a procedure of revisability. Such a procedure provides the forum for the making and unmaking of ideas. Or, at least, so I have argued here. And it may be, if what I say has any plausibility, that systems theory provides a framework within the context of which Levi's ideas themselves will have their day again!

NOTES

[1] *Dixon v. Bell* , 5 Maule & Selwyn 198 (1816).

[2] *Langridge v. Levy* , 2 Meeson & Welsby 519 (1837).

[3] *Winterbottom v. Wright*, 10 Meeson & Welsby 109 (1842).

[4] *Longmeid v. Holliday*, 155 Eng. Rep. 752 (1851).

[5] *Thomas v. Winchester*, 6 N.Y. 397 (1852).

[6] *MacPherson v. Buick Motor Co.*, 217 N.Y. 302, 111 N.E. 1050 (1916).

[7] *Donoghue v. Stevenson*, [1932] A.C. 562.

[8] *Anns v. London Borough of Merton*, [1978] A.C. 728

REFERENCES

Levi, E.H., 1948. 'An Introduction to Legal Reasoning', 15 *The University of Chicago Law Review*, pp. 501–574.
Luhmann, N., 1990. *Die Wissenschaft der Gesellschaft*, Suhrkamp, Frankfurt, p. 275.
Spencer Brown, G., 1969. *The Laws of Form,* Allen and Unwin, London.

Emmanuel College
Cambridge
England

GEOFFREY SAMUEL

ONTOLOGY AND DIMENSION IN LEGAL REASONING

It would be idle to suggest that lawyers have not asked themselves questions either about the ontological or about the epistemological basis of their discipline. Yet it is tempting to say that these questions have become pressing from a technical point of view only since the arrival of Artificial Intelligence (AI) and expert systems research. Before these new concerns appeared, ontology and epistemology were, it might be argued, merely aspects of ideology and philosophy; they were not fundamental concerns of legal science because legal science was not, in the end, a real science. Law was simply the product either of its own history or of some special branch of logic concerned with, for example, deontics or rhetoric. Even if this is a somewhat simplistic view, it is fair to say not only that the modern world is still largely ignorant, despite a millennium of Roman legal scholarship, of the habits of mind and thought processes of the Roman jurists themselves[1], but that epistemological models of legal reasoning still find themselves trapped within a particular knowledge assumption. That assumption is that legal knowledge is to be found only in propositional rules.

It will not, it must be stressed at once, be the purpose of this paper directly to challenge the assertion that legal knowledge is propositional. From both an historical and a methodological viewpoint there is no denying that the tradition of law has given a central rôle both to a régime of legal rules and to a deductive approach to the solving of certain legal problems. Moreover most knowledge can at some point (even if only descriptively) be reduced to propositions. Rather the aim will be to indicate that modern developments in epistemology suggest that knowledge, learning and action are much more complex phenomena not easily reducible to a single theoretical structure. Consequently, before a workable epistemological theory can be developed in respect of expert systems in law, a distinction will have to be made between, for example, the teaching and the practice of law, and between case-law reasoning and the administrative ordering of society.

These general epistemological themes will be pursued by way of an introduction (Section 1) and will be followed by the argument that there is a gap between legal ontology and the legal syllogism (Section 2). Here the paper will try to show that the activity of legal reasoning is not just a matter of the application of learned (knowing-that) legal knowledge; it is, as far as

Z. Bankowski et al. (eds.), Informatics and the Foundations of Legal Reasoning, 205–224.

the Common Law is concerned at least, more a mixture of descriptive, inductive and deductive techniques operating within an epistemological framework which is not necessarily best represented through a two-dimensional (pyramid, hierarchy, knowledge tree) model (Section 3). By way of conclusion (Section 4) it will be stressed that legal reasoning is as much an historical phenomenon as a logical one and, accordingly, that each historical epoch of reasoning technique must be understood not just in its own right but as an element which goes to make up today's legal science. It may be, therefore, that methodological differences to be found in the various legal systems are simply differences of emphasis within an epistemological model that is common to Western legal science as a whole; the problem is that the model is not one that can be conceived, without internal contradiction, within a two-dimensional structure.

1. INTRODUCTION

The idea that the starting point for an epistemological theory of law is to be found in the notion of a legal rule is so deeply embedded in legal thought that it has become almost impossible to conceive of any alternative conceptual model capable of describing the phenomenon of law (Susskind 1987). The science of law is a science of norms which exist as a major premise separated from the world of fact which exists as the minor premise in the legal syllogism (Schroeder 1978). Legal theorists no longer argue that legal reasoning is simply a matter of deductive logic, nor would many begin to claim that the logic used in formulating the legal syllogism is of the same kind as that used in formal analytical reasoning (Bergel 1989, paras. 246–258). The traditional distinction between formal and dialectical logic has been resurrected in order to explain the nature of legal reasoning (Perelman 1979). Yet despite the recognition that the formulation of the premises in legal logic is a matter of interpretation rather than strict science, it is still the view that the syllogism is *un outil irremplaçable* (Schroeder 1978, p. 117) and that anyone who 'would deny that strictly deductive reasoning is a genuine and important element in legal justification... must show that there is some alternative theory' (MacCormick 1978, p. 52).

The moment a problem can be analysed in terms of the application of a rule the easier it becomes to see a central rôle for the syllogism. However, just because it is so difficult to deny the rôle of rules and syllogisms this in itself raises an epistemological question. Is there not a danger that the whole notion of a rule is one that might form what Bachelard called an epistemological obstacle (Bachelard 1938)? Or, put another way, if one says that the act of knowing itself can be a cause of stagnation and even regression, to what extent is the presentation of legal knowledge through the notion of a legal rule as a major premise an obstacle to jurists having anything other than a very dogmatic view of legal knowledge? If one starts from the position that law consists of 'laws' then every time it is asserted that the syllogism has a central rôle to play in legal reasoning this will have the effect of reinforcing the starting position itself: the syllogism requires an epistemology that law is reducible to a language of 'laws' universally valid within a given domain.

Such an epistemology is not without its value with respect either to philosophy or to legal science. Thus the idea that there exists a régime of rules and principles from which the good judge can, and must, determine individual rights is a philosophy that not only defines a political ideal but is one that attempts to be deterministic in the scientific sense (see Dworkin 1977). Equally the notion that law is a pyramid of norms serves not just as a scientific model establishing a logical connection between the stating of a problem and its solution, but as a philosophy for political institutions. Indeed one lesson that can be drawn from the attempts to establish a science of law is that the line between epistemology and ideology becomes ever more uncertain the more one moves from the natural to the human sciences. This, it must be said at once, is not to deny that science and technique have their ideological aspects (see generally, Goffi 1988), but the great advantage of the natural sciences is that they can traditionally be tested empirically in terms of 'verification' and 'falsification'. Testing an epistemological theory of law is quite a different matter and it is only with the advent of AI that the issue has arisen in a practical context. But this practical context must not be underestimated. For not only is it likely to challenge existing legal theories simply by exposing them to the cold reality of technological hard and software, but a practical verification or falsification of legal technique might well have a profound effect on how legal knowledge is represented both to practitioners and students. Technology might, in other words, force its own philosophy on the phenomenon of law (cf. Samuel 1994, Chap. 4).

In fact, of course, technological thinking (on which, see Goffi 1988, pp. 31–51) has already influenced legal philosophy and this becomes increasingly evident the more that legal theory is seen in the context of the history of legal thought. The parallels between developments in the history of scientific thought and developments in the history of legal thought are, at the level of a history of reasoning in general, close enough to discern identical patterns of development from a descriptive, via an inductive and then deductive, to an axiomatic stage (see Blanché 1983, p. 65; Blanché 1973, no. 42.) Moreover the influence of mathematicians on the development of legal thought forms an important era in the history of Western law (Stromholm 1985; Jones 1940). However any relationship between legal and scientific rationality is to an extent limited because although both rationalities can be reduced to 'laws' the ontological and empirical questions facing each are really very different. Epistemological obstacles and scientific revolutions, while no doubt capable of being perceived in the history of legal thought (Atias 1985, no. 101), are likely to be perceived in a rather different way from those in the natural sciences simply because the discourse of law is both the science and the object of science (Linant de Bellefonds 1985; Atias 1985, no. 19). This means that legal science can control its object in a much more fundamental way than is often possible in many of the physical sciences. Legal scientists do not need theoretical revolutions in quite the same way because their 'empirical' world is one over which they have had complete control since Roman jurists developed legal science as 'a kind of reality imposed upon the social world, putting it into order', and which, as a result, ended up 'by becoming more "true" than the facts' of the real world itself (Ellul 1982).

Given this confusion between legal science and its object the temptation to reduce the phenomenon of law itself to a set of 'laws' universally valid within a particular domain was, and is, overwhelming. On the Continent such a temptation was irresistible both to the political ruler keen to use law as an active means of directing society (Ellul 1982, pp. 344–347), and to the teacher keen to acquire a general and systematic view of the discipline in order to master its contents (Astolfi and Develay 1989). And as a result of the close relationship between law, the state and the universities the notion of the legal rule, together with the technique of the syllogism, is particularly strong in the Civilian tradition (David 1982). In the Common Law tradition, on the other hand, the universities have, historically, had little rôle in the development of legal thought and as a result English legal science is that of the practitioner, that is to say, from a science point of view, it is a 'patchwork' of disunited elements and concepts (Astolfi and Develay 1989, p.114; Samuel 1994, chaps 3 and 10–11). Nevertheless despite the distrust of logic in favour of 'common sense' and despite the much narrower conception of *la règle de droit* it would be a great mistake to underestimate the influence of the syllogism in the Common Law. Just as in Continental law, it has been said that the methodology in English law is a matter of logic 'with the major premise consisting of a pre-existing rule of law (either statutory or judge-made) and with the minor premise consisting of the material facts of the case under immediate consideration'.[2] Admittedly this major premise does not consist solely of a legal rule. The facts also play a rôle in the development of the law by providing a basis for reasoning by analogy. Thus 'frequently the new law will appear only from subsequent comparison of, on the one hand, the material facts inherent in the major premise with, on the other hand, the material facts which constitute the minor premise.'[3] However the rôle of analogy is not so much to reach decisions as to develop the legal rule and in consequence it becomes difficult to see analogy as anything other than a technique which itself is based on principle (MacCormick 1978, p. 186). In other words legal reasoning by analogy becomes subservient to a rule-based epistemological model.

The problem with subjecting the technique of analogy to the legal syllogism is that it misrepresents both the technique itself and the actual process of legal reasoning in that it implies that the *rapport* between two particular factual situations is reducible to a common denominator that can accurately be expressed or encapsulated in a rule. This is not to say that the technique of legal reasoning cannot logically be reduced to rules —such a process is logically possible in law just as it is, say, in painting. What is being suggested is that if one does reduce the notion of the *ratio decidendi* to a process of rules acting as major premises, this will produce a model that does not represent the process of English legal reasoning. And it does not do so because any model of such rules acting as the basis for logical deduction would be so complex as to be of little practical value in that it would lack commonsense knowledge and give incorrect responses to questions slightly outside the domains for which it was programmed (Reeke and Edelman 1988; Bechtel and Abrahamsen 1991). No doubt it is desirable that law *ought* to be a matter of rules and one can sympathise with the criminal or contract lawyer who dreams of the perfect legal syllogism. Yet the quest to make sense of facts, to grasp them in a rational science in order that the future can be predicted, ought not in itself to be allowed to dictate both the philosophy and the epistemology of law, since the rôles of the two theories are very different. An epistemological theory must embrace the notion of the *ratio decidendi* and reasoning by analogy in relation not just to 'rules' but to all other legal concepts, relations between concepts, institutions, categories, procedures, strategies, techniques and the like. And this can be done only via a meta-language which is not part of the object to be theorised (Blanché 1983, p. 120).

If the meta-language is the rule itself the technique of analogy and of the syllogism become misrepresented because their full rôles get either hidden or exaggerated. Now to say a rule is extended by analogy is, at one level, not in any way incorrect and so it is perfectly reasonable to declare that 'for the purpose of the rule in *Rylands v. Fletcher* electricity is analogous to water'.[4] However it has to be remembered that in reducing this analogy to a rule one is eclipsing the operation of another analogy which has allowed the facts (minor premise) to be amenable to a *Rylands v. Fletcher*[5] analysis before the major premise is actually brought into play. But this second analogy has operated within the minor premise to produce the isomorphic pattern of a relationship between *persona* and *res* capable of giving rise to the possibility of a 'liability for things' approach in the first place. Now it is of course possible to reduce the idea of liability for a thing to a rule; but this second analogy cannot be reduced to a rule in the same way because the discourse of law does not accommodate in any formal sense how isomorphic patterns are to be determined. There is no rule as such that dictated that *Donoghue v. Stevenson*[6] had to be treated as a factual situation consisting of four independent legal subjects (manufacturer, seller, purchaser and consumer) with no sale relationship between consumer and seller; it is quite feasible that such a situation could have thrown up a different isomorphic pattern resulting in a different legal situation.[7] Indeed cases have been lost simply on the basis that counsel did not present to the court a feasible pattern out of which a cause of action analogy could be constructed (Samuel 1983). Of course one can produce procedural rules to try to determine how facts ought to be analysed and what ought to be done if some alternative pattern of liability is suddenly discovered within the facts.[8] But the point that needs stressing is that the formulation of the minor premise, the facts, is an essential part of legal method and yet is a part of the phenomenon of law that falls quite outside of a rule-based theory of reasoning as such (cf. Samuel 1994).

2. LEGAL ONTOLOGY AND THE LEGAL SYLLOGISM

The inadequacy of a rule-based epistemology is appreciated not just by some modern jurists (Bergel 1989, paras. 275–277). It is a 'rule' (*regula iuris*) to be found in the great historical source of legal science itself: *non ex regula ius sumatur, sed ex iure quod est regula fiat.*[9] A rule is not law but a means of conveying a *brevis rerum narratio* of legal decision-making which can prove dangerous the moment it is treated as some kind of truth.[10] What is revealing about this Roman adage is that it suggests that the notion of a science of law —and it must be remembered that the same Roman mind conceived of law as a rational discipline whose object was to make sense of a chaotic world[11]— is not something that can ever be adequately detached from its object, in the sense that the actual object itself can only be defined in terms of the legal science. This of course is true of aspects of the natural sciences as well, for example with regard to probability theory (Blanché 1975, pp. 133–150). But the point to be stressed with respect to legal science is that either the rules define their own domain of application or a huge array of factual categories are wielded in order to make a mass of rules seemingly workable. In both situations the rules as major premises become meaningless in any sense of explaining or predicting the future because one will always need another set of 'rules' to explain why, for example, a set of facts was interpreted as contractual rather than tortious[12], or why one factual category is to be preferred to another[13]. Such 'meta-rules' are often capable of being identified, but they may well conform to a reasoning system that is entirely different from the one to which the legal rules themselves conform. Thus it may be that both the French and the English courts will interpret the facts or the law, or both, in such a way that favours consumers, but as soon as one tries to construct a meta-rule about consumers it is likely to prove extremely 'brittle' (Bechtel and Abrahamsen 1991, p. 227), because there will be many other situations where the courts will for example either fail to recognise the possible existence of a 'consumer' or decide to apply some other meta-meta-rule which might contradict the meta-rule about consumers. None of this is to suggest that legal reasoning cannot be described in terms of a complex system or set of systems. Indeed this was a topic pursued in an earlier publication (Samuel 1991a). What is being suggested is that there is an ontological starting point to legal reasoning that is based on isomorphic patterns within facts that, although no doubt influenced by the nature of régimes of rules and principles existing as major premises (Bergel 1989, no. 276), nevertheless remains outside of any rule-based epistemological theory.

It is this epistemological gap between ontology and syllogism that makes the grasping of the *ratio decidendi* an impossible task in terms of a rule-based theory of legal knowledge. Of course rule-based definitions can be advanced, and for the purposes of legal practice they may be more or less satisfying (MacCormick 1978, pp. 82–86, 215–216). But the notion of a rule cannot at any point contain the knowledge of what will be the isomorphic pattern of legal institutions and relations in any particular set of facts. That knowledge is something that falls into a separate system which may well be explainable only by reference to a theory of probability. A knowledge of all the rules will of course help the jurist determine this probability question and the rôle of legal argument itself is to encourage the judges to make this or that analogy. Yet the decision will actually be dependent upon how the pattern of facts falls to be decided and the analogy chosen and applied is not something that, in itself, can be determined by any rule-based theory of law. There is no rule of law that says that the escape of electricity must be envisaged in terms of an isomorphic pattern that is analogous to the pattern of liability based upon the idea of control and escape of a thing, even although there might be a strong probability that, because of the existence as a major premise of the rule in *Rylands v. Fletcher*, lawyers will end up making the appropriate analogy.

It is the existence of this gap between syllogism and ontology that allows for genuine creativity in law. Thus the lawyer who can convince a court that ships are like cars[14] or that a house is like a bottle of ginger beer[15] is doing much to predetermine the outcome of a case. More subtly, if a barrister can present the facts in such a way that they create the same isomorphic pattern as exists in a previous precedent then again this may help determine the final decision of the case. For example in one recent case[16] a local authority invited tenders, the form of tender containing an exclusion clause to the effect that the authority 'do not bind themselves to accept all or any part of any tender'. The plaintiffs put in, by hand, a tender before the required deadline, but owing to the carelessness of the authority the letter box containing the tender was not cleared until after the deadline for consideration. The authority accepted a tender lower than the one submitted by the plaintiffs and the plaintiffs brought an action for damages against the authority. What makes this case of interest from a legal knowledge point of view is that a range of rules and principles could potentially be applicable. A damages claim might succeed on the basis that the authority were negligent or had acted in bad faith, thus preventing them from relying on their rights, or that the invitation to tender was a binding promise made to the world. Equally the action might be refused on the ground that it was merely an invitation to treat or that there was no causation or that the authority had the right to disregard any tender they wished or that it was an example of pure financial loss giving rise to no duty of care. How should the barrister influence the court to arrive at a decision in his or her favour? At one level by an appeal to the rules themselves —the difference for example between contractual obligations and mere expectations.[17] At another level it was a question of producing the required ontological pattern in the minds of the judges, not by an appeal to the rules, but by getting them to enter the facts themselves and to try out different formulations of fact situation in the hope that they would finally be prepared to make an unexpressed analogy with the administrative law fact pattern of public body behaving in bad faith towards worthy citizen. Nowhere in the case, so it would appear, does one find express reference to public law rules as such. But it is pretty evident that this particular defendant would be allowed to stand on its rights only if it had acted in good faith[18], a requirement not normally found in commercial contracts[19]. It was, then, not the rule or the syllogism that fully determined this damages action in favour of the plaintiff. It was the 'ontological' pattern adopted by the judges which went to make up the minor premise.

The gap between ontology and rule does not mean that there are no rules capable of acting as a means for predicting the outcome of litigation. There are some rules which use mathematics —for example the drinking and driving laws— and here the syllogism is more than capable of acting as the means for predicting a decision. One can say, of course, that these rules are importing into law the science of mathematics and thus the logical method here tells us little about legal reasoning in general. Yet there are other, non-mathematical, rules which might seem to be just as good as indicators of the outcome of possible litigation problems. Take the rule that the display of goods in shop windows or on supermarket shelves does not constitute a binding offer: does this rule not in itself act as a major premise capable of explaining certain legal decisions[20] and of predicting the outcome of a range of possible factual situations? There is no doubt that such a law can go some way in assuming the rôle played by a scientific 'law', that is of explaining and predicting. However even such an apparently clear rule will not of itself answer the question of whether an action for damages brought by a supermarket customer, in respect of an injury caused by a product exploding while in the supermarket basket before the customer has reached the checkout, will be successful. This question will be dependent, *inter alia*, upon how the facts are presented to, and accepted by, the court. It may be that the court will hold the supermarket strictly liable[21] on the basis of a collateral contract or it may decide the problem in tort on the basis of *res ipsa loquitur*; equally it could decide that the explosion was an accident involving no liability on the part of anyone or, perhaps, that the explosion was caused by the plaintiff's own unreasonable behaviour. The point to be stressed is that no single rule can contain the information necessary to know what pattern of institutional relationship will emerge out of the facts. Will the problem be seen as one of liability for a thing; will it be seen as an occupier's liability problem; will it be seen as an implied promise between supermarket and customer in a sale contract said to be perfected when the thing exploded; or will it be seen as a case of contributory negligence? All of these possible approaches can, individually, be related to a rule, but whether any particular rule will or will not be applicable is in part dependent upon formulating a factual pattern that will allow itself to be fitted into the paradigm pattern associated with any particular rule. Rules, in other words, act only as a very imperfect means of storing legal knowledge because they are incapable of containing knowledge about the creative isomorphic possibilities of the elements which go to make up the factual patterns in litigation (Samuel 1994).

3. EPISTEMOLOGY OF THE COMMON LAW

It must be emphasised that this alternative view of legal knowledge is not suggesting that rules and principles have no rôle; rather it is arguing that a system of rules is inadequate as a system of legal knowledge. No doubt it may seem quaint that one might appear to be advocating a return to Classical Roman law thinking in order to formulate an epistemological theory suitable for the era of AI. Yet it is worth remembering that modern systems thinking itself is looking at pre-cartesian methods of reasoning such as analogy (Durand 1992). Moreover the position is not as simple as it might appear. The great contribution of the Renaissance thinkers to jurisprudence is that they took law from the inductive to the deductive stage of scientific thought (see Samuel, 1991b), and this in itself was a valuable contribution in that it made clear that law was not just a descriptive science. It could create not only its own laws but also its own subject and object of these laws. But this movement was not so much a *développement* as, following Bachelard (Bachelard 1934 pp. 42, 53; Blanché 1975, p. 151), an *enveloppement.* By this is meant that if one sees the development of legal reasoning as conforming to the same law of development as reasoning in the sciences, it would be a question of the descriptive and inductive stages being embraced, rather than replaced, by the deductive stage.

Such an envelopment is particularly clear in the Common Law system. Indeed Maitland's observation (Maitland 1909), that the forms of action may be dead but they continue to rule from the grave, was, and is, indicative of the tension between descriptive, inductive and deductive modes of problem solving. In fact this tension is to be found in the methods of individual jurists. In one case Denning LJ attacked what might be said to be a descriptive approach to problem-solving when he stated that he would 'be sorry to think that, if a wrong has been done, the plaintiff is to go without a remedy simply because no one can find a peg to hang it on'; for that would 'be going back to the days when a man's rights depended on whether he could fit them into a prescribed form of action'.[22] Yet a couple of years later, in *Southport Corporation v. Esso Petroleum*[23], the same judge was happy to dismiss a claim in trespass on the ground that the discharge of oil which caused the plaintiffs' damage was not done directly on to the plaintiffs' beach; it was carried by the tide to the plaintiffs' land and this was consequential not direct. In other words Denning LJ was prepared to use descriptive reasoning techniques when the occasion required. One might add that in more recent times Lord Denning (as he became) is found adopting an axiomatic approach to reasoning when he justified the issuing of an injunction, *inter alia*, on the ground that 'a man who is carrying on a lawful trade or calling has a right to be protected from any unlawful interference with it'.[24]

Now the point of these examples is not to highlight judicial contradiction. The point is simply to indicate how different kinds of reasoning from different stages of development can co-exist in a legal system at one and the same time. In the *Esso* case the reasoning was rooted firmly in the concrete; as Southport Corporation had pleaded only trespass, nuisance and negligence of the captain it could not then go on to argue, at the appeal stage, that the facts themselves disclosed a right to compensation on the basis that Esso, as a legal person in itself, had been careless in putting to sea an unseaworthy ship [25]. The corporation lost their case, therefore, not because they failed to show an invasion of their 'rights', but because they failed to put forward a descriptive category which matched a legal category that was equally descriptive in the way it was formulated. This was not rule-based reasoning as such: it was reasoning by description —that is to say it was reasoning by a process of matching one descriptive situation with another and using this matching process as the sole means of determining the plaintiffs' 'right' to an action. By contrast in *Ex parte Island Records*[26] the descriptive process proved quite unsuitable because none of the existing legal categories appeared —to the Court of Appeal at least[27]— applicable to the facts in issue. The issue was whether a civil remedy would be available in situations where a person in contravention of a criminal statute made 'bootleg' recordings of live performances by famous pop musicians. Having admitted that these facts did not fall within any of the existing categories of liability within the law of tort, Lord Denning changed the basis of his reasoning and posed a different question: 'has the plaintiff a particular right which he is entitled to have protected?'[28] This change of question allowed Lord Denning first to induce out of a whole range of what might be termed interference cases 'a right which is in the nature of a property right'[29] and, secondly, because it was now an issue of a 'right' and thus a concept seemingly applicable without further justification (*ubi ius ibi remedium*), to apply in effect a legal axiom. Liability was not a matter of matching one set of facts to another, but of applying the institutional and axiomatic relationship between person and thing (*dominium*) and this had been achieved by turning a live musical performance into a legal object (*res*).

Lord Denning's approach was not, however, just a matter of switching from a descriptive to an abstract form of reasoning. It was a process of moving from one degree of rationality to another; it involved, in the language of the natural sciences, starting out from facts organised according to one logical structure in order to arrive at a structure founded upon quite a different set of logical relations (Blanché 1975, p. 152). One had moved from liability arising from a 'wrong' (founded on a legal relation or *iuris vinculum* between two legal subjects) to one arising out of the interference with a 'right' (founded on the relation between legal subject and legal object). This reorganisation of the rationality in turn involved a process whereby the new category of 'rights' could be constructed out of an older category of 'wrongs' and this process itself is important in the understanding not only of the notion of *enveloppement* but of the institutional structure of legal thought itself. This institutional structure and its epistemological implications have been analysed in more detail elsewhere (Samuel 1991c; see also Samuel 1994); suffice it to say here that the induction is not just a question of moving from one level to another but of rearranging the emphasis with regard to legal relations within a model which cannot without logical contradiction be seen to be functioning only in a two-dimensional world.

Take once again the *Island Records* case. Lord Denning starts out by analysing the legal relations between two legal subjects (*personae*)[30] and ends up basing his decision on the axiomatic relationship (*dominium*) between legal subject (*persona*) and legal object (*res*)[31]. This change of emphasis in the legal model is difficult to conceive of in a two-dimensional structure of institutions and relations because of the logical contradiction between *in rem* and *in personam* relations; to talk in terms of a 'right which is in the nature of a right of property' is to say that the service performed by the pop musicians is an object quite separate from the musicians themselves. Yet in the law of contract there is a great difference between the contract to convey a thing capable of being owned and the contract to perform a service[32]; and, more generally in patrimonial law, there is a fundamental difference between actions arising out of the relation between person-and-person (actions *in personam*) and actions arising out of the relation between person-and-thing (actions *in rem*)[33]. In the latter action all that a plaintiff need assert is interference with the property relation in order to have a remedy (Jolowicz 1957). Consequently the legal model has to make a sharp division within the notion of *res* between things capable of being the subject of ownership and things that are not. Now if one turns to the law of property the whole problem at the heart of the *Island Records* case was that live performances were not things capable of being owned in the same way as a car or a house; and even today it is clear that they are still more a question of personal rather than real rights.[34] Yet once it is appreciated that the legal remedy itself (*actio*) is capable of acting as an active institution within an institutional legal model that is three-, rather than two-, dimensional in structure the easier it is to appreciate how legal thought can be carried from *obligatio* (the relation between two legal subjects) to *dominium* (the relationship between legal subject and a legal object capable of being owned) via the concept of an 'interest' which is a notion that attaches to the relation between legal subject (*persona*) and legal remedy (*actio*).[35]

By emphasising the 'interest' relationship that a legal subject has with a legal action the *in rem* and *in personam* dichotomy can be suppressed in favour of a different institutional structure which uses the obligational relationship (*iuris vinculum*) as a legal object (*res*) so as to construct, in effect, a property bond between person and thing (*res*), the 'thing' here serving as an object both for a 'right' (a right *to* something) and for a property bond (*dominium*). In a two-dimensional model this kind of transition is particularly difficult to envisage because it seems continually to give rise to internal contradiction; thus when one tries to construct in patrimonial law a coherent system of 'rights' *in rem* and *in personam* one comes up against logical difficulties (Ginossar 1960, pp. 1–18). Yet if one moves to a three-dimensional structure it becomes possible to see how the notion of a 'right' can act as a legal object capable at one and the same time of embracing corporeal and incorporeal property, the latter including not just obligations[36] (Ginossar 1960, pp. 43–46) but, if need be, the 'interest' relationship between legal subject and legal action.[37] The moment one moves back to a two-dimensional world the more difficult it becomes to distinguish between a right and an interest simply because the two institutional relationships become eclipsed by each other.[38]

It should be more evident now how reasoning has moved from one epistemological stage to another: the legal action (*actio*) is no longer descriptive in function in a way that it was in the *Esso* case —that is to say it is no longer a means of encapsulating a descriptive set of facts to which the litigation facts are matched. It has become an institution in itself capable of supporting its own logical relationship. A legal subject might thus be entitled to a legal action if the subject has a 'sufficient' or 'legitimate interest' and this 'interest' is in turn supported by the relationship between legal subject and legal object, this latter now appearing as a 'right' in turn being supported by the 'interest' created in its turn by the relationship not just between *persona* and *actio* but between the state (an institution capable of being a legal subject) and the private legal subject in respect of a criminal remedy. 'I am satisfied', said Waller LJ in his judgment supporting Lord Denning in *Island Records*, 'that in equity there is jurisdiction for a court to grant an injunction to a person who claims that he has suffered special damage to a property interest of his by a crime'.[39] In terms of precedent this statement may no longer be good law[40], but in terms of legal reasoning its logical structure, if viewed within a model that can escape the limitations of the two-dimensional, is a perfectly sound piece of legal argumentation and rationality functioning on a level somewhat removed from the one in the *Esso* case.

It may seem strange to use latin words to discuss institutions in an English case, but the point to emphasise is that at the level of institutional discourse the gap between the Common Law and Civil Law may not be so wide as to be unbridgeable. Indeed the idea of an 'inner relationship' between English and Roman law, noticed by several Continental writers, may well be indicative of the fact that the main difference between Roman and English law on the one hand and modern Continental law on the other is simply one of progression in the concrete-abstract process.[41] Yet in terms of *enveloppement* it has to be remembered that English law, in not reaching an axiomatized stage, has never been able to suppress the former stages of epistemological progression. Accordingly the pre-institutional system modes of thought have survived to co-exist alongside the institutional modes. And it is here that the rôle of analogy becomes crucial.

In a descriptive stage analogy forms the pre-institutional screen behind which the discourse of law can gradually develop an isomorphic structure. In the inductive and deductive stages this structure forms sufficiently to function as a system capable of creating what are now its own institutions. The notion of a legal action is, as we have seen, fundamental here because it acts as the vehicle by which legal rationality can move from descriptive sets of facts to an institution capable of creating its own legal subjects (towns become persons when given legal remedies; see Jolowicz 1957, pp. 127–139) and legal objects (for example debts[42]). Yet once the legal action has achieved this restructuring of rationality the institutional system can largely take over the rôle formerly played by analogy; accordingly analogy in the Civil Law systems, along with the legal actions themselves (Jolowicz 1957, pp. 75–81), find themselves relegated to more minor rôles.[43] The survival of analogy in English law as an important means of reasoning is, then, evidence in itself of its earlier stage of development in the epistemological progression from the descriptive to the axiomatic and this helps explain the survival of the legal action as an important institution. It is not so much that the forms of action rule from the grave, as that the action itself has not really bequeathed its true heritage to the later generation. English law has moved on from the descriptive stage and is well into the process of allowing the institutional system to act as its own ontology; yet it has not reached a stage where the inductive process has given rise to a set of 'universal laws' acting as propositions which simply envelop the older forms of rationality to such an extent that they suppress the structural dimensions and inner workings of the institutional system itself (and see Samuel 1994, chap. 10–11).

4. LEGAL REASONING AS AN HISTORICAL PHENOMENON

In Continental legal technique this envelopment is, then, very much harder to perceive than in the Common Law because of the dominance of the syllogism linked to a general system of legal axioms whose abstract character is seemingly confirmed by their ability completely to transcend the social facts.[44] All the same while the *Code civil* has proved somewhat adept in moving from an agricultural to an industrial society, that is to say in not being entrapped by an ontology concerning the nature of things, this has not been without its cost when it comes to the analysis of factual situations in legal reasoning. Published French judgments, which have emphasised the axiomatic stage by their very brevity, have been criticised on the basis that they simply do not contain anything more than a *brevis rerum narratio* (Touffait and Tunc 1974). This criticism is aimed not so much at the decision-making itself, as at what might be said to be the envelopment of traditional legal reasoning by a style that is rooted in a view of legal science that simply does not reflect what judges actually do or should be doing. In keeping with the idea that each article of the code acts as an axiom within a strictly deductive system the gap in legal knowledge becomes so evident that the deductions end up patently contradicting themselves in a way that the science itself implies is impossible (Touffait and Tunc 1974, no. 10). In truth of course the French courts are constructing their own social reality in the same way as Roman and Common Lawyers; but because the French method operates at the level of the legal discourse itself this hides even more effectively both the operation of analogy when it comes to the qualification of the facts and the functioning of the institutional model. In the Common Law there is, as we have seen, much less of an awareness of law as an axiomatic science and this means that the syllogism has not yet had the chance to subvert reasoning by analogy. Like Roman law, English law has not moved on from the inductive stage of development with the result that its epistemological awareness is actually different from that to be found in France. Equally, however, it would be dangerous to say that the epistemological position in the Common Law is identical to that of Classical Rome (Samuel 1995). Common Lawyers are, seemingly, tempted to think that legal knowledge is a matter of rules and thus they are projecting onto the rules themselves reasoning techniques such as analogy. To an extent, as we have seen, this is workable; but it must be borne in mind that, when viewed from the position of the syllogism, analogy was and is a device designed, so to speak, to function within the minor premise, the facts. The point then of advocating a return to the Roman thinking is not so much an attempt to recapture a notion like the nature of things as an attempt to explain that it is rationalism itself which has helped to create the 'ontological' gap and the 'brittleness' in many existing rule-based expert systems.

From an historical and ideological viewpoint the idea of a universal body of 'laws' is perfectly understandable in that such a system has as its primary purpose the production of a normative discourse that aims to encourage actual human persons to act in certain desired ways as well as helping such persons to make sense, within an institutional framework, of what they actually do (Blanché 1975, p. 161). This goal must not, however, be confused with the process of litigation which involves neither real people nor real things. The facts in litigation are a rational construction that involve elements of an abstract science that are, however concrete the science may appear to be[45], nevertheless quite detached from the actual world of social reality. Law may be made for the human person[46], but the physical person only has a rôle to play vis-à-vis the science of law as a whole. This science, in its turn, has no rôle vis-à-vis real people and real facts. These latter are created by the science itself and once this is appreciated it becomes possible to see how legal science creates its own ontology. All the same this ontology is not a set of rules. For rules are merely an attempt to describe and to proscribe; they are the information processed by a system of institutions where interrelations and elements form the subjects, objects and actions and thus even in axiomatized systems the syllogism must be treated with care since it can easily mask the creative rôle of the institutional model in legal argumentation (Samuel 1994, chap. 9).

Legal reasoning is, accordingly, as much an historical phenomenon as a logical one and in order to appreciate its structure and operation it is necessary to study in detail each stage of its development in the long process from the descriptive to the axiomatic stage. Moreover it is also necessary to appreciate the anti-historical tendency of the axiomatic stage itself. This is where the Common Law can make a major contribution in that it is a legal system that has not experienced the effects of axiomatisation. The process of *enveloppement* thus remains evident, for all to see, in the reasoning itself. Yet in order for the epistemologist (and AI researcher) to be able fully to appreciate the complexity of this 'geological' record (so to speak) it is necessary not only to abandon the two-dimensional world of pyramids, hierarchies and knowledge trees, but to have a thorough understanding of how legal rationality has actually moved from the descriptive to the inductive stage. This is why the forms of action, or their successors, causes of action, should not be buried; they must be preserved for the systems theorist, epistemologist and AI specialist because they hold the key to the understanding of the relationship between legal and social reality.

NOTES

[1] See references in (Samuel, 1991a).

[2] Lord Simon in *FA & AB Ltd v. Lupton* [1972] AC 634, 658.

[3] *Ibid.*, p.659.

[4] Lord Simon, *op.cit.*, at p.659.

[5] (1866) LR 1 Ex 265; (1868) LR 3 HL 330.

[6] [1932] AC 562.

[7] See e.g. *Lockett v. A & M Charles Ltd* [1938] 4 All ER 170.

[8] See e.g., *Esso Petroleum Co Ltd v. Southport Corporation* [1956] AC 218; cf *Nouveau Code de Procédure Civile* art. 12.

[9] Digest 50.17.1.

[10] Digest 50.17.202.

[11] Digest 22.6.2.

[12] Paris 14.12.1961 (Gaz. Pal. 1962.1.135); Cass .civ. 20. 10. 1964 (D.S.1965.62), in (B. Rudden, 1991) pp. 310–312.

[13] Compare e.g., *Smith v. Eric Bush* [1990] 1 AC 831 with *Caparo Plc v. Dickman* [1990] 2 AC 605.

[14] *Esso Petroleum Co Ltd v. Southport Corporation* [1956] AC 218.

[15] *Dutton v. Bognor Regis U.D.C.* [1972] 1 QB 373; cf *Murphy v. Brentwood D.C.* [1990] 3 W.L.R. 414.

[16] *Blackpool & Fylde Aero Club Ltd v. Blackpool B.C.* [1990] 1 W.L.R.1195.

[17] *Ibid.*, at pp. 1200-1201.

[18] *Ibid.*, at p.1204.

[19] It has been said that a person is entitled to exercise a right under a contract 'for good reason or a bad reason or no reason at all': *Chapman v. Honig* [1963] 2 Q.B. 502, 520.

[20] *Fisher v. Bell* [1961] 1 QB 394; *Pharmaceutical Society of Great Britain v. Boots* [1953] 1 Q.B. 401.

[21] See now *Consumer Protection Act 1987* ss. 1–5.

[22] *Abbott v. Sullivan* [1952] 1 KB 189, 200.

[23] [1954] 2 QB 182 (CA); cf [1956] AC 218.

[24] *Ex parte Island Records* [1978] Ch 122, 136.

[25] [1956] AC 218.

[26] [1978] Ch 122.

[27] The reasoning of the majority of the Court of Appeal was subsequently doubted by the House of Lords in a later case: *Lonrho Ltd v. Shell Petroleum Ltd* [1982] AC 173.

[28] [1978] Ch at p.136.

[29] *Ibid.*

[30] [1978] Ch at pp.134-135.

[31] *Ibid* at pp. 135-137.

[32] See e.g., *Supply of Goods and Services Ac*t 1982, ss 1, 4, 12, 13

[33] Digest 44.7.3pr.

[34] *Copyright, Designs and Patents Act 1988*, s. 194.

[35] See e.g., *Nouveau Code de Procédure Civile* art. 31.

[36] See (Ginossar, 1960) pp. 43–46; Gaius, *Institutes* 2.14.

[37] See e.g., *Chief Constable of Kent v. V.* [1983] QB 34; cf *Pickering v. Liverpool Post Plc* [1991] 2 WLR 513, 524-525.

[38] See e.g., *IRC v. National Federation of Self-Employed and Small Businesses Ltd* [1982] AC 617.

[39] [1978] Ch at p.144-145.

[40] *Lonrho Ltd v. Shell Petroleum Ltd* [1982] AC 173.

[41] See generally (Samuel 1994, chap. 3) and references therein. It should however be pointed out that this book also examines important differences in the institutional structures of Classical Roman law and the Common Law. (See also Samuel 1995.)

42 On which see *Beswick v. Beswick* [1966] Ch 538 (CA); cf [1968] AC 58; (Samuel 1994, chap. 9).

43 See, generally, (Secretan, 1984).

44 See e.g., Cass. civ. 21.2.1927; D.P.1927. 1.97.

45 'The concrete, said Langevin, is the abstract rendered familiar by usage.' (Blanché, 1980, p. 104).

46 Digest 1.5.2.

REFERENCES

Astolfi, J-P. and M. Develay, 1989. *La didactique des sciences*, P.U.F.

Atias, C., 1985. *Epistémologie juridique*, P.U.F.

Bachelard, G., 1934. *Le nouvel esprit scientifique,* Alcan.

Bachelard, G., 1938. *La formation de l'esprit scientifique*, Vrin.

Bechtel, W., and A. Abrahamsen, 1991. *Connectionism and the Mind*, Blackwell.

Bergel, J.-L., 1989. *Théorie générale du droit*, 2e. éd., Dalloz.

Blanché, R., 1975. *L'induction scientifique et les lois naturelles*, P.U.F.

Blanché, R., 1978. *Le raisonnement,* P.U.F.

Blanché, R., 1980. *L'axiomatique*, 6e éd, P.U.F.

Blanché, R., 1983. *L'épistémologie*, 3e éd., P.U.F;

David, R., 1982. *Les grands systèmes de droit contemporains*, 8e éd., Dalloz.

Durand, D., 1992. *La systémique*, 5e. éd., P.U.F.

Dworkin, R., 1977. *Taking Rights Seriously*, Duckworth.

Ellul, J., 1982. *Histoire des institutions: 3 — Le Moyen Age*, 9e éd., P.U.F.

Ginossar, S., 1960 *Droit réel, propriété et créance,* L.G.D.J., Paris.

Goffi, J.-Y., 1988. *La philosophie de la technique*, P.U.F., Paris.

Jolowicz, H. F., 1957. *Roman Foundations of Modern Law,* Oxford University Press.

Jones, J.W., 1940. *Historical Introduction to the Theory of Law*, Oxford.

Linant de Bellefonds, X., 1985. *L'informatique et le droit*, 2e. éd., P.U.F.

MacCormick, D.N., 1978. *Legal Reasoning and Legal Theory,* Oxford University Press.

Maitland, F. W., 1909 (reprinted). *The Forms of Action at Common Law*, Cambridge University Press.

Perelman, Ch., 1979. *Logique juridique: Nouvelle rhétorique*, 2e éd., Dalloz.

Reeke, G.N. and G.M. Edelman, 1988. 'Real Brains and Artificial Intelligence', in S.R. Graubard (ed.), *The Artificial Intelligence Debate*, M.I.T..

Rudden, B., 1991. (ed), *A Source-book on French Law*, 3rd ed., Oxford University Press.

Samuel, G., 1983. Note: 'Owning Elvis', 99 LQR 182.

Samuel, G., 1991a. 'The Challenge of Artificial Intelligence: Can Roman Law help us discover whether Law is a system of rules?' *Legal Studies*, Vol. II No. 1.

Samuel, G., 1991b. 'Historical Jurisprudence and the New Rationalism', in T. O'Hagan (ed.), *Revolution and Enlightenment in Europe*, Aberdeen.

Samuel, G. 1991c. 'Epistemology and Legal Institutions,' [1991] *International Journal for the Semiotics of Law*, 309.

Samuel, G. 1994, *The Foundations of Legal Reasoning*, Metro/Maklu/Nomos.

Samuel, G. 1995, 'System and Systematics in Roman Law and the Common Law', *Zeitschrift für Eüropäisches Privatrecht* [forthcoming].

Schroeder, F.-M., 1978. *Le nouveau style judiciaire*, Dalloz.

Secretan, P., 1984. *L'analogie,* P.U.F.

Stromholm, S., 1985. *A Short History of Legal Thinking in the West*, Norstedts, pp. 175–191.
Susskind, R., 1987. *Expert Systems in Law*, Oxford University Press, pp. 154–155.
Touffait, A. and A. Tunc, 1974. 'Pour une motivation plus explicite des décisions de justice notamment de celles de la Cour de cassation', *Revue trimestrielle de Droit civil*, 487.

Department of Law
University of Lancaster
England

GREGORY PIPE

COMMON LAW CONCEPTS — THE PROBLEM OF INDEFINABILITY

Cases are tried because plaintiffs seek remedies that defendants contest. In litigation there can be little doubt that the availability of a remedy is the central concern of the jurist. When, however, legal advice is dispensed to clients outside the sphere of litigation there is much talk of rights, duties, powers etc.; often without reference to possible remedies. This is a confusing phenomenon. It obscures essential juridical reasoning. Any jurist knows that to advise a client that he or she possesses a legal right is inappropriate unless there is some legal remedy concurrent with that right. The only justification for the assertion that there exists a legal right, duty or power is that some remedy is available for failure to respect the right, for breach of the duty, for misfeasance or nonfeasance in the exercise of the power. Hence, at one level at least, discussion of the legal position of a party in a non-litigious situation involves just as great a consideration of the availability of a remedy as does consideration of his fate in litigation itself. A theory of legal argumentation must therefore seek to explain that process by which a decision that a remedy should be awarded in given circumstances can be taken and justified.

This paper treats the award of a remedy as the paramount issue of law. The model of legal reasoning that I propose has at its core the notion that what must be explained is both how a decision to award a remedy is reached and how that decision is justified.

1. LEGAL PROCESS: DECISION AND JUSTIFICATION

The distinction between what has come to be known as the heuristic process and the justificatory process is of fundamental importance for any analysis of legal reasoning. By heuristic I mean the process by which a jurist actually decides that a remedy ought to be awarded. This is the decision making process. It must be contrasted with the justification given for the award of a remedy. The latter is an explanation, an articulated reason for making the decision. The distinction must be made because not to make it would be to assume that the reason for making a decision and the reason given for making a decision are one and the same. It may of course be that the two reasons are the same, but there again it may not.

Z. Bankowski et al. (eds.), Informatics and the Foundations of Legal Reasoning, 225–244.

Anecdotal evidence of everyday life illustrates that the assumption is not always valid and suggests that we must guard against or, at least, test the same assumption in relation to juridical decisions. Let us take as an example a small schoolboy caught by his headmaster whilst attempting to climb to the top of the boot-lockers. The boy's decision to climb the lockers was made on the spur of the moment or, at best, with very little conscious thought. He simply found the idea attractive. The boy, of course, knows that the true answer to the master's question 'Why did you climb the lockers?': 'No reason,' or 'I do not know,' or 'Because I wanted to,' is unsatisfactory. He knows that he must somehow justify his decision. The answer he actually gives must be one which is both credible and acceptable. Credible in that it is a reason that the master believes explains why he made the decision. Acceptable in that it is a reason which is not inconsistent with the master's understanding of the school's code of discipline.

We probably all hope that in the legal context the decision that a remedy should be awarded is not merely based on partiality. There ought to be some good reason which guides the jurists decision. In the case of the judge at least he ought to reach a decision by a process of 'legal' argumentation. Whether he ought to or not, however, it cannot be assumed that he does, nor that he reaches that decision by the route mapped out in his judgement. Assertions that the existence of a written or oral reasoned judgement is evidence that the decision process involved a reasoned argument are by no means conclusive. The judgement is no more than a justification which, like the boy's answer, is successful if it is credible and acceptable: credible such that the legal community can believe that it is a reason for the decision and acceptable such that it is not inconsistent with the legal community's understanding of the law.

In the discussion which follows I shall attempt, within a model of common law reasoning, to keep the heuristic and justificatory processes distinct and to show, in some respects, how the two relate. What I hope to show is that the nature of common law thinking and the language used to justify its decisions are such that the concepts used in the award of remedies are not concrete but instead are subject to a continuous metamorphosis. In this way I hope to show a fundamental problem associated with the development of a mechanical legal decision making system.

The starting point of any case is an allegation of facts by the plaintiff which he claims entitles him to a remedy, together with an allegation of facts, possibly the same facts, by the defendant which he claims prevent the plaintiff from succeeding. The finishing point is the decision whether a remedy should be awarded to the plaintiff or refused, together, normally, with a justificatory reason. Much could be said about the process by which the 'raw' facts as alleged by the parties become the facts which are accepted by the jurist and upon which he then proceeds to determine the case. I shall content myself here to examine only the latter part of the process.

From a statement of fact and a statement of claim the method by which a jurist explains his decision is one in which he ascribes particular legal significance to the facts in order to show that they support the remedy, or alternatively, one in which he refuses to ascribe the required significance to the facts on which the remedy depends. In the English law of contract, for example, a claim for contractual damages will normally depend upon whether the jurist can credibly and acceptably state that the facts disclose a contract and a breach of that contract.

The ascription of legal significance is itself typified by the application of legal labels to the facts. It is a naming process. There is little difference between the legal process and that which we all do every day in using language. If, for example, I am asked how many chairs I have in my study, my answer will depend on which of those objects, on which I and my visitors sit, I label 'chairs'. I must decide whether or not each potential candidate for the appellation is to be labelled 'chair' or whether it must remain known as 'carpet', 'desk', 'window-ledge' etc. In the same way, if I am asked whether damages for breach of contract will flow from a particular concatenation of events, I must decide whether I would be justified in labelling the facts contract and breach.

Of course to say that the justification for awarding or refusing to award a remedy is simply whether or not the required labels can be applied is a superficial approach. It must be expanded by considering the possibility that despite all the required labels being applicable the remedy is still refused because some vitiating factor arises. In the contract example, there may be a contract and there may be a breach, but there may also be a frustrating event which makes an award of damages unjustifiable.

The possibility of facts arising which undermine what would otherwise be an acceptable justification for an award indicate that the application of the required labels to the facts is only a prima facie justification for the award of a remedy. It is defeasible. In order, however, to defeat a prima facie justification, more justification is needed. Hence refusal to grant an otherwise justified award of a remedy must be explained by the ascription of legal significance, to facts, of a nature that is acceptable to justify the refusal of a remedy to which the plaintiff is prima facie entitled. The mode of justification used to defeat the award is clearly the same as that used to justify the award itself. It is nothing more than the application of legal labels to facts.

If liability or non-liability is justified by the application of legal labels to facts, the answers to the following questions will form the substance of a legal justification.

i. What labels are required to justify a particular remedy?
ii. How are the labels to be applied?
iii. Do the labels apply to the accepted facts?
iv. Can any defeating conditions be argued?
v. What labels do the defeating conditions require?
vi. How are the labels to be applied?
vii. Do the labels apply to the accepted facts?

Schematically, the justification may be represented as in figure (1).

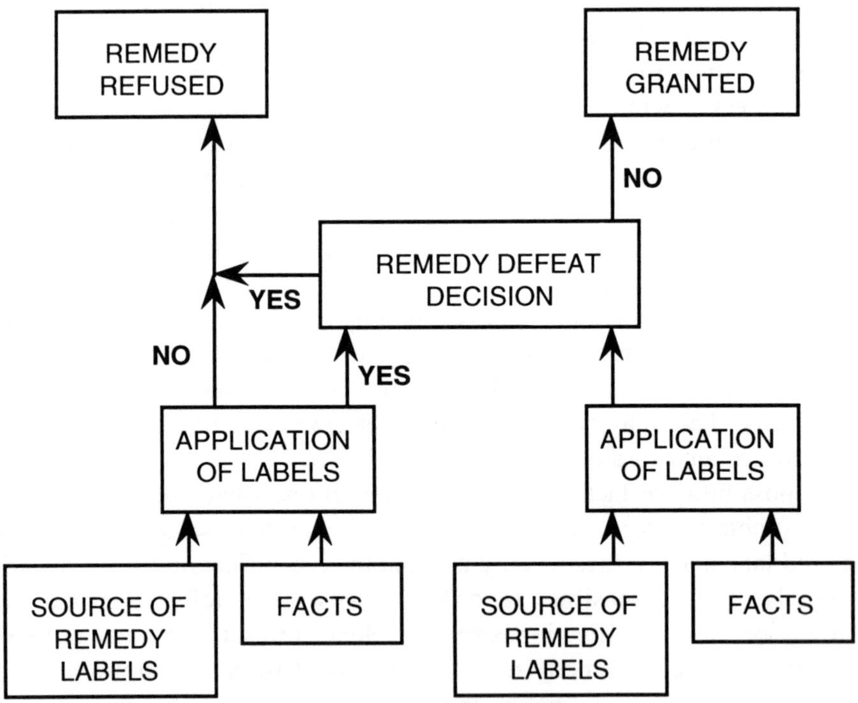

Figure 1.

The justification for the grant or refusal of a remedy is the ability to show that the labels apply to the facts. There may be any number of labels on which the justification depends. The labels may be alternative or contingent conditions. Thus the part of the diagram representing the application of labels must be expanded. Figure (2) represents a three-possibility justification for a remedy.

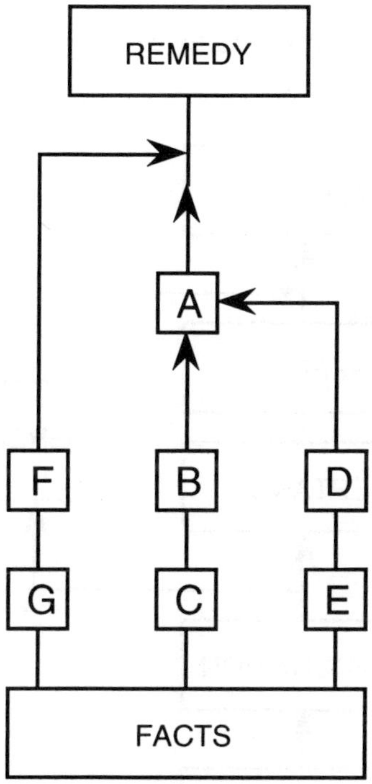

Figure 2.

The grant of a remedy is justified, given the facts if:

i. labels *A* AND *B* AND *C* can be applied, OR
ii. labels *A* AND *D* AND *E* can be applied, OR
iii. labels *F* and *G* can be applied.

The diagram represents only one possible structure: the same approach may be adopted no matter how complex the justification.

A practical example is illustrated by the remedy of damages for breach of contract. It has already been observed that the two basic requirements are contract and breach. If we look more carefully at contract the case law shows that it represents (with no pretence at exhaustiveness) the following labels:

((offer AND acceptance) OR agreement)
AND consideration
AND intention to create legal relations

This can be represented diagramatically as in figure (3).

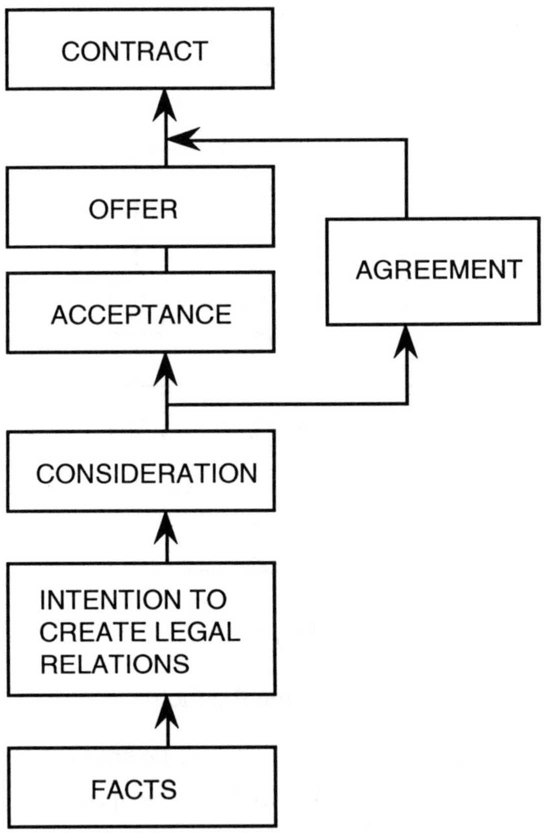

Figure 3.

It would be unusual if a case at bar involved disputes as to the application of all the labels required to justify the grant of a remedy. It is far more common for a case to turn on the application of a small number of labels from all those required. The arguments of counsel are directed at the application of the labels which are controversial. Most of the judgement concerns these labels with only cursory, if any, attention to the other necessary labels, the application of which is often conceded.

At this point it is important to attempt to link the justificatory process with the heuristic process. The application of a label justifies the granting of a remedy but the jurist applies the label because he understands a concept which the label merely represents. We must, therefore, see labels as nothing more than the signs for concepts as understood by the jurist. The concept and the label are at a point of correlation between the heuristic and the justificatory. The two are interdependent; any change in one in some way affects the other.

If a jurist decides that the concept that he understands covers the facts, he will apply the label. He must then justify the application. To do so he must provide an insight into his understanding of the concept. There are a number of ways in which he can do this. He may reason by analogy to attempt to show the factors which influenced the formation of the concept in his own mind in the hope that the analogy will create a similar concept in the mind of those who read his judgement. Alternatively, he may assume that the concept will be shared by those who read his judgement to the extent that the definition of the label in the context of the problem raised at bar will suffice to show why the label fits the facts. Both forms of reasoning are commonly found in the same cases, but it is probably true to say that the more long standing the label, and the more accepted the concept, then the more the judge will use the latter form of reasoning than the former.

In long developed areas of the common law the particular labels which are required to justify the grant of a remedy are often well settled. It would be surprising, for example, to see counsel arguing that consideration was not an essential element in a claim for damages for breach of contract and it would be more surprising still if a judge accepted the argument. It is not quite so unusual, however, to find cases in which the application of a well established label is called into question.[1] Again, though, it is true to say that the more long-standing a label the less likely its application is to be challenged.

It might appear therefore that the common law can reach a stage where the meaning of a label is incontrovertibly explained and, hence, that the concept that it represents is fixed. If this were so, barring legislative intervention, there might be some ultimate hope for certainty in the prediction of the outcome of a case. I shall argue that this is not possible.

A label is a word or a short phrase. It represents a concept. The first observation that must be made is that the label only represents the concept when the words from which it is formed are used in the relevant context of the legal labelling process and, indeed, in the area of law in which the concept comes to exist. The context sensitivity of labels is important. The meaning of a label can only be properly investigated in the correct legal context. Failure to pay attention to this issue will lead to the justificatory/heuristic correlation being overlooked and the true signification being lost. If at some later date the correlation is restored the acontextual explanation of the label will distort the original concept.[2]

Despite the assertion that the label is merely a sign for the concept and therefore that the concept should determine the meaning of the label, nevertheless it appears to be the case that the label exerts some influence over the concept. Because the judge must be able to justify his use of the concept, recorded explanations of the meaning of the label can confine that use. A concept which may originally have been unbounded in one direction can be very effectively circumscribed by an appellate judgement. The first instance judge may believe that the concept covers the facts, but not be able to justify the application of the label to the facts because of an explanation from which he is unable to depart. Ultimately it is then a small step to say that he has misperceived the concept, i.e. he has misperceived it as it truly is in the context of the law. Thus the wrong concept is being used if the application of its label leads to a justification that is inconsistent with the explanation of the label given by higher authority.

2. THE PROBLEM OF DEFINITION IN PRACTICE

The difficulties associated with providing an exhaustive definition of a label can be illustrated by the approach of English courts to the explanation of the meaning of the label 'consideration'. Although the consideration rule had a somewhat inconsistent historical rôle in the English law of contract[3], for the purposes of discussion, it is fair to say that the rule that consideration is an essential element for the grant of a contractual remedy has been generally accepted since the beginning of the nineteenth century.

An early attempt to explain the meaning of consideration was made in Selwyn's *Nisi Prius* (Selwyn 1831) which was subsequently adopted by the courts[4] in 1836. In 1893, Bowen LJ, in *Carlill v Carbolic Smoke Ball Co.*[5], treated this as a definition, quoting it as follows: 'Any act of the plaintiff from which the defendant derives benefit or advantage, or any labour, detriment, or inconvenience sustained by the plaintiff, with the consent...of the defendant.' On the facts, it was decided that the plaintiff who had used a smoke ball inhaler for a protracted period had suffered a detriment; and that the manufacturer whose sales had been promoted by its use had gained a benefit. There was, therefore, consideration for the manufacturer's promise that users of the smoke ball would not suffer from influenza, which was, thus, enforceable.

Selwyn's definition, used in Carlill, had already been de jure qualified before that case was decided. In *Thomas v Thomas*[6] it was held that a promise to convey a cottage could not be enforced if it was motivated merely by sentiment. In the words of Patteson J, 'A consideration, such as is recognized and known to our law, means a consideration of some value, moving from the plaintiff.' The argument that the satisfaction of a purely emotional desire could constitute a benefit was rejected. The Court here contemplated 'value' as economic value, and was able to treat the promise as enforceable because the widow had agreed to pay a ground rent of £1 per annum. The effect of *Thomas v Thomas* is to limit the broad definition of consideration put forward by Selwyn. It amounts to saying that the definition covered more cases than did the word it purported to explain.

It might be thought that the Thomas qualification, requiring a consideration to have economic value, would have vastly circumscribed the use of the label. It did not. The judges maintained a very open mind to the term 'value'. *Thomas v. Thomas* does not appear to have been intended to curtail that approach which was evident in *Bainbridge v Firmstone.*[7] In that case the defendant promised to reassemble two valuable boilers in return for the plaintiff's permission to weigh them. The defendant failed to reassemble the boilers and it was held that the plaintiff could enforce the defendant's promise. He had given consideration for the promise by allowing the defendant to weigh them. No enquiry was made by the court as to the value of the weighing to the defendant. It is now generally accepted that if some value can possibly be construed, it will be sufficient to satisfy the consideration test. The adequacy of the value will not be investigated. Thus, although something which is of no value cannot be termed consideration, the real extent to which a definition of consideration needs to accommodate this rule is limited.

A similarly liberal approach has been taken to the treatment of the requirement of benefit itself. In *Chappell & Co. Ltd. v Nestle Co. Ltd*[8], Lord Reid held that benefit could arise either directly or indirectly. In that case records were offered for sale as part of a chocolate promotion. The price was stipulated as a money payment together with three chocolate bar wrappers. His Lordship, with the majority of the House of Lords, found that the wrappers constituted consideration despite their lack of intrinsic value. The wrappers conferred a direct benefit on the manufacturer in so far as their acquisition in many cases was the result of sales that otherwise would not have taken place. They also conferred an indirect benefit, by way of advertising, which was of equal significance for the purposes of consideration. Thus any valuable benefit, whether direct or indirect can be labelled consideration.

In the cases considered thus far, consideration has been discussed as something tangible which had moved from the promisee before he sought to enforce the promise. Many contracts are, however, still at an executory stage when the breach occurs. In other words, the promisor has made his promise, the promisee has made a promise in return, the promisor has refused or failed to honour his promise and the promisee wishes to claim a contractual remedy against the promisor before actually performing his own promise. The consideration rule inevitably requires that for the promisee's claim to be successful, he must have given consideration. The Courts have overcome the apparent problem by regarding the promisee's promise as consideration: as Bowen LJ said in *Re Casey's Patent*[9], 'The consideration must be something other than...[what is to be done]...in the future. It is the promise...[to so act]...that constitutes the consideration.' In *Thomas v Thomas,* referred to earlier, it was the promise to pay the £1 ground rent which constituted consideration, not any subsequent payment itself. Thus the definition must be extended to allow the label to be attached to a promise.

A promise, or action. may, in certain circumstances, confer an undoubted benefit on the promisee, yet may not amount to consideration. There are two well known examples. First, the benefit may have been given before the promise was made. Second, there may have been a pre-existing legal obligation on the promisee to do the act which is subsequently done as putative consideration for the promise given. Both will be considered.

The rule that executed consideration does not support a subsequent promise is found in *Roscorola v Thomas.*[10] In that case a horse had been sold for £30. Subsequently, the vendor warranted it as 'sound and free from vice'. The horse did not comply with the warranty. It was held that the purchaser could not claim under the warranty because he had given no consideration. The sale was a past event which could have no effect on the vendor's subsequent promise which was thus gratuitous. Clearly the promisee had conferred a benefit but it was not such as amounted to consideration. Hence, the meaning of consideration must be understood to exclude, without more, past actions (and promises).

Cases in which attempts to argue that the performance, or promise to perform, pre-existing legal obligations can amount to consideration fall into three categories. The obligation can arise by operation of law, from a contract with a third party, or from a contract inter-partes.

As a general rule, the performance of an obligation that arises by operation of law does not constitute consideration. In *Collins v Godefroy*[11], a promise to pay a subpoenaed witness to testify was held unenforceable for want of consideration as he was doing no more than he was already bound to do. Similarly, in *Stilk v Myrick*[12] it was held that the performance of an obligation that has arisen from an inter partes contract does not amount to consideration for a new promise. In both types of case it has long been accepted that a promise, that would benefit the promisee or act as a detriment to the promisor by creating different legal rights would constitute consideration. Thus, in *The Atlantic Baron*[13], a promise to pay more than was necessary under a contract inter partes was in principle enforceable, consideration being a promise to perform the contractual obligation together with a new contractual obligation. Consideration in such cases appeared to involve a benefit or detriment in law rather than merely in fact.

In cases where the obligation arose from a contract between the promisee and a third party, on the other hand, the courts have encountered little difficulty in finding consideration. In *Pau On v Lau Yiu Long*[14], the Privy Council held that a promise to perform such a duty could amount to consideration for a new promise because it would give the new promisor 'the benefit of a direct obligation.' The benefit would be a factual benefit. A recent attempt has been made by the Court of Appeal to apply the factual benefit approach found in *Pau On* to the inter-partes scenario. In *Williams v Roffey*[15], a promise by a contractor to pay a sub-contractor more than he was obliged to pay was held enforceable. *Stilk v Myrick* was approved, yet only one of the three Lords Justices, Russell LJ, indicated that the consideration was a change of legal rights. The other two members of the court based their arguments on factual benefits.

The cases concerning the performance of a pre-existing legal obligations, have in the past, in the first two scenarios mentioned, regarded consideration as a change in legal rights. This clearly placed a further constraint on the meaning of consideration in some circumstances which the decision in *Williams v Roffey* is not, by itself, strong enough authority to reject.

Having reviewed the cases, several points have become clear:

1. Selwyn's 'definition', quoted in *Laythoarp v Bryant*[16] and subsequently in the Carlill case, is not a definition in the sense of an inflexible statement of meaning because it does not cover all the cases.
2. If there is a definition of 'consideration', it must accommodate all the cases mentioned above, given that they were not decided per incuriam.
3. Any definition must be sufficiently flexible to accommodate different judicial opinions on the same point, for example, the varying opinions on the nature of benefit present in *Williams v Roffey*.
4. The approach of the Courts has not been to lay down a definition and to adhere strictly to it, but rather to develop an intelligent understanding of when the term 'consideration' should apply; to develop that understanding in the light of new circumstances; and to develop that understanding flexibly.

To understand why the Courts cannot give a fixed definition of the term we must examine the status of 'definitions'.

3. MEANING AND ANALYSIS

Take a simple question 'What is a straight line?' The answer is apparently simple and uncontroversial: 'The shortest distance between two points on a plane surface.' The form of the question is common. It is applied almost universally when there is doubt whether a particular label ought to be applied to something. If for example the question is raised as to whether Stockhausen is a musician, it would not be surprising if the answer was approached by asking the further question 'what does musician mean?' The form of the answer is equally common. If an unknown word is read, the reader will, no doubt, search for its meaning in his dictionary —a meaning given in familiar language which is expected to exactly replicate that of the unknown word. If an interrogator asks for a word to be explained, the interrogatee will attempt to give a precise explanation of the word in the form of a definition. This approach appears to work very well in some instances; the straight line was a good example. It is not, however, universally effective, and what is at issue is the accuracy with which the putative definition conveys the meaning of the word.

Let us take another simple question 'What is a square?' Several answers come immediately to mind:

1. It is a plane bounded by two pairs of equilateral sides which intersect at right-angles.
2. It is a pitch on which cricket is played.
3. It is a conservative person who does not follow current trends.

Each answer is very different from every other answer, yet each answer describes a 'square'. None of the answers is incorrect, given the question. How might one of the answers be incorrect? Let us examine a statement and a question. If I take a friend to a cricket match I may observe 'The player on the far side of the square is the captain,' to which my friend may respond 'What is a "square"?' In those circumstances, only answer (2) is correct. The other two answers are excluded by the context of the question, i.e. by the context in which the word 'square' is used.

Let us now compare two of the answers, (1) and (3). Answer '1' explains when the word 'square' is applied in a geometrical context. It is an unusual form of explanation of a word because it is absolutely definitive. Anything which falls within answer (1) is a square in this context; anything which does not is not a square. There can be no debate; there can be no extension of the meaning. Answer (3), in contrast, is entirely different. It describes the meaning of the word square in a novel context. But it is far from absolutely definitive. To say that a square is a conservative person who does not follow current trends is to give only a vague idea of the meaning of square. Further questions inevitably arise: 'Must a person follow all current trends if he is to avoid being a square?', 'If not, which trends can he safely avoid?', 'To what sort of person can the term apply?', 'Can a three month old baby be a square?', 'Can a sixty year old solicitor avoid being a square?' etc. Answer (3) is incomplete, it may exclude some squares, but include some persons who cannot truly be labelled 'square'. It is no more than a rough approximation of the actual meaning of the term 'square'.

When an attempt is made to explain the meaning of a word the process used is usually analysis. The word in question is treated as a complex term which can be exactly represented by a number of other words. This approach has enjoyed recognition by laymen and philosophers alike. The ideal, in this process, is an exactly equivalent reduction of the word into others which can be reduced no more. If this could be achieved the meaning of the word in question would be unambiguous. Various attempts have been made at reductive analysis which can, for convenience be divided into two main groups. The first of the two is typified by the work of G. E. Moore; the second is the early logical analysis practised by the Atomists and the Positivists.

Moore's approach (Moore [1903] 1993) was to identify words for which he could find no equivalents: examples were 'red' and 'good'. The meaning of such terms, he believed, must be intuited. This approach produced a simple negative result: some terms could simply not be explained. The logical analysts (see Urmson, 1952), on the other hand, saw as their fundamental unanalyzables empirical data and the labels of objects. Their approach was more sophisticated than that of Moore: they worked on the basis of using logical operators to demonstrate the equivalence of apparently different representations of the same meaning and, by so doing, to demonstrate the irreducible representation of a complex term. In practise they were unsuccessful. Apparently complex terms such as 'nation' eluded precise analysis. Their theories simply did not work.

In *Philosophical Investigations* (Wittgenstein 1958), Wittgenstein identified two major reasons for the failure of analysis; indeed, two reasons for the impossibility of absolute reductive analysis. He dismissed the possibility of finding a logical framework underlying natural language, which was necessary for analytical purposes. He rejected the notion of exact, unquestionable definitions.

Logical analysis was premised on the basis that natural language rested upon a substantially logical framework. This can be attributed to an extension of Frege's belief (Baker and Hacker 1984) that human thought processes are based upon logic: this was extended by Russell to a theory that human language had a similar basis. (Russell 1972). If logic was the basis then it would have followed that exact linguistic equivalents could be produced and analysis could thereby take place. Russell had made the assumption of a logical basis. Wittgenstein argued that the assumption was groundless:

> Logic does not treat of language in the sense of which a natural science treats a natural phenomenon, and the most that can be said is that we construct an ideal language. (Wittgenstein, 1958, §81.)

Extra-linguistic factors, in the form of 'context' were too influential on the meaning that could be ascribed to a term to make the belief that some logical structure within language itself is capable of explicating meaning acceptable. The analysts, in Wittgenstein's opinion, had failed to take account of the vital influence of context.

If an ideal language was in operation, logical analysis and definition would clearly be possible. Frege had created such a language,

'Begriffsschrift', (Frege [1879] 1972), to process scientific results. If we return to the definition of the square, answer (1) represents a logical analysis. It does so because it refers to the square in the context of geometry where the term 'square' is no more than a logical construction. Answers (2) and (3) on the other hand refer to 'squares' in natural language where there is no logical basis to specify an absolute definition.

The impossibility of absolute reduction in natural language was further emphasised by the fact that it is always possible to conceive difficulties with a definition. Thus although answer (3) begins to explain the meaning of 'square', in doing so it raises more questions. Wittgenstein drew an analogy with the rules of a game:

> We can easily imagine people amusing themselves in a field playing with a ball so as to start various existing games, but playing many without finishing them and in between throwing the ball aimlessly into the air....And now someone says: the whole time they are playing a ball game and following rules at every throw. (Wittgenstein, 1958, §83.)

The past ball-play could be described by formulating rules to explain it, but those rules may well require amendment if they are to cover variations of play made in subsequent games. A definition, in other words, can only cover what its author currently understands and this understanding may be subsequently increased requiring the definition to be corrected.

4. LANGUAGE AND LAW

The conclusion drawn in the last section was that a word in natural language is not capable of precise, exhaustive definition, unlike a term in logical language. What, then is the status of a word in legal language? Can it be said that legal language is a logical language?

It is submitted that legal language is essentially natural language. Terms of legal art do not appear to have acontextual meanings. The label 'consideration' is an example in point. The four observations made above in relation to a definition of consideration indicate the rôle that definitions play in this subject. It is a different rôle from that of the geometrical definition of the square. It does not determine absolutely what is and what is not consideration; rather, it is flexible and can be amended as our understanding increases. It is a description of a concept in the mind of the jurist. It is much more like the third definition of the square given above. It represents a natural language approach.

The consideration cases show how the meaning of 'consideration' has been developed. The situation is very similar to that of the rules of Wittgenstein's game. All the decided cases could be reviewed and a definition of consideration produced that fits them all. If a case arises in the future involving a new aspect of consideration, the existing definition might well prove inappropriate. This is consistent with what has been seen in the consideration cases. Definitions have not been treated as determinative of meaning, unlike the geometrical definition, (1), of the square. In view of the new case, the definition would need amendment. The initial definition of consideration could not determine absolutely whether or not the facts of the new case could be labelled 'consideration' because the natural basis of legal language prevents total explication of the concepts involved. A putative definition of a legal term, it seems, is derived from nothing more than observations of how that term has been used thus far. Thus, although, as indicated above, the definition, especially if from a higher court, may limit the expansion of a concept in some respects, it does not precisely describe or confine it. It is not a definition that will bind us to invariably use the label in a particular way in the future.

The truth of the matter is that judges do not, as an observable phenomenon, justify their decisions by rigorously analysing the meanings of the labels that they have applied and by then showing why the definition covers the facts. Instead, they indicate little more than is necessary to explain why the label does or does not apply to the given facts. This is not necessarily a purposive approach; the courts have been careful to avoid being drawn to the non-legal merits of the claims.[17] Whether the label will be applied depends upon the judges understanding of the concept. This will not necessarily be capable of being put exhaustively into words; the case at bar will however enable the judge to express part of his understanding as the meaning of the label. It is from a synthesis of these parts that in many cases an attempt to express a general explanation of meaning can be made, but, because we are dealing with natural language, the explanation cannot be exhaustive.

Linguistically, the legal approach to the meaning of words is not analysis but synthesis. The meaning is gradually developed as new cases arise. This is appropriate: the words could not be exhaustively analysed, even if this were desired, in the context of the natural language of the law.

5. APPLICATION TO ALGORITHMS

To determine the availability of a remedy mechanically, it appears essential to analyse the process of justificatory legal reasoning into the most simple unambiguous steps in order to produce a comprehensive algorithm which follows the 'logic' of the justificatory process. The justificatory rule 'If *X* then *Y*', where *X* is a label and *Y* is a remedy, must form the basis of the algorithm. Normally, *X* will be one of several labels that must be capable of being applied to the facts in order to create a particular legal consequence. Each label may be more or less complicated. 'Consideration', like other complex labels, must be broken down into its components if we are to be able to adopt a mechanical process to determine whether or not it is to be applied. We might like to say that '*X*'' is equivalent to '*a* and *b* and either *c* or *d* or *e*', where *a*, *b*, *c*, *d*, *e* are simple unambiguous terms. This is why the process of definition is so crucial, for the judicial definition is the analysis from which the unambiguous terms, together with the relevant logical operators, are derived.

The nature of legal language and the inter-relation between the heuristic and justificatory processes presents serious obstacles to the creation of this type of algorithm. We cannot do so for two reasons: *a*, *b*, *c*, *d*, *e* cannot be unambiguous because they are elements of natural language; we cannot be sure that there is perfect equivalence because there is no logical operation on which it can be grounded. Furthermore, the ability of explanations of labels to curb concepts is only partial. Because the labels are part of natural language, it is not possible to provide an exhaustive definition of the way in which a label is used. It is not possible therefore for the justificatory judgements of the court to precisely define the limits of the concepts that lie behind the labels. It will always be possible for someone with an understanding of the concept to say that the concept fits a new factual situation which the definition of the label did not envisage. Although we may look at the cases and define label '*X*' as some configuration of *a*, *b*, *c*, *d* and *e*, we can have no a priori inkling that another component, *f*, say, is required. The requirement of *f* is the result of subsequent juridical synthesis at the justificatory level.

If the algorithm cannot be based on acontextual, linguistic meaning alone, it may be argued that it could be effective if it included those factors which indicate the context, i.e. which determine the direction that synthesis will take. Factors which influence the direction include social policy, morality, and political culture. It is not claimed that this list is exhaustive; the list merely indicates the diversity of extra-legal phenomena that influence the development of the law. For a mechanical application of these considerations to be possible, the range of factors together with their influence must be defined. Unfortunately, the common problems associated with natural language will have as great an effect on attempts to define the meaning and, therefore the application, of these factors as it has been shown to have in other areas. Attempts to define when and how the factors will affect synthesis will, on this understanding be, fundamentally uncertain. Furthermore, it is difficult to see how the type of factor that could be relevant could be exhaustively defined —contexts may change. An attempt to produce an algorithm that overcomes the uncertainty of meaning of a legal label resulting from the contextual nature of language by attempting to isolate the factors that influence the way in which the language is construed would merely move uncertainty one stage further on.

6. THE PROBLEM IN PERSPECTIVE

From what has been said thus far, it would appear that it is impossible to know with certainty from previous justifications whether or not an existing label will be applied to the facts of a new case and hence the notion of constructing an algorithm based on existing justificatory reasoning which will take the same decisions about the award of remedies as would a jurist giving a justification is impossible. An existing definition of the label can give some indication of how the meaning of the label must be changed if it is to include or exclude the new case. Definitions of the effect of the extra-legal factors will give some indication of whether the label should be applied. Neither of these will indicate, for certain that the label must be applied. This represents a conceptual limit on what can be achieved by mechanical jurisprudence. No matter how developed the algorithm, there is no proof against new, thus far unconsidered, factors appearing which would result in a jurist solving a legal problem in a credible and acceptable way that is contrary to the mechanical solution and which makes clear that the latter is unacceptable.

Whilst this is a conceptual obstacle to the creation and application of algorithms, it does not follow that in practise it should be regarded as dealing a mortal blow to the their value. If, instead of attempting to produce a system which would in fact be an idealised syllogistic common law decision maker, we attempt to produce a system which takes the same decisions as would such a super-jurist in a very large proportion of cases, the project of mechanisation begins to look very attractive. It must be remembered that the importance of precision is, in practice, relative.

The attempt to determine the outcome of cases from mechanical tests for the application of significant legal labels has been castigated because, in new cases, it may be wrong: it may fail to recognise an important new factor. This should be compared with attempts at the 'intelligent' human determination of the outcome of a case. This may also prove unsatisfactory on either, or both, of the twin criteria of credibility and acceptability: the new factor may not be noticed, its significance may be over or underestimated, insufficient care may have been taken to produce the existing meaning of the label into which the new factor must be consistently incorporated, an extra-legal influence may have been misused. It is no exaggeration to say that the intelligent justifiable determination of the outcome of cases is a 'Herculean' task; given that it is performed by mortals there is a significant probability of error. Mechanical decision-making also involves the probability of error. It would be rash to claim that the latter probability is inevitably higher than the former.

NOTES

1 Issues concerning the application of the label 'consideration' recently went to the English Court of Appeal in *Williams v Roffey* [1990] 1 All ER 512.

2 It is arguable that this is the cause of the problem of validity of the so called Romalpa clauses(See *Aluminium Industrie v Romalpa Aluminium* [1976] 1 WLR 676). The label 'property' has been used historically in several ways i.e. to refer to several concepts. Difficulties have arisen as a result of modern attempts by vendors to become unregistered, secured creditors by reserving 'property' in contracts of sale. In certain contexts it is clear that property can be reserved, e.g. in cif contracts and under S.19 Sale of Goods Act 1979. It is by no means clear that what is meant by 'property' in such a valid reservation is the same thing as is meant by 'property' in Romalpa clauses.

3 Originally, the consideration was itself the cause of legal obligations. Latterly, it has become the generally accepted view that obligations arise as a result of the contractual promise; they are given legal effect if consideration is present. See (Atiyah, 1979).

4 *Laythoarp v Bryant*, (1836) 3 Scott 238 at 250

5 [1893] 1 QB 256 at 271.

6 (1842) 2 QB 851.

7 (1838) 8 A & E 743.

8 [1960] AC 87.

9 [1892] 1 Ch 104.

10 (1842) 3 QB 234.

11 (1831) 1 B & Ad. 950.

12 (1809) 2 Camp. 317.

13 [1979] QB 705.

14 [1980] AC 614.

15 [1990] All ER 512.

16 (1836) 3 Scott 238.

17 As an example of this judicial reluctance, see the judgement of Bingham LJ in *Blackpool and Fylde Aero Club v Blackpool B.C.* [1990] 3 All ER 25.

REFERENCES

Atiyah, P., 1979. *Rise and Fall of the Freedom of Contract,* Oxford University Press, pp. 139–154, 448–455.

Baker, G.P. and Hacker, P.M.S., 1984. *Frege: Logical Excavations*, Blackwell, Oxford.

Frege, G., [1879] 1972. *Begriffsschrift,* trans. *Conceptual Notation and Related Articles,* T.W. Bynum (ed.), Oxford 1972..

Moore, G.E., [1903] 1993. *Principia Ethica,* (revised edition, ed. T. Baldwin), Cambridge University Press.

Russell, B.A.W., 1972. 'Logical Atomism I', reprinted in *The Philosophy of Logical Atomism,* D. Pears (ed.), London.

Selwyn, W., 1831. *An Abridgement of the law of Nisi Prius*, 8th edn, London.

Urmson, J.O., 1956. *Philosophical Analysis*, Oxford University Press.

Wittgenstein, L., 1958. *Philosophical Investigations*, ed. and trans. G.E.M. Anscombe, R. Rhees, G.H. von Wright, 2nd edn, Blackwell, Oxford..

Faculty of Law
University of Leeds
England

GARRETT BARDEN

FORMALIZATION, INVENTION, JUSTIFICATION

1. ONTOLOGICAL AND EPISTEMOLOGICAL CONDITIONS

In any instance of justification there is a conditioned, *X*, whose conditions are said to be fulfilled. Thus: *X*, if the set of conditions, *C*. And *C*. Therefore, *X*. This justificatory structure holds in every domain.

The conditioned, *X*, is a proposition. There is a distinction between ontological and epistemological conditions. Tarski's suggestion (Tarski [1944] 1949) that the proposition expressed in the sentence 'Snow is white' is true iff it is the case that snow is white, denotes the ontological condition of the truth of the proposition. The ontological condition does not epistemologically justify the proposition. If I am asked why I claim that snow is white, I do not answer simply: 'Because it is white'. Rather I give an answer like: 'Because when I look out my window and see what I have been taught to call "snow", I get the impression that it is the colour that I have been taught to call "white".' This may not be thought to be a very satisfactory answer, that is, the questioner may not think that this is sufficient evidence for affirming the proposition, but the sole present point is that it is a different kind of answer from the ontological answer. When presented with any proposition whatsoever one knows at once the ontological condition of its being true; namely, that what it affirms is the case. Contrariwise, one does not immediately know the epistemological conditions of whatsoever proposition. To know the relevant epistemological conditions is to know the domain within which the proposition belongs.

In the formal expression of the basic form of inference, '*X* if *C*, And *C*, So *X*', the major premiss, '*X* if *C*', asserts not that *C* holds but that *C* is the relevant condition. The minor premiss, 'And *C*', asserts that *C* holds. The justified conclusion asserts that *X* holds because *C* holds and *C* is the relevant condition of *X*.[1].

2. THE STRUCTURE OF THE CONDITIONED ENTITLEMENT

What holds for every domain, holds for the jural domain, but to distinguish the jural domain it will be necessary to describe the character of the conditioned, *X* and the set of relevant conditions, *C*.

In the jural domain the internal structure of the conditioned is *RxAy*, where *x* and *y* are legal persons; *A* is the entitlement or what is due; and *RxAy* is that

Z. Bankowski et al. (eds.), Informatics and the Foundations of Legal Reasoning, 245–269.

x is entitled to A from y. Thus, $RxAy$ if C, where C is the set of relevant conditions and $RxAy$ is the consequent relation of entitlement.

This is an empirical claim about rules of justice and decisions of courts. It pretends to denote what is, as a matter of fact, the case, not what must be the case. Thus, it is perfectly possible to imagine a criminal process where the conclusion of the Court is simply of the form: '*x* is guilty of the crime of which he stood accused', or: '*x* is not guilty . . .', or: 'The accusation against *x* is not proven'. But, as a matter, not of necessity but of fact, this type of judgement, although it forms an important part of the Court's process, is not its conclusion. The conclusion is of the type: '*x*, having been declared guilty of the crime of which he stood accused, is sentenced to *S*,' where *S* is what, in the judgement of the Court, is due to *x* from the State.[2]

This analysis accepts the division between crime and tort which, again, is a division of convenience, perhaps of great convenience and of considerable antiquity; it is certainly not a matter of necessity. Thus, where *S* is interpreted as '*S* is due to *x* from the State' this is a particular application of the general structure $RxAy$ of a particular criminal procedure in which x is 'the Criminal', y is 'the State' and A is 'the Sentence'.

The analysis illustrates that, even where, at first glance, the Court's decision is not of the form $RxAy$, it turns out to be so on closer investigation.

In any attempt to use the structure $RxAy$ it will be necessary to specify what stands for x, what for y and what for A. Some further specification is given below.

3. ENTITLEMENTS AND RULES

Not all *rules* are of this kind.

Rules such as 'Do not drive vehicles in this park', 'Do not park on this side of the road', 'No smoking', 'Ships must display shapes by day and lights by night', are not of this kind.

There is no suggestion that is uninteresting to study such rules. But they are not *rules of justice* and it is misleading to confuse them with rules of justice and to take them or their like as paradigms when discussing justice and its administration.[3]

Suppose a Court to be confronted with someone accused of driving a vehicle in the park where the only rule is 'Do not drive vehicles in this park'. The Court could consider the evidence and come to the conclusion that the accused was or was not in contravention of the rule but it could go no further; it could not assign an entitlement for the clear and simple reason that no entitlement goes with a rule of this kind. It is part of the Court's task to determine whether or not the accused is in contravention of the rule but the Court is not in fact content with this and continues its work the goal of which is to assign entitlements in the light of the discovered situation. [4]

It might be objected that Courts are concerned with such rules but that they might assign entitlements entirely of their own invention. This is patently not in fact the case but even hypothetically it is mistaken. Were the Court's task to assign entitlements in case of the contravention of a rule such as 'Do not drive vehicles in this park', then the real structure of the rule, *as it concerns the Court*, is: 'Anyone driving a vehicle in this part is liable to an entitlement to be settled by the Court.'[5]

The answer to the objection shows how rules of this kind may be transformed into rules of justice with which the Court may be concerned, namely, by the addition of an entitlement associated with breaking the rule, e.g. 'Anyone bringing a vehicle into this part is liable to a fine of ECU50'.

This form of such transformed rules is:

$(x)\ Fx \rightarrow RxAy$, where

Fx : x brings a vehicle into this park etc.

$RxAy$: x is in a relation of entitlement with y with respect to liability to a fine of ECU50.

As a corollary, and in passing, since this is not the present concern, it may be asked if the legislature deals with rules or laws of the form 'Do not bring vehicles into this park'. It is clear on brief examination of legislative practice that the legislature is certainly not concerned *only* with rules of this kind. It would seem that most of the rules emanating from a modern legislature include associated entitlements. However, it does seem that there are rules or laws of this kind. Constitutional provisions often seem not to include any associated entitlement. Thus, if the State or its representatives breaches a Constitutional provision the Court will often simply require that it annul or cease from its action in breach of, and act in accord with, the Constitution.[6]

Notice, too, that the *political purpose* of many rules, including rules of justice, is to prevent certain activities or to ensure the possibility of others. But the Court is not directly concerned with these issues.

4. TWO-PLACE RELATIONS

As applying within the jural domain the relation $RxAy$ reads: x is a legal person; y is a legal person; A is an entitlement; $RxAy$ states that x is entitled to *A* from *y*. The meanings of 'legal person' and of 'entitlement' remain to be defined.

From the formalism, the relation of entitlement, however it is to be further specified, is a three place relation; a legal person is whatever may stand for *x* or *y*; an entitlement is whatever may stand for *A*.

It is proposed that the relation *RxA* (*x* is entitled to *A*) is either a short version of the three place relation *RaXy* or is jurally meaningless. An expression in common speech such as 'Everyone is entitled to enough food' is not meaningless but neither is it a jural statement. Many political rights or claims are expressed as two place relations of the form *RxA*; endless confusion is generated if it supposed that these rights or claims are jurally meaningful. They become jurally meaningful only when transformed into the three place relation, *RxAy*, and become specific only when *x* and *y* are specified. For this, among other reasons, jural relations are institutional.

Two place relations such as 'Everyone is entitled to enough food' or 'Every citizen is entitled to enough food' are politically meaningful as claims precisely because they envisage a second political person or persons from whom everyone or every citizen is so entitled; they envisage eventual legislation when they become rules of justice in which both entitlements and jural persons will be specified. When it is impossible to envisage a second political person or persons as in, for example, 'Every state within the EC is entitled to exactly the same amount of sunshine and rainfall' the claim becomes politically and jurally absurd.[7]

5. ENTITLEMENT AND *IUS*

An entitlement is whatever is due to a legal person within the relation *RxAy*. *Justitia est constans et perpetua voluntas ius suum cuique tribuere* —which may be translated as: 'The virtue of justice is the constant and enduring willingness to give to each that to which they are entitled (or, that which is due to them).'

The Roman formulation is interesting for two reasons. First, a similar expression: *suum cuique tribuendi* ('to give to each what is theirs') occurs without *ius*. Secondly, certainly in early Roman law, the central paradigm or exemplar of the entitlement or what was due was a material thing, an object, viz., a house or a piece of land or a slave and so the term *res* is used and only gradually becomes extended to include non-material things. The term *ius* at the beginning of the Institutes is, I suspect, a quite deliberate attempt on

Tribonian's part to invent a technical term to indicate the deep jural structure of what was due.

Roman Law is a flexible, subtle and fallible attempt to describe and determine society as a network of jural relations between citizens and others.[8] In other words, it is an attempt to see society from the perspective of what is mine, what is yours, what is ours, what is theirs etc. when 'what is mine' may be different from 'that which I now physically hold' (even if physical possession was and remained a powerful image of ownership to the extent that claiming a slave as one's own included the gesture of putting one's hand on him and manumission became the technical word for giving a slave freedom). The distinction between physical possession as the sole criterion of ownership[9] and *ius* is an indication of an institutional theory of law operative implicitly in Roman jurisprudence (or perhaps it would be better to say that the institutional theory of law provides a good interpretation of Roman jurisprudential practice —as, of course, if correct, it should!)

A rule of justice, then, determines, at a certain level of generality, what, in the society, belongs to whom. Litigation between parties is always a dispute, now at a very specific level, about who owns what, who is entitled to what, what is due to whom. Litigation always emerges within a society institutionally defined by the rules of justice that state the jural relations between its members. (The quarrel between jural philosophers may often be about the nature, extent, specificity and applicability of that institutional definition to the instant case).

In the formalism the relationship of entitlement is already interpreted to be a three place relation. A brief indication of why this interpretation is chosen should be given.

First, there is good traditional precedent. The jural relation is explicitly three place in Aristotle. In the Roman formulation above it is implicitly so.

Secondly, there are good independent reasons for following this tradition. Jural relations are relations between people. But what distinguishes them from, say, the relation of friendship is that they regard what is owned by each person. Although he uses similar terms with a meaning quite different from their meaning here, Hobbes clearly and correctly saw that what are here called jural relations simply did not exist in the solitary state. Possession and dispossession did exist, for the solitary was not alone, but possession was not ownership in the sense of *ius*. (What Hobbes called 'law' (Hobbes, 1651). Confusingly, from the limited point of view of this essay, Hobbes uses the Latin *ius*, which he translates as 'right', to refer to a pre-institutional characteristic of the solitary state. But 'right' for him was the freedom to possess whatever one could possess and was conducive to one's own survival. Neither Hobbes nor anyone else has ever pretended that his meaning of *ius* is close to the Roman.) Thus, in a jural relation there is always a third thing called here an *entitlement*, and in Roman law commonly a *res*, but in the *Preamble* already quoted a *ius*.

Expressions such as 'I have worked hard and am entitled to my dinner/ a drink/ a swim etc.' are both commonplace and meaningful. They are not, I think, jural. And once again the empirical test is to ask what a Court can do with such entitlements if no third element (a second person) can be found.[10]

Finally, there are everyday expressions of three place relations that are not jural. Thus, 'A horse is entitled to humane treatment from its owner' is not properly jural since a horse (as a matter of fact in most jurisdictions, not as a matter of principle) is not a legal person. An entitlement is defined as between legal persons. What is meant by 'legal person' is not carried by the formalism and must be examined later.

6. ENTITLEMENTS AND INSTITUTIONS

Entitlements are institutional. They may be so in a variety of ways.

Like many terms taken from common speech to serve as terms of art, 'institutional' can mislead. An institution may be imagined to be a third thing, separate from the actors, within which people interact. Properly an institution should be understood as analytically distinct from, but not separate from, the actors. Thus, for example, if two people, NN and AA, enter into a relation of lending and borrowing so that NN lends her car to AA, and correlatively, AA borrows NN's car, then NN and AA have established between them the institution of lending and borrowing even in case this institution had never before existed.

Lending and borrowing is an institution that is constituted by and through the meaning of the participants. We can now ask what entitlements are involved in the institution but it should be made clear that the entitlements will not be tacked on to the institution; the network of entitlements is the institution.

What if AA fails to return NN's car? Perhaps NN will try to recover it by force. If there are no further institutional arrangements this or something like it will be the outcome, as Hobbes plainly saw. Or it may be that an effective adjudicative institution will be established that, once again, will have a number of entitlements constituting its meaning. For example, the disputants may be entitled to an authoritative hearing and to the public enforcement of its decisions. Or they may be required to submit to this procedure, i.e. they may be required to live in that relation with one another. Clearly the question of authority and coercion arises in this context yet it is not the present question.[11]

In case no such institution exists and NN claims that she is entitled to an effective adjudicative hearing, what is the status of her claim? It is simply a claim. It is meaningful to propose that a certain entitlement should exist but it is needlessly confusing to assert that an entitlement exists when, as a matter of institutional fact, it does not.

Finally, the old question of a distinction between natural and conventional entitlements is not a matter of a distinction between natural and institutional entitlements. All entitlements are institutional. Some are natural, i.e. they arise from the nature or character of the institution. Some are conventional, i.e. they are invented to decide between matters of indifference. That NN retains ownership of her car is natural to the institution of lending and borrowing; that AA is to return the car after one week is conventional.

7. ENTITLEMENTS AND THE DEONTIC

Jural relations are sometimes thought to be more properly analysed deontically. While I do not agree with this position, it is not to be thought that jural relations are totally dissociated from deontic relations. The relation between the two seems to me to be:

$$RxAy \rightarrow y \text{ should give } A \text{ to } x.$$

'Should give' may be 'must give' or 'may give'. This may be written $\mathrm{O}yAx$. Accordingly,

$$RxAy \rightarrow \mathrm{O}yAx\,.$$

This may be generalized to read:

$$(x)(y)(A)RxAy \rightarrow \mathrm{O}yAx.$$

I take this last expression to exhibit the meaning of the Roman formula: *iustitia est constans et perpetua voluntas ius suum cuique tribuere*. The virtue or deontic element in the formula is expressed by *iustitia est constans et perpetua voluntas ... cuique tribuere*, and the categorical element by *ius suum*. Implicit, but patent, in the Roman formula is that whatever whosoever is entitled to, that they should be given. This universal element is expressed in the formalism by $(x)(y)\,(A)$.

The formalization as so far elaborated seems to derive *ought* ($OyAx$) from *is* ($RxAy$). In fact it does not but this must be made clear.

The formalization, like the Roman formula, simply defines what the virtue of justice is: if you wish to be just then you must give to each what is due to them (on the particular occasions when it is relevant to you to be just). So if AA is entitled to something from NN, it follows that NN should give that something to AA only in case NN should be just. Thus the full deontic formalization becomes:

$$O\{(x)(y)(A)RxAy \rightarrow OyAx\}.$$

This states not simply what the virtue of justice is but that one ought to be just. Thus, there is no reason, other than the convenience of the occasion, to be just on a particular occasion unless it is the case that in general one ought to be just and that one ought to be just generally cannot be derived from the fact that another is entitled to something from oneself. Still, if for whatever reason, y wants to be just, then y should give A to x because x is entitled to A from y. To be just is to give someone what they are entitled to from you; so, if one decides to be just, this is what one must do.[12]

The question as to why one ought to be just properly arises —this is an important question in Hobbes, the 'obscure heart of his, (and any) moral theory'— but it is not the present question.

Under the general rubric that each participant in a jural community should be just we have that the reason AA should give X to NN is that NN is entitled to X from AA. Thus, $OyAx \rightarrow RxAy$, where $OyAx$ is: 'y should give A to x' . Conversely, if NN is entitled to X from AA, then AA should give X to NN. Thus, $RxAy \rightarrow OyAx$.

Why is the fact that NN is entitled to X from AA *a reason* for AA to give X to NN? Because, in the social world in which entitlements exist, that AA should give X to NN is part of the meaning of the fact. Entitlements that were never in fact honoured might be pointless but they would not be meaningless; entitlements that were in principle never honoured would be meaningless: if a promise, in principle, never commits the promissor, the institution is, not only pointless, but meaningless.

8. LEGAL PERSONS AND HUMAN PERSONS

Entitlements have been defined as terms in a relation between legal persons. A legal person is anything that can fill the places x or y in the expression $RxAy$.

It can happen that not every human person is a legal person. Slaves, wives and children in Roman Law were not, and there have been cases in more recent times where women have been denied that status. Things that are not human persons can be legal persons. There are mediaeval examples of animals being legal persons. And, importantly, corporations, cities, states are legal persons. What is or is not a legal person is determined within a jural system. Thus, a legal person is institutionally determined.

There can be dispute within a community as to what should or should not be a legal person and further dispute as to how the matter is to be settled; but it is crucial to recognize that an adjudicative system does not simply jurally organize legal persons but constitutes them for the first time as legal persons. Thus, in a promise, I constitute myself as a promissor.

Since to be a legal person carries entitlements, to be a legal person is itself an entitlement. Thus it may be that, within a jural system, provisional and limited status may be granted to allow a claim for personhood to be heard. So, a question could and did arise about the status of the commercial organization called a company: was a company a single thing? was it a legal person? But here it is plain that 'legal person' means *capable of legal relations*, i.e. substituting for either of the variables, x or y, in the relation $RxAy$. A candidate for legal personhood will present arguments in favour of its candidature (there will be, therefore, an argumentative or reasonable source for personhood); there will be also decision (and, therefore, a responsible or voluntary source).

Notice that although not every human person has always been institutionally determined to be a legal person and not every legal person is a human person, still, because legal persons must be capable of legal relations (either independently or through representation), it follows that only those things that are independently capable of legal relations are potentially legal persons by nature, and no legal system will exist without the participation of things that are potentially legal persons by nature. Thus, although legal personhood is institutional, it includes and must include the actualization of a natural potentiality in the sense outlined.

9. LEGAL PERSONS AND ENTITLEMENTS

Accordingly, in the relation $RxAy$, where x and y are legal persons, A is an entitlement and R is a relation of entitlement, the relation defines the terms and the terms the relation such that anything is a legal person that can fill the place x or y and anything is an entitlement that can fill the place A.

Conversely, anything that is entitled to nothing is not a legal person and anything to which no legal person is entitled is not an entitlement.

10. JURAL CONDITIONS

RxAy is conditioned. *C* is the set of conditions. The formal structure of the jural institution is $C \rightarrow RxAy$ (or $RxAy \leftarrow C$). Formally, anything is a condition that can fill the variable *C*. Materially, anything whatsoever can fill the variable *C*, e.g.

> If the wind is in the right quarter,
> Sophie is entitled to maintenance from Peter.

This curiosity is simply the application to a jural context of the material conditional.

Since, materially, anything can be the condition for anything, the actual jural conditional will, and must, be a matter for argument and decision. Jural reflection and decision will, and must, be in response to the fundamental jural question: *what condition goes with what entitlement?*

What kind of thing can be a jural condition? The formal answer is that anything can be a condition that can fill the place *C* in $C \rightarrow RxAy$, and that nothing is a jural condition that cannot fill the place *C*. Since we know that, materially, anything can be the condition for anything, it becomes clear that what is or is not a jural condition is, once again, a matter of jural reflection and decision.

Take the condition, 'If the wind is in the right quarter'. Can this be a jural condition? The answer, however bizarre it may seem at first sight, is, quite unequivocally, affirmative. This answer indicates, perhaps, that the question is not very useful and the more useful question is: *Is* it a jural condition? This is an empirical question about actual jural systems. And we can also ask: is it the kind of thing that is a condition within actual jural systems or within an actual jural system? The courts or the legislature, however, are sometimes faced with yet another question when it is claimed that something, which is not yet a condition for a given entitlement, should become one. Thus, it may be claimed that a described mistake voids a given contract. Here *C* is the described mistake; the entitlement claimed is that the contractual relation between *x* and *y* (*RxAy*) is voided, i.e. $\sim(RxAy)$.

Associated Japanese Bank (International) Ltd v. Credit du Nord SA and another[13] involves the law of common mistake and will be helpful in the approach to discovering what kind of thing can become a condition within

English Common law. My purpose is not to discover precisely the present English law of common mistake but to examine some uncontroversial and accepted features of mistake in order to discover what kind of a thing mistake is. In the course of his judgement Steyn J. writes:

> Lord Atkin held ([1932] AC 161 at 218, [1931] All ER Rep I at 28): 'a mistake will not affect assent unless it is the mistake of both parties, and is as to the existence of some quality which makes the thing without the quality essentially different from the thing as it was believed to be.'[14]

I think it is commonly agreed that a mistake will or may affect the contract if it is the mistake of both parties as to the existence of some quality which makes the matter of the contract, without the quality, essentially different from what it was believed to be. Three features are to be noticed: (1) there is mistake; (2) the mistake is common to the contracting parties; (3) the mistake regards the contract. The spontaneous response to the third feature would be, I suspect, that it is so obvious that it is not worth reporting. Of course, the mistake must regard the contract. Were the contracting parties mistaken about the result of a football game that had nothing to do with their contract, this common mistake would be irrelevant. What the isolation of the feature and the response to the isolation shows is that a relation of relevance between condition and conditioned (between C and $RxAy$) is fundamental. (Some of the humour in both Lewis Carroll and Franz Kafka, however widely different in other respects their humour is, has its source in their refusal of anticipated relevance). It is the relation of relevance that moves the conditional from being simply material to being potentially jural.

What kind of mistake is relevant to a contract? Certainly, a mistake without which the contract or some detail of the contract would not have been made or would have been different. This may not be enough (indeed, in English law it is not enough). But it is a necessary condition and is an attempt to define relevance in mistake.

Common mistake is 'naturally' relevant to the contract. This does not mean that the proposition 'Common mistake is "naturally" relevant to the contract' is naturally known; the claim is simply that when one examines contract and mistake about the matter of the contract it will seem reasonable to make the judgment that mistake is relevant to the contract. However, despite its natural relevance to contract, this must be discovered and instituted for mistake to be jurally relevant.

The first feature, (1), that there is mistake, is equally banal. Still, the banal is sometimes worth a glance and we can note first that the mistake is entirely with respect to C. It is not a mistake about the major premiss: $RxAy \leftarrow C$. It is a mistake about the nature of the world (including, of course, the social world) not about the law. A distinction is commonly made between law and facts. Facts are *C*. There is no suggestion that jural perspectives are not used in describing a fact or determining whether or not something was a fact; but if something is, or purports to be, a fact, then it fills the place *C* in the conditional $RxAy \leftarrow C$.

Jurists generally, and for excellent reasons, take (1) and (3) for granted, to concentrate on (2) which contains the meat of English doctrine. It is in (2) that English law may differ from other laws. (1) and (3) are common to all legal systems.

A condition, *C*, is then a state of affairs relevant to a jural entitlement. A potential condition is a state of affairs potentially relevant to a jural entitlement. A state of affairs can be pronounced not to be a condition if it has been determined not to be relevant to any jural entitlement. A state of affairs may be pronounced not to be a condition in a restricted domain if it has been determined not to be relevant to any jural entitlement within that domain.

Rules of justice, then, establish mutual entitlements (*RxAy*) within states of affairs (*C*). Legislation does so at a level of generality; courts at a specific level.

The proposal that *C* is a state of affairs requires further work for it is still shorthand. Suppose that having been born in Ireland is legislated to be a sufficient condition for Irish citizenship. That state of affairs is not a sufficient condition for one's citizenship to be recognized; the sufficient condition for recognition is the judgement that one was born in Ireland and, as we saw above, the fact of having been born in Ireland is the sufficient and necessary ontological condition for the truth of the judgement that one was born in Ireland but is not the epistemological condition for affirming the judgement.

This analysis leads to an aporia that recalls Lichtenberg's aphorism that the difference between an insane person who thinks himself a prince and a prince is that no-one accepts the insane person's definition of himself. Suppose that a person, *X*, fulfils the condition for citizenship but cannot show this, is he a citizen? He has none of the entitlements that flow from citizenship; should he attempt to claim something on the basis of citizenship he may be arraigned for fraud. In practice he is not a citizen; as far as others are concerned he is like Lichtenberg's deluded person. And yet the rule does not say that one is a citizen if one can show that one fulfils the condition; the rule states that one is a citizen if one fulfils the condition. The distinction between ontological and epistemological condition is again useful. One's being a citizen rests on the fact; one's being recognized as a citizen rests on the judgement.

A distinction between 'being' and 'being recognized' is the condition of the possibility of the court being mistaken.

It may be asked if *C* is an ontological or an epistemological condition in $C \rightarrow RxAy$. It would seem that we must distinguish. 'Being born in Ireland' is an ontological condition for the entitlement 'Irish citizenship'. The Court will require epistemological conditions to affirm the proposition '*X* was born in Ireland' and it is the judgement '*X* was born in Ireland' that is the relevant condition for the granting of the entitlement 'Irish citizenship'. Thus, the Court's affirmation of the proposition '*X* was born in Ireland' is the ontological condition of the Court's granting the entitlement 'Irish citizenship' to *X*.

The conclusion of the Court is that *RxAy*. To arrive at this conclusion the Court relies on the major premise $RxAy \leftarrow C$ [the rule of justice] and on the minor premise that *C* [the judgement that the conditions are fulfilled].

11. SPECIFICITY AND CLARITY

Stated conditions may incline towards the pole of specificity (SC) or towards the pole of non-specificity (NC); cases may tend towards the pole of being clear and uncontroverted instances of the relevant conditions (ci) or towards the pole of being non-clear instances of the relevant conditions (ni). The following combinations are possible:

(1) SC/ci; (2)SC/ni; (3)NC/ci; (4)NC/ni.

(1) When the conditions tend towards specificity and the instance is clear the matter often does not appear before the Court. Social security regulations are frequently of this kind. (2) Litigation in this situation will concentrate on persuading the court that the situation is plausibly described or not described as an instance of the conditions. (3) This is the situation that occurs when something is, for example, manifestly unreasonable[15], although 'unreasonable' is a condition tending towards non-specificity. (4) Finally, and to stay with the same example, it often happens that it is difficult to settle whether some action was, in the circumstances, reasonable or not.

12. NEW SITUATIONS OF ENTITLEMENT

It is now possible to give a formal analysis, in the terms and relations worked out here, of a genuinely new situation. A situation will be new only in three cases: (1) where *C* is new; (2) where *RxAy* is new; (3) where *RxAy*←*C* is new.

(1) *C* is new when the proposition represents a state of affairs never before considered within the jurisdiction. Perhaps surrogate parenthood is an appropriate example.

(2) *RxAy* is new when (2a) an entitlement never before considered is claimed or when (2b) a new candidate for personhood is proposed. An example of (2a) is the claim first made in 1969 by a group of Australian Aborigines of the Pitjajanjara group in Leonora, Western Australia, that the group owned, within the meaning of Australian law, land considered sacred to it. An example of (2b) is the discovery, which can be fairly precisely dated, in Roman Law that a city or town can own something and thus be a legal person.[16]

(3) *RxAy* ←*C* is new when it is proposed to relate *RxAy* to a *C* with which it has never been related before. If Steyn J's analysis is correct then the emergence of mistake (*C*) as sufficient to void a contract (*RxAy*) is an example. He writes in the case quoted: 'In the early history of contract law, the common law's preoccupation with consideration made the development of a doctrine of mistake impossible.'[17]

13. POSSIBILITIES OF FORMALIZATION

Much can be said about the possibilities of formalization. The pertinent question here is whether anything can be said of it in the light of the foregoing analysis.

The fundamental distinction made here has been between *C* and *RxAy*. They are said to be linked as condition and conditioned. Thus, there are only two jural questions:

> (1) if the conditions are such, what are the entitlements?

and

> (2) if such an entitlement or entitlements are sought, what are the conditions?

These may be written: (1) *C* →? and (2) *RxAy* ←? The form of a settled rule of justice is *RxAy*←*C*.

Useful, therefore, would be a decision support system that would associate (1) and (2) in such a way that an enquirer could key in either an entitlement or a condition and be given the relevant conditions or entitlements. Thus, for example, an estranged wife could key in 'C = estranged wife', and expect to be informed of the associated entitlement. Now it might well be that this C on its own brings with it no entitlement while still being one condition, even perhaps a necessary condition, in a set of conditions. A decision support system would have to be able to distinguish between sufficient conditions and relevant but insufficient conditions. In the example, the system would not simply answer 'No entitlement' but would answer, say, '*RxAy' where '*' indicates that C is relevant but insufficient. In case '*' appeared the system would then move to giving the set of sufficient conditions for $RxAy$. It might well be that the condition, C, is relevant to many entitlements and the system would, therefore, answer $RxAy$, RxA_1y, $RxAy_1$ etc. some of which might be starred, some not.

From both the jural and the computing side the work involved is considerable and requires considerable subtlety. On the computing side there is, I think, no doubt but that the theory is sufficiently advanced to cope with the task. On the legal side there are doubts, both practical and theoretical. The practical question is whether the task is worth the effort. The theoretical question is whether the expertise at present exists to formalize a legal system, or even an interesting part of a legal system, in this way. The contention here is that this is the deep structure of a legal system even if this is not always apparent.

14. ANALOGY

A final question regards analogy as an inventive method. Zenon Bankowski's work on analogy ((Bankowski 1995) in this collection) discovers the following structure:

$$[(C \rightarrow RxAy) \& (C_1 \approx C)] \rightarrow (C_1 \rightarrow RxAy)$$

where $C_1 \approx C : C_1$ is sufficiently like C.

Analogy, as Bankowski analyses it, operates in type (1) newness, since, by definition, C_1 represents a set of conditions not yet considered within the jurisdiction. Just as human judges perceive analogies so, too, may human advocates. Indeed, advocates often suggest them to judges. What of non-human decision support systems?

In many contemporary jurisdictions an estranged long-term partner is treated like an estranged spouse because it has been successfully argued that a long-term partner is analogous to a spouse. There is no theoretical problem about incorporating the result of successfully proposed analogies but there is considerable theoretical difficulty surrounding the discovery of new ones.

One reason for the affirmation of an analogy between spouse and long-term partner is, as Bankowski shows in his analyses of other examples, that a feature by feature description of the one overlaps considerably with a feature by feature description of the other.[18] But if the machine has no more than the terms 'spouse', 'wife', 'husband' —even if it has established correlations between these— it must either reject the term 'long-term partner' as unrecognized or, if it is programmed to accept new terms, as merely a new term with no association whatsoever with the others.

Bankowski's analyses suggest that one should programme the machine not simply with the terms 'spouse', 'wife', 'husband' and with relations between these but also with descriptions of these so that when a new term accompanied by an appropriate description is introduced, the machine would correlate descriptions and so link 'long-term partner' to 'spouse'.

Appropriate description is not automatic and if Bankowski's analyses indicate a solution, they likewise point to a difficulty present from the outset. How is one to derive a rule of justice from a particular case?

The famous Scottish case of *Donoghue v. Stevenson* (without at least mention of which no discussion of English law can, it seems be complete) is considered by Bankowski. In the form RxAy→C this can come out as: 'If there is a snail in the consumer's ginger beer, then the consumer is entitled to compensation from the manufacturer.'

But already the named protagonists appear as the anonymous 'consumer' and 'manufacturer' and 'compensation' replaces the actual result of the particular case.

'*C*' is replaced by 'there is a snail in the consumer's ginger beer'. Would 'mouse in oatmeal' equally well replace '*C*' in this particular specification of $C \rightarrow RxAy$? The human advocate would surely say that if this were not certain at least it would be worth a trial; the decision support system, on the other hand, would see no relation whatsoever between 'snail in ginger beer' and 'mouse in oatmeal' unless 'snail in ginger beer' and 'mouse in oatmeal' were inserted into the same set and the relation $(p)(q)(Fp \ \& \ Fq) \rightarrow (p=q)$ were an operative feature of the set, that is, if p is a member of the set F and q is a member of the set F, then, for defined purposes, p and q are jurally equivalent.

But what is the relevant set? This is a jural, not a computational, question. Is the relevant set to be defined:

(1) animal in food, or
(2) foreign body in food, or
(3) foreign body in consumer good, or
(4) some otherwise defined set?

Sets (1), (2) and (3) are invented so that (p){[(1)$p \rightarrow$ (2)p] & [(2)$p \rightarrow$ (3)p]} while the reverse does not hold so ~(p)[(3)$p \rightarrow$ (1)p]. Thus (3) contains (2) and (2) contains (1) but not the reverse.

(1) is not the least comprehensive plausible set imaginable —(0) animal in drink in opaque bottles, is possible for example— but, assuming that the three are accepted as reasonable suggestions and that (1) is accepted as the least comprehensive likely within the jurisdiction (that this is so will, of course, be an expert jural assessment of the character of the jurisdictional context), into which of the three sets should 'snail in ginger beer' be placed *before later cases bringing further settled determinations are decided*?

The answer is quite plain: we simply don't know. And we don't know not for epistemological reasons only but for ontological reasons. Within the jurisdiction (2) will be the correct set if and only if the court determines that (2) is the correct set and, by hypothesis, this determination has not yet taken place; in other words, the ontological conditions for the truth of the judgement 'Case "snail in ginger beer" is a member of set (2)' do not yet exist. In still other words, the judgement is not a judgement of fact (although syntactically indistinguishable from one) but an educated guess.[19 20]

A guess, educated or not, is often expressed in the future tense, —e.g. 'Desert Orchid will win the Gold Cup'— but, even so, syntactically, looks like a proposition. In fact, epistemologically, a guess about the future is not a proposition precisely because the ontological conditions for its truth do not yet exist. Paradoxical puzzles about truth and falsity arise here only when guesses (statements about the future, prophecies, predictions) are treated as propositions. 'Desert Orchid will win the Gold Cup' is neither true nor false —but for a very simple and radical reason: it is not a proposition and only propositions are true or false.

Neither is an advocate's opinion concerning the likely outcome of a case, unlike the medical doctor's opinion on the patient's condition. The former is not a proposition, for the ontological conditions for its truth or falsity do not yet exist. In the case of medical diagnosis the ontological conditions exist but the evidence for the diagnosis may be insufficient and the proposition, while genuinely a proposition, may be mistaken. Still, an educated guess differs from an ignorant, wild or random guess and there is no reason that I can see not to include educated guesses but it would seem wise to distinguish syntactically between them and propositions. So, for example, an educated guess might be preceded by the signal '!'. The advantage of doing this —besides its undoubted theoretical nicety— is that it would allow the introduction of several educated guesses that, were they propositions, would be unacceptably[21] incompatible.

The structure of the decision support system would then be as follows:

(a) Settled case: snail in ginger beer (Cl) → entitlement (El)

(b) ! (1) animal in food → entitlement (El)

! (2) foreign body in food → entitlement (El)

! (3) foreign body in consumer good → entitlement (El)

(c) Case under consideration: oily rag in oatmeal → ?(El)

Question: Is 'oily rag in oatmeal' a member of the set Cl?

Answer: If the set Cl is defined at least by !(2), then affirmative.

If the set Cl is defined by !(1), then probably not.

A second example may indicate more clearly that the suggested procedure may be developed generally.

Rule: Only a native citizen of the United States is eligible to become President of the United States.

Condition: Native born citizen.

Entitlement: Eligibility to become President of the United States.

What is the condition 'native born', i.e. what prejural facts will be jurally determined to fulfil the condition? A native citizen of the United States will be a person who is a citizen by reason of birth and was

(1) born in a place that was part of the United States when the person was born there;

! (2) born in a place that is now part of the United States but was not a part of the United States when the person was born there (e.g. Hawaii, Alaska);

!(3) born in Puerto Rico after Puerto Rico became a U.S. protectorate;

!(4) born in Puerto Rico before Puerto Rico became a U.S. protectorate;

!(S) born in an Embassy of the United States;

!(6) born in the country in which their parents were serving in the Embassy of the United States in that country although not in the Embassy itself;

!(7) born outside the United States and not in the country in which their parents were serving in a United States Embassy but while their mother was on the business of the Embassy;

!(8) as for !(7) but born while their mother was outside the country not on Embassy business;

!(9) born in a military installation of the United States;

!(10) born in an Indian reservation.[22]

Specification (1) is deliberately not preceded by '!'. This indicates that this is considered to be settled law. (There is no suggestion of infallibility.) Notice, however, that the condition 'native born U.S. citizen' must have some possible specification to be jurally meaningful. If no set of prejural facts can be adduced to specify *C*, then the condition, *C*, is jurally meaningless; if no set of prejural facts is known to specify the condition, then the condition's meaning is unknown.[23]

The condition, *C*, will not have an infinite number of possibly relevant specifications, but it will have many, and the general point is that a decision support system will be more valuable the more '!' specifications of *C* it contains. Since the conditions in any jural system swing between the poles of greater and lesser specification, the invention of '!' specifications will be more important in some parts of the system than in others.

I have taken the relatively simplistic and trivial matter of the meaning of the condition 'native born citizen' to illustrate the point that even in apparent clarity, specifications are less certain than they may seem. Contemporary jural treatment of anti-trust law in the United States is a more realistic and important example. Antitrust jurisprudence has developed two manners of dealing with alleged violations: where the violation is considered per se in which case the law is more or less algorithmically applied; where the alleged violation is treated according to a principle of reasonableness and an effort is made to investigate the effect of the alleged violation on the economy. In the one case, the legislation is taken to be at the pole of specificity and clarity (SC/ci); in the other case, the legislation is taken to be at the pole of specificity and unclarity (SC/ni).[24] It has been suggested (see Meehan 1991) that the jurisprudence is tending towards treating anti-trust legislation increasingly as SC/ni; in other words, the legislation is specific (i.e. there are clear instances of its meaning) but the actual cases presented to the courts are less obviously instances.

When a jurisprudence develops in this way it may be expected that any features in the legislation that tend towards being non-specific will be concentrated on and, after some time, anti-trust jurisprudence will tend towards being NC/ci.

The greater the specification, the more numerous the applications, the longer the rule has been in place, the less inventive need a human adjudicator be; for in such cases the adjudicator decides almost algorithmically. The lesser the specification, the greater the uncertainty, the greater the likelihood of new situations, the less algorithmic the operation and, consequently, the larger the place left for human inventiveness, assessment and responsible decision.

The computation of law is retrospective. In as much as the future repeats the past (and scientific prediction, as Hume saw clearly, is based on this assumption[25]) this retrospective computation is adequate; in as much as the future differs from the past, computation yields to invention or, if one's institutional position is not that of the deciding Court, to the informed inventive guess normally called 'counsel's opinion'. Because there is always jurisprudence, because there are specifications and traditions and argument some algorithmic analysis is both possible and useful. Because a true future —that is, a future that is not simply the repetition of the past— is always possible within a legal system, a total algorithmic computation of the law is not a possibility.[26]

Finally, and to end on a question, the informed inventive guess is often expressed thus: 'As far as I can see the possible outcomes are *A*, *B*, *C*, *D* and of these the most probable is *B*; the least probable is *A*; and *C* and *D* are somewhere in between'.

The question is this: in what sense is *B* the most probable?[27]

NOTES

1 The formal analysis does not distinguish ontological from epistemological conditions. Epistemologically the formalism is to be interpreted as: The proposition, *X*, may be affirmed, if the epistemological conditions, *C*, are fulfilled. And the epistemological conditions, *C*, are fulfilled. Therefore, the proposition, *X*, may be affirmed. Notice that the epistemological conditions for affirming the proposition that snow is white is not the proposition 'When I look out of the window etc...' ; the epistemological conditions are the experience of looking out of the window etc...' This does not involve me in the position that the proposition 'When I look out of the window etc...' is infallible —a position to my mind convincingly refuted by Wilfred Sellars; it does, however, involve the claim that the evidence for the proposition 'Snow is white' and the evidence for the proposition 'When I look outof the window etc....' may be the same. Whether or not looking out of the window etc. is, in fact, sufficient evidence for affirming the proposition, 'Snow is white', is not the present issue.

2 An empirical claim is about a defined range of data. Introducing here the notions of 'criminal justice', 'the State', 'the Court' defines the range as, perhaps, European and derived adjudication procedures. Whether the theory applies to any other range of data is an open question. How the general structure of justice, the just and adjudication applies to another range of data can be determined only by an investigation of that range of data. However, it seems that every society is a network of entitlements; that in every society there is sometimes dispute about entitlements; that commonly some method of resolving such disputes is instituted.

3 The argument here is not that there is no relation between rules of this kind [commands] and rules of justice; nor is the argument that sentences such as 'Do not drive vehicles in this park' cannot be translated into sentences not in the imperative mood, for example: 'Vehicles are not to be driven in this park'. Many hortative or imperative sentences are rhetorical versions of indicatives, e.g. in car manuals one can come across: 'Do not fill with petrol of less than an octane rating of 87' which seems to be a command but, in the context of car manufacturer and car owner, is not although, of course, in other social circumstances it may be; it is, rather, a version of: 'If the car is filled with petrol with an octane rating of less than 87, the engine will knock and may be damaged'. However, I fully accept that commands do exist and a deontic or modal logic may be required for their formal analysis.

4 It is not only possible but easy to imagine a task the goal of which was simply to discover whether or not a person was guilty as accused. But what of the announcement of the discovery? Is the accused person, the accuser or the community, in the imaginary universe, entitled to the publication of discovered innocence or guilt? There is a crucial distinction between a task the goal of which is to discover only and one the goal of which is to discover and promulgate. In some small, face to face societies the goal of what at first sight seems to be the equivalent of a European court is, indeed, to discover and promulgate guilt or innocence and the community then responds accordingly. In such a situation I should prefer to analyse the entire community as the equivalent of a European court and the smaller group whose task it is to discover and promulgate as the equivalent of that part of the process in a European criminal court that concludes with the promulgation of the discovery: 'Not guilty' etc.

5 This is the structure of many jural rules, perhaps of most. In many jurisdictions the situations in which the Court has no discretion in the assignment of entitlements are rare; where the Court has discretion the discovery of the appropriate entitlement is the work of prudence or epieikeia.

6 Two examples from the Constitution of Ireland are relevant. Since 1937 and despite an attempt to remove it by referendum, there is a provision in that Constitution forbidding divorce. But to say that divorce is forbidden is in fact odd for one can forbid only that which it is possible to perform. More accurately, the Constitution makes divorce impossible, i.e. prevents the institutional possibility; the Constitution ensures that the institution of divorce cannot exist. By a recent amendment to the Constitution, the Oireachtas was forbidden to legislate in favour of abortion; once again it is more accurate to say that the Oireachtas cannot do so than that it may not do so; if the Oireachtas purports to pass legislation allowing abortion, the Supreme Court will strike it down, not on the grounds that it should not have been done, but on the grounds that the purported legislation is not in fact legislation. Thus, there is a sense that legislation allowing abortion or divorce cannot exist; divorce, being institutional, thus cannot exist; abortion, being a pre-institutional practice, can exist, and therefore, can be forbidden.

7 The example is deliberately bizarre to illustrate the serious point that it is jurally meaningless to assert that someone is entitled to something unless, in case the person is lacking it, we can specify from whom they are entitled to it. Stepping beyond the circle of metropolitan or international law to the containing circle of morality we find the same structure; it is morally meaningless to claim that, say, starving people are entitled to food unless one adds that they are entitled to it from some identified or in principle identifiable moral person or persons. Sometimes a significant moral discovery in a person's life is that they are the person from whom the other is entitled; this is the responsible discovery or invention of oneself; indeed, the fundamental moral question is: what am I responsible for?

8 Roman Law, considered as a collection of jural rules for determining the just within Roman society, hardly raises the question of the justice of the society itself. In this it differs no whit from other legal systems. An adjudicative system that put its containing setting focally in jeopardy in every dispute would be unworkable just as a science that put its containing

presuppositions or paradigms in focal jeopardy at every moment would collapse in confusion; containing paradigms can be questioned but they cannot be questioned all the time.

9 To speak more strictly: physical possession as 'ownership' is already an institution. In itself, physical possession is merely physical possession. Thus, when Hobbes writes of having a right to what one physically possesses, he does not mean that this is the way in which he understands the participants in the natural condition understand themselves. It should be recalled, however, that physical possession among animals is not a chaos but a natural order discovered in ethological enquiry.

10 Even such commonplaces do in fact have a second person. The claim: 'I am entitled to a drink' differs from 'I want a drink' and translates the desire to another sphere: I am entitled to a drink from myself. In this tiny and very ordinary example, is repeated the passage from desire and possession to 'ownership'; desire and possession are the matter of civil society; entitlement is the form.

11 Both Hobbes and Hume considered justice a coerced virtue since they each, in their different ways, presumed that natural spontaneity or sentiment militated against justice. This attitude has to a great extent been taken for granted as patently correct; I think it is not correct but I may be mistaken; here I would note only that it is an empirical statement about humans not a given axiomatic truth. Perhaps precisely because it has been taken to be plainly true, much legal philosophy has concentrated on coercion. Hume and Hobbes were both correct, of course, to assert that we are commonly tempted to act unjustly and that sometimes we shall not do the just thing unless coerced; the issue of coercion thus properly arises and shows that any account of human community that does not face the issue of coercion or force is sentimentally utopian.

12 The general deontic formula:

$$[(p \rightarrow Oq) \rightarrow O(p \rightarrow q)] \;\&\; [O(p \rightarrow q) \rightarrow (p \rightarrow Oq)]$$

disposes of the objection that 'ought' is being derived from 'is' but, obviously, does no more than posit the 'ought'. The question as to whence the obligation derives is left untouched. However, as Andrew Jones has pointed out to me, there are very considerable problems about this formula. When analysed it is discovered to suggest that whatever is ought to be —a result at once unintended and undesired. I have not yet discovered a way out of the impasse.

13 All ER [1988]3, pp. 902-915.

14 All ER [1988]3, p. 910 @ h

15 'Manifestly unreasonable' is a social criterion; that is manifestly unreasonable which 'everyone' finds manifestly unreasonable. Of course, 'everyone' may be wrong but the Court is not infallible and the pursuit of justice is asymptotic.

16 I am indebted to Geoffrey Samuel for this reference.

17 All ER [1988]3 p. 909 @ g

18 Bankowski does not claim that a feature by feature analysis is the only method of establishing analogy. It is also worth remarking that the discovery of the relevant features requires intelligence. Suppose 'John buys an orange from Jane'. This is an institutional account of a set of physical actions that have taken place between John and Jane. Suppose now that a set of very similar physical actions go on between Paul, Priscilla and a car. The enquirer with the appropriate institutional background or context will understand the set of actions as 'Paul buys a car from Priscilla'. Is there some common feature linking 'car' and 'orange'? No; 'car' = 'orange' because both can be understood as 'commodities' in the institutional relation 'selling and buying'. When we understand the transaction between John and Jane we understand the particular transaction —John at this time, Jane at this time, this orange— as an instance of the form: 'buying and selling goods'. The feature by feature analysis recalls Wittgenstein's remarks

on the resemblances between games; the discovery of forms with their instances recalls the method opposed by Wittgenstein. Wittgenstein made, I think, a genuine discovery but was mistaken to think it radically opposed to the other method which it rather supplements. See (Barden, 1976)

19 If someone guesses on Wednesday and Desert Orchid wins on Thursday can we not say that the person propounded a true proposition on Wednesday? We cannot; because the person propounded no proposition on Wednesday. What the person uttered was a sentence that on Wednesday expressed the guess; on Thursday the same sentence can express the true proposition concerning Desert Orchid's success. Aristotle in his discussion of the sea battle in *Peri Hermenias* makes a similar point: if on Wednesday I know [in the strict sense] what will happen on Thursday, the Thursday's event is determined; similarly, if a proposition about Thursday's event is true on Wednesday, then that event is determined because, following Tarski again, the ontological condition of the proposition being true is the actuality of the state of affairs denoted by the proposition.

20 There is a crucial difference to be noticed between medical diagnosis and the anticipation of the Court's decision. The structure of medical diagnosis is: if such symptoms are observed, then such a disease is present. Let the set of symptoms be A, B, C, D, E, F. These may be associated in many ways, e.g. [A & B & C & D & E & F]; [A ∨ B ∨ C ...]; [A & (B ∨ C) ...]; [A & (B→C)...]. The more sophisticated the array the more sophisticated and delicate must and can the diagnostic programme be. Commonly enough medical diagnosis is tentative but notice that the ontological conditions already exist or do not already exist, i.e. the patient either has or has not measles. The diagnosis, 'This patient has measles' is tentative not because the ontological conditions for the truth or falsity of the proposition do not exist but because the epistemological conditions for affirming the proposition do not yet exist, i.e. the diagnostician does not yet have enough evidence. In the anticipation of the Court's decision the ontological conditions for the truth of the judgment that the Court will decide in such and such a way do not yet exist and so there simply cannot be enough evidence for affirming the proposition: 'The Court will decide in such and such a way' because there cannot be enough evidence for affirming something for which the ontological conditions are absent. More simply, there cannot be enough evidence for affirming that something is the case when it is not the case. Thus, medical diagnosis on slender evidence is ontologically dissimilar from legal anticipation; there cannot be a categorical judgement about a contingent future unless one presumes the future to be conformable to the past. On this both Aristotle and Hume concur; and are correct. See notes 19 and 21.

21 'Desert Orchid won the Gold Cup in 1990' is unacceptably incompatible with 'Desert Orchid did not win the Gold Cup in 1990'. But guesses are not incompatible in the same way as those who place bets on different horses to win the same race, in practice, know. I may seem to be claiming that sentences in the future tense are not propositions and are neither true nor false. My claim is that sentences in the future tense obliquely express propositions that are more perspicuously expressed in sentences in the present tense. Propositions apparently about the future are properly about the present. Thus 'Desert Orchid will win the Gold Cup' may express the proposition more perspicuously expressed as: 'I anticipate that Desert Orchid will win the Gold Cup' and this proposition is either true or false and unacceptably incompatible with 'I anticipate that Desert Orchid will not win the Gold Cup' since so to anticipate requires that one not anticipate that Desert Orchid will win. But the ! specifications are not judgements; they are hypotheses.

22 Although American Indians are citizens by birth since 1923 (were those who became citizens in 1923 'native born citizens'?), reservations are in some respects not legally part of the United States. There is no jurisprudence on American Indian citizenship in the following situation: a child born in a reservation within the geographical landmass of the United States but to Canadian parents. The child is not a US citizen from the parents. The child was born in a

reservation that in some respects is not part of the United States. So the question must yet be settled as to whether or not the reservation is part of the US for the purposes of gaining citizenship. (The term 'Native American' is now commonly used but this term includes Hawaiians and Esquimaux or Inuit.)

23 It is not necessary that the relevant prejural facts be realized, e.g. the condition 'native born citizen' is jurally meaningful even if there are no native born citizens; the condition is jurally meaningless in case there is no possible situation denoted by 'native born citizen'; the condition is effectively jurally meaningless in case no situation denoted by 'native born citizen' can be identified. To know what 'native born citizen' means jurally is to know what situations the condition denotes. Accordingly, the term 'native born citizen' is not completely understood, i.e. its meaning is not wholly known, until every situation that it denotes is known. To know what 'the legislator' meant by the term is to know what situations the legislator considered the term to denote. There are well known difficulties surrounding the attempt to discover what the legislator meant or would have meant; I have adopted here the position that the legislator's meaning in this sense is not the criterion of the meaning of the condition. The criterion is the reasonable understanding of the social world. On this account, analogy is one method of posing the question: if condition *C* denotes situation *S*, then is it reasonable to understand condition *C* as denoting S^1? For example, if a person born in a place that was part of the United States when the person was born there is a native born citizen, is a person (who would otherwise qualify for citizenship) born in an Embassy of the U.S.A. a native born citizen? To ask about what the legislator would have meant had the legislator considered this situation is no more than a subterfuge to conceal the real situation that one must take the responsibility oneself.

24 See !11 above where the terms SC/ci etc. are introduced.

25 See for example (Hume [1777] 1974): '... all our experimental conclusions proceed upon the supposition that the future will be conformable to the past.'

26 The argument behind this is very simple: if the problem is in principle not solvable by an algorithm, it is of no use to seek a more sophisticated algorithm. For example, if Turing's solution of the halting problem —a theorem showing that the halting problem is not algorithmically solvable— is correct, as most contemporary mathematicians take it to be, then there is no point in seeking a more sophisticated algorithm to solve it algorithmically. Notice that it is no part of my argument that it is impossible to build a non-algorithmic machine that thinks in every way as we do. With respect to human thinking, my position is that it is not wholly algorithmic and so algorithmic machines will not reproduce it.

27 The probability in question here is not necessarily the kind investigated in probability theory. There is at least one other common meaning of 'probable'. One may say that a judgement is probable rather than certain but the probability here is not statistical. Furthermore, although this is a different point, if it is discovered that a particular counsel is correct nine times out of ten, what is the probability of the opinion in this specific instance being correct? I suggest that there is no statistical probability attaching to this particular guess and yet we should, quite reasonably, incline to trust counsel whose opinion has been correct nine times out of ten, more than we should one whose opinion had been correct only three times out of ten.

REFERENCES

Bankowski, Zenon, 1995. 'Analogical Reasoning and Legal Institutions', in this collection.
Barden, Garrett, 1976. 'Discriminating Classes', *MAN*, Vol. 11, No. 3, pp. 345–355, London.
Hobbes, T., [1651] 1957. *Leviathan*, (ch. xiv), Ed. M. Oakeshott, Basil Blackwell, Oxford.

Hume, D., [1777] 1974. *Enquiry concerning Human Understanding*, (Section IV, part 2). *Hume's Two Enquiries*, ed. L.A. Selby-Bigge, 3rd edn ed. P.H. Nidditch, Oxford.
Meehan, James, 1991. 'Research, Joint-Ventures, and Anti-Trust Policy,' *Sloan Foundation Science-Technology Colloquium*, Colby College, 15 March 1991.
Tarski, A., [1944] 1949. 'The Semantic Conception of Truth and the Foundations of Semantics'. Trans. pp. 52–84 in: P. Feigl and W. Sellars (eds.), *Readings in Philosophical Analysis*, New York.

Department of Philosophy
University College, Cork
Ireland

ANDREW J.I. JONES & MAREK SERGOT

ON THE RÔLE OF DEONTIC LOGIC IN THE CHARACTERIZATION OF NORMATIVE SYSTEMS[1]

Two topics dominate this paper: the rôle of deontic logic in knowledge representation in the legal domain; and the rôle of deontic logic in the specification of computer systems. In both cases, we take the library regulations at Imperial College as an illustrative example. The essential point for which we then argue is that deontic logic —in some form or other— needs to be taken seriously as soon as one is forced to make explicit the distinction between what ought to be the case and what is the case, or as we also say, between the ideal and the actual. In conclusion we touch on the rôle of deontic logic in the development of the theory of normative positions —a theory which is of relevance both to legal knowledge representation and computer system specification. Our overall aim in this paper is to sketch the beginnings of a methodology for the use of deontic logic in the analysis and representation of normative systems.

It is a common misconception that deontic logic has been used to formalise reasoning in what are sometimes called 'legal expert systems'. Although there is enormous interest, and a considerable amount of published material is devoted to the representation of law in computer programs (see Sergot 1990 for an extensive survey), systems that have made explicit or implicit use of a deontic logic are few and far between. McCarty (1983, 1986) has presented a deontic logic based on an action logic which he sees as one component of a comprehensive theory of practical reasoning (McCarty 1989). The deontic logic is presented in detail but there are only hints as to the purpose to which it shall be put. There are miscellaneous proposals for incorporating some rudimentary deontic logic, usually resembling Standard Deontic Logic (SDL), in representational languages for legal domains (see e.g. Biagioli et al. 1987, Alchourrón and Martino 1989). In these proposals it is taken for granted that some kind of deontic logic is either essential or desirable in the formal representation of law, but neither motivation nor guidance on use is given. In his jurisprudential enquiry into the nature of legal expert systems, Susskind (1987) has argued that the occurrence of deontic modalities in the source texts must be recorded with the representation, though he gives little indication of why this is important, or how these markers will contribute to the reasoning of the system. Bench-Capon (1989) has suggested that reasoning with deontic modalities is only

Z. Bankowski et al. (eds.), Informatics and the Foundations of Legal Reasoning, 271–289.

necessary in the resolution of 'hard' legal questions where appeal must be made to general principles, and that deontic logic is not required if attention is restricted to the resolution of routine cases in mundane administrative legal domains. Of course deontic logic has long attracted attention in the jurisprudential literature. Tammelo (1978) is usually referred to in this context; MacCormick's writing (1990) is a more modern representative. Separately, the two of us have also remarked on the rôle of deontic logic in the representation of law. Sergot (1982, 1985) has argued that, for certain practical purposes, many fragments of law can be represented adequately without deontic logic, but that there are other fragments, and other purposes, where an adequate representation would demand a deontic logic. Jones (1990) has illustrated how some of the most subtle and difficult issues currently being investigated in the literature on deontic logic could arise naturally even in apparently mundane examples of law.

Our aim in this paper was originally to consolidate our earlier remarks, to comment on what is encountered in the literature and to address the rôle of deontic logic in the representation of law in computer programs. However, we now feel that this question cannot, and should not, be divorced from consideration of a much broader set of questions; we have been led to address the rôle of deontic logic in the representation (and analysis) of *normative systems,* of which law is only one species. Our reasons for broadening the scope of the paper in this way are presented by consideration of a small specific example, which we introduce in the next section.

We present no technical results in this paper. Our concern is rather with identifying the rôle of deontic logic, and moving towards a methodology for its use.

1. THE EXAMPLE

The main points we wish to make can be illustrated by reference to one rather straightforward example (cf. Sergot 1982) —a fragment of the Library Regulations at Imperial College, consisting of four rules and a specification of 'book allowances'.

LIBRARY REGULATIONS

1. A separate form must be completed by the borrower for each volume borrowed.
2. Books should be returned by the date due.
3. Borrowers must not exceed their allowance of books on loan at any one time.
4. No books will be issued to borrowers who have books overdue for return to the library.

Book allowances:	Undergraduates	6
	Postgraduates	10
	Academic staff	20

The small size of the example is an advantage, making the discussion to follow more manageable, and avoiding unnecessary clutter; from this it should not be inferred that the example is too *simple.* It will prove to be rich enough to permit the expression of a number of representational options and subtleties.

Before proceeding, it is necessary to forestall the possible objection that, despite its merits, our example is after all not a piece of *legislation,* so whatever conclusions we may draw by using it could not readily be extended to apply to the genuinely legal domain. To this we would reply that, in common with much of the law, our example contains formulations of norms, designed to regulate the behaviour of individuals —in this case borrowers and library administrators. Furthermore, our example exhibits a number of the features which are often said to be characteristic of the law; although these features will *not* be our focus of attention here, they are worth mentioning at this point, just to help forestall the objection. For instance, the Library Regulations exhibit 'open texture'. (When is a book *returned*? What counts as a *member of Academic Staff*?) The Library Regulations are part of a 'seamless web' of regulations, governing the College. (We happen to know that no degree may be conferred on a student who has books overdue for return to the Library). The Library Regulations do not exist in a vacuum, divorced from a wider context of laws and principles. (The Librarian would not be allowed to fix a smaller allowance of books for black students.)Particular cases may arise, perhaps not explicitly mentioned in the Regulations, on which decisions will have to be made by the administrators of the Library. (Andrew becomes a Visiting Researcher at the Department of Computing —it is decided to classify him as a member of Academic Staff.) And there exist committees authorised to change the Regulations, decide on difficult cases, and hear appeals against allegedly unfair treatment. We find, in short that there are no clear reasons for refusing to accept the applicability of what we are about to say to the genuinely legal domain.

The example has a further advantage in that it is easy to imagine how a computer system might be introduced to automate part of the library's operation. This allows us to raise a different set of problems: problems that arise in the specification of computer systems.

Imagine the following scenario. The Chief Librarian wishes to improve the efficiency of the library, and asks us to construct a computer representation of the library regulations.

One way to proceed would be to choose some appropriate formal language, use this to formulate a precise representation of what we think the regulations say, and then animate the representation with an automated reasoning system: given a description of some real or hypothetical state of affairs, this computer program would derive what legal, here quasi-legal, consequences would seem to follow. It could be used, for example, to advise on the specific obligations and rights that borrowers and librarians have in given circumstances. This is the kind of program that most immediately comes to mind in discussing artificial intelligence applied to law. It would be an example of a 'legal analysis program', or an 'academic legal expert system' in the terminology of (Susskind 1987) —'academic' because here there is no attempt to simulate the actual reasoning of an expert lawyer.

But is this the kind of computer system the Chief Librarian has in mind? A legal analysis program might be an effective complement to distributing the library regulations on paper, but still it would describe the library as it currently exists; operations in the library would remain as before. Perhaps what the Chief Librarian has in mind is a *different* library, a library where some of the operations are carried out by computer. In the second case, the library regulations are given to us as a description of how the new library ought to function, after computerization.

At the very least, we must ask the Chief Librarian to choose between two different options. (1) Does he want us to construct a system that advises on the obligations and rights of the various users of the library as it currently exists? Or (2), does he want us to take the regulations as a specification of how the library ought to function, giving us the task of constructing a computer system which automates the library, at least as regards the issuing and returning of books? We shall examine the second of these two possibilities first, since that will allow us to introduce, in a simple way, a fundamental distinction which will figure prominently throughout: the distinction between the actual and the ideal.

2. THE LIBRARY REGULATIONS AS SYSTEM SPECIFICATION

For the first scenario, let us suppose that the Chief Librarian wants us (the system engineers) to introduce a system of computers and other administrative procedures so designed and constructed as to guarantee that the library functions in the way that it should. The Chief Librarian wants us to view the Library Regulations *as a specification of how the system should operate.* Accordingly, we may call this the *systems specification* scenario. The task here facing the system designer is to construct a library system which actually behaves in the way the Library Regulations require.

Taking the Chief Librarian at his word, we might consider how we can *force* actuality and ideality to coincide in this example. Recognizing that librarians cannot be forced to perform like automata, and that borrowers cannot be trusted to return their books on time, we might try to shift the entire operation onto a device which can be expected to perform according to our requirements.

Here is a design proposal: first, maintain a database of who borrowed what and when, incorporating 'integrity constraints' to filter out spurious input. Then, acquire the appropriate hardware so that, in order to issue a book, the borrower's library card is first inserted, whereupon the machine calculates the current allowance, either from information stored in the card, or from personal details in the database, or both. If the allowance is already used up, the card is ejected, and will not be accepted again by the machine until either the borrower's book allowance has been increased, or else the borrower returns at least one book. If the allowance is not already used up, the system makes an electronic version of the requested book available to the reader, on appropriate equipment, for precisely the period of time specified by the Chief Librarian. The borrower may exercise his or her right to 'return' the book prior to expiry of the maximum loan period, by tapping in an appropriate message.

If this is what the Chief Librarian wants, and this is what the engineers provide, then we have an example of 'representation of the Library Regulations' only in the sense that conformity to these regulations is implemented in the system. In fact regulation 1 now becomes obsolete, because forms were part of the old library's system for borrowing books and play no rôle in the new system. Regulation 4 is also obsolete because it is just not possible to have a book overdue. And at first sight what corresponds to regulations 2 and 3 are the facts that books *are* 'returned' by date due and that borrowers do not exceed their allowance.

We were given a specification for how the library should function. We designed a computer system accordingly. How can we demonstrate that our proposed implementation meets the Chief Librarian's requirements as expressed by the regulations, or at least systematically investigate the claim? Deontic logic has been proposed as a component in formal specification languages for computer systems (see e.g. Minsky & Lockman 1985, Khosla & Maibaum 1987, Fiadeiro & Maibaum 1991). But is deontic logic required here?

In addition to saying what is meant by 'meets the requirements', there are two things that we need to express precisely: (a) the Chief Librarian's specification of how the library system should be; (b) our specification of how the computer system should be.

For the Chief Librarian's specification, we would say that a deontic logic is necessary. One immediate reason is that at least one of the regulations (regulation 4) only applies in the case of a violation (of regulation 2). The distinction between the ideal and the actual is the province of deontic logic; the language we use to formulate this specification must allow for the consistent expression of violation, that is to say, the case where actuality and ideality are different.

For specification of our proposed computer system, the need for a deontic logic depends on what the specification encompasses. If we assume that all components of the computer system work flawlessly, and assume that no other kind of violation can occur, or if we choose to ignore the possibility of violation and make no provision for it in the specification, then there is no need to distinguish between the actual and the ideal, and no need for deontic logic either.

But let us examine the assumptions about the computer system we are proposing. Even for the extreme kind of implementation where all library operations are delegated to automata, *and even if we assume that all these automata work flawlessly,* there is still the possibility of violation, because of the influence of extraneous factors.

Leaving aside the possibility that regulations (the Chief Librarian's requirements) change, here are two examples of violations that can arise in the proposed implementation:

- Andrew leaves Imperial College, while he has books on loan from the library. His allowance goes to zero and is therefore exceeded. Either we admit the possibility of violation, or we must arrange for an extension of the library's computer system (so that access to the library's electronic 'books' is automatically cancelled when a person leaves Imperial College, for example).
- Marek is promoted (or demoted) by the Department of Computing, and his library allowance reduces as a result. (If this is fanciful, we might mention that at the time of writing there is a research assistant in the Department who has applied to become a full-time PhD student. If his application is successful, his allowance will reduce from the 20 books allocated to Academic Staff to the 10 books allocated to postgraduate students.) Whatever, Marek is demoted, his allowance changes, and is exceeded because he has a number of books on loan at the time. Again, either we admit the possibility of violation, or we design the system so

that the possibility of violation is eliminated: the library's computer system removes Marek's access to books, or somehow we arrange for it to block the demotion until the right number of books is 'returned'.

We see that, even where we opt for an implementation where everything is performed by automata, the possibility of violation remains:

— because of faults in components of the system;
— because of the influence of extraneous factors over which we have no control.

If we were now to design the computer system with the possibility of violation in mind, we might wish to include in the specification additional provisions for dealing with cases of violation as they arise; to express these provisions precisely we need a deontic logic.

The implementation we proposed is very extreme, and might not be acceptable to the Chief Librarian for any number of reasons. In practice, we would probably not automate the entire operation, but introduce computer systems only for part of it. The methodological points we have been making would still apply.

Here is another design proposal. As before, we maintain a database of who has borrowed what and when, with the appropriate 'integrity constraints'. We also keep the procedure whereby the borrower's library card is inserted and the remaining allowance is computed from details recorded in the database. But now instead of access to electronic books, the borrower is given the actual book, which he can take away. The librarian sweeps the book across an optical reading device; if the allowance is not exceeded and the borrower has no book overdue for return, the system updates the database of what is out on loan and the book is 'issued'. (This is in fact almost exactly the system currently in operation at Imperial College.)

Notice that this library system has no control over the behaviour of borrowers: in particular it cannot guarantee that books are returned by date due. In the context of the previous discussion, the borrowers are either components of the library system who cannot be assumed to perform flawlessly, or extraneous factors over which the library system has no control. The actual behaviour of the librarians is irrelevant (but see section 4.0). Assuming no faults in the computer, no book is issued to a borrower who has a book overdue, or to one who is at the limit of his allowance: any attempt to record such an update will be rejected by the library's database.

How might we implement such a system? As part of the database, we clearly need integrity constraints to filter spurious input. At the very least, an attempted update saying that book b has been issued to borrower x can only be accepted if (i) *b is* a book in the database (or we trust the optical reading device); (ii) *x* is a borrower in the database (or we trust the library card); (iii) borrower *x* is not currently at the limit of his allowance; and (iv) borrower *x* has no book overdue for return. These conditions could all be expressed with standard integrity constraints.

But consider now the possibility of violation, because of extraneous factors. Suppose Andrew leaves Imperial College while he has a book out on loan, and the librarian attempts to record his departure in the database. The integrity constraint requiring that books can only be on loan to borrowers is violated: either the update is rejected, in which case Andrew's departure cannot be recorded; or the update is accepted, and the database enters a state where at least one of its integrity constraints is not satisfied.

Although there are other possible ways of dealing with updates like these, one promising approach is to introduce 'softer' *deontic* integrity constraints. These are constraints that *ideally* all database states should satisfy; they differ from the standard ones in that we accept sub-ideal states of the database which do not satisfy deontic integrity constraints, whereas we reject states of the database which do not satisfy the standard ones. Deontic integrity constraints were suggested in Sergot's earlier discussion of the library regulations (Sergot 1982) but the idea is not developed there. Weiringa et al. (1989) have also proposed distinguishing a class of deontic integrity constraints though the intended purpose of these seems somewhat different to what we have in mind. We have been led to consider what kind of logic would be adequate for treating the deontic integrity constraints we want. Though the investigation is not complete and we have no space to present the details here, it looks as if a rudimentary deontic logic might suffice for the deontic part: it may even be that the features which make SDL inadequate as a theory of deontic reasoning in general (see section 3.2) are not problematic in the context of databases. Note that the checking of deontic integrity constraints would require a (simple) automated theorem prover for whatever deontic logic we use to express them.

In summary, we have identified in this section three rôles for deontic logic in the *systems specification* scenario.

(1) We might require a formal language in which to express precisely the specification of an organisation (here the library together with its computer and other administrative procedures). Such a specification must usually make provision for the possibility of violation, where actual behaviour deviates from the ideal, and for this a deontic logic is necessary.

(2) We might require in addition a formal language in which to specify precisely the intended operation of a computer system. A deontic logic is necessary for specifying computer systems if we want to make provision for violations —whether resulting from faulty components or from extraneous factors. We should like to be able to reason with these specifications, for example to test the internal consistency of the specification, or to determine whether one is a logical consequence of another. And —without meaning to give the impression that we underestimate the task— we should *like* to be able to investigate systematically whether the specification of a computer system meets the specification of the organisation into which it is introduced.

(3) We might wish to use an automated theorem prover for a deontic logic as a means of *implementing* some of the (software) components of a computer system. We have given one very simple indication of such a use in the remark on the checking of 'soft' deontic integrity constraints in databases. (Another example comes in section 3.2.)

3. THE LIBRARY REGULATIONS AS NORMS DIRECTED AT USERS

We turn now to the other scenario, where the Chief Librarian wants us to construct a system which is capable of giving advice to users and librarians concerning their obligations and rights, or more generally of reasoning with a normative representation of the regulations. Of course the example is so small, and the general process of borrowing books from libraries is so familiar, that it is difficult to imagine that anyone would actually want to construct a system of this type for practical purposes. But the points we shall be making are easily extended to more complicated and less familiar domains where such systems have been seen as a valuable aid.

We divide the discussion in this section into two parts, both relating to species of naivety which we believe can be detected in the existing literature. First there is a naive view of where deontic logic is needed; and second, there is a naive view of how to do deontic logic when it is needed.

3.1 The definitional component

Sergot has observed (1982, 1985) that for many practical purposes, substantial amounts of legislation are, or can be taken to be, essentially definitional in nature. By this is meant at least the following: that many regulations, including many embodied in legislation, may be viewed as *qualification norms,* which specify the conditions under which some entity *x* counts as an entity of a particular type *F*. Thus, to cite the best known example in the current literature (Sergot et al. 1986), the main point of the British Nationality Act 1981 is to spell out the conditions under which an entity (in this case, a person) qualifies as a British citizen. For certain purposes (to be discussed shortly), the norms may be represented in the following form:

british_citizen(x) ← born_in_UK(x)
british_citizen(x) ← parent_of(x,y) & british_citizen(y) . . . and so on.

The actual norms are of course much more complicated than this but the simplified version retains all the features that are presently of interest. Likewise, norms qualifying a person as entitled to Supplementary Benefit (Bench-Capon a *al.* 1987) may be cast in the form:

entitled_to_supp_ben(x) ←. . . . (conditions)

And part of the Library Regulations may be viewed as defining borrowing allowances:

allowance(x, 6) ← undergraduate(x)
allowance(x, 10) ← postgraduate(x)
allowance(x, 20) ← academic staff(x)

As in the last example, some qualification norms may be seen as specifying the definition of a *relation* but nothing turns on this. The British Nationality Act also lays down the conditions for determining whether two persons fall in the 'parent of' relation; and as a matter of fact, it defines four different categories of British citizen, and so the representation referred to above actually resembles the form:

british_citizen(x, category l) ← ... (conditions)
british_citizen(x, category 4) ← ... (conditions)

Substantial fragments of legislation have been represented as logic programs in this fashion; it is the ability of these programs to deal with the mass of detail that gives them their practical utility. Of course, logic (here predicate logic) is not universally accepted as an appropriate representational formalism even for norms of the qualificatory type. Others have preferred to use other kinds of representational devices and the literature on artificial intelligence and law abounds with a wide variety of proposals. But the points we wish to make here are independent of such considerations. We wish to make three fundamental points about the representation of qualification norms, in whatever formalism.

Our first point concerns the *surface formulation* of qualification norms. Qualification norms are often expressed in legislation and regulations using a form of words where apparently deontic modal auxiliaries occur. ('A person shall be a British citizen if....', 'A person shall be entitled to Supplementary Benefit if....', 'A postgraduate shall have an allowance of 10 books'.) This has led some to suggest (see in particular Susskind 1987) that these modalities must be captured somehow, else the representation does not give a faithful account of what the legislation says. We argue almost the opposite. Where legislative texts are taken to compress qualification norms, the occurrence of deontic modalities may be ignored, for most practical purposes, in the representation. For *which* purposes? Well, obviously, if one is interested in designing a system which will *in fact* classify entities in a manner which *conforms* to the norm stipulated, then the distinction between what *shall be* and what *is* becomes redundant. And for many practical purposes, in public administration, or in the administration of a library, for instance, one might indeed be interested in achieving just that. There may be simply no point in designing a system which fails to classify x as a British citizen even though x ought to be classified as a British citizen —and likewise for the other examples.

This is not to say that deontic modalities in the formulation of qualification norms should always be ignored, for all purposes. Legislation that specifies a definition can sometimes be seen as a directive also: so the British Nationality Act might be seen as expressing an obligation on the judiciary, or on the immigration authorities, or on other citizens, to recognise as a British citizen anyone who satisfies the conditions laid down in the Act. And if the purpose of the representation is to capture this reading then the directive force of the legislation, and the possibility of violation, cannot be ignored. But this has nothing to do with the form of words used in the text. The same would apply if a different form of words had been chosen and no deontic modality appeared in the text. It is naive to expect a meaningful representation of a legislative text to emerge by mechanically replacing all occurrences of the word 'and' by logical conjunction; it is no less naive to replace all occurrences of 'shall' or 'must' by the obligation symbol of a deontic logic.

The second point we wish to make concerns the *limitations* of restricting attention to norms of the qualificatory type. The point is a very obvious one, but we feel it needs to be made explicitly to avoid misunderstandings that have apparently arisen before. A representation of the conditions under which a person is (or ought to be) classified as a British citizen is precisely that, and no more. It does not attempt to say what else follows from the classification of a person as a British citizen: what package of rights, or obligations, or duties or privileges British citizenship confers on an individual. But then neither does the British Nationality Act. A more complete representation of the British legal system might be constructed that presents in addition the norms expressed in the Immigration Act or in the (unwritten) Constitution —but this would be a separate exercise. Similarly, a representation of the qualification norms that classify a person as entitled to Supplementary Benefit does not represent what follows from such a classification. And a representation of the definition of borrowing allowances in the Library Regulations does not pretend to be also a representation of the other regulations.

It might be felt that restricting attention to qualification norms and definitions is pointless, because to ignore the existence of norms that refer to these definitions is to ignore everything of any essence. This is a separate consideration, because it concerns the adequacy of a representation relative to its intended purpose. Clearly, we could not insist that representation of the British Nationality Act is pointless unless every norm in the British legal system of relevance to British citizenship is represented as well. Somewhere a line must be drawn, and a decision must be made about what needs to be represented and what does not. Perhaps the essential problem in determining whether to issue a British passport to a given individual reduces in practice to the problem of determining whether the person ought to be classified as a British citizen. Perhaps the problem of determining whether to grant Supplementary Benefit requires consideration of the qualification norms only. And perhaps the main problem in administering the Library Regulations is the computation of an individual's borrowing allowance, not reasoning about what the other regulations say. If the last example seems ridiculous, then imagine a system which deals also with the definitions of 'undergraduate' and 'academic staff' and takes into account the precedents that have been set by authoritative rulings in the past. As an aside, we believe it is fair to say that the existing literature on artificial intelligence and law has been largely preoccupied with the representation of norms of the qualificatory type, where the main focus has been on questions of vagueness and 'open texture' and the adequacy or propriety of the various techniques that have been proposed. This would certainly account for the —perhaps surprising— fact that so little attention has been paid to deontic logic in 'legal expert systems'.

The third point we wish to make is a practical suggestion. The following section (3.2) will be concerned with the representation of norms proper, that is to say, norms not of the qualificatory type. What we suggest here is a way of avoiding the representation of genuine norms, and stretching the applicability of techniques that apply only to qualification norms. The suggestion relies on the observation that many of the norms encountered in complex statutes and regulations can be factored into two components: a genuinely normative component, and a component that is definitional only.

Consider the following example (which is a simplified form of section 74 of the Road Traffic Act 1972):

> All four-wheeled vehicles shall carry two white lamps at the front. All two-wheeled vehicles shall carry one white lamp at the front.

Factoring these two norms yields the following paraphrase:

> All vehicles shall carry the requisite number of white lamps at the front. The requisite number of white lamps is: for four-wheeled vehicles, two; for two-wheeled vehicles, one.

Now, for some practical purposes, it might be sufficient to represent only the definitional component: 'vehicle', 'white lamp', 'at the front', and now also 'requisite number of lamps'. Of course, the resulting representation would ignore the normative component; but as already discussed, a line must be drawn somewhere, and there are circumstances where restricting attention to a definitional component is enough.

3.2 The normative component

For certain purposes it would not be realistic to ignore the distinction between what actually happens and what ideally happens, or more simply, between the actual and the ideal. And the Chief Librarian may not be satisfied with a system that restricts itself to a representation of the definition of 'allowance' but requires a system that can reason about the permissions and obligations of borrowers and library staff, some of whom, some of the time at least, fail to abide by the rules; indeed, as already observed, one of the regulations (regulation 4) applies only in the case where a violation has occurred.

So at the very least there is a need to mark the distinction between what shall be done and what is done, between what shall be the case and what is the case. Some appear to have suggested that there is no need to do more, that some kind of syntactical marker is enough. For example, MacCormick has proposed distinguishing a special class of predicates which he calls *normative* predicates. (See MacCormick 1978, MacCormick 1990, MacCormick 1992, and Dewitz 1995 in this collection). But he provides neither an axiomatic nor a model-theoretic characterization of the logical properties of this special class of predicates. Such a syntactical marker might be of some value as part of the documentation of a representation, but it obviously does not contribute to an analysis of deontic reasoning.

It is one thing to insist that uninterpreted syntactic markers fail to supply an analysis of deontic reasoning; it would be quite inappropriate to go on from that truism to the claim that we must always set our sights on achieving an *elaborate* theory of deontic reasoning. For certain purposes it is conceivable that no more than a very *rudimentary* deontic logic would be required – one which, say, allowed the consistent assertion of 'ought A' and 'not-A', and the derivation of 'permitted A' from 'ought A', but which otherwise remained silent on the logical properties of the deontic modalities. (Perhaps something as elementary as this was all that was required for the ESPLEX system, for instance Biagioli et al. 1987.) But if, on the other hand, something fancier is needed, then there are very good reasons for supposing that some tricky problems can easily emerge.

Although there are perhaps as many competing hypotheses about how to deal with these problems as there are deontic logicians, there is nevertheless one point on which there is a good deal of agreement: and this is that SDL —a normal modal system of type KD in Chellas' classification (Chellas 1980)— is unable to provide an adequate theory of deontic reasoning. Criticism of SDL has been the point of departure for much recent work in the field, and since the proposed alternatives to SDL often differ markedly, it is not surprising to find that the shortcomings of SDL receive various types of diagnosis in the literature. See, e.g., (Aqvist and Hoepelman 1981), (Loewa and Belzer 1983), (Jones and Pörn 1985), (Meya 1988). But here again one point is quite generally agreed upon: that SDL lacks the means for supplying an acceptable analysis of deontic *conditionals,* for instance of sentences of the type 'if A then it ought to be the case that B'.

Much of (Jones 1990) was concerned with the task of showing that problems with deontic conditionals easily infect rather mundane application areas. In both the Library Regulations and statute law (e.g., in contract law) one finds structures of what Chisholm called the 'contrary-to-duty' type (Chisholm 1963), in which the conditional obligation to do B has, as its condition, the violation of some other obligation. Here, for instance, is a translation of parts of two sections of the Norwegian Sale of Goods Act of 1988, slightly simplified:

> The goods shall be delivered within a reasonable period of time following their purchase. (section 9(1))

> If the seller is prevented from completing the transaction within the appropriate time period, he shall inform the buyer of the delay....If the buyer does not receive this information within a reasonable period of time, then the buyer may demand compensation for any loss which could have been avoided had he been given reasonable notice of the delay. (section 28)

Given the occurrence of structures of these kinds, it is by no means far-fetched to suppose that scenarios of just the type Chisholm described could easily arise in actual practice (the point is more fully developed in Jones 1990). The formal characterization of such scenarios involves confronting some central problems of deontic logic. The point here is not to make claims about how these problems should be solved: it is simply to indicate that they can easily arise.

In fact it can be argued that genuine problems of deontic logic arise even before one gets to 'contrary-to-duty' conditionals and the Chisholm scenario. For just the matter of deciding on which detachment principles to accept for deontic conditionals itself raises questions of a nontrivial kind. Suppose, for instance, that it ought to be that *A*, and that it ought to be that *B* given that *A*. Do we then accept a deontic detachment principle by means of which we conclude that it ought to be that *B*? Or do we say, rather, that the logical conclusion is not that it actually ought to be the case that *B*, but merely that it ought *prima facie* to be the case that *B*? But then how is the distinction —if accepted— between *actual* and *prima facie* obligation to be articulated?

Or suppose that it ought to be that *B* given that *A*, and that *A* is in fact the case; do we then accept a factual detachment principle by means of which we conclude that it ought to be that *B*? Would we accept that such an inference can be made *unrestrictedly*, i.e., no matter what else, apart from *A*, is true of the circumstances at hand? Or should we, rather, view the conditional as holding by default only —as holding only in regard to the typical, nonexceptional circumstances in which *A* is true, being possibly defeated/overruled in other, exceptional circumstances? An affirmative answer to the latter question would lead the analysis into the thorny problems of default reasoning. But can the logic of deontic conditionals fail to be confronted by such issues? (For further discussion of these points, see Jones and Pörn 1991. For the moment, the only aim here is to indicate how easily the analysis of deontic reasoning leads quickly into deep, in parts uncharted, waters.)

The argument of this section may also be used as a basis for critical response to the central thesis of (Bench-Capon 1989). For the problems here indicated, concerning the proper analysis of reasoning with and about deontic conditionals, are by no means confined to the domain of so-called 'hard' cases, where there is some lack of clarity regarding what the facts of the case are, or regarding which rules to apply, or both. For even if it *could* be argued that the Chisholm scenario is relatively eccentric, problems about how to define detachment principles for deontic rules are clearly going to arise quite independently of whether particular cases are straightforward or hard.

4. NORMATIVE POSITIONS

The Library Regulations, in common with many other sets of regulations, leave a number of questions about the rights and obligations of the participant agents unanswered. For instance, when it is said (regulation 2) that books should be returned by the date due, this is ordinarily taken to mean that a borrower *b* is under an obligation to return his books on time. But if we look at this regulation from a relational point of view, in terms of the relationship between the borrower *b* and a librarian *a*, then it is natural to ask also what the regulation says about the position of librarian *a*. The librarian *a* is not under an obligation to return *b*'s books, although presumably *a* is permitted to do so. And furthermore, in most libraries, the librarian *a is* obliged not to prevent borrower *b* from returning books on time. Likewise, if there was a rule saying that *b* was permitted to borrow books up to the limit of his allowance, this would ordinarily be understood to mean, not only that *b* is not prohibited from borrowing books, but also that librarian *a* was under an obligation to issue him the books he asks for, up to his allowance. There are other pairs of agents one could pick on, including the Chief Librarian, or the library authorities, or Imperial College. The point is that the Library Regulations do not completely specify the relative *normative positions* of librarian and borrower, or librarian and library, or borrower and library, vis-à-vis the particular types of acts that are involved in the business of the library.

Now it may appear that, for the example at hand, nobody would ever have a practical interest in mapping out in complete detail the normative positions concerned. Whether or not that is true, there are clearly other contexts in which a complete specification of this kind might be deemed highly desirable. In (Morris and McDermid 1991), for instance, the central task is to map out the relative normative positions of the agents in a hospital (doctors, nurses, clerical staff, patients...) vis-à-vis the act of accessing patients' medical files. And in the context of artificial intelligence and law, Layman Allen in particular has long advocated this type of approach to the analysis of legislation, arguing that there are important nuances and ambiguities that remain undetected otherwise (see e.g. Allen and Saxon 1986).

The tools of deontic logic and the logic of action have been applied to the task of developing a theory of normative positions. (See Lindahl 1977 which expounds and develops the pioneering logical work of Stig Kanger, in the jurisprudential tradition deriving from Bentham and Hohfeld.) The theory provides a means for investigating systematically the logical space of possible normative positions concerning, for instance, a given pair of agents and a given act type. The advantages to be gained from using the theory as an aid in designing an adequate specification of a set of regulations for a given domain are clearly brought out in the paper by Morris and McDermid. It is interesting to note that no more than rather rudimentary deontic and action logics are needed in order to define the basic principles of the theory (although it would no doubt be possible to push the further development of the theory in directions which would call for more elaborate underlying logics, capable, for instance, of coping with some of the tricky issues mentioned above in 3.2).

The theory of normative positions has its origins in the study of *legal* positions and *legal* relations, but it is clear that it can find application in the description of many types of organisations. The agents whose behaviour is governed by these organisations may be human individuals, or individual components of computer systems, or human collectivities, or collections of components of computer systems, or any combinations of these. While there is no doubt that the formal characterization of these agents' behaviour will be a matter of some considerable complexity, it is also clear that, at a certain level of abstraction, their behaviour may be viewed as norm-governed. At this level of abstraction, these organisations are all normative systems and deontic logic will have a key rôle to play as an analytical and representational tool.

ACKNOWLEDGMENT

Andrew Jones was supported by a Visiting Fellowship from the United Kingdom's Science and Engineering Research Council.

NOTE

[1] An earlier version of this paper was published under the title 'Deontic Logic in the representation of law: Towards a methodology', in *Artificial Intelligence and Law* 1: pp 45–64 (1992).

REFERENCES

Alchourrón, C.E. and Martino, A.A., 1989. 'A sketch of logic without truth.' *Proc. Second International Conference on Artificial Intelligence and law*, Vancouver, ACM Press.

Allen, L.E., and Saxon, C.S., 1986. 'Analysis of the logical structure of legal rules by a modernized and formalized version of Hohfeld fundamental legal conceptions.' *Automated Analysis of Legal Texts*, Martino, A.A., Socci, F., (eds). North-Holland, Amsterdam, pp. 385–451.

Åqvist, L. and Hoepelman, J., 1981. 'Some theorems about a "tree" system of deontic tense logic.' *New Studies in Deontic Logic*, Hilpinen, R., (ed.) Synthese Library 152, D. Reidel, Dordrecht, Holland.

Bench-Capon, T.J.M., 1989. 'Deep models, normative reasoning and legal expert systems.' *Proc. Second International Conference on Artificial Intelligence and Law,* Vancouver, ACM Press), pp. 37–45.

Bench-Capon, T.J.M., Robinson, G.O., Routen, T.W., Sergot, M.J., 1987. 'Logic programming for large scale applications in law: A formalisation of Supplementary Benefit legislation.' *Proc. First International Conference on Artificial Intelligence and Law,* Boston, ACM Press, pp. 190–198.

Biagioli, C., Mariani, P., and Tiscornia, D., 1987. 'ESPLEX: A rule and conceptual based model for representing statutes.' *Proc. First International Conference on Artificial Intelligence and Law,* Boston, ACM Press, pp. 240–251.

Chellas, B.F., 1980. *Modal Logic – An Introduction.* Cambridge University Press,.

Chisholm, R.M., 1963. 'Contrary-to-duty imperatives and deontic logic.' *Analysis* 24.

Dewits, Sandra, 1995. 'Using Information Technology as a Determiner of Legal Facts', in this collection.

Fiadeiro, J. and Maibaum, T.S.E., 1991. 'Temporal reasoning over deontic specifications.' *Logic and Computation.*

Jones, A.J.I., 1990. 'Deontic logic and legal knowledge representation.' *Ratio Juris* 3.

Jones, AJ.I. and Pörn, I., 1985. 'Ideality, sub-ideality and deontic logic.' *Synthese* 65.

Jones, AJ.I. and Pörn, I., 1991. 'On the logic of deontic conditionals'. Paper submitted to the workshop on Deontic logic in Computer Science, Amsterdam December 1991.

Khosla, S. and Maibaum, T.S.E., 1987. 'The prescription and description of state based systems.' In *Temporal Logic in Specification*, Banieqbal, B. et al., (eds), Lecture Notes in Computer Science 398, Springer-Verlag, Berlin, Germany.

Lindahl, L., 1977. *Position and Change – A Study in Law and Logic.* Synthese Library 112, D.Reidel, Dordrecht, Holland.

Loewer, B., Belzer, M., 1983. 'Dyadic deontic detachment.' *Synthese* 54, pp. 295–319.

MacCormick, D.N., 1978. *Legal Reasoning and Legal Theory*, Oxford University Press.

MacCormick, D.N., 1990. 'Legal Reasoning and the Institutional Theory of Law.' Paper presented to the ESPRIT Working Group on Foundations of Legal Reasoning, Cork.

MacCormick, D.N., 1992. 'Legal Deduction, Legal Predicates and Expert Systems', *International Journal for the Semiotics of Law*, Vol. 14, 1992.

McCarty, L.T., 1983. 'Permissions and obligations.' *Proc. Eighth International Joint Conference on Artificial Intelligence*, Karlsruhe, pp 287–294.

McCarty, L.T., 1986. 'Permissions and obligations: An informal introduction.' *Automated Analysis of Legal Texts*, Martino, A.A. and Socci, F., (eds), North-Holland, Amsterdam, pp. 307–337.

McCarty, L.T., 1989. 'A Language for Legal Discourse I. Basic features.' *Proc. Second International Conference on Artificial Intelligence and Law,* Vancouver, ACM Press, pp. 180–189.

Meyer, J.-J., Ch., 1988. 'A different approach to deontic logic: Deontic logic viewed as a variant of dynamic logic.' *Notre Dame Journal of Formal Logic 29.*

Minsky, N.H., Lockman, A., 1985. 'Ensuring integrity by adding obligations to privileges.' *Proc. 8th International Conference on Software Engineering,* August 1985, pp. 92–102.

Morris, P and McDermid, I., 1991 'The structure of permissions: A normative framework for access rights.' Paper submitted to the workshop on Deontic Logic in Computer Science, Amsterdam, December 1991.

Sergot, M.J., 1982. 'Prospects for representing the law as logic programs.' *Logic Programming*, Clarke, K.L. and Tamlund, S.-A., (eds). Academic Press, London.

Sergot, M.J., 1985. 'Representing legislation as logic programs'. In *Machine Intelligence II*, Hayes, J.E., Michie, D., Richards, J., (eds). Oxford University Press, pp. 209–260.

Sergot, M.J., 1990. 'The representation of law in computer programs: A survey and comparison.' *Knowledge Based Systems and Legal Applications*, Bench-Capon, T.J.M. (ed.) Academic Press.

Sergot, M.J., Sadri, F., Kowalski, R.A., Kriwaczek, F., Hammond, P., Cory, H.T., 1986. 'The British Nationality Act as a logic program.' *Communications of the ACM* 29, 5, pp. 370–386.

Susskind, R.E., 1987. *Expert Systems in Law: A Jurisprudential Inquiry.* Oxford University Press.

Tammelo, I., 1978. *Modern Logic in the Service of Law.* Springer-Verlag.

Wieringa, R., Meyer, J-J., Weigand, H., 1989. 'Specifying dynamic and deontic integrity constraints,' *Data and Knowledge Engineering* 4.

(For Andrew J.I. Jones)
Department of Philosophy, and
Norwegian Research Centre for Computers and Law
University of Oslo
Norway

(For Marek Sergot)
Department of Computing
Imperial College, London
England

JOXERRAMON BENGOETXEA

AI, LEGAL THEORY AND EC LAW: A MAPPING OF THE MAIN PROBLEMS

In the present paper I would like to examine some of the relations between Artificial Intelligence, especially Expert Systems, and the law of the European Communities. My analysis will be carried out from a legal theoretical point of view and will be exploratory in character. I shall first sort out some areas and background problems of EC law of particular interest to the legal theorist acting as an advisor on basic problems concerning the design of systems of the expert domain or decision support systems. Secondly I shall follow the late Jerzy Wróblewski and critically reconstruct his analytical model of the application of the law as applied to the law of the European Communities pointing out the epistemological and phenomenological moments where Artificial Intelligence can provide some help.[1]

1. PROBLEM AREAS OF EC LAW

There are, in my view, three main problems concerning the analysis of EC law for any knowledge-representational and decision-supporting purpose:

1. *Formal level:* devising a foundational legal theory for EC law,
2. *Substantive-conceptual level:* knowing EC law and dealing with comparative law,
3. *Dynamic level:* reasoning with and within EC law.

The specific help which can be obtained from artificial intelligence in EC law will be left to the second part of this paper. This first part deals with the main problems which EC law poses for any legal analysis. The three problem areas pointed out are not exclusive to EC law, but special problems arise when those questions are raised within EC law. Of course, one needs a foundational legal theory for any law, not just for EC law. But the question will be whether current legal theories available can also explain EC law. Likewise, one needs working legal knowledge in any law, but the question is whether knowing EC law involves something different from knowing, say German law or Irish law. Finally, problems of legal reasoning are common to all laws, but when it comes to EC law one needs to consider whether and to what extent reasoning with EC law involves special techniques.

Z. Bankowski et al. (eds.), Informatics and the Foundations of Legal Reasoning, 291–309.

The argument runs that Expert Systems or Decision-Support Systems in EC law will be flawed if they are built on a weak theoretical foundation unfit for EC law (level 1), if they do not adequately represent EC legal knowledge (level 2) and if they do not reflect the legal methods specific to EC law (level 3). Such Expert Systems will improve considerably if they are built on a sound ontological theory of EC law —i.e. a theory of the types and structure of the norms that make up the EC legal system, and of the formal features of this system— (level 1), if their knowledge base includes information about legislation in the Member States and about possible European standards (level 2), and if their inference engine reflects the specificities of EC legal reasoning (level 3). To my knowledge, very little work has been done regarding the application of AI to EC law, and one will be aware of the immense difficulties involved. But at least one can point out the main problems which would have to be solved for any such project to get started. This is what I am set to do.

1.1. A foundational theory for EC law?

The level of *basic research* implies the adoption and elaboration of a legal theory which will account for the peculiarities of the legal order of the European Communities and which will provide an ontological and epistemological foundation and method for carrying out particular analyses or dogmatic studies (level 2) of the different areas or institutions of EC law e.g. the law of agriculture, the law of competition, the law of goods, the freedom of establishment, etc., which are the subject-area where Expert Systems might eventually develop. We have already suggested that EC law might require a special legal theory to account for its specificity, and many of the legal theories 'on offer in the academic market' have been developed in too close relation to the idea of the state for them cogently to explain EC law. This leads us to distinguishing between different layers of theory.

First, there is what I call *Grand Legal Theory* or Philosophy of Law which tries to account for the law in its integrity taking into account its linguistic, logical, phenomenological, structural, social, political aspects. Most Grand Legal Theory versions have given a privileged position to state sovereignty and official coercion, and they need important re-adjustments in order to account for EC law, or else they deny its juridicity —they deny it the status of law.[2] One can have doubts about the interest of such Grand Legal Theory and as regards EC law it seems to me that it will take some time before a Grand Theory of EC law is put forward.

Secondly there is a less comprehensive, *middle range legal theory* or legal science which works as the background theory of any legal dogmatics. This is a theory about the sources of law, about the units that make up a legal system, about the validity conditions of those units, about norms and relations between norms, etc. Legal science would deal with these elements in the abstract without considering their concrete applications or instantiations in a given law or area of law. Some authors are happier than others about the term 'legal *science*' but we can skip this problem now. Some such middle range legal theory is the minimum necessary for any formal treatment of the law with a view to its representation, storage, retrieval, or decision support.[3]

Finally there is a much more concrete, less extensive layer of legal theory or *legal dogmatics* which is really legal theory applied to a given field of law. Legal dogmatics presupposes a background or foundational legal theory which is then applied to analyse and treat the content and structure of certain laws systematically, e.g. criminal law, private law, public law or even given institutions of EC law. The fact that most legal dogmatics is being carried out without much awareness of its theoretical background does not mean that such background theories are lacking. It is plausible to argue that legal dogmatics would considerably improve in quality were it to be conducted in full awareness of its theoretical background. One of the tangential virtues of devising an Expert System in a restricted area of law or legal institution is that it makes background middle range legal theory inescapable and brings it to the fore, and thus contributes to the improvement of legal dogmatics, and possibly also of legal theory itself.

In my view the type of legal theory one needs for EC law is *middle range legal theory.* Grand Legal Theory would be too broad, it would provide us with important critical knowledge, but not enough formal or 'scientific' methods for understanding law. Legal dogmatics would provide too detailed knowledge about what the law says in certain areas, but not enough knowledge about how the law says what it says. We shall therefore point out some of the major questions which have to be addressed by a middle range legal theory. It must be said from the outset that all the problems involved cannot be identified now. We shall at least indicate some.

Any legal theory has to account for the normativity of law, for the elements that make up the law and for their origins and interrelations. There is first of all an ontological question: what makes up the law? what are its units? how are they related? One can provisionally answer that norms make up the law. The next question imposes itself, but what are norms? how does one identify a norm? what are the sources of norms? where does one look for a norm?

Problem (a): There is a great diversity of theories about norms. The two poles would be to consider (1) that a norm is a linguistic sequence or fragment found in a 'normative text' or normative material e.g. a rule stated in an article of an act or statute, or regulation or the like, in which case there is an approximation between the norm and the source of the norm; or else (2) that the norm is the meaning of a linguistic sequence or fragment or of a series of fragments contained in 'normative materials', in which case a certain jump is produced from the source of the norm or normative material to the norm itself. (See the papers by Bell and MacCormick in this collection.)

Neither pole is uncontroversial. Both approaches would probably coincide in practice in situations of clarity or *isomorphy,* i.e. situations where there is a definite written and controllable normative material organised on the basis of typical normative sentences of the type $p \rightarrow q$ (if p is the case then q follows) where p and q do not require any form of interpretation beyond linguistic understanding according to the semantic, syntactic and pragmatic conventions operative in a given natural language (interpretation in the large sense).[4]

There is a problem with the $p \rightarrow q$ type of normative sentence. The problem is what does one do with the normative or deontic element that would identify this formula as a norm as opposed to e.g. a descriptive sentence or proposition? One can opt for a normativity in the background $D(p \rightarrow q)$ where D stands for the deontic element: *obligatory*, *forbidden*, or *permitted*. Here we have normativity as a pragmatic element and it need not be represented in an Expert System. The other possibility is to make normativity a semantic feature, so to speak, in which case the formula would be $p \rightarrow Dq$ and in this case the deontic element would have to be represented in an Expert System. (See Jones and Sergot in this collection.)

But in *situations of doubt* where the meaning of a normative material is unclear and interpretation in the strict sense is required, the two poles mentioned above would lead to very different results. Does one represent the problematic hard text contained in the source as it stands with its ambiguity (pole 1) or does one perform an interpretation and represent the meaning one ascribes to the normative material (pole 2)? In this second case it might be that the problem normative material has already been given a concrete meaning institutionally, e.g. by some judicial organ. One would then have to decide whether to represent the normative material with the institutionalised interpretation. But what if the institutional interpretation is controversial or there are institutionalised interpretations that differ for the same normative material? Does one then opt for one of the contending interpretations or does one represent all of them as viable hypotheses? These are real problems when designing the knowledge base of an Expert System.

Problem (b): The very identification of a piece of normative material can itself be a very complicated interpretative activity. It presupposes a given theory of legal sources which will partly at least depend on a Grand Theory because problems of political philosophy are involved. A theory of the sources of law requires a secondary norm of recognition, and that norm is a matter not only of middle range legal theory but also of political theory: are judicial precedents a source of law? —is the Constitution the major source of law? —what are the rankings between different legislative materials? —is international law a source of law? —is legal doctrine or dogmatics a source of law? —is comparative law a source of law? These are all problems of a legal theory of the sources of law which imply deep and hard questions of political morality —to use a term coined by R. Dworkin. (Dworkin 1977, 1984a, 1986b). To mention but one of the problems involved, if precedent is a source of law there might be difficulties about identifying the norm contained in a precedent. The norm finally distilled will be closer to pole 2 than to pole 1, even if there is an authoritative theory of precedent.

Problem (c): The next major issue is the question of the validity or existence of the norm. It is usually accepted that norms do not exist in isolation: rather, they are elements or units of systems of norms. This takes us directly into two main areas of questions: when does a norm belong to a system? and what are the main features of a system of norms? The first question has partly been dealt with in relation to the sources of law and to the norm or rule of recognition. But being extracted from an accepted source of law is not enough. In order to belong to a system and thus be valid, a norm might have to fulfil certain systemic criteria or secondary rules like consistency with other valid norms of the system (legal positivist version of validity), coherence with the principles inspiring the law or the given area of law (axiological version of validity), and even rational acceptability to the organs who apply the law (legal realist version of validity). (See Bengoetxea 1992 and 1991a.) For representation purposes this implies that preferably not all norms which can be extracted from the sources or normative materials should be represented, but only those that are valid according to given criteria of validity.

Problem (d): The next problem is the structure of norms. It is classical, especially since Dworkin, to distinguish between two main types of norms: rules and principles. Rules would be norms with the form $D(p \rightarrow q)$ or $p \rightarrow Dq$. They have an all or nothing character, they either apply or do not, but if they do they hold all the way with all the consequences so that it is logically incorrect to affirm the antecedent or protasis and deny the consequent or apodosis at the same time. Rules lend themselves to formal chaining of the type $D((p \rightarrow q) \,\&\, (q \rightarrow r) :: \mathrm{O}(p \rightarrow r))$ which is useful for decision support systems. Needless to say that the formulae needed in practice tend to be much more complex. But when principles are involved matters get even more complicated. Whereas the conflict between two rules is solved in the sense that the application of one rule excludes the application of the other, principles have a dimension of weight and call for a (non-monotonic) weighing and balancing process: if two principles conflict, one principle does not overrule the other but might outweigh it. Principles have a formal structure of the type Dp, which could be read 'prima facie $\mathrm{O}p$' or 'it is desirable that p be the case'. This poses serious difficulties for any knowledge or expertise representation and requires special forms of reasoning and 'inference' engines. Whereas reasoning with rules does not differ substantially across different legal systems, reasoning with principles does, according to the relevance of principles in a system.

Problem (e): Groups of norms dealing with different aspects of a common subject area are structured into legal institutions. Citizenship, residence, marriage, inheritance, contracts, etc. are all examples of legal institutions. One of the virtues of the concept of legal institution is that it allows for some simplification, classification and systematisation of the many norms there are in a legal system into more workable compounds. But this theory still has to clarify how to identify institutions, how general can institutions be. For instance, contract can be seen as a very general institution, and contract of employment as a specific institution, but how does one distinguish the two?

The concept might also be useful as regards the range of application of a decision support system, given that it is highly unlikely that a decision-support unit will cover subject areas that are too large. Legal institutions are compounds of two sets of norms[5]: (1) constitutive norms, i.e. standards relating to the existence (coming into being or termination) of an instance of the institution, and (2) consequential norms, relating to the legal consequences that follow from the instantiation of an institution. These sets of norms are themselves structured according to systemic criteria like the ones mentioned above.

The problems listed above are common to any middle range legal theory. Now we shall mention, following the classification set out above, some of the specific problems involved when devising a legal theory for EC law: (a) norms of EC law, (b) identification of the sources of EC law, (c) existence or validity of EC law norms and EC legal system, (d) structure of EC norms, and (e) institutions of EC law.

Problem (a): The first question for an EC legal theory will concern the adoption of a concept of legal norms of EC law. In particular, one has to make a choice between normative materials and the meaning ascribed to them after interpretation in the strict sense. Is a norm of EC law a *fragment* of the normative material of EC law, or is it the *meaning* of such a fragment? If it is a fragment, what fragment? An article, a group of articles, a paragraph in an article? Does the preamble of a normative material of EC law count? How does one deal with judgments of the European Court of Justice, do they constitute norms? These might seem rather naïve questions, but they are really quite controversial. I personally see no special problem in calling such judgments norms, as long as we are aware of the special nuances that appear when they are unclear. Still, this will remain a terminological problem.

Does one opt for the *meaning* of a fragment of normative material? This has the advantage of making knowledge representation easier and more systematic, but it has the disadvantage, in cases of strict interpretation at least, of giving the fragment of normative material a meaning which might not coincide with the meaning the main interpreter of EC law —the ECJ— might give it eventually. In any case I think it would do no harm to bracket-in the original problem text so that the user is made aware of the reconstruction performed by the expert. This solution is also ideologically sound in that it remains faithful to the *rule of law,* which is an institutional regulative ideal. After all, the norm making agent has opted for that given text in all its indeterminacy, and this might be a conscious, explicit choice.

In my opinion, the *fragment* of normative material —rule text or physical or canonical text— can be directly reproduced if the text is pragmatically and tendentially clear and precise. This will be the case for some articles of the Treaties establishing the Communities, for articles of EC Regulations and articles of Directives capable of producing direct effect according to the doctrine of the ECJ (including its *acte clair* doctrine[6]), for individual decisions of the ECJ, or even for the *dispositif* of some ECJ judgments. But as regards fragments of normative materials which call for interpretation, the expert acting as an advisor when building a knowledge base will have to interpret many of those fragments to extract a norm or rule content. Of course the expert will have some guidance in this sense: previous ECJ judgments, preambles of normative materials, doctrine, even the fragments of normative materials which, according to the doctrine of the ECJ, would lack direct effect, and especially the doctrine of interpretation operative at the ECJ.

Problem (b): The second problem will consist in identifying the sources of EC law from which fragments —rule texts— of EC law are extracted or from which norms of EC law are derived. I have already mentioned a few. How does one deal with recommendations, declarations, resolutions and the like, which can be termed *soft law*? These work, at the very least, as guides to interpretation. There are specific problems as regards the preambles of the Treaties, of Regulations and of Directives. The ECJ often has recourse to such preambles as guides to interpretation or even as justifying reasons accompanying other norms of EC law.

There is the further theoretical problem whether judgments of the ECJ count as precedents and consequently the practical problem whether norms can be extracted from them to be eventually represented in a knowledge base. Theoretically it is generally accepted that judgments of the ECJ are not strict precedents, but in practice they work as precedents, and therefore they should be represented in any knowledge base when they turn on basic questions of EC law, and in the particular knowledge base when they deal with the particular institution or area of law which is being represented.

Further problems regard the status of legal doctrine as a source of EC law, or even the status of comparative law. They are both useful aids to interpretation, especially comparative law, and they might be usefully represented subsidiarily in support of a given interpretation when the text of EC law is unclear.

Problem (c): The third question consists in deciding what are the systemic norms of EC law from which we can derive criteria of validity or existence of EC legal norms. What are the systemic features of EC law which will have to be taken into account when rearranging groups of norms in a particular area of EC law or even when interpreting norms of EC law? We have already pointed out that norms do not exist in isolation, rather they belong in normative systems, and legal norms are no exception. The existence and validity of a norm of EC law will therefore be a question of its belonging to the legal system of the EC.

The first thing one has to ask is whether there is Community *competence* on the given area of law one wants to represent. There are several possibilities here. If there is clearly exclusive Community competence, then one moves down to consider the other systemic features. If there clearly is no Community competence on the subject, then one goes to domestic law. If there is doubt as to whether there is exclusive Community competence, one has to resolve the doubt and interpret EC law with the help of the doctrine of the ECJ and especially according to the guiding principle of *subsidiarity*. If there is shared competence between the Community and the Member State then special problems arise: EC law might provide the general normative framework or minimum standards common to all Member States, but then domestic law will fill the details as long as those minimum standards are not jeopardised. The expert representing a knowledge base will then have extra work: the minimum standards will remain the same for all domestic laws, but a different knowledge base will have to be designed for every domestic law, and in that case any problem of interpretation or validity between domestic details and community standards will have to be interpreted away by the expert inspired by the principle of *primacy* of Community law and by the doctrine of interpretation of the ECJ. This might lead to serious difficulties in practice.

The next systemic feature is *consistency*: norms of EC law must not contradict each other; conflicts will be solved according to the criteria of hierarchy —the higher norm derogates the lower one, temporality —the more recent norm derogates the older one, and speciality —the more specific norm derogates the general one. But what is the hierarchy in EC law? Is a Regulation higher than an individual decision? Is it higher than a Directive?

Unity of EC law is the next systemic feature which guides any arrangement of norms of EC law into a system. This is fairly unproblematic. In practice it leads to the notion, operative in the doctrine of interpretation of the ECJ, that the terms and notions used by norms of EC law have an *autonomous* Community meaning, and in theory it would tend to block access to comparative law, though in practice it does not.

Completeness of EC law can be understood not as a completeness of qualification —for there are gaps and these cannot always be successfully filled— but rather as a completeness of validity and of decision: in principle it is possible to decide whether any norm of EC law is valid, if it belongs to EC law.

The final systemic feature of EC law is material, rather than formal. EC law is to be treated as a *coherent* whole: a norm has to be interpreted so that it is made coherent with EC law, so that it hangs together with the rest of the valid norms of EC law, e.g. it is inspired by the same background principles.

Coherence can also guide the choice of validity of a norm: a norm will be treated as valid if, apart from formally belonging to EC law, it is also substantially coherent with it.

Problem (d): The fourth problem lies in the complex and varied structure of norms of EC law: principles feature prominently in EC law and are made great use of by the ECJ, normally as *justificatory reasons* in support of an interpretative decision, but in some cases even blocking rules as *exclusionary reasons.* They tend to ensure the coherence of EC law but they present special problems as regards legal reasoning.

Rules of EC law are not free of nuances: many of them are addressed to various subjects and require the normative intervention of those subjects for their full effect: this is the case with Directives, addressed to domestic norm-making authorities, but which can be used by domestic law-applying authorities, even in the absence of developing norms, if the norms of the Directive can have direct effect. Many rules are hypothetical or conditional in character and their conditions of application depend on a time lapse, and this requires a logic of time to be introduced into the system. The lack of direct enforceable sanctions (rules addressed to enforcement officials as a guarantee for the primary rules addressed to individuals) might also be seen as a further element of indeterminacy regarding the qualification as rules of many norms of EC law, although some have seen this as a virtue.

Problem (e): Finally there is the question of institutions of EC law and the systematisation of the norms constituting and regulating those institutions into workable compounds on the basis of which decision support systems can be designed. All the specific problems of EC law could be included here. I shall only insist on the complicated process of analysing and systematising institutions for which there is shared competence between the EC and the Member States.

1.2. A knowledge base in EC law

In contrast with the points made above I shall now be rather brief. Knowing EC law involves operating with a given background legal theory to analyse and rearrange the norms of EC law into systematised institutions. Therefore the problems mentioned above should be taken into consideration here. But knowing and understanding EC law involves a further distinctive element.

The element I want to mention as specific to EC law is the need to adopt a comparative law approach at all times. At the substantive level, all areas of

EC law, even the Treaties themselves, display or are the product of a tension between two poles: (1) legal concepts and legal ideas brought from the legal traditions of the Member States, and (2) legal ideas which are meant to be specific to Community law and to have an autonomous Community meaning.

This makes EC law a perfect setting or laboratory for comparative approaches. In order to understand EC law one needs important notions of constitutional and administrative law as they have developed in the French and German legal traditions, notions of the law of obligations that go as far back as Roman law, notions of the US law of competition, procedural rights notions from the Common Law tradition, etc. This comparative approach is inevitable when one considers that the officials who make up the staff of the EC come from very different legal traditions, and their understanding of EC law will necessarily be impregnated with concepts and legal reasoning characteristic to their legal backgrounds. The ECJ is no exception. When interpreting EC law it does not openly proclaim in the *justification* of its decisions its use of the comparative method, but the comparison of the different laws of the Member States in order to arrive at interpretative decisions is a constant element of the *heuristics* of decisionmaking at the Court.

The comparative law approach poses a practical problem for any representation of EC law. Should one develop models which can deal with the translatability problem among different databases from the different Member States? The information thus assembled and organised can be extremely useful at a legal conceptual level (legal theory and legal dogmatics), at the lawmaking or legislative drafting level of the European Communities (COREPER and the Commission) and at the decision-making level.

Any interpretation of EC law by an expert will take into account the solutions adopted in the different Member States. The practical problem is how much weight to give to comparative materials: should one opt for an autonomous Community meaning or should one follow the meaning of legal concepts in the Member State traditions; and if so, which solution should be followed, the majority solution or the solution which best seems to further the aims and objectives of EC law? This second alternative is followed by the ECJ, and therefore it should be followed by the expert as well. But a lot of discretion is involved here.

At the norm-making level, the norm-making institutions of the EC are aware that the implementation of EC law at the domestic level will be easier if the concepts and methods of EC law are rooted in the legal traditions of the

Member States. But this ideal can never be fulfilled because those traditions differ a great deal, and one always runs the risk that EC law will be interpreted and understood differently in the different Member States. Still EC law is a perfect laboratory for comparative law also in the sense that EC law, being also the law of the Member States, is achieving a certain approximation or convergence of the different legal traditions of the Member States, and the work of the ECJ is notable for moving in this direction. When the EC Treaties or even the ECJ make reference to the common standards of the Member States, the first question one has to ask is whether there really are any such common standards, and the second question will be how to find them. Comparative law is essential for both purposes. Therefore the expert acting as an advisor in the representation of legal knowledge will have to be also an expert in comparative law. Even if the autonomous Community meaning prevails, one cannot really know what that meaning amounts to if one does not distinguish it from the domestic meaning.

1.3. Reasoning with EC law

Once one has a knowledge base available with universalised formulations of legal norms, one is ready to work with it formally, devising inference engines towards the resolution of concrete cases involving particulars. This is the domain of legal reasoning. Of course legal reasoning has also featured prominently in the elaboration of the knowledge base, in the reconstruction of the system of norms. and in the re-formulation of the norms in situations of doubt. But legal reasoning is typically the type of reasoning one needs for applying norms to particular cases (reasoning with norms and reasoning with facts in legal contexts), the paradigm of which will be the judicial application of the law —to which we now turn.

2. AN ANALYTICAL MODEL OF THE APPLICATION OF EC LAW

This second part will explain the late Prof. Wróblewski's analytical model[7] of the application of the law and consider how it applies to EC law and what the contribution of Expert Systems and computers might be in this area.

2.1. The model of justification

First we shall reconstruct the law-applying decision with the help of a diagram (see Figure 1).

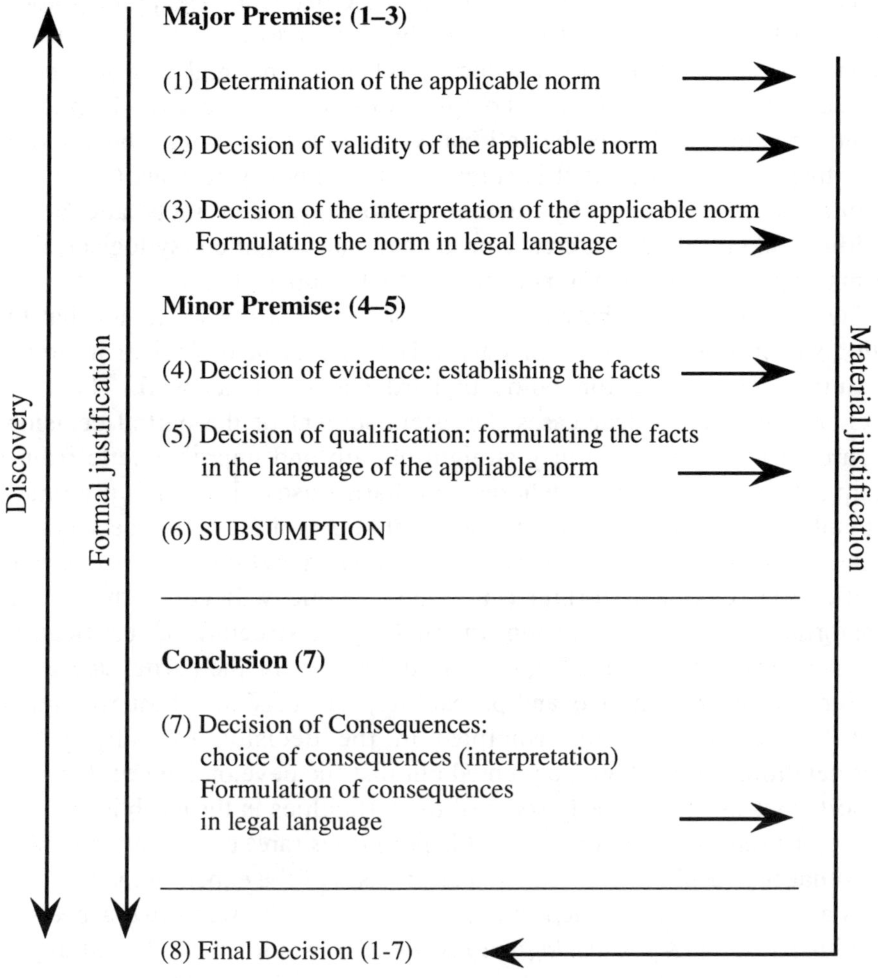

Figure 1. Analytical Model of the law-applying decision

We cannot here go into the details of this model. I shall only make brief and general comments, and then move on to consider in what particular moments of the decision computers, information technology or expert systems can be of help. In general the term 'decision support systems' is more appropriate because we are trying to see how the law-applying *decision* can be *supported* by machines.

By way of general comments about the analytical model devised one must say from the outset that the model reconstructs the process of justification of the law-applying decision. It does not try to capture the process of discovery or heuristic process which actually leads to the decision. The point is not to underrate the importance of discovery but rather to control law-applying decisions from a justificatory standpoint. Whatever the 'real' reasons behind the decision[8], whatever the psychological or cognitive process which led to it, the decision will only be rationally acceptable if it can be justified according to the model, if it is supported by authority reasons (valid law, adequately interpreted), by factual reasons (proven facts adequately qualified) and by a valid inference or logical transformation (syllogism) from the major premise plus the minor premise to the conclusion.

The main difference between clear cases and hard cases is not that the syllogism only applies in clear cases. The syllogism or logical inference leading to the conclusion holds in hard cases just as well. The main difference is that in clear cases the establishment of the partial decisions (Figure 1, 1–5 and 7) is fairly straightforward and unproblematic from a pragmatic point of view, whereas in hard cases there are pragmatic difficulties or doubts as to the establishment of any of the partial decisions.

Decision support systems can work with a syllogistic structure of justification. Classical formal (monotonic) logic will cover the overall transformation to the conclusion, the underlying structure of justification, and special non-monotonic logics can be devised for the partial decisions, e.g. for reasoning with facts and probability, for decisions of interpretation, even for reasoning with principles in the decision of validity and interpretation. It must here be pointed out that the development of decision-support systems might clarify some of the difficulties in the establishment of the Major Premise where the applicable norm(s) is (are) technically complex. The situations resulting can be called clear cases of the expert domain.

As a final general comment we shall distinguish between two aspects of legal justification. A *formal-logical justification* would check the validity of the transformation from the premises to the conclusion. A law-applying decision will be formally justified if the syllogism supporting the conclusion is valid or logically correct. Since the formal reasoning here involved is monotonic the conclusion will either be valid or invalid.

Material or substantive justification checks the establishment of the premises or partial decisions, i.e. whether they are rationally acceptable. The reasoning process involved here is not logical in the classical sense, it is non-monotonic, and therefore the premises or partial decisions will not be either valid or invalid —although in some cases they could be invalid, e.g. if they contradict valid law or if they ignore a proven fact or grossly misqualify a proven fact— but rather more or less acceptable. Of course criteria of acceptability vary and one has to take into account the criteria operative at a given context, say the ECJ.

Thus legal justification of a law-applying decision requires a two-fold justification: formal and substantive. In any case the formal and substantive legal justification of a law-applying decision does not prejudge its justification within a different normative system like ethics or politics and outside the legal system which is being applied. Legal justification is justification within the law, *internal* to a particular legal system, but not an *external* justification across different normative systems be they legal, ethical or political.

2.2. The use of computers

We shall now move to the final part of this paper and consider how the support of the partial decisions can profit from recent developments in information and computer science. I am no expert in this area, so my suggestions are made and should be taken with great caution.

(1) As regards the determination or individuation of the applicable norm the problem is to find a norm of the system which tendentially covers the problem for which we want a legal solution. This takes us to the process of discovery because the first type of information we need is to know what happened. We shall feed the basic facts to the computer and think of an area of the law that might apply to those facts. A document retrieval system would be most useful here. The system will give us a list of the possible norms that might apply to the problem case at hand. The document retrieval system will store norms in their physical sense, i.e. the fragments of normative materials, and the key words of the facts we feed into the system when interfacing with it will act as cues to search for the relevant information. Once we have individuated a norm as a possible candidate to govern the case at hand we move on to the decision on the validity of the selected norm.

(2) The decision of validity requires an examination of the norm according to systemic criteria of validity. While document retrieval systems solve the problem of locating and identifying the applicable norm they do not solve the problem of validity. Here we need systemic reasoning:

> A norm of EC law will be valid
>
> — if it belongs to the EC legal system,
> — if it is contained (explicitly) in a normative material of EC law according to an accepted theory of the sources of EC law partly determined by a secondary rule of recognition,

— or if it can be implicitly extracted from such material,
— and if it does not contradict a norm of EC law declared as valid,
— or if it does contradict any valid norm then the antinomy must be solved according to some acceptable criterion.

A system representing norms rather than normative materials will have solved these problems. The representation of these norms could follow the physical norm found by the document retrieval system as a *reformulation* of the physical text, not strictly as an interpretation of it.

(3) The decision of interpretation is the next problem. If the applicable norm seems clear enough for pragmatic purposes after an interpretation in the large sense, then there are no major difficulties and strict interpretation can be bypassed. But if there are pragmatic doubts as to the meaning of the norm then it has to be interpreted in the strict sense. There might be different readings of the same physical text. These could all be represented as alternative norms. The system could look something like this:

physical text: PN
(proposed readings of PN)
N': $Ax\,(Fx \rightarrow Cx)$
N": $Ax\,(Fx \vee F'x \rightarrow Hx)$

This information can be represented by the system and the user will know that if one interpretation is chosen certain consequences will follow. Interpretation will be carried out according to the specific doctrine of interpretation operative in a given legal system, e.g. the doctrine of interpretation operative at the ECJ.[9] If the Court has already pronounced itself on the question, one of the proposed alternatives can be suggested as more plausible. If there is a *jurisprudence constante* of the ECJ then only the official interpretation need be represented. Once a given interpretation is chosen then the norm can be formulated in the legal language with a view to its application to individuals.

(4) Establishing the facts is the next step. This is often called the decision on evidence and depends on the law of evidence. This is an area about which the law, at least in the continental tradition, normally has little to say. The proof of the facts is left to the wise discretion of the judge or of the jury. A document retrieval system could perhaps indicate what type of information is relevant to prove facts, and how information about facts can, may and may not be obtained. This is an area of the law-application process into which needs more basic research needs to be done, especially in relation to the computation of probability and evidence.

(5) The qualification of the facts is the next decision. The particular facts, once proven, have to be labelled or qualified according to the universal terms or concepts used by the applicable norm as formulated after interpretation. (See Pipe and Barden in this collection) This is an operation for which computers cannot provide much help, because it is a discretionary decision, or even an intuitive operation, the modelling of which is very difficult. Of course a document retrieval system can give information about how similar facts have been previously qualified by the Court, and this is valuable information especially if there is a consistent line of precedents. But, as in the case of alternative interpretations, alternative qualifications can be represented, and the legal consequences, which will differ according to how the facts are qualified, can also be represented:

Formulation of the applicable norm:
$Ax\ (Fx \rightarrow Gx) \vee Ax\ (F'x \rightarrow Hx)$
Facts proven: *a* is the case
Qualification of the facts:
a is *F*, *a* counts as *F*
a is *F'*, *a* counts as *F'*

(6) Subsumption is a mechanical operation which will be carried out by the inference engine. We shall not deal with this question.

(7) The decision of consequences is related to the decision of interpretation. If the legal consequence or apodosis foreseen by the norm is clear for pragmatic purposes, then the consequence will be represented in the Major Premise adequately. But if the apodosis of the norm is unclear then it has to be interpreted according to the accepted doctrine of interpretation. The different alternative consequences proposed can be represented and the user will have to chose among them.

Applicable norm: $Ax\ (Fx \rightarrow Gx)$
Doubt: *Gx*?
Alternative readings of *Gx*: *G'x*, *G"x*

(8) The final decision will depend on the partial decisions we make throughout the process, especially on the alternatives we chose in the decisions as to interpretation (of the protasis of the norm), as to qualification and as to consequences. Each partial choice will have to be argued for. While the system cannot replace the user in making those arguments it can at least offer them to the user. This is a general point addressed to those who see expert systems as possible threats to human decision-making: the decisions

will be made by human beings, but the system will help them along or support them through the labour intensive business of identifying the relevant material, and will suggest possible solutions from which to choose. Of course the greater the alternatives offered the wider the scope for leeway. In any case this should depend on the state of legal knowledge and legal science and not on the whims of the expert. Discretion will not be eliminated, and we should not see this as a shortcoming of decision-making.

Thus the system will suggest an interpretation and tell the user what are the arguments in favour of and against this or that choice. The same goes for the qualification of facts and the choice of consequences. Of course these arguments offered by the system will be reconstructions of a Court's theory of justification, and this again requires of the expert designing the system a thorough knowledge and understanding of the doctrine of justification operative at a Court: what arguments must be advanced, what arguments should be advanced, what arguments may, and what arguments may not, be put forward.

This last point takes us back to the general message of this paper, which is that legal theory can provide very valuable help to the expert designing a decision-support system. I can only hope that the interaction between legal theorists, legal experts and computer experts will continue and lead to a fruitful cooperation.

NOTES

[1] The views here put forward were first presented at meetings of the ESPRIT Group, and I would like to thank all the members who made comments on my presentation, and especially Carlos Alchourrón, Garrett Barden, John Bell and Ian White. Many of the ideas here expounded are reconstructions of the ideas of Jerzy Wróblewski to the memory of whom I would like to pay tribute in this article.

[2] For a criticism of such theories see (Bengoetxea 1991b).

[3] This is the range of theory which has been examined and adopted by e.g. (Susskind 1987). A higher level or grander theory is not needed for representational and programming purposes. The type of legal theory which was being pursued within the ESPRIT group on the foundations of legal reasoning, and which is intended as a foundation for the possible applications of AI in law is also middle range legal theory.

[4] We are here following the late Prof. Wróblewski, in his many articles and books; see in general (Wróblewski, 1992).

[5] My analysis differs here from that of MacCormick and Weinberger who consider terminative rules as a distinct set of rules. See (MacCormick & Weinberger 1986) and (Bengoetxea 1991a).

[6] See (Bengoetxea 1992) and (Bengoetxea 1990).

[7] Wróblewski explained this theoretical model in many works. One of the first versions of his model can be found in (Wróblewski 1967).

[8] I do not hereby imply that the justificatory process is somehow 'unreal'. It is no less real and very significant from a social-theoretical perspective in the light of the general legal requirement that judicial decisions be motivated. Art. 33 of the Statue of the European Court of Justice provides: 'Judgments shall state the reasons on which they are based'.

[9] For a detailed study of the doctrine of interpretation operative at the European Court of Justice, see (Bengoetxea 1992).

REFERENCES

Barden, G., 1995. 'Formalization, Invention, Justification.' In this collection.
Bell, J., 1995. 'Policy Arguments and legal reasoning.' In this collection.
Bengoetxea, J., 1990. 'The Justification of Decisions by the European Court of Justice', *Paper 202 Europa Institut der Universität des Saarlandes*, Saarbrucken.
Bengoetxea, J., 1991a. 'Institutions, Legal Theory and EC law', *ARSP* Vol. LXXVII/Heft 2
Bengoetxea, J., 1991b. 'Legal System as a Regulative Ideal', *IVR World Congress*, Göttingen, Aug. 1991.
Bengoetxea, J., 1992. *The Legal Reasoning of the European Court of Justice*, Oxford.
Dworkin, R. 1986a. *A Matter of Principle*, Oxford.
Dworkin, R. 1986b. *Law's Empire*, London.
Dworkin, R., 1977. *Taking Rights Seriously*, London.
MacCormick, N., 1995. 'Defeasibility in Law and Logic.' In this collection.
MacCormick, N., and O. Weinberger, 1986. *An Institutional Theory of Law,* Dordrecht.
Pipe, G., 1995. 'Common Law Concepts — The Problem of Indefinability.' In this collection.
Susskind, R., 1987. *Expert Systems in Law,* Oxford
Wróblewski, J., 1967. 'Il modello teorico della applicazione della legge', *Rivista Internazionale di Filosofia del Diritto.*
Wróblewski, J., 1992. *The Judicial Application of Law* (*Sadowe Stosowania Prawa*), trans. & ed. by Zenon Bankowski and Neil MacCormick, Kluwer.

Department of the Philosophy of Law
University of the Basque Country
San Sebastian
Spain

LILIAN EDWARDS

BUILDING AN INTESTATE SUCCESSION ADVISER: COMPARTMENTALISATION AND CREATIVITY IN DECISION SUPPORT SYSTEMS [1]

1. INTRODUCTION

Mr McConnell, a prosperous businessman, dies on the 13th December by foolishly walking out into the path of a motorcar proceeding in excess of the speed limit along Leith Walk. Even more unfortunately, he dies without making a will, having been of the opinion there was plenty of time yet for such considerations. Mr McConnell is a domiciled Scotsman and dies leaving a wife and two children. What shares in his estate will they take under the Scots law of intestate succession? Will anyone else benefit?

The Intestate Succession Adviser is a computer program which was built by the writer to solve problems of the type above, i.e. the distribution of the estate of a deceased person who has died without leaving a valid will which applies to the whole of his estate. The program deals only with the Scots law of intestate succession which is to be found primarily in the Succession (Sc) Act 1964, and differs considerable from the system found in England. This paper attempts to explain why this domain was seen as suitable both from a pragmatic and a philosophical perspective for the development of a so-called 'expert system' or decision support system, and examines certain features of the implementation of the domain which proved unexpected.

2. CHARACTERISTICS OF LEGAL DOMAIN

The characteristic expertise of the Scottish succession rules lies in understanding several interconnected elements. First, there are not one but three distinct types of right which arise out of the deceased's estate. Secondly, these rights rank, so that prior rights are exacted from the estate before legal rights and the latter before free estate rights. Thirdly, these rights are not exacted evenly from the estate as a uniform whole but are taken differently from different aspects of the estate (e.g. the matrimonial home) and from the heritage (immoveable) and moveable portions of the estate. There is therefore a need for a certain methodology to be followed in working out the intestate succession calculation: some rights must always take precedence over other rights; the value of some rights is dependent on

Z. Bankowski et al. (eds.), Informatics and the Foundations of Legal Reasoning, 311–323.

whether other rights are taken; and heritage and moveables must be tallied separately till a certain point in the problem.

The example above may help clarify. Suppose Mr McConnell died leaving a house in joint title whose net value after paying off the mortgage was £150,000 and net moveables of £70,000, which include £10,000 of household contents. His widow takes the first slice of the cake in the form of an assortment of rights known as 'prior rights'. These give her the right to (a) the deceased's share in the matrimonial home (£75,000), (b) the deceased's share in the furniture and plenishings of the home (£10,000), and (c) a certain financial right (cash sum) from the estate which she is in theory able to continue to maintain herself in the home just as she did before her husband died (here, £21,000). The policy of the legislation is clear but the details, shaped by the complexities of life, are not. For example, it is thought inequitable for a widow (or widower —the provisions apply without sex discrimination) to do well just because the matrimonial home is particularly opulent. So there are cash limits on the house and plenishings right. (But there are no minima where the house was, say, particularly under-furnished.) The financial right varies depending on whether there are children to consider. There are problems of two-home couples to consider, and so forth. The financial right is also not entirely straightforward to calculate since it must be derived according to the rules rateably from the heritage and moveables remaining at that stage of the game.

This last point is particularly significant because the second stage of the distribution on intestacy involves the extracting of 'legal rights' from the estate, which are rights only exigible from moveables not heritage. (The reason for this is that legal rights date from an early stage of development in Scots succession law when heritage was controlled by feudal law and only moveables descended according to civil law.[2]) So the portion of the estate that goes into the legal rights kitty varies from estate to estate according to its particular make-up and not always in accordance with what might be seen as common sense or equity. Legal rights can be claimed by the surviving spouse of the deceased and the children (including representatives of any children who pre-decease), and can be disclaimed, which can be advantageous where the alternative is to claim a legacy.

Finally if any estate remains after the prior and legal rights are taken then what remains (the 'free estate') is distributed among the first surviving class of relatives on a list of ranked relatives, headed by the children. Thus if, for example, a brother or sister of Mr McConnell were to ask what they would gain from the estate, the problem would be trivial if there were children

—they would get nothing— but if there were no children the whole question of the rights of the widow would have to be examined before the rights of the sibling could be established.

The Succession Adviser was conceived as a tutoring aid for students, who often find the intestacy domain deceptively simple and tend to learn to deal with it in a rather ritualistic (and therefore easily unsettled) fashion. The point perhaps that is most under-appreciated is that while each possible permutation of the distribution of the estate is relatively simple, the number of ways in which the outcome may be varied by the differing characteristics of the estate and the surviving family is not. The purpose of the Adviser was to make the required methodology explicit to students of property law by formalising the operation of the rules of the domain in the form of a rule-based deductive computer program.

The program was written over a fairly short development period using a simple 'expert system' shell, CRYSTAL (© Intelligent Environments, Richmond, Surrey) which is rule based and provides a backward-chaining inference engine, churning simple propositional logic. (CRYSTAL is one of the best known expert system shells on the UK PC-based market and is widely known in legal computing as the system used by Susskind and Capper (1988) to build the Latent Damage System.) CRYSTAL provided a pleasant and flexible user interface and considerably minimised the programming effort that would have been necessary to have generated the Succession Adviser from scratch.

The intestate succession area was regarded as suitable for implementation in computable form because it was believed the domain was one which although syntactically complex and of social and legal significance was nonetheless semantically clear, and that therefore the difficulties typically found when modelling legal norms for implementation in decision support systems would not be applicable here. These difficulties are well documented in the literature: pre-eminent among them are the problems of open texture in the Hartian sense, arising from the inherent fuzziness of many legal concepts, and the problem of extracting legal rules from a common law which is not formalised as legislative rules are, is dynamic and is at worst internally contradictory.

However, the domain of intestate succession seemed peculiarly unafflicted by the open texture problem. This was partially due to the fact that while policy considerations (as we have seen above) informed the development of the law, the law itself is primarily expressed in terms of concrete objects and actors with clear, almost mathematically phrased relationships between them.

Concepts like ‘children’, ‘parent’, ‘estate’ are apparently matters of clear fact. This is of course not true; but the most obvious areas of fuzziness (does a child include an adopted child, a step-child?) are comprehensively dealt with in the statute. There is little room for judicial discretion or play for concepts that are inherently opposed to formalization in Boolean logic such as reasonableness and intention. (There are of course still a few problems, such as the definition of ‘heirlooms’ in the Act which is couched, rather oddly, in deontic terms.[3]) In many ways, the domain seemed akin to an area such as tax law, where expert knowledge is required to deal with the complexity of the law (and its relationship to a computational problem) but not primarily to deal with semantic or policy-oriented problems. (See (McCarty 1980) on the suitability of tax law for expert systems development.) To adopt Susskind’s paraphrase of Hart, the domain seemed to be one where the difficulties for the lawyer lie in ‘clear cases of an expert domain’ (Susskind 1987), i.e. where cases arise frequently which while posing no real problems of semantic interpretation still demand expert knowledge and strategy to solve.

Another promising aspect of the domain was that unusually for a core area of private law, the rules largely derived from a single statute which was unusually devoid of interpretative case law. Since the Act has been in force almost twenty years, we appeared genuinely to be dealing with a domain where statutory rules operated efficiently without need for case-law exposition, as opposed to a piece of new legislation where case-law has not yet accrued; here typically ambiguities and lacunae do exist but are simply yet to be exposed, and hopefully plugged, by the advent of contentious cases. (An alternative explanation for the lack of case-law however might be that almost by definition intestate estates do not contain a great deal of money —otherwise a valid will would have been commissioned— and therefore do not repay contentious litigation. The only reported case[4], in fact, is one where winning the case did make for relatively substantial financial gain for the litigant.)

These assessments of the domain largely proved correct. It did indeed prove to be the case during the implementation phase that no serious problems arose concerning the issues of open texture, and case law currently remains notable only for its absence from the domain. However there are more aspects to the task of engineering expertise than these, including problems to which there is less attention in the documented projects of computers and law. We shall now consider in some detail two problems which arose in implementation in relation to (a) the preliminary compartmentalisation of the domain and (b) the pragmatic context in which the rules were likely to operate.

3. COMPARTMENTALISATION

Compartmentalisation has been identified as a desirable attribute for a domain which can be successfully translated to an expert system (Capper and Susskind 1988). In a rule-based system especially, it is essential that a defined limitation can be placed on the area which is to be formalised so that within these limits the structure can be seen and/or imposed which can be represented in the typical decision-tree form. If the area becomes an unbounded network rather than a delimited tree then it will be impossible for inference to be carried out[5]. The problem is also one of simple pragmatism: in the McConnell example which began this paper, for example, the facts disclosed not only 'core' issues to do with intestacy but also a peripheral issue of whether the relatives might have a claim in delict which could be considered as an item in the deceased's estate. It would be impossible for the Adviser to contain sufficient expertise to deal with all such arising questions. Most definitions of expert systems take it as a simple assumption that the domain must be and can be selfcontained.[6] However the experience during the implementation stage here was that this was not a trivial assumption even in an apparently favourable domain.

Intestate succession seemed at first to be an obviously delimited area —the Succession (Sc) Act 1964 in its standard edition is only 17 pages long (not all of this exclusively to do with intestate succession) and as previously mentioned, the case law is minimal. However the first act of the system has to be to separate cases of testacy from those to which it applies, namely, intestate deaths. Intestacy results not only where there is no will, but, of course, also where there is a will which for some formal or substantive reason is invalid, either wholly or partially, or simplest of all, does not deal with all the property in the estate. But this leads to the difficulty of stating positively, and comprehensively, what processes might result in any portion of the estate falling into intestacy. Some of these are obvious e.g. lack of formality in execution; invalidity of particular legacies due to (for example) ademption[7] (factual), vagueness (a problem of open texture) or rule of public policy (a problem of defeasibility), essential invalidity of a will which excludes legal rights of surviving spouse and children. However an expert system, unlike a book, is put in this instance in the position of having to enumerate all its exceptions rather than of being able to state a single rule; in other words, the positive legal state of intestacy, which a human expert could recognise without difficulty, can only be regarded by the rule based program as a collection of exceptional circumstances. Intestacy, which seemed at first glance to be one half of a simple dualism, will or no will, turns out instead to be a concept of uncertain content. It seems in strict theory that a system that deals with the domain of intestacy must in fact deal with the whole of the law of testacy too. In real life, the system fudges this issue by throwing itself on the discretion of the user, aided by the system in help mode.

The special destination problem

One example of this type of difficulty is of particular note. In Scots law, property can be bequeathed to person or persons not only by a will but by a quasi-testamentary device known as a special destination. Such a destination is usually found as a clause in the written title to heritable property governing its passage on the death of the owner. If the property is still in the hands of the owner on death then it will pass on that event to the person(s) named in the clause and will not form part of the intestate estate even where the deceased otherwise dies without testamentary provision. (See Macdonald 1990).

The paradigm special destination is where the matrimonial home is taken in joint title by husband *A* and wife *B* with a destination clause in the title 'to *A* and *B* and the survivor' (known as a survivorship destination). This implies a contract between A and B that on the death of one, his or her half will pass to the other. There is obviously scope for conflict here between the assumed right of a testator to leave his property to whom he wishes by writing a legacy into his will and the automatic transfer of the half-share of the property imposed on death by the special destination in the title. This conflict is resolved by complex rules which decide who is empowered to revoke ('evacuate') a special destination in their will and leave their portion of the property instead to their named heirs —rules in other words which determine when there is no contractual reliance between the parties and therefore no bar on breaching the destination. This is regarded as a difficult and problematic area of law, with much muddied case law, and is currently under review by the Scottish Law Commission. (See Scottish Law Commission 1990). However it might reasonably be expected not to be the problem of the builder of an intestate succession system who assumes with relief that if there is no will, the destination will operate without problems, while if there is a will, any conflict can fairly be characterised as a problem outside the law of intestacy.

In fact however a worst of all worlds scenario can be devised in which the problem becomes both one of interpretation of the case-law concerning whether there has been a valid evacuation of a special destination, and one of applying the rules of intestacy. Suppose *A* and *B*, a married couple, own a house in joint title with a special destination clause in the title 'to *A* and *B* and the survivor of them', as in the paradigm above. *A* and *B* therefore each own a *pro indiviso* half share of the house; during lifetime each can sell or gift this half to a third party without the other's consent. But what is the situation on death? Say husband *A* paid the whole of the price for the house. From *Perrett's Trs* 1909 SC 522 and *Hay's Trs* 1951 SC 329, it appears that in these special circumstances there is no implied contract between *A* and *B* to follow the destination, and not to evacuate it, and *A* has a valid power to evacuate the destination —although only from his half of the house. So *A*, thus advised by his lawyer, leaves his half of the house in his will to his friend *X*. Unfortunately, *X* dies before *A*. By the law of testacy, then, when *A* dies the legacy to *X* lapses. Who gets *A*'s share of the house?

There are two possibilities. Either there has been a valid evacuation of the destination, under current case-law which appears to base the entitlement to a power to evacuate on the grounds of who financially contributed to the purchase of the property —in which case there has simply been an ordinary case of lapse of legacy (due to *X*'s death) and the halfshare of house will fall either to *A*'s residuary legatee, if any, or if there is none, into intestacy. (And hence into the ambit of the Intestacy Adviser.)

Alternatively, an argument could be envisaged that there has indeed been no valid evacuation of the special destination —that in fact, not only is there a requirement of exclusive funding of the purchase of the property as prerequisite for a power to evacuate, as signposted by the current cases, but there is also another requirement, of a living third party to receive the diverted legacy. Or as MacCormick puts it (MacCormick 1995, in this collection), the previous conditions for a power to evacuate were no more than 'presumptively sufficient' conditions of the legal consequence in question. Such an argument might be given authority by the Scottish policy argument that in areas of uncertain interpretation of the law of wills, the testator's intention should be the guiding principle, in which case could the testator not be assumed to have only preferred the claim of the specified third party *X* to that of his wife *B* who would otherwise have taken? In other words, while he might want *X* to inherit rather than *B*, if he had known *X* would die before him then he would have been happy to leave the special destination to operate in his wife's favour.

Such an argument, one might feel, would be enormously bolstered if the situation were that *A* had indeed left no residuary legatee so that if *A*'s claim failed, the house-share would fall into intestacy. Given the strength of another policy argument, the Scottish presumption against intestacy, there would then be a good case for arguing that a special destination could only be validly evacuated on death in favour of a living and indicated legatee.

The instance given is interesting as a practical example of the type of case where it can not easily be discerned whether a policy argument is being used to provide an extra condition for a legal consequence or as a defeasance of a claim based on a set of legal conditions which had already been met. The situation is comparable to that in the *Connor*[8] case discussed by MacCormick and other contributors to this volume. In *Connor*, a woman applied for a widow's pension on the grounds that her husband was dead. The unusual circumstance about the case was that the husband was dead because his wife had killed him. In interpreting the pensions legislation, the court found that the principle that the law will not uphold rights arising directly out of criminal acts should apply and that therefore the widow was not a satisfactory claimant, although there was nothing explicit in the pensions legislation to warn her of this. There is a problem here of whether in formalising this new 'rule' to treat the issue as raising another pre-condition to the vesting of a right not previously contemplated, or whether to treat it as an exceptional case in which the already vested right is defeated or perhaps will not be enforced. For the expert system builder, the problem is a pressing and practical one since it indicates that no rule is ever 'safe' in the sense that its definition may only be fully revealed by the presence of an unprecedented set of facts, and thus that no system can ever aspire to be a complete formalization of the domain. (I consider in the concluding section what the positive aspects of this state of affairs may be for legal creativity.)

4. PRAGMATIC CONTEXT OF RULES

It is now a truism in the field of legal expert systems that almost all formally drafted rules however apparently clear do not in themselves represent unambiguous legal norms but will have a penumbra of uncertainty which can only be resolved by reference to the legal context in which they operate, embracing such factors as lawyer's assumptions, policy arguments, social context etc. Leith sums this argument well in his paper (Leith 1986), reminding us that 'legal rules are objects of discourse, not objects with a concrete nature which we can mysteriously formalise and "find" in the legislation or the weekly law reports'.

In the intestate succession domain, it was hoped that, at least in a system aimed at students and not intending to be or support an adjudicator, problems of context in law would not be abundant. However, several problems were found in the implementation process, with particular reference to the way in which the law would be applied in practice so as to maximise the benefit from the legislation which the heirs would take.

The negative-valued 'right' problem

In order to 'debug' the system, it was run during the building process with figures inserted for all kinds of composition of estate, however unlikely. One combination involved a deceased spouse leaving an estate composed of a matrimonial home burdened by a mortgage greater than its current value (perhaps as a result of re-mortgaging) and an amount of moveables greater than £33,000. The effect of this on running the system was that the surviving spouse took the negative value of the house (i.e. the debt) which was then 'added' to her financial provision settlement of £21,000 —so that her net sum was *less* than it would have been had she had not had the 'right' to her spouse's relevant interest in the matrimonial home. This also had controversial effects upon the calculation of the spouse's financial right in the estate, which is calculated by reference to the ratio of the heritage and the moveables in the estate at that stage of the calculation: the strict mathematical effect of a negative heritage value was that the spouse took more from the moveables than she would have done if the heritage value had been zero —to the detriment of the children of the deceased who take their rights in moveable estate *after* the spouse has taken hers.

It might be thought that a purposive interpretation of the statute would be possible so as to exclude this ambiguity; however the words of the statute seem sufficiently clear to discourage if not a judge then certainly the constitutionally unauthorised builder of an educational system. Section 8(1) of the 1964 Act clearly puts an upper monetary limit on the dwelling house right (of £65,000) but is silent on a lower limit; it might again be thought that the 'relevant interest' of the deceased which is taken excludes a negative-valued interest by common sense but s 8(5)(d) clearly states that a 'relevant interest' in relation to a dwelling house means 'the interest therein of an owner ... subject in either case to *any heritable debt* secured over the interest'.

In the real world context the practical solution to this is for the spouse to disclaim the dwelling house right. But there is no mention of the right to disclaim in the statute —it is merely inferred from common legal usage. Again this poses the question whether every formalization of the law relating to the conferring of a right, and its legal consequences, must also deal with the converse i.e. the legal consequences of the disclaiming of that right and perhaps also the requirements for an entitlement to disclaim. (For example, the dwelling house right in question is conferred by s. 8 of the 1964 statute and is intrinsically bound up with the right in the furnishings of the house also conferred by that section. The statute gives no guidance whether it would be competent to disclaim the dwelling house right and take the furnishings right, which would be financially worthwhile in the situation above.)

5. CONCLUSION

Building a legal decision support system of any kind reveals that the difficulties of legal formalization are not merely philosophical but essentially pragmatic. Even a system such as the Intestate Succession Adviser, built in what seemed the least ambiguous of areas and using a relatively unsophisticated tool, raises many problems of interpretation. But the implementation process also reveals that the problem of formalising law is a two-edged sword; it is indescribably difficult but it is also a fertile source of legal creativity. Many types of system, like the Intestate Succession Adviser and the Latent Damage System, act as a sort of legal fruit machine; they conjugate all possible permutations of the legal rules in the domain with all possible combinations of facts and in the end they produce the legal consequences as results, some predictable, some unexpected, some undesirable. It is not argued that these all represent, as it were, legal truths - these will not all be how the law will be decided though there will probably be a statistical certainty that these are how some cases —the clearest, with the least complications of policy and context— would be decided. But this uncertainty of outcome is not necessarily a bad thing. It means it is quite likely that with current technology we can never conceive of a computerised judge without human (probably human legally-trained) assistance. But this is purely to look on computerised systems as replacements for judges. They are far better seen as tools for an adversarial system, as generators of arguments for potential pursuers or defenders.[9]

The paper above gives examples of two areas where the comprehensive coverage of the domain produced by running the system engendered two examples of legal argument, even in a domain which appeared so settled and unambiguous that it has generated only one case of significance since its coming into force. These were generated by giving as input highly unusual sets of facts. It could be postulated that if a legal rule is seen as acting on all possible relevant facts so as to produce a set of all possible legal consequences, then there is a broad middle band of the most usual facts where the most predictable results will occur; while the more extreme facts will produce less predictable results. So the predictability of the application of the rule could be mapped as a U-curve. In this metaphorical landscape, I would argue that expert systems are highly useful tools for trying to map where legal difficulties may arise near the far ends of the U-curve. They act rather as a common law judge does, trying a rule for absurdity against instantiated examples, only faster and more frequently (but, of course, without human intelligence to interpret what follows from the results!) The system is not able to judge what the desirability of the results flowing from the unusual fact set will be. But it can alert the legal user/builder to the exact area of difficulty so that human legal reasoning and creativity can then be used to create new rules which can be built into the system where necessary. In this way, every consultation is a step to a better system.

On the contrary though there will be occasions in any domain landscape where the problem is not the application of the legal rule to unexpected facts, nor even the unexpected involvement of a supereminent principle or policy argument triggered by unusual facts in the case profile, but where the problem is the classic 'hard case' —where two applicable legal rules which could both be expected to apply, clash. There is little a rule based legal support system can do at this juncture except turn for assistance either to a human legal user, or, more problematic but perhaps more hopeful for the AI judge of the future, to the techniques of case based reasoning.[10]

There is no doubt that very many difficult problems remain to be solved before the current level of legal applications aspire even tentatively to the level of 'artificial intelligence'. But perhaps some consolation should be taken from the possibility that harnessed as a tool to human intelligence these systems can be used as generators for human legal creativity. To borrow from Ronald Staudt, himself borrowing from Papert, the father of the educational computer language LOGOL, they can be 'invitations to legal mindstorms' (Staudt 1991). That is an attractive invitation to be taken up by legal philosophers and legal educators alike.

NOTES

[1] An earlier version of this paper appeared in (1992) 3 *Journal of Law and Information Science*, p. 116, published by the Faculty of Law, University of Tasmania.

[2] See (Meston 1982) which sketches the history of legal rights in chapter 1.

[3] Succession (Sc) Act 1964, Section 8(6) (a) —'heirloom' in relation to an intestate estate means any article which has associations with the intestate's family of such a nature and extent that it ought to pass to some member of that family other than the surviving spouse of the intestate.

[4] *Kerr, Petitioner* 1968 SLT (Sh Ct) 61.

[5] Many researchers feel one of the strengths of modelling a legal domain within a hypertext-type system rather than a traditional rule decision-tree is that compartmentalisation need no longer be an issue, and that law can thus be modelled as an organic and expansionist network rather than in arbitrarily defined boxes. See for example the work of Eve Wilson, representative of which is (Wilson, 1990). Other researchers more anecdotally suggest however that hypertext involves its own risks of losing the user in 'hyperspace' e.g. (Leith, 1991).

[6] (Waterman 1986) cites the very narrow domain of expertise of expert systems as one of their 'inherent limitations'.

[7] Ademption occurs when the object of a legacy has been sold after the execution of the will but before the death of the testator.

[8] *R v. National Insurance Commissioner ex p. Connor* [1981] All ER 770.

[9] The Alvey-DHSS Demonstrator project, which ran from 1984 to 1989 explicitly recognised as one of its specifications that different systems would need to be designed, sharing only a common database, for adjudicators, policy makers and claimants. See (Bench-Capon 1991).

[10] Very simplistically, case based reasoning involves deriving answers to a consultation from analysis of decided instances (in the legal domain, actual or hypothetical cases) rather than from the churning of pre-formalised rules. There is research going on into systems which turn to case based reasoning when rules run out or are incapable of reaching a solution: see e.g. the review of the field in (Sanders 1991).

REFERENCES

Bench-Capon, T., 1991. (ed.) *Knowledge Based Systems and Legal Applications*, Academic Press.

Capper, P. and Susskind R., 1988. *Latent Damage Law: The Expert System* , Butterworths, London.

Leith, P., 1986. 'Fundamental Errors in Legal Logic Programming,' 29 *Computer Journal*, p. 545.

Leith, P., 1991. 'Towards Software for Lawyering', *Computers and Law* 8.

MacCormick, N., 1995. 'Defeasibility in Law and Logic', in this collection.

McCarty, L.T., 1980. 'The TAXMAN Project: towards a cognitive theory of legal argument' in B. Niblett *Computer Science and the Law* , Cambridge University Press.

Macdonald, R., 1990. *An Introduction to the Scots Law of Succession*, W. Green & Son, Edinburgh.

Meston, M.C., 1982. *The Succession (Scotland) Act 1964*, 3rd edn W.Green & Son, Edinburgh.

Sanders, K., 1991. 'Representing and Reasoning about Open-textured Predicates', *Proceedings of the 3rd International Conference on Artificial Intelligence and Law*, Oxford.

Scottish Law Commission, 1990. *Report on Succession,* Scot. Law. Com. No 124, 1990, Part VI.
Staudt, R.W., 1991. 'Legal Mindstorms: Lawyers, Computers and Powerful Ideas', 31 *Jurimetrics*, p. 171.
Susskind R. 1987. *Expert Systems in Law*, Clarendon Press, Oxford, pp 244–245.
Waterman, D., 1986. *A Guide to Expert Systems*, Addison-Wesley.
Wilson, E., 1990. 'A Guide to JUSTUS: an overview of a hypertext legal database'. In: *Proceedings of the 5th BILETA Conference*, Warwick.

Faculty of Law
University of Edinburgh
Scotland

ROBERT A. KOWALSKI

LEGISLATION AS LOGIC PROGRAMS

The linguistic style in which legislation is normally written has many similarities with the language of logic programming. However, examples of legal language taken from the British Nationality Act 1981, the University of Michigan lease termination clause, and the London Underground emergency notice suggest several ways in which the basic model of logic programming could usefully be extended. These extensions include the introduction of types, relative clauses, both ordinary negation and negation by failure, integrity constraints, metalevel reasoning and procedural notation.

In addition to the resemblance between legislation and programs, the law has other similarities with computing. It needs for example to validate legislation against social and political specifications, and it needs to organise, develop, maintain and reuse large and complex bodies of legal codes and procedures. Such parallels between computing and law suggest that it might be possible to transfer useful results and techniques in both directions between these different fields. One particularly promising possibility explored in this paper is that the linguistic structures of an appropriately extended logic programming language might indicate ways in which the language of legislation itself could be simplified and made easier for people to understand.

1. INTRODUCTION

The characteristic feature of the language of legislation is that it uses natural language to express general rules, in order to regulate human affairs. To be effective for this purpose, it needs to be more precise than ordinary language and, as much as possible, it needs to be understood by different people in the same way. In this respect legislation can be viewed as programs expressed in human language to be executed by humans rather than by computers.

Thus the language of legislation might also serve as a model for computing, suggesting ways in which programming languages might be made more like human languages, while still remaining machine executable. In this paper I shall focus on a comparison between the language of legislation and the language of logic programming. I shall argue that although logic programming fares well in this comparison, it needs to be improved by incorporating such extensions as types, relative clauses, both ordinary negation and negation by failure, integrity constraints, metalevel

Z. Bankowski et al. (eds.), Informatics and the Foundations of Legal Reasoning, 325–356.

reasoning, and procedural notation. I shall also argue that in some cases legislation itself can be improved by re-expressing it in a style more closely resembling such an extended logic programming form.

I shall investigate three examples, which between them illustrate a range of legal drafting styles. The first consists of several sections from the British Nationality Act 1981; the second is the University of Michigan lease termination clause; and the third is the London underground emergency notice. The first example was investigated earlier by the author and his colleagues (Sergot et al. 1986) as an illustration of the use of logic programming for representing legislation. The second was investigated by Allen and Saxon (1984) as an example of the use of logic to eliminate ambiguities in the formulation of a legal contract. The third was identified by the author (Kowalski 1990) as an example of a public notice which is meant not only to be precise but also to be as clear as possible to ordinary people.

In our earlier investigation of the British Nationality Act 1981 (H.M.S.O. 1981) we emphasized both the prospects of using logic programming to build legal applications as well as the problems of attempting to use logic programming for knowledge representation. In this paper I am concerned only with the second of these matters, but more specifically with investigating linguistic similarities and differences between logic programming and legislation, and more generally with exploring other parallels between computing and the law.

2. THE BRITISH NATIONALITY ACT 1981

The following four examples from the British Nationality Act 1981 illustrate some of the complexity and precision of legal language. They also illustrate the treatment of time, default reasoning, negative conclusions and reasoning about belief.

2.1. Acquisition by birth

The first subsection of the British Nationality Act 1981 deals with the case of acquisition of citizenship by virtue of birth in the United Kingdom after commencement (1 January 1983, the date on which the Act took effect).

1(1) A person born in the United Kingdom after commencement shall be a British citizen if at the time of the birth his father or mother is —

(a) a British citizen; or

(b) settled in the United Kingdom.

The English of this clause is already close to logic programming form, even to the extent of expressing the conclusion before (most of) the conditions. Using infix notation for predicates and upper case letters for variables, 1(1) can be paraphrased in logic programming form by:

X acquires british citizenship by section 1.1
if X is born in the uk at T
and T is after commencement
and Y is parent of X
and Y is a british citizen at T or
Y is settled in the uk at T

This has the propositional form

A if [B and C and D and [E or F]]

which is equivalent to two rules

A if B and C and D and E
A if B and C and D and F

in normal logic programming form.

In this paper I shall use the term *logic program* to refer to any set of sentences which is equivalent to a set of universally quantified implications in the *normal logic programming form*

A if B_1 and ... and B_n

where A is an atomic formula, B_i for $0 \leq i \leq n$ is an atomic formula or the negation of an atomic formula, and all variables, e.g. X_1, ..., X_m occurring in the implication are assumed to be universally quantified, i.e.

for all X_1, ..., X_m [A if B_1 and ... and B_n].

The negation 'not B' of an atomic formula is interpreted as *negation by failure* (Clark 1978):

not B holds if and only if B fails to hold.

This interpretation of negation is based on the so called 'closed world assumption' that the program contains an exhaustive collection of rules enumerating all of the conditions under which the conclusion B holds. It is under this assumption that it is justifiable to conclude that not B holds, if and only if none of the rules with B as conclusion succeeds in establishing B.

Negation by failure is closely related to many of the formalisms developed for nonmonotonic reasoning in artificial intelligence.

The logic programming representation of 1(1) can be made more like the English, while remaining formal, by introducing types and various forms of syntactic sugar. For example:

a person who is born in the uk at a time
    which is after commencement
  acquires british citizenship by section 1.1
    if a parent of the person is a british citizen at the time,
    or a parent of the person is settled in the uk at the time.

Here 'person' and 'time' are type identifiers; 'a person' is the first occurrence of a variable of type 'person'; 'a time' is the first occurrence of a variable of type 'time'; 'the person' and 'the time' stand for later occurrences of the same variables. The relative pronouns 'who' and 'which' also stand for additional occurrences of the variables they follow. 'who' stands for an occurrence of type 'person', whereas 'which' stands for an occurrence of any type of variable.

Relative clauses in expressions of the form

... V which P_{***}

for example, are syntactic sugar for

(... V***) if V P

where V is a variable, and P is a predicate which applies to V.

Similarly an expression of the form

...a R of T P_{***}

is syntactic sugar for

(... V P_{***}) if V R of T

where R is a binary predicate, T is a term, and V is any variable not occurring elsewhere in the sentence.

Notice that the two transformations described above need to be combined with the simplification of formulae of the form

(A if B) if C

to the form

A if B and C.

This kind of typing and syntactic sugar can be defined more precisely and can be extended to deal with several variables of the same type, pronouns, and more flexible kinds of relative clauses. In this way English can serve as a model to improve the naturalness of logic programming without sacrificing the precision of its logic.

I shall argue elsewhere in this paper that, conversely, the conclusion-conditions form, which characterises the syntax of logic programming, can sometimes serve as a model to improve the clarity of natural languages such as English.

2.2. Representation of time

In the representation of 1(1), time has been represented by an explicit parameter of type 'time'. The expression

... after ***

is interpreted as short-hand for

... at a time which is after ***

i.e. ... at T if T is after ***

This explicit representation of time contrasts with modal representations, where temporal relationships are represented by modal operators, and time itself is implicit rather than explicit.

As mentioned for example in (Kowalski and Sergot 1986) to reason about time, an explicit axiom of persistence can be formulated to express, for example that

a property holds at a time
    which is after another time
  if an event occurs at the other time
  and the event initiates the property
  and it is not shown that
    another event occurs at yet another time
      which is between the time and the other time
    and the other event terminates the property.

'a person acquires british citizenship by section 1.1' initiates 'the person is a british citizen'.

The phrase 'it is not shown that' is used here as an English expression of negation by failure. Its use in the axiom of persistence has the effect of ensuring that once a property is initiated, it then persists by default, until some event is shown to terminate the property.

Here the expressions 'a time', 'another time', and 'yet another time' are intended to introduce different variables of the same type 'time'. Notice that these English expressions suggest that the variables refer to distinct individuals, whereas the usual logical convention is that different variables of the same type can refer to the same individual. This is one of several discrepancies which would need to be attended to in a more rigorous correspondence between symbolic logic and unambiguous English. Perhaps the persistence axiom is an example where the complexity of the English is sufficiently great that a more symbolic representation might actually be easier to follow.

Notice also in the two axioms above how events and properties are treated metalogically as names of sentences.

2.3. Abandoned children and default reasoning

The second subsection of the British Nationality Act is conceptually one of the most complex sentences of the Act.

1. (2) A new-born infant who, after commencement, is found abandoned in the United Kingdom shall, unless the contrary is shown, be deemed for the purposes of subsection (1)-

(a) to have been born in the United Kingdom after commencement; and

(b) to have been born to a parent who at the time of the birth was a British citizen or settled in the United Kingdom.

Under the procedural interpretation of logic programs, conclusions of sentences are interpreted as goals and conditions as subgoals. According to this interpretation, the conclusion of a sentence identifies its purpose. Thus we can interpret the phrase 'the purposes of subsection (l)' as a metalevel reference to the logical conclusion and goal of 1.1, namely to acquire British citizenship. Moreover the object level phrases 1.2a and 1.2b above are exactly the logical conditions of 1.1. Thus we can regard the entire subsection 1.2 as a mixed object level and metalevel sentence which expresses that

the conditions of 1.1 shall be assumed to hold for a person
if the person is found new-born abandoned in the uk at a time
  which is after commencement
and the contrary of the conditions of 1(1) are not shown.

This can be reformulated at the object level alone by using a technique similar to the partial evaluation of meta-interpreters. (Gallagher 1986, Takeuchi and Furukawa 1986)

a person who is found newborn abandoned in the uk at a time
    which is after commencement
acquires british citizenship by section 1.2
if   it is not shown that it is not the case that
        the person is born in the uk at a time
        which is after commencement
and either it is not shown that it is not the case that
        a parent of the person is a british citizen at the time of birth
    or it is not shown that it is not the case that
        a parent of the person is settled in the uk
        at the time of birth

Notice that although I have used the expression 'either...or' as a kind of parentheses, in order to eliminate ambiguity, its English meaning as exclusive 'or' is at variance with its intended logical meaning as inclusive 'or'. This example shows how difficult it is to avoid ambiguities in ordinary natural language, without an adequate analogue of logical parentheses. Nonetheless, for simplicity's sake in the remainder of this paper, I will use 'either...or' in English when I actually intended inclusive 'or'.

Notice also that this example seems to be a case where the mixed object level meta-level sentence is easier to understand than the purely object level representation.

Conditions of the form

it is not shown that it is not the case that P

in the object level sentence above, can be interpreted as combining negation as failure 'not' ('it is not shown that') and ordinary negation '¬' ('it is not the case that'), i.e.

not ¬ P.

Thus, for another example, the statements

A bird flies if it is not shown that it is not the case that the bird flies.
It is not the case that an ostrich flies.

can be formalised by

a bird flies if not ¬ the bird flies
¬ an ostrich flies

Just such an extension of logic programming to include both negation by failure and ordinary negation has been investigated by Gelfond and Lifschitz (1990) and by Kowalski and Sadri (1990).

Negation by failure is a form of default reasoning and is non-monotonic. Thus a person who acquires citizenship by 1.2 might non-monotonically have citizenship withdrawn in the light of new information. It is unlikely, however, that parliament intended that people be deprived of citizenship in this way. Both such an intention and the opposite intention can be catered for by introducing an extra layer of time concerned with the time for which beliefs are held in addition to the historical time for which properties hold true in the world. A logic programming approach to such a joint representation of belief time and historical time has been developed by Sripada (Sripada 1991).

Thus, for example, it is possible to apply to 1.2 either the metarule

> a conclusion of a rule is believed at a time
> if the conditions of the rule are believed at the time

or the alternative metarule

> a conclusion of a rule is believed at a time
> if the conditions of the rule are believed at another time
> which is before the time.

In the first case, citizenship would be withdrawn as soon as a belief in any one of the conditions which originally justified citizenship is withdrawn. In the second case, citizenship would persist even after the grounds for citizenship were removed.

It is important to clarify that when formalising legislation as (extended) logic programs we do not attempt to define concepts which occur in conditions of rules in the legislation but not in conclusions. Thus, for example, we do not attempt to define the concept 'new born infant' which occurs in the conditions of 1.2. This means, as a consequence, that a formalisation of the British Nationality Act has only limited applicability by itself. To be used in a particular case it would need to be supplemented, if not by a set of definitions of such vague terms, at least by a set of 'facts' which express judgements about whether or not such terms apply to the case in hand.

2.4 . Deprivation of citizenship and negative conclusions

Except for its occurrence in conditions of the form

not ¬ P

ordinary negation '¬' seems to be needed only in the conclusions of rules. In such cases, a negative conclusion typically expresses an exception to a general rule, as in the example

it is not the case that an ostrich flies

which expresses an exception to the general rule that all birds fly.

Exceptions, expressed by sentences with negative conclusions, are common in legislation (Kowalski 1989). The provisions for depriving British citizens of their citizenship exemplify this use of negation:

40. (1) Subject to the provisions of this section, the Secretary of State may by order deprive any British citizen to whom this subsection applies of his British citizenship if the Secretary of State is satisfied that the registration or certificate of naturalisation by virtue of which he is such a citizen was obtained by means of fraud, false representation or the concealment of any material fact.
40. (5) The Secretary of State –
(a) Shall not deprive a person of British citizenship under this section unless he is satisfied that it is not conducive to the public good that that person should continue to be a British citizen; ...

40(1) has the logical form

P if Q

whereas 40(5) has the form

¬ P if not R.

If both conditions Q and not R hold, then by ordinary logic it would be possible to deduce a contradiction

P and ¬P.

But this is not the intention of the English, which is rather that the exception should over-ride the rule, or equivalently that the rule should be understood as having an extra, implicit condition

P if Q and not ¬P.

In fact, the metalevel phrase 'subject to the provisions of this section' at the beginning of 40(1) can be regarded as a caution that the meaning of 40(1) cannot be understood in isolation from the rest of the section as a whole.

The extension of logic programming to allow negative conclusions, for the purpose of representing exceptions, has been investigated by Kowalski and Sadri (1990). They also show that such extended logic programs can be transformed into normal logic programs. In particular a rule with a single exception

P if Q
¬P if not R

can be transformed into the simpler rule

P if Q and R.

Both representations can be useful for different purposes. A representation in terms of rules and exceptions is often easier to develop and to maintain. However, the simpler representation as normal logic programs is usually clearer and easier to understand. The first representation, accordingly, might be preferred by a draftsman, who codifies the law; the second might be preferred by an administrator who executes the law.

In this discussion of the provisions for deprivation of citizenship we have considered only the propositional structure of the English sentences. We have not considered the meaning of such conditions as

> he is satisfied that it is not conducive to the public good that that person should continue to be a British citizen.

This is partly because it would be very difficult to do so; but also because we have restricted our attention to representing formally only what is expressed already in the English.

Nonetheless, it is hard to resist the temptation to try to understand the thinking processes of the Secretary of State. Moreover, to a limited extent at least, such reasoning about thinking is the subject matter of logics of knowledge and belief.

2.5. Naturalisation and the representation of belief

Like the provisions for deprivation of citizenship, the provisions for naturalisation contain conditions concerning the Secretary of State's thoughts. In addition, however, they contain rules governing the subject matter of those thoughts. This leads us to consider whether we can establish a logical connection between the two.

Section 6(1) contains the main provision for naturalisation:

6. (1) If, on an application for naturalisation as a British citizen made by a person of full age and capacity, the Secretary of State is satisfied that the applicant fulfils the requirements of Schedule 1 for naturalisation as such a citizen under this subsection, he may, if he thinks fit, grant to him a certificate of naturalisation as such a citizen.

At the propositional level this is equivalent to a sentence in conclusion-conditions form:

> the secretary of state may grant a certificate of naturalisation to a person by subsection 6.1
>
> if the person applies for naturalisation
>
> and the person is of full age and capacity
>
> and the secretary of state is satisfied that
>
> the person fulfils the requirements of schedule 1 for naturalisation by 6.1
>
> and the secretary of state thinks fit to grant the person a certificate of naturalisation.

The last two conditions vest considerable powers of discretion in the Secretary of State. The last condition is totally inscrutable and can only be given as part of the input for a given case. But the meaning of the penultimate condition ought at least to be constrained by the meaning of Schedule 1. This schedule is quite long, and it is convenient therefore to summarise its content:

> a person fulfils the requirements of schedule 1 for naturalisation by 6.1
>
> if either the person fulfils residency requirements specified in subparagraph 1.1.2
>
> or the person fulfils crown service requirements specified in subparagraph 1.1.3
>
> and the person is of good character
>
> and the person has sufficient knowledge of english, welsh, or scottish gaelic
>
> and either the person intends to reside in the uk in the event of being granted naturalisation
>
> or the person intends to enter into or continue in crown service in the event of being granted naturalisation.

To understand the connection between 6.1 and Schedule 1, it is necessary to understand the connection between meeting the requirements for naturalisation specified in Schedule 1 and satisfying the Secretary of State that those requirements are met. Fortunately, this can be done in part at least by regarding satisfaction as a kind of belief. The appropriate rules of belief can be formalised in both modal logic and metalogic. The following formalisation in metalogic has the form of a meta-interpreter.

a person is satisfied that P
if the person is satisfied that P $\Leftarrow$ Q
and the person is satisfied that Q

a person is satisfied that P $\wedge$ Q
if the person is satisfied that P
and the person is satisfied that Q

a person is satisfied that P $\vee$ Q
if the person is satisfied that P
or the person is satisfied that Q

Here '$\Leftarrow$',' $\wedge$', and ' $\vee$' are infix function symbols naming implication, conjunction, and disjunction respectively.

We may safely assume that

the secretary of state is satisfied that P
if P is a representation of the meaning of a provision of the british nationality act 1981

Thus the Secretary of State is satisfied in particular that the implication which represents the meaning of Schedule 1 holds. This assumption and the meta-interpreter above are all we need in order to establish a logical connection between 6.1 and Schedule 1. This connection can be simplified, however, if we transform the meta-interpreter using the technique of partial evaluation (Gallagher 1986, p. 26]:

The secretary of state is satisfied that a person fulfils the requirements for naturalisation by 6.1
if either the secretary of state is satisfied that
the person fulfils residency requirements specified in subparagraph 1.1.2
or the secretary of state is satisfied that
the person fulfils crown service requirements specified in subparagraph 1.1.3
and the secretary of state is satisfied that
the person is of good character
and the secretary of state is satisfied that
the person has sufficient knowledge of english, welsh, or scottish gaelic

and either the Secretary of State is satisfied that
the person intends to reside in the uk
in the event of being granted naturalisation
or the Secretary of State is satisfied that
the person intends to enter into or continue in crown service
in the event of being granted naturalisation.

The result is an explicit, though somewhat tedious, statement of what it means to satisfy the Secretary of State concerning the requirements for naturalisation. Clearly the statement could be made a little less tedious if we used the pronoun, 'he' or 'she' for all references to the Secretary of State after the first.

This example shows how a comparison between legal language and computer language not only might guide the improvement of computer languages, but might even clarify the natural language analysis of the law.

The English of the British Nationality Act 1981 is for the most part extraordinarily precise. It is also very complex. Most of this complexity is inherent in the meaning of the Act. However, some of the complexity can be reduced by the explicit use of conclusion-conditions form and by the use of meaning-preserving transformations of the kind illustrated in the last two examples.

By comparison with ordinary language and even with legal language in general, the Act is also surprisingly unambiguous. However, as we have already seen it does contain vague terms and undefined concepts. Such vagueness is often incorrectly viewed as ambiguity. Although, like genuine ambiguity, vagueness causes problems of interpretation, it is generally benign, because it allows the law to evolve and adapt to changing circumstances.

Genuine ambiguity, on the other hand, generally serves no useful purpose, except perhaps to make the expression of thought less troublesome for the communicator, or to enhance the poetic or humorous quality of the communication. Moreover, whereas logic can easily accommodate vagueness, it cannot so easily tolerate ambiguity.

The University of Michigan lease termination clause, presented in the next section, was originally investigated by Allen and Saxon (Allen and Saxon, 1984) to illustrate the use of logic to formulate a precise interpretation of an ambiguous legal text. I shall argue that the use of logic programming conclusion-conditions form has the further advantage of rendering many of the possible interpretations logically implausible.

3. THE UNIVERSITY OF MICHIGAN LEASE TERMINATION CLAUSE

The clause consists of a single, long sentence which has the underlying, logically ambiguous form

A if Al and A2 or A3 or A4 or A5 or A6 or A7
unless Bl or B2 or B3 or B4 or B5 in which cases B.

Different ways of introducing parentheses produce different interpretations. Some of these are logically equivalent because of the associativity of 'or', for example. After accounting for these equivalences, Allen and Saxon identify approximately 80 questions that might need to be asked in order to distinguish between the different parenthesizations. As a result of this analysis they identify one intended interpretation which has the form

((A if ((Al and(A2 or A3)) or A4 or AS or A6 or A7))
if not(Bl or B2 or B3 or B4 or BS)) and
(if (Bl or B2 or B3 or B4 or BS) then B)

where 'unless' has been translated as 'if not'. It is interesting that this interpretation has a logic programming form. Indeed if we can assume that other interpretations that do not have logic programming form are highly unlikely, then this eliminates many of the ambiguities.

The logic programming representation can be simplified if, as Allen and Saxon maintain, conditions Bl–B5 are the only ones under which conclusion B holds. In that case the conditions not (Bl or B2 or B3 or B4 or BS) can be replaced by the simpler condition not B. Thus the intended interpretation can be represented by the simplified, normal logic program:

A if Al and A2 and not B
A if Al and A3 and not B
A if A4 and not B
A if AS and not B
A if A6 and not B
A if A7 and not B
B if Bl
B if B2
B if B3
B if B4
B if BS

This logical analysis of the propositional structure of the sentence should be compared with the English text:

> The University may terminate this lease when the Lessee, having made application and executed this lease in advance of enrolment, is not eligible to enrol or fails to enrol in the University or leaves the University at any time prior to the expiration of this lease, or for violation of any provisions of this lease, or for violation of any University regulation relative to Resident Halls or for health reasons, by providing the student with written notice of this termination 30 days prior to the effective time of termination, unless life, limb, or property would be jeopardized, the Lessee engages in the sales or purchase of controlled substances in violation of federal, state or local law, or the Lessee is no longer enrolled as a student or the Lessee engages in the use or possession of firearms, explosives, inflammable liquids, fireworks, or other dangerous weapons within the building or turns in a false alarm in which cases a maximum of 24 hours notice would be sufficient.

Notice how the conclusion A of the first half of the sentence is split into two parts by the insertion of the conditions Al–A7. Notice also that the English of the sentence is so complicated and so confused that the drafters mistakenly wrote 'maximum of 24 hours' when they must have meant 'minimum of 24 hours'.

In fact I have slightly misrepresented Allen and Saxon's analysis of the sentence. In addition to identifying the intended placement of parentheses, they analyse for each of the three occurrences of 'if' in the apparent meaning of the sentence whether or not 'if and only if' is really intended. They conclude that in the first two cases (of the words 'when' and 'unless') it is not intended, whereas, in the third case (of the words 'in which cases') it is. Thus their real analysis of the intended interpretation has the form

> ((A if ((Al and (A2 or A3)) or A4 or AS or A6 or A7))
> if not(Bl or B2 or B3 or B4 or B5)) and
> (if (Bl or B2 or B3 or B4 or B5) then B)
> and(if not(Bl or B2 or B3 or B4 or B5) then not B).

In contrast, with this change of representation using ordinary logic, the logic programming representation does not change to reflect this change of interpretation. In the logic program there is no difference between the representation of 'if' and the representation of 'if and only if'. The difference between the two interpretations depends upon whether or not the 'closed world assumption' is applied.

Thus a sentence of the form

C if (C_1 or C_2 or ... or C_n)

is interpreted as

C if and only if (C_1 or C_2 or ... or C_n)

under the closed world assumption that C_1, C_2,...,C_n are the only conditions under which the conclusion C holds. Otherwise the sentence is interpreted literally as stated.

In 'when', the interpretation 'if and only if' is not intended because there are other situations referred to elsewhere in the lease under which the University may terminate the lease with 30 days written notice. But in the case of the words 'in which case', the interpretation 'if and only if' is intended because there are no other cases under which the University may terminate the lease with 24 hours notice. In the case of the word 'unless', the question is not relevant because in the context in which it occurs the closed world assumption is not applicable.

Allen and Saxon argue that the logical representation of the lease termination clause does not express what the drafters actually intended. After all the ambiguities have been resolved, the English text expresses that for the University to be able to terminate the lease with 30 days written notice, not only must one of the conditions

(Al and(A2 or A3)) or A4 or A5 or A6 or A7

hold but none of the conditions

Bl or B2 or B3 or B4 or B5

under which it may terminate the lease with 24 hours notice, should hold. But these extra negative conditions play no useful rôle. They serve only to make the conditions under which conclusion A holds exclusive of the conditions under which conclusion B holds.

The simpler rules

A if ((Al and(A2 or A3)) or A4 or A5 or A6 or A7)
B if(Bl or B2 or B3 or B4 or B5)

are more flexible. Compared with the original rules they give the University the extra option of giving students 30 days notice in cases where they would otherwise only be able to give 24 hours notice.

Using indentation, and the expressions 'both ... and', and 'either ... or' in place of parentheses, this new interpretation can be written in a form which arguably has both the precision and simplicity of logic programming and the naturalness of English:

> The university may terminate this lease by providing the lessee with written notice of the termination 30 days prior to the effective time of termination
>
> if both the lessee has applied for and executed this lease
>   in advance of enrolment
>
> and either the lessee is not eligible to enrol
>
> or the lessee fails to enrol
>
> or the lessee leaves the university at any time
>   prior to the expiration of this lease
>
> or the lessee violates any provisions of this lease
>
> or the lessee violates any university regulations
>   relative to residence halls
>
> or there are health reasons for terminating this lease.

> The university may terminate this lease by providing the lessee with notice of the termination a minimum of 24 hours prior to the effective time of termination
>
> if life, limb or property would be jeopardized by continuation of the lease
>
> or the lessee engages in the sale or purchase of controlled substances in violation of federal, state or local law
>
> or the lessee is no longer enrolled as a student
>
> or the lessee engages in the use or possession of firearms, explosives, inflammable liquids, fireworks, or other dangerous weapons within the building
>
> or the lessee turns in a false fire alarm.

The University of Michigan lease termination clause is not a good illustration of our thesis that legal language can be a good guide for improving computer languages. If anything, it seems to suggest the converse, that some computer languages might be a useful guide for improving the language of the law.

In fact, few legal documents are written to the standards of precision found in the acts of parliament; and hardly any legal documents at all are written not only to be precise but also to be clear and easy to understand. However, public notices, which are meant to be understood by ordinary people, are for the most part an important exception to this rule; and the London underground emergency notice, in particular, is a good example of such an exception.

4. THE LONDON UNDERGROUND EMERGENCY NOTICE

The notice has many characteristics of a logic program, but with some interesting differences:

> EMERGENCIES
>
> Press the alarm signal button to alert the driver.
>
> The driver will stop immediately if any part of the train is in a station.
>
> If not, the train will continue to the next station, where help can more easily be given.
>
> There is a £50 penalty for improper use.

From a knowledge representation point of view, the first sentence is probably the most interesting. Expressed in a procedural style, it shows that a procedural form of expression can sometimes be more appropriate than an 'equivalent' statement in declarative style:

> You alert the driver
> if You press the alarm signal button.

Notice, however, that the procedural form can be regarded as a compiled version of the procedural interpretation of the declarative form. Like most compiled representations of knowledge, it requires less thought for the reader to understand the communication and to put it into practice. It is also more concrete than the uncompiled form, and is possibly more natural for the communicator.

This example and others like it suggest that logic programming could be made more like natural language if it allowed both declarative and procedural syntax. Under the procedural interpretation of logic programming both the declarative syntax

> A if B and C

and the procedural syntax

> to do A do B and do C

would be equivalent. In fact both styles of expression would have the same declarative meaning

> A if B and C

and the same procedural meaning

> to do A do B and do C

A procedural syntax for logic programs would not, however, allow arbitrary imperative programming language constructs. It would not, for example, without further extension, include such purely imperative statements as

press the alarm signal button.

All imperative statements in a logic programming language would have to be imbedded in a procedure, which contains an expression of its purpose. I shall discuss the possible extension of logic programs to include purposeless procedures, viewed as integrity constraints, in sections 5.1 and 5.2.

To simplify the discussion of the emergency notice, I have ignored and, for the most part, will continue to ignore the temporal relationships between the different actions and situations referred to in the notice. We should note however, that to be accurate the title of the notice should be interpreted as an extra qualification of its conclusion

press the alarm signal button,
to alert the driver to an emergency

The second sentence of the notice is expressed in impeccable logic programming form. However, even allowing for the fact that the phrase

the driver will stop immediately

is short hand for

the driver will stop the train immediately,

the sentence fails to express its intended meaning, because it is missing an entire condition. The meaning of the sentence can be made explicit, by supplying the missing condition from the conclusion of the previous sentence:

the driver will stop the train immediately
if You alert the driver to an emergency
and any part of the train is in a station.

Certainly this precise expression of the meaning of the sentence is more cumbersome than the English. However, it is hard to see how the logic programming representation could be simplified so that it more closely resembles the English, without losing its logical precision.

The third sentence begins with an allusion to the explicitly stated condition of the previous sentence. Ignoring for the moment, the comment at the end, the sentence with all its conditions made fully explicit has the logical form:

> the train will continue to the next station
> if You alert the driver to an emergency
> and not any part of the train is in a station.

But this alone cannot be all that it is intended by the English, because the train will generally continue to the next station whether or not the driver is alerted to an emergency. Surely, what is meant is that the train will stop at the next station and that help will be given there. This is part of the meaning of the phrase

> where help can more easily be given.

Moreover, presumably help will be given at a station whether it is the next station or not. Thus we can obtain a better approximation to the intended meaning of the third sentence with the two sentences

> the train will stop at the next station
> if You alert the driver to an emergency
> and not any part of the train is in a station.

> help will be given in an emergency
> if You alert the driver to the emergency
> and the train is stopped in a station.

The second sentence of this revised formulation of the original sentence captures part of the meaning of the comment at the end of the sentence. Presumably the rest of its meaning could be expressed by the metastatement that this procedure for getting help is better than the alternative procedure of stopping the train when it is not in a station.

The last sentence of the notice has a simple meaning in conclusion-conditions form:

> there is a £50 penalty
> if You use the alarm signal button improperly.

This contrasts with a purely imperative statement, which expresses a prohibition without expressing a purpose:

> do not use the alarm signal button improperly.

In contrast with the purely imperative statement of prohibition, the procedural interpretation of the English sentence contains a clear expression of purpose:

> if You want a £50 penalty,
> then press the alarm signal button improperly !

Notice, by the way, how different the procedural syntax of a sentence can be from its declarative meaning. The English procedural sentence

> if You want A, then do B

actually has the underlying declarative meaning

> A if B.

Although the English of the London underground notice can be improved, it is undoubtedly clear and easy to understand. I believe its clarity is due to at least three characteristics: (1) the explicit use of conclusion-conditions form, (2) the appropriate use of procedural syntax, and (3) the use of ellipsis to avoid unnecessarily stating the obvious.

The first two characteristics can usefully be applied to the design and improvement of computer languages today. The third characteristic is harder to achieve, although some progress along these lines might be possible in the future.

5. OTHER COMPUTING PARADIGMS

The preceding examples illustrate some of the typical characteristics of legislative language and its remarkable similarity to logic programming form. It is also possible, however, to find suggestions of other computing paradigms.

5.1. Condition-action production rules

Condition-action rules were developed by Newell and Simon (1972) as a model of human psychology and have been used to implement expert systems (Waterman and Hayes-Roth 1978). They can also sometimes be found in the language of public notices. For example, the following notice is displayed in the carriages of the London underground

> Please give up this seat if an elderly or handicapped person needs it.

This is a distinct improvement over the earlier, ambiguous, and potentially disturbing notice

> Please give up this seat to an elderly or handicapped person.

But even with the explicit use of the word 'if', the sentence fails to have logic programming form, because the apparent conclusion

> please give up this seat

is imperative rather than declarative. Moreover the sentence does not express a purpose.

The condition-action form in which the rule is expressed can be converted into logic programming form by making the purpose, e.g.

> to do a good deed

explicit rather than implicit. The resulting statement can be expressed procedurally

> to do a good deed give up this seat if an elderly or handicapped person needs it

or declaratively

> You do a good deed
> if You give up Your seat to a person
> who needs Your seat and
> who is elderly or handicapped.

The claim that every command has an explicit or implicit purpose is an important theory in legal philosophy. The use of logic programming form, which forces purposes to be made explicit, is in the spirit of this theory. Associating explicit purposes with commands makes it possible to reason about the relative merits of conflicting commands, to reason whether a command is appropriate, and even to issue a command to oneself when the purpose of the command is included among one's own goals.

Nonetheless, natural language does allow the expression of commands without purpose, and there even seems to be a computing analogue of this in the form of integrity constraints. Moreover, the transformation which we have just seen between commands without purpose and procedures with purpose seems to be analogous to a transformation, which has been found to be useful in computing, between integrity constraints and implications in logic programming form.

5.2. Integrity constraints

For many years the London underground has displayed the following notice above the automatic doors of its carriages

> Obstructing the doors causes delay and can be dangerous.

In other words

> there can be a delay
> if You obstruct the doors.
>
> there can be danger
> if You obstruct the doors.

As long as delay and danger are considered to be undesirable, a thinking person will conclude that obstructing the doors is undesirable too.

But the London underground authorities have recently changed the wording of the notice on some of its trains. The new sign reads

> Do not obstruct the door.

A sad reflection of our changing times. Either delay and danger are no longer considered undesirable, or travellers cannot be relied upon to reason about the consequences of their behaviour.

But for a logic programmer the new notice is worrying, not only because it indicates the possibly deteriorating state of British underground society, but also because it seems to suggest a move away from a libertarian, logic programming style of communication to a more authoritarian, imperative style. But on closer consideration, the change of wording seems to be similar to recent efforts which have been made to extend logic programming by the inclusion of integrity constraints.

This extension is motivated by database applications of logic programming. For these applications, a number of studies (Bry et al. 1988, Lloyd and Topor 1985, Reiter 1990, Sadri and Kowalski 1987) have investigated the nature of integrity constraints in logic programming and the development of efficient integrity checking methods. In all of these approaches integrity constraints are viewed as properties which a database or program must satisfy as it changes over the course of time. To the extent that the contents of a database describe a state of the world, commands, which impose obligations or prohibitions on states of the world, can be interpreted as integrity constraints on states of the database.

An integrity constraint can be expressed in the form of any sentence of first-order logic including a denial. Thus the command

do not obstruct the doors

might be represented by a denial

¬You obstruct the doors

which expresses an integrity constraint on descriptions of events which take place in the world.

Similarly the condition-action rule

please give up this seat if an elderly or handicapped person needs it

can be interpreted as an integrity constraint which has the form of an implication

You give up a seat to a person
if You are sitting in the seat
and the person needs Your seat
and the person is elderly or handicapped

Thus, given a database that records events that take place in the world, the integrity of the database will be violated if the database records that a person is sitting in a seat which an elderly or handicapped person needs and the database does not contain a record of that person giving up the seat to the elderly or handicapped person. It is another problem, if integrity has been violated, to decide how integrity should be restored. Perhaps this is where ‘purpose’ or ‘sanctions’ might play a useful rôle.

Thus commands without purpose viewed as integrity constraints seem to be compatible with logic programs viewed as deductive databases.

Moreover, there is even a transformation between integrity constraints and logic program rules, which is analogous to a transformation between commands without purpose and procedures with purpose:

Given an integrity constraint expressed as a first-order sentence

C

introduce a new predicate S and convert the constraint to the rule

S if not C

together with the new constraint

¬S

The new predicate can be interpreted as a 'sanction' which applies if the original constraint is violated. This transformation has been used in the literature on integrity constraints in deductive databases to convert arbitrary first-order integrity constraints into denial form. Similar techniques for converting rules with conditions which are arbitrary formulae of first-order logic into normal logic program rules have been developed by Lloyd and Topor (1984).

The analogy between this transformation and the legal doctrine of sanctions suggest the possibility of adapting legal techniques for dealing with violations of commands to the problem of restoring integrity in deductive databases. This is an intriguing possibility that merits closer investigation.

5.3. Object-oriented programming

The paradigm of object-oriented programming has become increasingly important in computing in recent years. It is interesting to investigate, therefore, to what extent it has analogues in natural language and in legislative language more particularly.

We have already seen some characteristics of object-orientation in English when we saw the use of common nouns such as 'person', 'time' and 'lessee' as a kind of object-oriented typing of variables. Other manifestations of object-orientation seem to be more difficult to find in the actual language of legislation, but easier to find both in descriptions of individual cases and in the organisation of law as a whole.

In natural language descriptions, it is common to group sentences together around a single topic, which is located at the beginning of the sentences. Such topics seem to help organise communication similarly to the way that objects organise knowledge in computing.

Compare, for example, the pair of sentences

> The Prime Minister stepped out of the plane.
> Journalists immediately surrounded her.

with the pair

> The Prime Minister stepped out of the plane
> She was immediately surrounded by journalists.

Psycho-linguists have shown that most people understand the second pair of sentences more easily than the first, despite the fact that the second pair uses the passive rather than the active voice. The two sentences in the more comprehensible pair have the same topic, whereas the two sentences in the other pair have different topics. Such examples suggest that organising knowledge around objects makes the knowledge more coherent and easier for humans to understand.

In the domain of law, it is common to organise the different areas of law into hierarchies, which are similar to hierarchies of objects. Thus a country might have one statute governing criminal law in general, another statute covering behaviour in public places, and yet another dealing with behaviour in public buildings. Assault and battery, for example, might be prohibited everywhere, whether in public places or not. Going about naked, however, might be prohibited only in public places, but allowed in the privacy of one's own home. Smoking, on the other hand, might be prohibited only in public buildings but be allowed everywhere else.

Thus natural language seems to support two notions of objects: objects in the small, which are used like types and topics to organise descriptions of individuals; and objects in the large, which are used to organise whole areas of knowledge. From this point of view, logic programming and object-orientation correspond to different features of natural language and are complementary.

However, the notion of object in computing has other characteristics, such as message passing and change of state, which do not have such obvious counterparts in natural language. These characteristics seem to be more closely associated with simulating the behaviour of objects in the world than with describing their behaviour.

There have been several attempts to apply object-orientation to legal reasoning. Some of these, like Gordon's Oblog (Gordon, 1987), are based on a view of objects as types and topics, which is entirely compatible both with logic programming and with the representation of natural language meanings. Others, like the treatment of patent law by Nitta et al (Nitta et al. 1988) are based on the use of objects to simulate behaviour.

The use of objects for simulation in the patent law example is especially interesting because of the way in which patent procedures, obligations and prohibitions are used to generate and filter changing states of the simulation of a patent application. It seems possible that, if the changing states of the simulation are viewed as database states, then the obligations and prohibitions expressed in the patent law might be viewed as integrity constraints. This possibility would establish an interesting correspondence between the changing status of an object and the changing states of a theory. Moreover under this correspondence imperative statements in object-oriented programming would seem to correspond to integrity constraints in deductive databases and logic programming.

No matter what the outcome of a more detailed investigation of these possibilities, there can be little doubt that legislation provides a rich domain outside computing science itself within which relationships between different computing paradigms can be studied. These studies need not be confined to programming languages alone, but could usefully be extended to many other aspects of computing.

6. OTHER RELATIONSHIPS BETWEEN COMPUTING AND LAW

To the extent that we can truly regard legislation as programs to be executed by people, we can also expect to find analogues in the law of such other computing matters as program specification and software management.

6.1. An analogy between specifications and policies

In the same way that programs are written to meet specifications, laws are drafted to achieve social, political or economic policies. The purpose of the British Nationality Act 1981, for example, was 'to make fresh provisions about citizenship and nationality, and to amend the Immigration Act 1971 as regards the right of abode in the United Kingdom', and in particular to restrict immigration to the United Kingdom by residents of the former British colonies. The purposes of the University of Michigan lease termination clause presumably include such goals as discouraging unsociable behaviour in the halls of residence, restricting residency to legitimate students, and avoiding undue hardship for individuals who are obliged to terminate their residence. The rules for dealing with London Underground emergencies, on the other hand, are designed to facilitate the provision of help as effectively and quickly as possible in the case of genuine emergencies and to avoid inconvenience and unnecessary trouble in the case of false alarms.

Program specifications have many characteristics in common with the policies of legal documents. In the same way, for example, that the primary obligation of a program is to meet its specification, the primary duty of a legal document is to achieve its social and political objectives. In both cases, moreover, specifications and policies are often ill-defined, inconsistent, or the result of compromise between conflicting demands.

The formal methods developed in computing to verify that programs meet their specifications are much more advanced than any corresponding methods developed for the law. A pilot study of the possibility of adapting formal methods of software verification to the problem of verifying social security regulations has been made by Bench-Capon (Bench-Capon, 1987).

Thus the transfer of techniques for-program verification is one area in which the field of law might be able to benefit from its similarities with computing. In other areas, such as software management, both fields might benefit more equally.

6.2. An analogy between software maintenance and maintenance of the law

In the same way that programs need to be modified to meet changing specifications, legislation needs to be modified to meet changing social and political and economic needs. But programs are both difficult to construct and difficult to change. So much so in fact, that programs are often still in use long after they have outlived their specifications.

The situation is not much better in the law. In democratic societies legislation often lags far behind social, political, and economic changes. Obsolete and incorrect legislation is enforced simply for the sake of 'law and order'.

But the drafters of legislation have developed some ingenious devices for adapting modifying and revising old legislation. The liberal use of vague and undefined terms such as 'good character', 'life, limb or property would be jeopardized' and 'improper use' greatly contribute to the flexibility of legislation and to its ability to adapt to change. Such use of vague terms is reminiscent of the use of data abstraction and encapsulation in computer programming, which allow the lower levels of a program to change, while leaving the higher levels intact.

Much new legislation is explicitly concerned with the repeal or amendment of earlier legislation. The British Nationality Act 1981, for example, repeals the British Nationality Acts 1948 to 1965 and amends the Immigration Act 1971. Amendments in particular are typically expressed by metalevel statements which describe how an old piece of text should be edited to create a new text. Metalevel statements are also used to create a new provision from a similar provision in the same act.

Section 6(2) of the British Nationality Act 1981, for example, makes special provision for naturalisation of people who are married to British citizens. The requirements are similar to those for people who apply under section 6(1), but include shorter residency requirements, omit the requirement of having sufficient knowledge of English, Welsh, or Scottish Gaelic, and include

> 'the requirement specified in paragraph l(l)(b)'

this metalevel reference to l(l)(b) is in fact a reference to the requirement

> 'that he is of good character'.

This particular use of metalanguage is rather unusual in that the English use of the metalinguistic form is actually longer than the equivalent object level expression. Usually the metalinguistic formulation is more concise than the object level formulation.

Thus the source code of legislation often mixes object level statements about the domain of discourse with metalevel statements about the text of other legislation or of other provisions in the same legislation. The principal objective of using such metalevel statements in preference to equivalent object level statements is to make explicit the relationship between different but similar texts. This technique contrasts with the alternative technique, used more commonly in computing, of defining concepts more abstractly and of obtaining similar cases by creating different instantiations of the abstraction.

The language of legislation also employs remarkable techniques for reusing previous legislation. In the British Nationality Act 1981, for example, it states that one of the conditions for being a British citizen by descent under the 1981 Act is to be a person who

> under any provision of the British Nationality Acts 1948 to 1965, was deemed for the purposes of the proviso to section 5(1) of the 1948 Act to be a citizen of the United Kingdom and Colonies by descent only, or would have been so deemed if male

The last phrase is an example of a counterfactual condition. A metalogical interpretation of such counterfactuals has been developed by Bench-Capon (1989). It is possible to imagine how metaprogramming might be used to implement such counterfactual reuse of software in a logic programming environment.

6.3. The relationship between case based and rule based reasoning

In artificial intelligence a contrast is sometimes made between case-based and rule-based reasoning and a conflict is often held to exist between these two (Schank 1983) People, it is argued, reason by means of analogies between different cases rather than by means of deductive rules.

The distinction between these two kinds of reasoning also lies at the heart of law. To some extent it is even reflected among the distinguishing features of the two main western legal traditions. Common law systems, such as those in England and the United States, place greater emphasis on reasoning by means of cases. Civil law systems, such as those on the continent of Europe, place greater emphasis on reasoning by means of codified rules. In fact, in both systems of law the two kinds of reasoning are complementary.

In rule-based legislation, for example, case-based reasoning plays a fundamental rôle in determining the meaning of vague concepts. Previous cases of a concept serve as precedents for new cases.

On the other hand, in case-based legal argumentation, the justification for a decision in a precedent-setting case is often expressed in general terms and appeals to general principles. Moreover, authoritative restatements of case law effectively reformulate the precedents set in individual cases into general, rule-based form. Indeed it can be argued that there is a natural evolution in the law from reasoning by means of cases to reasoning by means of rules. The technique of explanation-based learning or generalisation (Mitchell et al. 1986) developed in artificial intelligence seems to be a model of this kind of evolution.

7. CONCLUSION

The similarities between computing and law seem to cover all areas of computing software. Moreover, the linguistic style in which legislation is drafted combines in one language the expressive power of computer languages for such diverse areas as programming program specification, database description and query, integrity constraints, and knowledge representation in artificial intelligence. This linguistic style might be a good guide therefore to how these different areas of computing might be unified in the future.

The similarities between computing and law go beyond those of linguistic style. They extend also to the problems that the two fields share of developing, maintaining and reusing large and complex bodies of linguistic texts. Here too, it may be possible to transfer useful techniques between the two fields.

In this paper I have concentrated on similarities between logic programming and legislation. I have indicated several ways in which the language of legislation suggests that the basic model of logic programming can usefully be extended, to include types, relative clauses, both ordinary negation and negation by failure, integrity constraints, metalevel reasoning, and procedural notation. I believe that with the aid of such extensions logic programming can provide the foundations for a future, single computer language that will be suitable for all areas of computing in the same way that natural language is suitable for all areas of law.

ACKNOWLEDGEMENT

This work was supported initially by the Science and Engineering Research Council and more recently by the ESPRIT Basic Research Action, 'Computational Logic'. I am especially indebted to my colleagues, Trevor Bench-Capon, Fariba Sadri and Marek Sergot, whose work on legislation and logic programming has provided much of the background for this paper.

REFERENCES

Allen, L. E., and Saxon, C.S., 1984. 'Computer Aided Normalizing and Unpacking: Some Interesting Machine-Processable Transformation of Legal Rules', *Computing Power and Legal Reasoning,* C. Walter (ed.), West Publishing Company, pp. 495–572.

Bench-Capon, T.J.M., 1987. 'Support for policy makers: formulating legislation with the aid of logical models', *Proc. of the First International Conference on AI and Law,* ACM Press, pp. 181–189.

Bench-Capon, T., 1989. 'Representing Counterfactual Conditionals'. *Proceedings of Artificial Intelligence and the Simulation of Behaviour,* A. Cohn (ed.) Pitman Publishing Co.

Bowen, K. A. and Kowalski, R. A., 1982. 'Amalgamating Language and Metalanguage in Logic Programming', in *Logic Programming*, Clark, K.L. and Tamlund, S.-Å., (eds), Academic Press, pp. 153-173.

Bry, F., Decker, H., and Manthey, R., 1988. 'A uniform approach to constraint satisfaction and constraint satisfiability in deductive databases', *Proceedings of Extending Database Technology*, pp. 488–505.

Clark, K. L., 1978. 'Negation by failure', in *Logic and databases*, Gallaire, H. and Minker, J. (eds), Plenum Press, pp. 293–322.

Gallagher, J., 1986. 'Transforming Logic Programs by Specializing Interpreters', *Proc. of 7th European Conference on Artificial Intelligence*, pp. 109-122.

Gelfond, M. and Lifschitz, V., 1990. 'Logic programs with classical negation', *Proceedings of the Seventh International Conference on Logic Programming*, MIT Press, pp. 579-597.

Gordon, T. F., 1987. 'Oblog-2 a Hybrid Knowledge Representation System for Defeasible Reasoning'; *Proc. First International Conference on Artificial Intelligence and Law.* ACM Press, pp. 231-239.

H.M.S.O., 1981. British Nationality Act 1981, Her Majesty's Stationery Office, London.

Kowalski, R. A. and Sergot, M. J., 1986. 'A logic-based calculus of events', *New Generation Computing* Vol. 4, No. 1, pp. 67-95.

Kowalski, R.A., 1989. 'The treatment of negation in logic programs for representing legislation', *Proceedings of the Second International Conference on Artificial Intelligence and Law*, pp. 11-15.

Kowalski, R.A., 1990. 'English as a Logic Programming Language', *New Generation Computing*, Volume 8, pp. 91-93.

Kowalski, R. A. and Sadri, F., 1990. 'Logic programs with exceptions', *Proceedings of the Seventh International Conference on Logic Programming*, MIT Press, pp. 598-613.

Kowalski, R. A., Sergot, M. J., 1990. 'The use of logical models in legal problem solving', *Ratio Juris*, Vol. 3, No. 2, pp. 201-218.

Lloyd, J. W. and Topor, R. W., 1984. 'Making Prolog more expressive', *Journal of Logic Programming* Vol. 3, No. 1, pp. 225-240.

Lloyd, J. W. and Topor, R. W. 1985. 'A Basis for Deductive Database Systems', *J. Logic Programming*, Volume 2, Number 2, pp. 93-109.

Mitchell, T. M., Keller, R. M. and Kedar-Cabelli, S., 1986. 'Explanation-based Generalization: A Unifying View' *Machine Learning*, Volume 1, pp. 47-80.

Newell, A. and Simon, H. A., 1972 *Human problem solving*, Prentice-Hall.

Nitta, K., Nagao, J., and Mizutori, T., 1988. 'Knowledge Representation and Inference System for Procedural Law', *New Generation Computing*, pp. 319-359.

Reiter, R., 1990. 'On asking what a database knows', *Proc. Symposium on Computational Logic*, Springer-Verlag.

Sadri, F. and Kowalski, R. A., 1987. 'A theorem proving approach to database integrity', in *Foundations of deductive databases and logic programming,* J. Minker, (ed.), Morgan Kaufmann, pp. 313-362.

Schank, R. C., 1983. 'The current state of AI: One man's opinion', *AI Magazine*, Volume 4, No. 1, pp. 1-8.

Sergot, M. J., Sadri, F., Kowalski, R. A., Kriwaczek, F., Hammond, P. and Cory, H. T., 1986. 'The British Nationality Act as a logic program', *CACM*, Vol. 29, No. 5, pp. 370-386.

Sripada, S. M., 1991. 'Temporal Reasoning in Deductive Databases'. Department of Computing, Imperial College, London.

Takeuchi, A. and Furukawa, K., 1986. 'Partial evaluation of PROLOG programs and its application to metaprogramming', *Proc. of IFIP 86*, North-Holland, pp. 415-420.

Waterman, D. A. and Hayes-Roth, B., 1978. *Pattern-directed Inference Systems*, Academic Press, New York.

Department of Computing
Imperial College, London
England

SANDRA DEWITZ

USING INFORMATION TECHNOLOGY AS A DETERMINER OF LEGAL FACTS

As a visiting professor at the University of Texas Law School in 1990, Neil MacCormick led a seminar on artificial intelligence and legal reasoning. In this seminar and in a working paper that we discussed at the time (now published as MacCormick 1992), he maintained that legal reasoning is, at least in part, a deductive process, but that the degree to which we can use computers to perform this deduction is quite limited. I concur with MacCormick's first assertion but will demonstrate here that, when legal acts are performed on an electronic network, it may be feasible to use information technology to automate a wider spectrum of legal reasoning activities than has been suggested.

On an electronic network, legal acts are performed through the transmission of electronic documents that have legal effect. For example, electronic data interchange (EDI) supports the transmission of highly standardized, computer-readable business documents over a telecommunications network.[1] Graham Rowbotham, an attorney specializing in EDI law, has noted that 'All EDI messages can be expected to have some legal effect, since even an answer to the smallest inquiry as to product liability or pricing constitutes provision of information' (Rowbotham 1988). I will discuss how we can use information technology to observe and evidence these electronic legal acts and to apply legal rules to determine the legal facts they bring about.

1. THE LIMITS OF COMPUTER-BASED LEGAL REASONING SYSTEMS

MacCormick has stated that the extent to which expert systems can be used in legal reasoning is limited because a major facet of legal reasoning is determining just what the facts of a situation are.[2] He describes the important rôle of a 'fact-determining authority' who works with four kinds of proposition to perform the various tasks of legal reasoning. These four kinds of proposition consist in predication by four kinds of predicates: purely descriptive predicates, descriptive-interpretive predicates, evaluative predicates, and normative predicates.

Z. Bankowski et al. (eds.), Informatics and the Foundations of Legal Reasoning, 357–369.

(1) *Purely descriptive predications* state empirically verifiable facts and require no evaluation except of evidence; for example, the predication

transmitted(bank, seller, letter_of_amendment)

requires evidence, i.e., testimony of someone who witnesses this act.[3]

(2) *Descriptive-interpretive predications* state legal, i.e. operative, facts derivable from certain purely descriptive predications and applicable legal rules; for example, the predication

amended(bank, seller, letter_of_credit)

can be derived from the purely descriptive predication above and a legal rule stating that, in certain circumstances, the act of transmitting a letter of amendment performs the legal act of amending the credit.

(3) *Evaluative predications* require reference to human values and interpretations made in legal precedents, for example,

reasonable(act)

or

proximate_cause(event1, event2).

(4) *Normative predications* describe the consequences of certain legal states being true; for example, the normative predication

obligation(bank, seller, amend_conditions)

can be derived from a legal rule and the legal fact stated in the descriptive-interpretive predication in (2), along with other established facts.

Given descriptive-interpretative predications and formalized rules for inferring normative predications, we can automate part of the legal reasoning process. In fact, numerous computer-based legal reasoning systems[4] have been developed to infer normative predications (i.e. legal conclusions) from descriptive-interpretive predications (i.e. legal facts). These legal reasoning systems assume that the legal facts are given (by human interpreters?) as input to which formalized legal rules are applied to infer a conclusion. The basic model for this aspect of legal reasoning is the logical rule *modus ponens*:[5]

Major Premise:	IF ‹ Operative Facts ›
	THEN ‹ Legal Conclusion ›
Minor Premise:	‹ Operative Facts ›
Conclusion:	‹ Legal Conclusion ›

But reasoning from purely descriptive predications to descriptive-interpretive predications is another matter. MacCormick contends that the truth of purely descriptive predications cannot be computed because these predications require evidence —e.g. observation and testimony that an event occurred. But computers generally cannot 'observe' events, nor can they evaluate evidence in order to determine 'that certain facts count as instances of a rule's operative facts', nor can they apply human values to an interpretation of legal rules. Thus MacCormick concludes that

> such determination can only be made by beings with intelligence and will as well as a capacity for evaluation of evidence and understanding of values implicit in rules. It is therefore arguable that only a person, not a machine, can possibly answer them (MacCormick 1992).

Few would disagree that, because we cannot imbue computers with human values, we should abstain from automating any reasoning processes that require reference to these values. However, if the computer is the medium through which an event occurs (e.g. an automatic teller machine's processing of deposits and withdrawals), it may be reasonable to contend that the computer can 'observe' the occurrence of this event and can evaluate evidence that the event occurred. Furthermore, it may be feasible to formalize rules mapping occurrences of particular computer-observable events (i.e., purely descriptive predications) to assertions that certain legal states (i.e., descriptive-interpretive predications) exist. If so, a computer can determine the truth of certain purely descriptive predications and can function as a fact-determiner to transform these purely descriptive predications into descriptive-interpretive predications. In fact, MacCormick's work with Ota Weinberger on the Institutional Theory of Law, specifically its analysis of brute and institutional facts, provides support for this proposition.

2. BRUTE FACTS, INSTITUTIONAL FACTS, AND LEGAL SPEECH ACTS

The Institutional Theory of Law (MacCormick and Weinberger 1986) distinguishes between *brute facts* —true statements about material, physical, observable acts or objects— and *institutional facts* —statements whose truth depends on the interpretation of an act or object relative to humanly established rules or conventions. For example, the assertion that 'Bank has transmitted a letter of amendment to Seller' is a brute fact whose truth can be verified empirically. In contrast, the assertion that 'Bank has amended its credit with seller' is an institutional fact whose truth can be verified only by consulting legal rules governing how to amend a letter of credit. In the Institutional Theory of Law, most institutional facts deal with legal concepts, such as a contract or amendment. These are 'institutions of law' or 'legal institutions': concepts 'regulated by sets of institutive, consequential and terminative rules', whose instances 'exist over a period of time, from the occurrence of an institutive act or event until the occurrence of a terminative act or event' (MacCormick and Weinberger 1986, p. 53). The 'institutive act' that creates most instances of legal institutions is a legal speech act.

The notion of a *legal speech act* is derived from Speech Act Theory[6], whose main tenet is that words can do more than just *describe* states of affairs in the world; they can be used to *change* these states of affairs. For example, the words 'I promise to deliver my paper at the conference' are used not to describe an existing state but to create a new state in which I am obligated to perform the promised action. This concept of a speech act has been generalized to include non-verbal acts, e.g. raising one's hand at an auction performs the act of bidding, and written words, e.g. a promissory note can be used to promise repayment.

Legal speech acts differ from ordinary speech acts in that they invoke legal rules and conventions to create rights and duties, which are consequences enforceable by law.[7] The law has long recognized that legal speech acts are actions, not merely statements. For example, in American Law, the *Federal Rules of Evidence*, 'exclude from hearsay the entire category of "verbal acts".'[8] Thus, an objective third party who witnesses the formation of an oral agreement can testify that a contract was formed. Testimony about what someone *said* is inadmissible hearsay; however, testimony about what someone *did* in performing a legal speech act is admissible as evidence (Tiersma 1986).

That so many legal acts can be performed by legal speech acts is what makes performing these acts on an electronic network feasible. On an electronic network, these legal acts take the form of computer-readable documents; thus, their occurrence is a brute fact that can be verified empirically. The framers of the *Uniform Rules of Conduct for Interchange of Trade Data by Teletransmission* (UNCID)[9] may have had this in mind when they required that each party using an electronic network to transmit business documents must 'ensure that a complete log is maintained of all trade data as they were sent and received, without any modification' (Article 10(a)). The brute fact that a particular document has been transmitted can be verified by referring to the log. Given this brute fact and a knowledge base of rules mapping from document transmission to legal speech acts, information technology can be used to identify the legal speech act(s) each document performs. And, more importantly, given evidence that a particular legal speech act has been performed, and a knowledge base of institutive, consequential, and terminative rules, information technology can be used to infer the legal consequences of these acts, i.e. institutional facts.

3. FROM ELECTRONIC DOCUMENTS TO LEGAL SPEECH ACTS AND LEGAL FACTS

In this section, I present an example to demonstrate the feasibility of using information technology to verify brute facts and to infer institutional facts. The application domain is international sales involving documentary credits[10], a payment method that involves a buyer (aka the account party), a seller (aka the beneficiary), a letter of credit, and at least one international bank (aka the issuing bank). Documentary credit procedures are performed exclusively through the creation, exchange, and evaluation of documents. Payment to the seller is made not on the delivery of the goods, i.e., not on the seller's actually satisfying his obligations under the sales contract by performing certain physical acts (e.g., having the goods inspected and insured, shipping the goods, etc.), but on the seller's satisfying the documentary conditions stated in the letter of credit, i.e., on the seller's presentation of stipulated documents that evidence the performance of the required physical acts.

Under the letter of credit, the issuing bank's only obligations are to issue the credit and to examine the documents tendered by the seller; empirically verifying that the seller has actually performed the physical acts evidenced by the documents is not the bank's concern. Thus, documentary credit procedures provide an ideal domain to illustrate the fact-determining capability of a computerized legal reasoning system: (1) the only legal acts of interest are legal speech acts performed by documents, (2) the only evidence requiring evaluation is present in documentary form, and (3) the evidence can be read and understood by the computer.

To act as a legal fact-determiner, the network's legal reasoning system must (1) maintain records of all documentary transmissions; (2) provide rules for mapping from documents transmissions to the legal speech acts they perform; (3) provide rules for evaluating whether the intended legal speech act was performed successfully; (4) provide rules for determining the legal facts brought about by a successful legal speech act; and (5) be endowed with fact-determining authority by those whose electronic transactions it will oversee. Below these requirements are more fully explained and illustrated using examples from documentary credit procedures.

3.1. Recording all Transmission

When documentary credit procedures are performed electronically on a telecommunications network, the brute facts about document transmissions can be maintained in a transmission log. This transmission log contains not only a record stating the time and other details of the transmission but also a record of the document itself, which provides the purely descriptive predications needed to determine whether a party has met his obligations under the letter of credit. For example, if the seller must provide documentary evidence that particular goods were shipped from a specified port on a certain date, these purely descriptive predications are stated in the marine bill of lading that the beneficiary presents to the issuing bank. According to the *Uniform Customs and Practice for Documentary Credits* (UCP), the seller has satisfied this requirement if the marine bill of lading 'appears' to be authentic[11] and to evidence the conditions required by the letter of credit, i.e., describes the particular goods having been shipped from the specified port on the certain date.

3.2. Mapping from Documents to Legal Speech Acts

The correspondence between documents and legal speech acts must be formalized if the legal reasoning system of an electronic network is to observe the physical act of a document transmission and to infer the legal speech act(s) this transmission performs. The basic model of the legal reasoning process required to perform this transformation is similar to the logical inference rule shown earlier:

Rule: IF Sender transmits a letter of amendment to Receiver,
THEN Sender has performed the legal speech act of amending his credit with Receiver.

Physical Act/Brute Fact:
Bank has transmitted a letter of amendment to Seller.

Legal Speech Act/Institutional Fact:
Bank has performed the legal speech act of amending his credit with seller.

The context in which a speech act occurs may colour the meaning of the act.[12] For example, raising one's hand at an auction does not perform the same speech act as raising one's hand in a classroom. Contextual factors are especially important in law, where the relationship between legal documents and legal speech acts is not isomorphic; a single document may perform different legal speech acts in different contexts. For example, assume a scenario in which Bank has issued a revocable letter of credit to the benefit of Seller. When Bank transmits a letter of amendment to Seller, this transmission performs the legal speech act of amending the letter of credit. However, if Bank has issued an irrevocable letter of credit to the benefit of Seller, then Bank's transmission of a letter of amendment performs the legal speech act of requesting Seller's permission to amend the credit.

Because the same document transmission can perform a different legal act depending on the context in which the transmission occurs, capturing this context is an important requirement in the network's fact-determining process. Thus, the original rule mapping from the transmission of a letter of amendment to the legal speech act of amending the credit must be modified to reflect the context in which the transmission occurs:

Rule: IF Sender transmits a letter of amendment to Receiver
WHERE the letter of credit is revocable,
THEN Sender has performed the legal speech-act of amending his credit with Receiver.

Brute Facts:
Bank has transmitted a letter of amendment to Seller.
The letter of credit is revocable.

Institutional Fact:
Bank has performed the legal speech act of amending its credit with Seller.

Additional rules would be needed to reflect the other contexts in which a letter of amendment might be transmitted and the other legal states that it might create; and, of course, similar rules would be needed for all the documents in the procedure.

3.3. Evaluating the success of a legal speech act

In a documentary credit procedure conducted on an electronic network, legal speech acts are performed by document transmissions. It would be more accurate to say that these document transmissions *attempt* to perform legal speech acts. The act of transmitting a document is a necessary but not a sufficient condition for successfully performing a legal speech act in this domain. Numerous institutive rules —both statutory rules stipulated in the UCP and transaction-specific rules stipulated in the letter of credit— must be satisfied for the attempted legal speech act to succeed.

One institutive rule for creating an instance of a letter of credit states that the credit 'must clearly indicate whether [it is] available by sight payment, by deferred payment, by acceptance or by negotiation' (UCP, Article 11(a)). Similarly, a letter of credit 'must state precisely the document(s) against which payment, acceptance, or negotiation is to be made' (UCP, Article 22(a)). Under the rules of the UCP, a document purporting to be a letter of credit but not containing the required indications may be construed as ineffective; in other words, its attempt to perform a legal speech act fails. Also important in evaluating a legal speech act's success is, again, the context in which the act was performed. Any attempted legal speech act must be a permissible move from the current legal state if it is to succeed. For example, transmitting a letter of amendment will fail to perform the legal speech act of amending the credit terms if the seller has already presented documents (i.e., the credit has been settled). Similarly, a letter of revocation will fail to revoke a credit if the credit was issued as irrevocable. As these examples illustrate, many legal speech acts are constrained by rules that stipulate the sequence in which they must be performed[13] and the conditions under which they may be performed.

3.4. Rules for determining legal facts and consequences

As H.L.A. Hart stated, human acts are not 'self-labelling': '[f]act situations do not await us neatly labelled, creased, and folded, nor is their legal classification written on them simply to be read off by the judge.' (Hart 1958). Instead, human actions must be analyzed and interpreted to determine their legal meaning. As MacCormick noted in his recent article (1992), this legal fact-finding process is performed by a designated 'determiner of fact' —a judge, jury, or other legally appointed authority imbued with the power to determine the truth of relevant statements about a legal situation. Following prescribed procedures, such fact-determining authorities work from brute facts to determine whether certain legal/institutional facts are true. An institutional fact is true only if the fact-determining authority finds it to be true, and it is legally true even if —given full knowledge— we could demonstrate that it is empirically false.

Here again the process of inferring legal facts from legal speech acts and contextual factors is formalized using the same inferencing structure shown earlier. What's different this time is that, instead of inferring institutional facts from legal rules and brute facts, this process involves inferring one institutional fact from legal rules and another institutional fact. Given a rule that infers from a descriptive-interpretive predication—

amended(sender, receiver, credit_id, amend_terms)

to a normative predication—

obligation(sender, receiver, credit_id, amend_terms)

and given the institutional fact—

amended(ABank, RBank, LC2, Expiration_Date_amended_to_05–31–94)

we can infer the truth of a second institutional fact—

obligation(ABank, RBank, LC2, Expiration_Date_amended_to_05–31–94).

3.5. Using Information Technology as a fact-determiner: the critical rôle of the Umbrella Contract

In order to use information technology as a fact-determiner on an electronic network, the users of the network must agree to give the network's legal reasoning system this authority. The required agreement is achieved through an *umbrella contract* that outlines the rules and procedures for acting on the network, i.e., that stipulates how to perform a particular speech act on the network and what the consequences of doing so are. The International Chamber of Commerce has noted that resolution by contract is probably the best way to handle the myriad legal issues likely to arise when parties from several types of businesses (e.g., suppliers, manufacturers, retailers, carriers) use an electronic network for 'direct open communication' (International Chamber of Commerce 1987). Thus, access to the electronic network would be conditioned on subscribers' having indicated their understanding and acceptance by signing the umbrella contract.

Endowed with fact-determining authority by the umbrella contract, the network can function as a 'trusted third party'[14] whose transmission log records all document transmissions and whose knowledge base contains rules for interpreting the legal meaning of these transmissions. The range of possible actions on the network is limited and pre-defined, the interpretations of these actions are pre-specified, and the designations of their effects are stated unambiguously in the umbrella contract and implemented in the network's knowledge base. In fact, the network's knowledge base is a kind of automated body of law and contractually appointed computer-based determiner of legal facts.

It should be noted that the legal reasoning system's fact-determining authority would not be the same as that of a judge: it is not the system's purpose to replace the judge–attorney–plaintiff–defendant system of litigation currently used to resolve disputes. Rather, its purpose is to avoid these disputes in the first place. Acting as an automated legal advisor and as a kind of front-line bureaucrat, the system possesses a good deal of legal knowledge and can interpret legal acts within a limited domain. However, its interpretations do not carry the force of legal verdicts, and parties who dispute its interpretations could have recourse to a human-based fact-determining authority (i.e., judge or jury) whose pronouncements would carry such force.

4. CONCLUSION

Perhaps the most significant contribution of this research is that it demonstrates how to push back the stage at which the legal reasoning process can be automated. The computerized legal reasoning system outlined here would exploit the structure and explicitness provided by EDI documents to perform more of the legal inferencing process than other legal reasoning systems are able to perform. Whereas most legal reasoning system require a human to interpret human actions and to transform these actions into a computationally tractable representation, the system described here operates directly on document transmissions, and is able to determine both the legal speech acts these documents perform and the legal meaning of these acts, and to apply rules to determine their consequences.

As modelled in Figure 1[15], legal reasoning involves (1) describing a situation or event in terms of its relevant legal facts (Identification and Interpretation), (2) searching for a legal norm that is applicable to this situation (Norm-search), and then (3) applying it to the situation (Norm-application).[16] Most computer-based legal reasoning systems focus on representing legal rules in a computable form and then finding and applying these rules to situations that human users have already interpreted and described as legal facts. Thus, in these systems, only the Norm-search and Norm-application stages are automated. However, the legal reasoning system described here automates the Identification and Interpretation stages as well.

That is, given a situation consisting of the exchange of EDI documents by certain parties within a certain context, this legal reasoning system can infer the legal facts entailed by this situation. Thus, at least in this narrow domain, information technology can be used to perform more of the legal reasoning process.

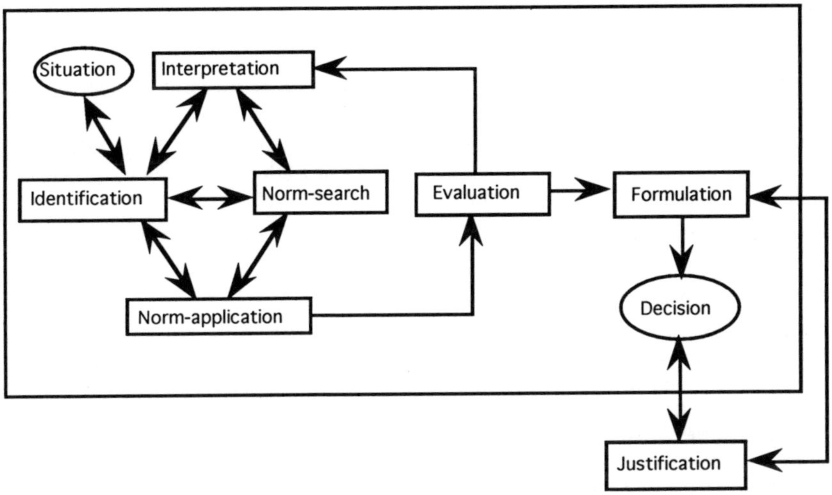

Figure 1. A Model of the Legal Reasoning Process

NOTES

1 See generally (Sokol 1989) for a full discussion of EDI.

2 (MacCormick 1989). See also (Burton 1985), (Leith 1986), and (Stamper 1988) for a discussion of the need to characterize the facts of a case as a precursor to legal reasoning.

3 Examples here are drawn from documentary credit procedures, which will be discussed briefly later in this article.

4 See, e.g., (Bench-Capon and Sergot 1985), (Capper and Susskind 1988), (Gardner 1987), (Gordon 1985), (Hustler 1982), (MacCarty 1966), (Meldman 1977), (Sergot et al. 1986), (Stamper 1980), (Susskind 1987), (Waterman and Petersen 1984), (Waterman et al. 1986).

5 The inference rule of *modus ponens* states that given the sentence $A \rightarrow B$ and the fact A, we can infer the conclusion B.

6 See, e.g., (Austin 1962/1975), (Searle 1969), (Searle and Vanderveken 1985).

7 See also (Dewitz and Lee 1989), (MacCormick and Bankowski 1986), (Tiersma 1986).

8 Article VIII, Hearsay. Rule 801: Notes of Advisory Committee on Proposed Rules, Rule 801.

9 (International Chamber of Commerce 1987) The UNCID is a set of guidelines, developed by the International Chamber of Commerce, that trading partners may adopt as a standard set of rules governing business transactions performed electronically.

[10] See *Uniform Customs and Practice for Documentary Credits*, 1983 version, (International Chamber of Commerce 1983), for a complete presentation of rules governing this domain.

[11] (International Chamber of Commerce 1983) See, for example, Article 9, which states that a bank is obligated to honour the credit by accepting the seller's documents as long as those documents '*appear on their face* to be in accordance with the terms and conditions of the credit'. Article 16 reiterates this point from a different perspective: 'If, upon receipt of the documents, the issuing bank considers that they *appear on their face* not to be in accordance with the terms and conditions of the credit, it must determine, *on the basis of the documents alone*, whether to take up such documents...' [Emphasis added].

[12] Support for this claim is provided by J. Searle's essential or constitutive rule, which states that utterance *X* counts as speech act *Y* in context *Z* (Searle 1969).

[13] Some industry guidelines for using EDI 'prescribe the sequence in which transaction sets [i.e. documents] can be communicated. If ... the 'wrong' transaction set is sent ..., it may have no legally binding significance.' (Baum 1990)

[14] See (Baum 1990) and (Baum and Perritt 1991) for fuller discussion of the 'trusted third party' concept

[15] Adapted from (Wahlgren 1989).

[16] Evaluation involves evaluating the outcome inferrable from the earlier steps in order to determine whether it seems to satisfy both the letter and the spirit of the law. Formulation is the process of stating —in oral or written form— the decision entailed by completing the earlier processes. Justification involves tracing the processes leading to the decision in order to demonstrate that the decision is both rational and desirable. These are distinctly human forms of reasoning commonly performed in a judicial setting but currently beyond the capabilities of computer-based reasoning systems.

REFERENCES

Austin, J.L., 1962. *How to Do Things with Words*, Oxford.

Baum M.S. and H.H. Perritt, Jr, 1991. *Electronic Contracting, Publishing, and EDI Law*, John Wiley and Sons, New York.

Baum, M.S., 1990. 'EDI Law', *The EDI Forum.*

Bench-Capon, T. and M. Sergot, 1985. *Towards a Rule-based Representation of Open Texture in Law*, Working Paper, Department of Computing, Imperial College of Science and Technology, London.

Burton, S.J., 1985. *An Introduction to Law and Legal Reasoning*, Chapter 3, Little, Brown and Company, Boston.

Capper, P.N., and R.E. Susskind, 1988. *Latent Damage Law: The Expert System*, Butterworth, London.

Dewitz S., and Lee, R., 1989. 'Legal Procedures as Formal Conversations: Contracting on a Performative Network', *Proceedings of the Tenth International Conference on Information Systems*, ACM Press.

Gardner, A. Von der Leith, 1984. *An Artificial Intelligence Approach to Legal Reasoning*, Bradford Book, MIT Press.

Gordon, T., 1985. 'Object-Oriented Predicate Logic and Its Rôle in Representing Legal Knowledge', in C. Walter (ed.), *Computing Power and Legal Reasoning*, St Paul, MN, West Publishing.

Hart, H.L.A., 1958 'Positivism and the Separation of Law and Morals', 71 *Harvard Law Review*, p. 607.

Hustler, A., 1982. *Programming Law in Logic*, University of Waterloo Department of Computer Science, Research Report CS–82–13.

International Chamber of Commerce (ICC), 1983. *Uniform Customs and Practice for Documentary Credits*, 1983 version.

International Chamber of Commerce (ICC), 1987. 'Draft Uniform Rules of Conduct for the Interchange of Trade Data by Teletransmission', *Computer Law and Practice*, January–February 1987, pp. 105–109.

Leith, P., 1986. 'Legal Expert Systems: Misunderstanding the Legal Process', 49 *Computers and Law*, pp 26–31.

MacCormick, D.N., 1978, *Legal Reasoning and Legal Theory*, Oxford University Press.

MacCormick, D.N., 1992. 'Legal Deduction, Legal Predicates and Expert Systems', *International Journal for the Semiotics of Law*, Vol. 14, 1992.

MacCormick, D.N., and Z. Bankowski, 1986. 'Speech Acts, Legal Institutions, and Real Laws', in N. MacCormick and P. Birks (eds.), *The Legal Mind: Essays for Tony Honoré*, Oxford University Press.

MacCormick, D.N. and O. Weinberger, 1986. *An Institutional Theory of Law,* Dordrecht.

McCarty, L.T., 1966. 'Reflections on TAXMAN: an Experiment in Artificial Intelligence and Legal Reasoning', 90 *Harvard Law Journal*, pp. 837–803.

Meldman, 1977. 'A Structural Model for Computer-aided Legal Analysis', 6 *Journal of Computers and Law*, pp. 27–71.

Rowbotham, G., 1988. 'EDI: the Practitioner's View', *International Financial Law Review,* August 1988, p. 33.

Searle, J.R., 1969. *Speech Acts: An Essay in the Philosophy of Language*, Cambridge University Press.

Searle, J.R., and D. Vanderveken, 1985. *Foundations of Illocutionary Logic*, Cambridge University Press.

Sergot, M.J., F. Sadri, R. A. Kowalski, F. Kriwaczek, P. Hammond, and H.T. Cory, 1986. 'The British Nationality Act as a Logic Program', *Communications of the ACM*, vol. 29, n. 5, May 1986, pp. 370–386

Sokol, P., 1989. *EDI: The Competitive Edge,* McGraw Hill, New York.

Stamper, R., 1980. 'LEGOL: Modelling Legal Rules by Computer', in B. Niblett (ed.), *Advanced Workshop on Computer Science and Law*

Stamper, R., 1988. 'The Dangers of AI in Information Systems as Exposed by the Field of Computers and Law', 3 *Journal of Information Technology*, pp 6–8.

Susskind, R.E., 1984. *Expert Systems in Law: A Jurisprudential Inquiry,* Butterworth.

Tiersma, 'The Language of Offer and Acceptance: Speech Acts and the Question of Intent', 74 *California Law Review*, 1986, pp. 189–232.

Wahlgren, P., 1989. 'Legal Reasoning —a Jurisprudential Description', *Proceedings of the 2nd International Conference on Artificial Intelligence and Law*, pp. 147–156.

Waterman, D.A., and Petersen, M.A., 1986, 'Evaluating Civil Claims: An Expert Systems Approach,' 1 *Expert Systems*, pp. 65–76.

Waterman, D.A., Paul, J., Petersen, M.A., 1986. 'Expert systems for legal decision making', *Expert Systems* 3, 4, pp 212–226.

College of Business
St Jose State University
San Jose, California
USA

INDEX

Alexy, R. 20, 76, 166, 168
amendments to legislation 352
analogical reasoning 27, 177–190, 198, 209
analogy 20, 26, 32, 163, 179, 219, 231, 259
argumentation theory 9, 19, 146, 153, 159–176
Aristotle 26, 249
Australian law 258

Bachelard, G. 206, 214
belief, representation of 334
British Nationality Act 41, 49, 280, 326
burden of proof (*see* proof, burden of)

Carroll, Lewis 25
case-based reasoning (CBR) 20, 24–8, 353
certainty, legal 10, 14, 88
change in law 19, 29, 196
Chisholm, R. 41, 45, 284
Civil Law 19, 208, 218, 354
clarity in law 103, 257
clear cases v. hard cases 8, 22, 35, 46, 304
Code civil 219
Coke, Chief Justice 61
Collins, H. 56
Columba, St 26
Common Law 19, 33, 206, 208, 214, 218, 301, 354
compartmentalisation (*see* self-contained parts of law)
conditions, legal (*see also* effects, legal *and* entitlements) 38, 120, 245, 254
conflicts in law 93, 121, 146
Connor, Mrs 44, 101
contrary-to-duty obligations 284
creativity in law 24, 34, 187, 212, 264

decision support systems 8, 47, 73, 74, 259, 262, 292, 303
decision, requirement to make 28, 75, 122, 200
deduction (*see* syllogism, legal)
defeasibility 9, 14, 22, 38, 60, 91, 95, 99–117, 227, 315
defeasibility, explicit v. implicit 99, 104
defeasibility, logic of (*see also* non-monotonic inference) 106, 113, 119–157
definitions, legal 36, 43, 232, 236
definitions, norms as (*see* qualification norms)
deontic logic 37, 40, 45, 164, 251, 271–290

distinctions between cases 4, 21, 28, 182, 192
draftsman, statutory (*see also* language, legal) 50, 83, 326, 334, 351
Dworkin, R. 77, 143, 186, 296

effects, legal 120
electronic data interchange (EDI) 59, 357–370
Engisch, K. 19, 162
entitlements 37, 246, 248
enveloppement 214
epistemology v. ontology 12, 32, 37, 205, 210, 245, 261
European Community Law 45, 291–309
exception v. qualification (*see* qualification v. exception)
exceptions to norms v. exceptions to effects 50, 131
exceptions to rules 18, 120, 146, 334
expert systems (*see also* decision support systems) 60, 115, 271, 311–323, 366

facts, legal determination of 208, 306, 357–369
family resemblance 22, 26, 32, 239
formal logic 153, 258, 304
Frankenstein 54
Frege, G. 238

German Federal Republic, Constitution of 162
Golding, M. 21, 181

Habermas, J. 167
hard cases v. clear cases (*see* clear cases v. hard cases)
Hart, H.L.A. 22, 99, 108, 142, 313, 364
heuristics 7, 46, 47, 142, 225, 231, 304
Hobbes, T. 249
Hohfeld, W. 13
Holmes, O.W. 107
Hume, D. 184, 264
hypothetical cases 23, 48, 183, 185

ideal, conformity to 42, 59, 275
imperatives and indicatives 19, 51, 346
indeterminacy in the law 31, 39, 40, 76, 141, 261
Institutional Theory of Law 12, 249, 296, 359
institutional fact 40, 58, 102, 216, 250
institutions 99, 296
integrity constraints 275, 347
International Chamber of Commerce 365
interpretation, legal 8, 46, 75, 84, 85, 164, 173, 294, 306, 314
isomorphic pattern (*see* pattern, discerning)

Italian Civil Code 15, 124–131, 149

James I of England (VI of Scotland) 61
justification, model of 7, 37, 46, 302

Kafka, F. 189
Kelsen, A. 76

language, legal 50, 53, 146, 325–356
Levi, E.H. 28, 192
LEX project 174
Lichtenberg, G. 256
logic programming 325–356

major premise (*see* syllogism, legal)
McConnell, Mr 311
mechanical procedure 54, 240
metalanguage and object language mixed 13, 131, 144, 330, 353
minor premise (*see* syllogism, legal)
monotonic inference (*see* non-monotonic inference)
Moore, G.E. 237

negation by failure 49, 327
new cases (*see* novelty in law)
non-liquet (*see* decision, requirement of)
non-monotonic inference 10, 27, 47, 134, 139, 144, 153, 304, 328, 332
non-refutanda (*see* proof, burden of)
normative position (*see* position, normative)
normative text (*see* text, normative v. physical)
Norwegian Sale of Goods Act 285
novelty in law 17, 29, 38, 49, 242, 258

ontology v. epistemology (*see* epistemology v. ontology)
open texture 22, 273, 313

parable 187, 189
paradox 23, 41, 191, 194, 285
pattern, discerning 32, 210, 214
pattern-matching 34
physical text (*see* text, normative v. physical)
policy arguments 8, 51, 73–97
Polya, G. 47
Popper, K. 60, 186
position, normative 113, 286
powers, legal 12, 13, 108
pragmatics 48, 100, 315, 318
precedent (*see* case-based reasoning)
principles and decisions (*see also* decision, requirement of) 8, 199
principles v. rules 142, 186, 296
probability 39, 48, 54, 243, 264
probanda (*see* proof, burden of)

proof, burden of 14, 104, 121, 127
prosthesis, social (*see* society, rôle of computers in)
public policy (*see* policy arguments)
purposes of laws 8, 51, 52, 78, 81, 173, 247, 346, 351
qualification norms 41, 59, 279
qualification v. exception 11, 16, 104

remedy, judicial 34, 215, 226
Roman Law 33, 214, 218, 220, 249, 301
rules v. principles (*see* principles v. rules)
rule extracted from case 25, 181, 209, 261, 296
rules, legal 7, 74, 91, 101, 205, 210, 246

self-contained parts of law (*see also* compartmentalisation) 315, 144, 273, 315
self-contained, the law as 29, 41, 76, 191
society, rôle of computers in 53, 55
society, rôle of law in 8, 58, 200, 351
Special Case Thesis 20, 76, 166
specifications of systems 41, 44, 52, 273, 287, 351
Spencer Brown, G. 194
Standard Case Method 22, 173
statutory interpretation (*see* interpretation, legal)
Stone, J. 11, 16, 104
substantial v. formal conditions 15, 136
syllogism, legal 32, 162, 46, 206, 245, 304
systems theory 191–204

Taylorism 56
text, normative v. physical 8, 82, 84, 294
time, stability over 59, 113
time, representation of 329
tradition 20, 184
Tübingen Seminar 161
Turing, A. 56

U.K. Magistrates Courts' Act 15
U.S. Federal Constitution 262
U.S. Federal Rules of Evidence 360
umbrella contract 59, 365
Uniform Customs and Practice for Documentary Credits 362
unpredictability in law 17, 261

values in law 80, 88, 101, 138, 201
violations of norms 41, 276, 284

Weber, M. 57
Weinberger, O. 359
Wittgenstein, L. 22, 31, 32, 238
Wróblewski, J. 45, 46, 302

Law and Philosophy Library

1. E. Bulygin, J.-L. Gardies and I. Niiniluoto (eds.): *Man, Law and Modern Forms of Life*. With an Introduction by M.D. Bayles. 1985 ISBN 90-277-1869-5
2. W. Sadurski: *Giving Desert Its Due*. Social Justice and Legal Theory. 1985 ISBN 90-277-1941-1
3. N. MacCormick and O. Weinberger: *An Institutional Theory of Law*. New Approaches to Legal Positivism. 1986 ISBN 90-277-2079-7
4. A. Aarnio: *The Rational as Reasonable*. A Treatise on Legal Justification. 1987 ISBN 90-277-2276-5
5. M.D. Bayles: *Principles of Law*. A Normative Analysis. 1987 ISBN 90-277-2412-1; Pb: 90-277-2413-X
6. A. Soeteman: *Logic in Law*. Remarks on Logic and Rationality in Normative Reasoning, Especially in Law. 1989 ISBN 0-7923-0042-4
7. C.T. Sistare: *Responsibility and Criminal Liability*. 1989 ISBN 0-7923-0396-2
8. A. Peczenik: *On Law and Reason*. 1989 ISBN 0-7923-0444-6
9. W. Sadurski: *Moral Pluralism and Legal Neutrality*. 1990 ISBN 0-7923-0565-5
10. M.D. Bayles: *Procedural Justice*. Allocating to Individuals. 1990 ISBN 0-7923-0567-1
11. P. Nerhot (ed.): *Law, Interpretation and Reality*. Essays in Epistemology, Hermeneutics and Jurisprudence. 1990 ISBN 0-7923-0593-0
12. A.W. Norrie: *Law, Ideology and Punishment*. Retrieval and Critique of the Liberal Ideal of Criminal Justice. 1991 ISBN 0-7923-1013-6
13. P. Nerhot (ed.): *Legal Knowledge and Analogy*. Fragments of Legal Epistemology, Hermeneutics and Linguistics. 1991 ISBN 0-7923-1065-9
14. O. Weinberger: *Law, Institution and Legal Politics*. Fundamental Problems of Legal Theory and Social Philosophy. 1991 ISBN 0-7923-1143-4
15. J. Wróblewski: *The Judicial Application of Law*. Edited by Z. Bańkowski and N. MacCormick. 1992 ISBN 0-7923-1569-3
16. T. Wilhelmsson: *Critical Studies in Private Law*. A Treatise on Need-Rational Principles in Modern Law. 1992 ISBN 0-7923-1659-2
17. M.D. Bayles: *Hart's Legal Philosophy*. An Examination. 1992 ISBN 0-7923-1981-8
18. D.W.P. Ruiter: *Institutional Legal Facts*. Legal Powers and their Effects. 1993 ISBN 0-7923-2441-2
19. J. Schonsheck: *On Criminalization*. An Essay in the Philosophy of the Criminal Law. 1994 ISBN 0-7923-2663-6
20. R.P. Malloy and J. Evensky (eds.): *Adam Smith and the Philosophy of Law and Economics*. 1994 ISBN 0-7923-2796-9
21. Z. Bankowski, I. White and U. Hahn (eds.): *Informatics and the Foundations of Legal Reasoning*. 1995 ISBN 0-7923-3455-8
22. E. Lagerspetz: *The Opposite Mirrors*. An Essay on the Conventionalist Theory of Institutions. 1995 ISBN 0-7923-3325-X

KLUWER ACADEMIC PUBLISHERS – DORDRECHT / BOSTON / LONDON